THE CAMBRIDGE ILLUSTRATED HISTORY OF *Religions*

The Cambridge Illustrated History of *Religions*

Edited by John Bowker

CAMBRIDGE
UNIVERSITY PRESS

PUBLISHED BY THE PRESS SYNDICATE
OF THE UNIVERSITY OF CAMBRIDGE
The Pitt Building, Trumpington Street,
Cambridge CB2 1RP, United Kingdom

CAMBRIDGE UNIVERSITY PRESS
The Edinburgh Building, Cambridge CB2 2RU, UK
40 West 20th Street, New York, NY 10011-4211, USA
10 Stamford Road, Oakleigh, Melbourne 3166, Australia
Ruiz de Alarcón 13, 28014 Madrid, Spain
Dock House, The Waterfront, Cape Town 8001, South Africa
http://www.cambridge.org

First published 2002

This book was conceived, designed, and produced by:
The Ivy Press Ltd
The Old Candlemakers
West Street
Lewes
East Sussex
BN7 2NZ

Creative Director: Peter Bridgewater
Publisher: Sophie Collins
Editorial Director: Stephen Luck
Designers: Chris Lanaway, Jane Lanaway, Tony Seddon
Editors: Mike Darton, Rowan Davies, Sarah Polden
Picture Researcher: Vanessa Fletcher
Captions: Viv Croot
Printed in China by Hong Kong Graphics and Printing Ltd

A catalogue record for this book is available
from the British Library

ISBN 0 521 81037 X hardback

Page 1: Jain temple complex on Mount Shatrunjaya (see also pages 62–63).
Page 2: The Western Wall, Jerusalem. It is normal practice to stand at the wall, except in cases of infirmity or long periods of prayer.
Page 3: Muslim women praying at morning service, Cirebon, Java.

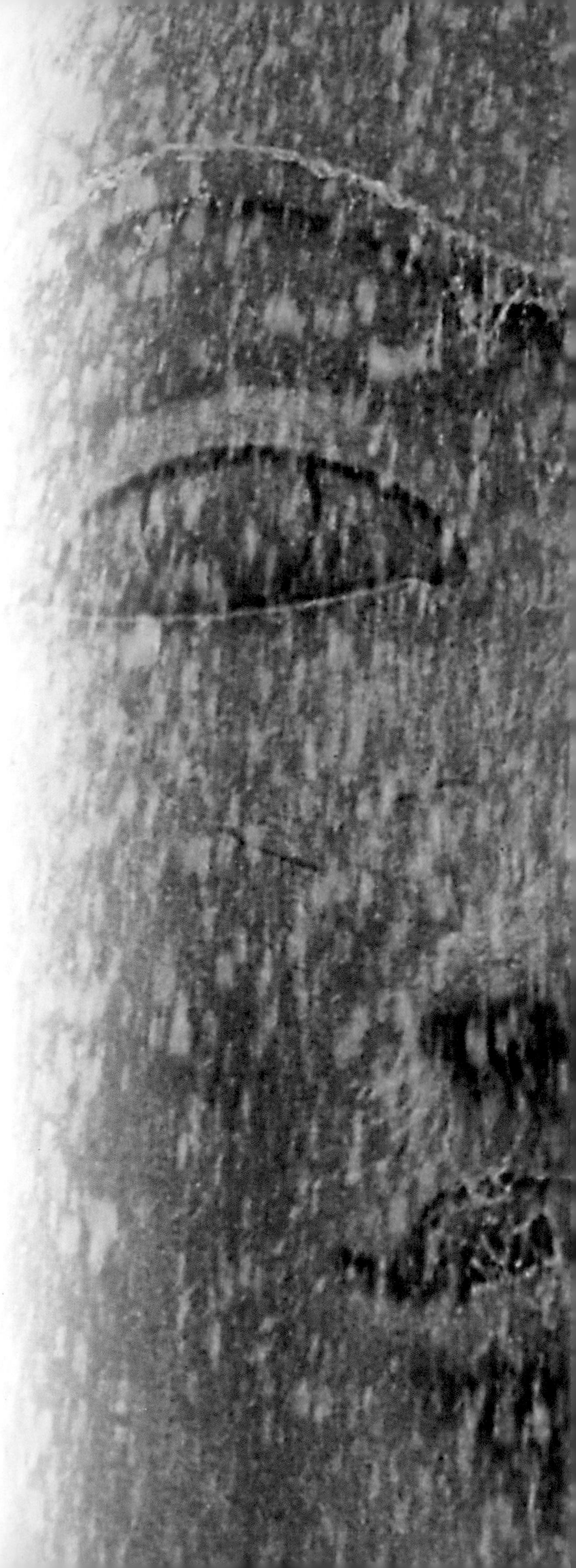

Contents

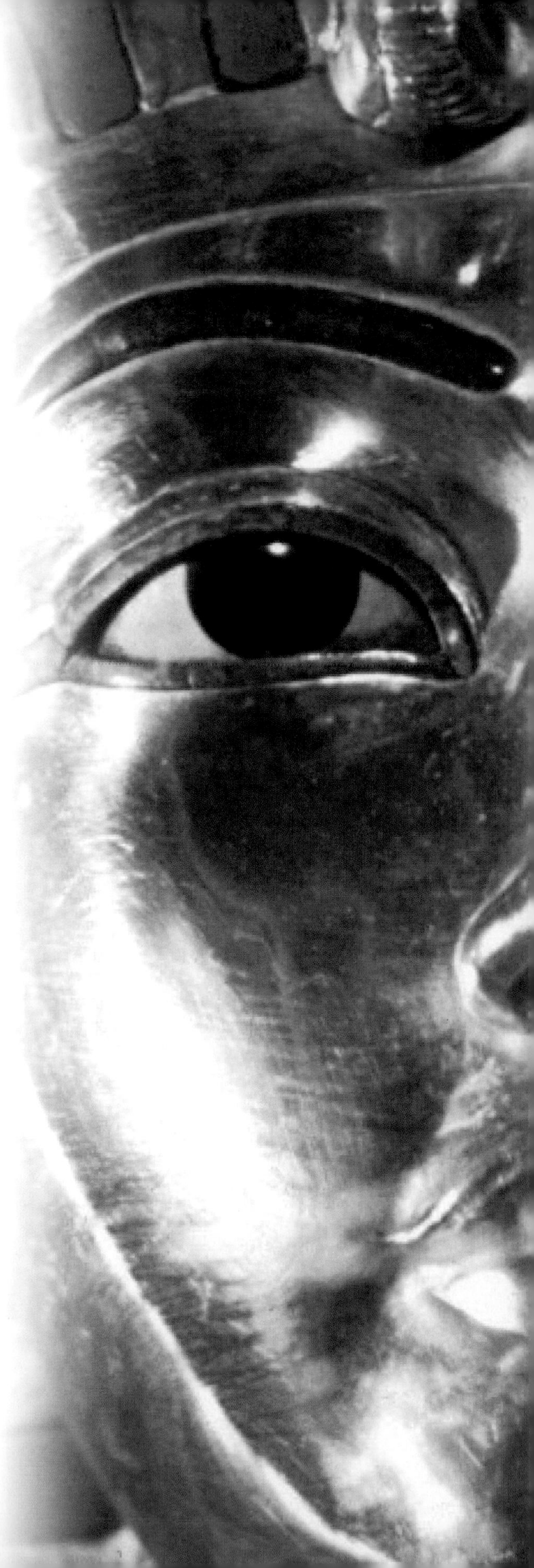

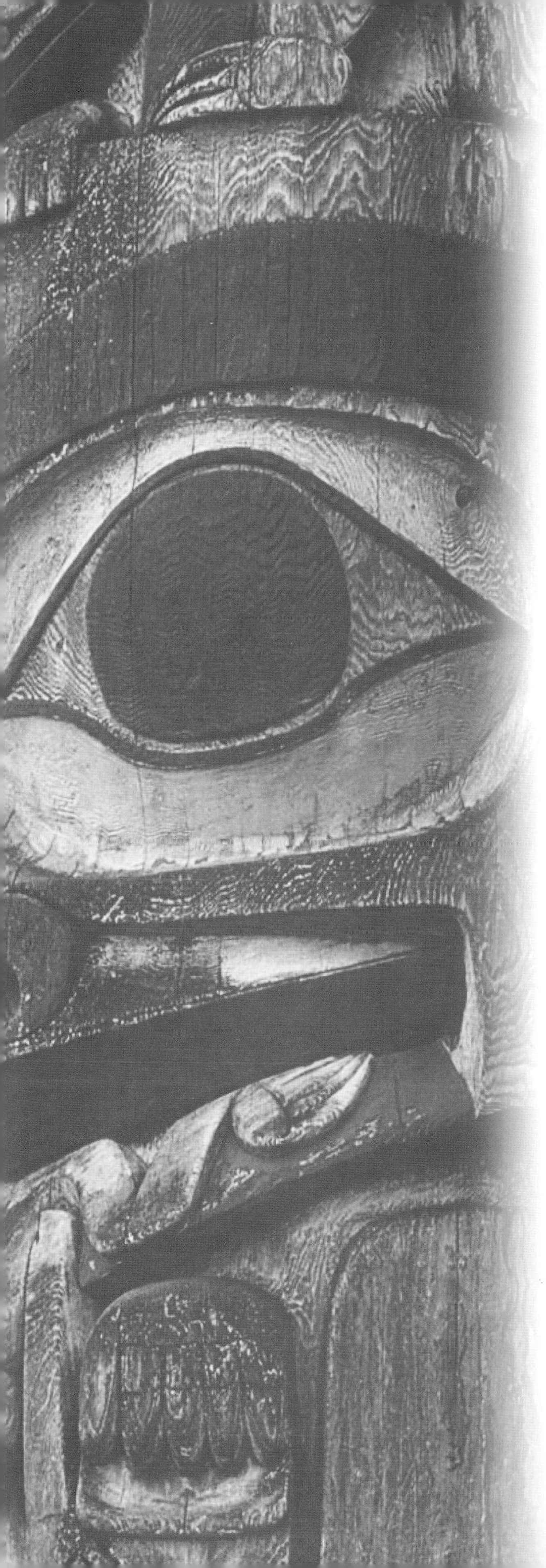

INTRODUCTION

JOHN BOWKER

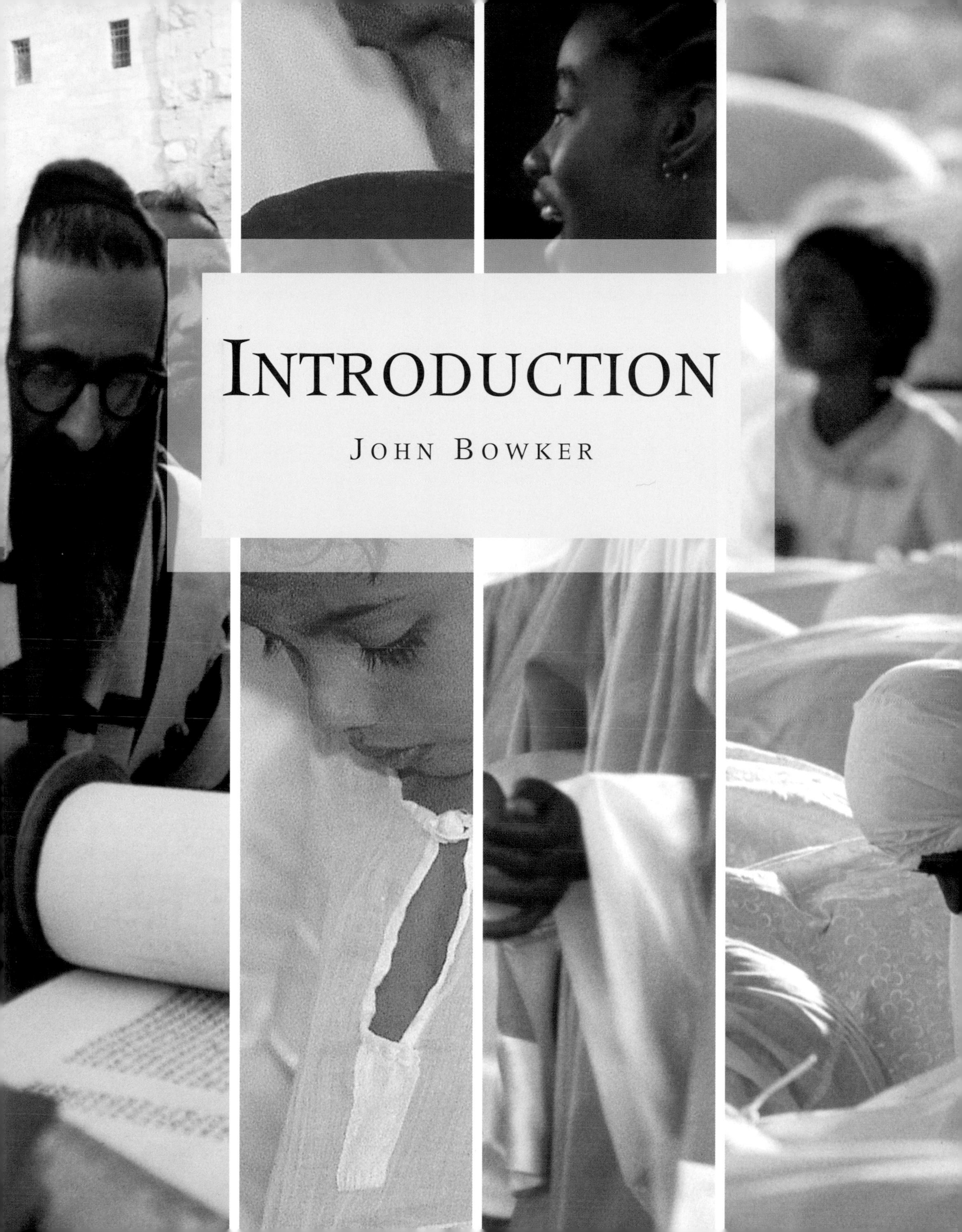

INTRODUCTION

THERE IS NO KNOWN SOCIETY in which religion has not played a part, and frequently a controlling and creative part. This seems to have been true of the earliest societies, but in their case the history of religions is not easy to write. Basically that is so because before the invention of writing, people passed on the record of events that occurred during their lives, as well as their understanding of their beliefs and practices, by word of mouth (oral tradition) and by means of paintings and carvings. Archeologists uncover the remains of buildings and recover artefacts of many different kinds, but the use and meaning of these things has to be inferred – or often simply guessed. The nature of those early religions can be glimpsed, perhaps even overheard as a distant whisper in the survival of myths around the world, but it cannot confidently be recovered.

THE HISTORY OF EARLY RELIGIONS

To take a well-known example, what are we to make of the Nasca lines of southern Peru (c. 200 BCE–200 CE), often referred to as 'the eighth wonder of the world'? These lines, covering nearly 1,000 square kilometres (400 square miles) of desert, are so vast and complex in design that they can only be seen completely from the air. Some are of geometrical design; others are of spiders, monkeys, and above all birds. What did the people who made these lines (and never saw them except in their imagination) have in mind? What did the lines mean to them?

Because there is no controlling record of text or inscription, archeologists can only infer the meaning. The archeologist Anthony Aveni dismissed the wilder guesses (for example, that the lines are copies of runways made by visitors from outer space) and argued, from a much wider knowledge of the whole area and its history, that the lines 'were used to partition the land to indicate the distribution of water rights'. Because rights of that kind could have been the cause of conflict, a ritual landscape was constructed in which the gods were pre-eminent over humans and thus had 'the last word' in any dispute. Clearly, that hypothesis is more probable, because warrants for its assertions are offered at every stage. Even so, it cannot be used with certainty in writing the early history of religions; suppose, for example, that these ancient peoples made some of the lines and images simply because they enjoyed doing so?

A map showing the location of Nasca in Peru, the location of the Nasca lines (see right), which are sometimes referred to as the 'eighth wonder of the world'.

CAVE ART AND SHAMANISM

That view has been offered as an explanation of much of the cave art that has been found in numerous parts of the world. It is likely that the people who put one of their hands against a cave wall and then traced its outline were fascinated by leaving

Petroglyphs scratched into the rock of Renegade Canyon, California, and possibly dating from before 1000 CE. According to some theories these figures could represent shamans enacting a ritual that mediates between the people and the forces of nature.

their mark outside themselves – much like the Greek soldier from Colophon who (in common with many tourists) sailed up the Nile and cut his name into the leg of the vast carving of an Egyptian Pharaoh at Abu Simbel.

Maybe, therefore, cave art came about simply because of the deep satisfactions that humans experience in their brains and bodies when they create or contemplate something that *feels* good. Feelings and emotions are deeply embedded in the human brain and body, and they are as fundamental to religion as they are to art. Art is unquestionably fun; but many other claims have been made about cave art, most of which connect it to the early history of religions. The archeologists Jean Clottes and David Lewis-Williams, for example, have argued that a good deal of cave art depicts the beliefs and practices that are connected with shamanism.

The term 'shamanism' has been used to describe a wide variety of early religious practices that have survived right down to the present day. In very general terms, shamans are inspired and charismatic individuals, both male and female, who enter into trance states, have the power to control spirits (often by incarnating them), and are also able to make journeys out of the body, to both 'heaven' and 'hell'.

The word 'shaman' is traced to the Tungus in Siberia (where shamanism is common), though the claim is also made that the origin is in the Sanskrit *śramaṇa* (meaning 'monk'), reaching China in the form of *shamen* and Japan as *shamon*. Tungus shamanism was described by S. M. Shirokogoroff, a pioneer in the study of shamanism, who pointed out that potential shamans are marked out by a traumatic episode or illness. If they can bring the spirit causing this under control, and can demonstrate trance states, then they are recognized as shamans. The spirits involved are not regarded as inherently either good or evil; the outcome depends on the context and on whether the spirits are controlled. Shamans remove threats to an individual or community by incorporating potentially destructive spirits into their own bodies and thereby neutralizing them.

The inducing of trance states is accomplished in various ways, including the exclusion of general sensory stimuli through such actions as drumming, dancing, or concentration on a mirror, and by means of tobacco, alcohol, and hallucinogens.

Modern Nepalese shamans, known as *jhankaris*, dress in traditional clothes to perform a ritual healing ceremony. Healing is an integral part of the shaman's work, as sickness is considered to have a spiritual as well as a physical dimension.

The word 'trance' is now used of a wide variety of people who enter these states, and make what are described as 'out-of-body' journeys. The ability to make journeys to upper or (more often) lower worlds is a part of the protective role of the shaman extended from its main focus on this earth.

The recent, careful study of shamanism has established the extent to which it is fundamental to the proper study of the history of religions; it has also had the effect of making the analysis proposed by Mircea Eliade (a major figure in the study of religion, 1907–1986) improbable, although this analysis has had considerable influence. Eliade argued (against observation) that 'the specific element of shamanism is not the incorporation of spirits by the shamans but the ecstasy provoked by the ascension to the sky or by the descent to hell: the incorporation of spirits and possession by them are universally distributed phenomena, but they do not necessarily belong to shamanism in the strict sense'.

Eliade then attempted to separate the two historically; he regarded the ascent as a survival of archaic religion, to be called 'pure shamanism' (other writers have called it 'white shamanism'), while he believed the contest against malevolent spirits to be an innovation ('black shamanism'). There is no serious warrant for this distinction in the practice of shamanism as observed; the imposition of it is more likely to be a creation of the modern mind.

It was this kind of problem that led the archeologist Jacquetta Hawkes to write in 1967, 'Every age has the Stonehenge it desires – or deserves'. Presumably people did not set up those huge stone blocks on Salisbury Plain in southern England (or for that matter the massive *moai*, or carved heads, that are such a distinctive feature of Easter Island) simply for fun. The early history of religions is difficult because we cannot answer the question why, in fact, people acted as they did. This has not, however, stopped people from claiming over the years that they *have* found the answer to this enigma, and that is what Jacquetta Hawkes meant by saying that each generation gets the Stonehenge (that is, the understanding of Stonehenge) that it either desires or deserves. There are more theories about the origins and meaning of Stonehenge than there are stones in its construction, and some of these (as in the detailed way in which the religion of the Druids is reconstructed and connected with Stonehenge) tell us more about contemporary religion than they do about the early history of Stonehenge (see P. Carr-Gomm for further discussion). Repeatedly, modern interpretations are imposed on ancient clues.

THE EARLY HISTORY OF RELIGION

In the absence of contemporaneous interpretation, how can the early history of religions be written? There have been two common ways of doing so: the identification of a common core at the heart of all present-day, observable religions, which is then 'read back' into whatever remains of earlier religions; and the use of the anthropological descriptions of small-scale contemporary religions that have not been affected by later 'civilization', on the premise that these may be an echo of the kind of religion practiced in the earliest times.

An important foundation of the first method was laid by Lord Herbert of Cherbury (1583–1648), who put forward the view that five beliefs are held in common by all people because they are innate: that there is a Supreme Being; that the Supreme Being is worthy of worship; that worship depends on a relationship with the Supreme Being, which requires, as a *sine qua non*, a life of virtue; that wrongdoing and sin are to be acknowledged and repented of; and that justice demands punishment after death for those who refuse to repent. In a more sophisticated form, the same kind of method underlay the attempt by Ninian Smart (1927–2001) to identify seven dimensions that can be found or inferred in every religion: practical and ritual; experiential and emotional; narrative and mythical; doctrinal and philosophical; ethical and legal; social and institutional; and material (art, architecture, and sacred places).

The second historiographical method, involving the use of anthropology, became prominent from the late nineteenth century onwards. From the description of the religion of the Aboriginals (a significant name in this context as it means 'from the beginning' in Latin, suggesting continuity), the sociologist Émile Durkheim (1858–1917) created his understanding of religious life as a response to the ways in which people experience society as having a life and power of its own. Thus society is, in many ways, independent of the particular individuals who happen to make it up at any one time; people create religion, and above all religious symbols, in order to state and affirm the values that sustain the social order, and the social structures and sanctions of any society will be a direct counterpart of its religious beliefs. Here again it was assumed that the observed tribal beliefs and practices had survived from a previous era, and that early religion could therefore be inferred from them. In this spirit, Durkheim called his most influential book on religion *Les Formes élémentaires de la vie religieuse: Le systeme totémique en Australie* (1912). Often this methodology was combined with the claim that some core belief could be identified from which all subsequent religious history derived – rather like believing that the growth of an oak tree can be traced and explained from the acorn.

This understanding of religious history was reinforced by the theory of evolution, expounded by Charles Darwin (1809–1882) in *On the Origin of Species* (1859), though in fact it came into being either before (in the case of the French mathematician and philosopher Auguste Comte, 1798–1857) or independently of (in the case of the English philosopher Herbert Spencer, 1820–1903) Darwin's work. Reinforced by Darwin, the method ran wild. In 1897, for example, Grant Allen published *The Evolution of the Idea of God*, in which he claimed that 'the protoplasm of religion is corpse-worship'.

The low point of this approach to the early history of religions was reached by the Scottish social anthropologist J. G. Frazer (1854–1941), in a long series of books (eventually 13 volumes, 1890–1937) called *The Golden Bough*: having formed a dismissive view of religion, he then looked around for evidence or anecdotes with which to illustrate it – not unlike the conduct of certain twentieth-century political trials, which first advanced their verdicts and then offered evidence to justify them. His method prompted one of Frazer's Cambridge colleagues to advise him to read the ancient author Epiphanius, because he would find in it 'a mine of folklore to be quarried'; another colleague recorded that Frazer once responded to a query by 'emptying out his notes higgledy-piggledy' in the hope of finding an answer.

To all this there was a far more serious side. Sir John Lubbock (1834–1913) combined anthropological observations (at that time anthropology as a discipline was still coming into being) with a strong commitment to evolution, and he argued that 'races in a similar state of mental development, however distinct their origins may be, and however distinct the regions they inhabit, have very similar religious concepts'. On that basis he proposed a six-stage evolution of religion: atheism (where there was no fixed system of belief or of mythology), fetishism (where an object is regarded with awe or reverence because of its inherent properties of power), totemism (where an object in nature is identified with a particular family group or tribe and may be worshipped), shamanism (where people with special properties are seen as mediators with spirits and other worlds), anthropomorphism (where other-world beings are invested with human or superhuman properties), and ethical monotheism (where there is a belief in only one God).

Carved totem poles and longhouses now preserved at Vancouver Museum, British Columbia, Canada. The Native Americans of the Pacific northwest shared a shamanistic religious tradition; totems were considered to both protect a tribe and embody its spirit.

These two historiographical methods grew out of contemporary beliefs about the nature of history itself. From the time of Sir Isaac Newton (1643–1727) onwards, there was a quest to find and describe laws of human behaviour that were as basic and invariable as the physical laws that Newton had described. If Darwinian theories could be extended to establish the laws governing the evolution of human beliefs, then it should be possible to write the early history of religions by observing religions that were believed to be 'survivals'. This was the word that was used by E. B. Tylor (1832–1917; he has been called 'the father of anthropology'), though he was also inclined to use the phrase 'unchanged savagery'. Tylor believed that the acorn from which all religion grew is 'the belief in Spiritual Beings', which he called 'animism'.

From universal animism, Tylor could write the early history of religions with confidence, because he had simply to trace the chain of cause and effect that had led to present-day religion. In *Primitive Culture* (1871) he quoted with approval the remark of an African chief in Bechuanaland (present-day Botswana) to a missionary called Casalis: 'One event is always the son of another, and we must never forget the parentage.' At the beginning of that book, Tylor made explicit his understanding of history as the tracing of law-bound sequences of events: 'None will deny that, as each man knows by the evidence of his own consciousness, definite and natural cause does, to a great extent, determine human action. Then keeping aside from considerations of extra-natural interference and causeless spontaneity, let us take this admitted existence of natural cause and effect as our standing-ground, and travel on it so far as it will bear us. It is on this same basis that physical science pursues, with ever-increasing success, its quest of laws of nature.'

The attempt to write history according to laws governing human behaviour had an immensely important influence during much of the twentieth century, because it created those disciplines which called themselves 'the social sciences'. History was to become scientific, as the English economist Alfred Marshall declared in 1897: 'Social science or the reasoned history of man, for the two things are the same, is working its way towards a fundamental unity; just as is being done by physical science, or which is the same thing, by the reasoned history of natural phenomena. Physical science is seeking her hidden unity in the forces that govern molecular movement; social science is seeking her unity in the forces of human character. To that all history tends; from that proceeds all prediction, all guidance for the future.' And, he might have added, 'all guidance to the past', since on this basis any gaps in the history of early religion could easily be filled in: by definition (as the essential nature of religion was defined in advance), all religions must exemplify that essence, albeit in variant forms.

Thus Max Müller (1823–1900), the great pioneer of the study of religions, argued for an extensive comparison of religions ('he who knows one knows none') in order that their histories could be worked out from their common origin. He believed that religion began when people first became aware of something beyond their immediate contact with the world, something 'not finite like all the rest', and when they felt a demand made upon them from that source. 'When men began to feel constrained to do what they do not like to do, or to abstain from what they would like to do, for the sake of some unknown powers which they had discovered behind the storm or the sky or the sun or the moon, then we are at last on religious ground'. The foundation of all religions is, therefore, 'the perception of the infinite under such manifestations as are able to influence the moral character of man', and this is the acorn from which the oaks of all religions grow.

The difficulties of this approach rapidly became apparent. A major problem arose as theories that were imposed on the past were contradicted when hitherto unknown scripts belonging to early religions were eventually deciphered; the inscriptions and texts revealed for the first time at least something of the beliefs of those religions, and showed that their histories were in fact far more complex and diverse than had been supposed.

OLMECS, AZTECS, AND MAYANS

An important example of this was the brilliant decipherment, over a period of many decades during the twentieth century, of Mayan script. The Mayans were one of the Mesoamerican peoples, living in a region encompassing parts of present-day Guatemala, Belize, Honduras, and Mexico, and they were close neighbours of the Aztecs and Olmecs to the north in present-day Mexico. The Olmec people, who flourished from about 1200 BCE to 300 CE, are usually regarded as the source of culture and religion in this area. They travelled great distances in order to obtain and transport basalt boulders (weighing up to 20 tons), from which they carved large heads, but the beliefs associated with these figures are unknown. They also made many artefacts depicting the jaguar.

The jaguar was widely understood as a symbolic focus and embodiment of power in South America; for the Aztecs *(see opposite)*, for example, the jaguar was the incarnation of the god Tezcatlipoca. In general, the jaguar was regarded as the father of all other animals, the Lord of Animals, the ruler of the spirits. To visit the spirits and to communicate with them, the shamans of South America transform themselves into jaguars, in which form they possess the jungle and command the forces that bring good fortune or distress. The jaguar, like the shaman, slips through the twilight shadows of the jungle as an almost invisible presence. The jaguar is the source of life, but it has become – not by its own choice – the enemy of humans, as the South American fire myth of Botoque records.

From such myths, it is possible to write a history of the diffusion of beliefs, and that at once opens up the question of historiography: *whose* history is the history of the historian? A history of events in chronological order is impossible for societies without written records, but other kinds of history, plotting the diffusion of myths and artefacts, might clearly be attempted. Thus it is not even known when or why the Olmecs declined and disappeared, but it is known that they influenced the Mayans in the building of temple complexes, in the use of hieroglyphs, and in their concern for the calendar and astronomy.

The Mayans took those innovations much further. During the Classic Period (c.300–900 CE), they built in Tikal alone about 3,000 different structures in a single square mile, including six temple pyramids. When Europeans explored and conquered the Mayan territory from the sixteenth century onwards, they found immensely impressive temples and many hieroglyphic inscriptions, only a few of which were explained before their use and meaning died out. Much was destroyed, but one book, *Popul Vuh* or *The Book of Council*, had been written in Quiché (a Mayan language), albeit in Spanish script, between 1554 and 1558, telling of creation, the gods, and the story of the Quiché people. What did all this mean? An English explorer, Alfred Maudslay, made seven expeditions between 1881 and 1894, and wrote careful descriptions of the major temple sites, including Tikal, Yaxchilan, Copan, Quiriga, Palanque, and Chichen Itza (the ruins of Bonampak were not discovered until 1946). Even in ruin, they were awe-inspiring. What did the people who worshipped there believe? More was known about the Aztecs, with whom the Mayans were therefore compared.

Ruins of the Northern Acropolis and Temple 1 at the Mayan site of Tikal, Guatemala. An unassuming village in 600 BCE, Tikal expanded to become an important centre of ceremony and administration with an estimated population of 10,000 (plus 50,000 living in the suburbs) between the seventh and ninth centuries CE. The site includes five pyramid temples and three palace-temple complexes clustered around impressive plazas. By the tenth century CE, it had fallen into disuse.

The Aztecs were descended from Mexica warriors who had been armed by Native Americans from further north, and who, in about 1325, had established a foothold on an island, Tenochtitlán, in Lake Texcoco. Calling themselves Tenocha, their influence spread through alliances and conquest and they began to call themselves Aztec, from the land (in legend) in which their ancestors had lived. The Aztecs flourished until the arrival of the Europeans in the sixteenth century. It was well known that the Aztecs were a warlike people who practiced human sacrifice; they attacked their neighbours for plunder, but they also campaigned to capture prisoners for sacrificial victims.

The Mayans seemed entirely different – but that judgement was reached before the Mayan script had been deciphered. On their own, the Mayan ruins suggested a more peaceful and rational people who had left behind Tylor's 'unchanged savagery'.

It was therefore claimed that the Mayans had reached a later and more advanced stage of religious and cultural history. They were, it was said, peaceful, engaging in war only out of necessity, coexisting with each other in city-states. In the temples, paternalistic rulers interceded for the people to the gods. From their strong interest in the calendar and astronomy, and from the fact that they were literate and numerate, the Mayan culture was likened to the height of civilization attained in Greece and Rome, and was indeed called 'the classical civilization of the Americas'.

When, however, Bonampak was discovered with its well-preserved murals depicting violence and the torture and sacrifice of prisoners, and when the Mayan script began to be deciphered, it became clear that the Mayans believed that all beings are possessed of a sacred power (*k'uel/ch'uel*) located essentially in the blood, much as the Aztecs did. Humans depended on the gods, but the gods depended also on humans to sustain them with the blood of sacrifices. Blood could be drawn from a person's own body, but far more efficacious was the blood of prisoners who had endured a long and painful torture.

This complete transformation of the understanding of early Mayan religion illustrates the problem of writing the history of cultures from which no written records survive, or whose script has not been deciphered.

AFRICAN RELIGION

This problem is exacerbated where the religions of a geographical area vary from tribe to tribe, even from village to village. This is a problem of the history of religion in Africa. Africa, like the Americas, is so vast that generalizations about religion are unwise. The geography of Africa ranges from rain forests to uninhabitable deserts; its peoples may be hunter-gatherers with no settled abode, but equally they may live in villages or in modern cities.

Native African religion is thus extremely diverse, and it has few written records. However, oral tradition thrives in Africa, and much has been recovered, not through the decipherment of scripts, but through the development of sophisticated analysis of oral history. The history of African religion is better known in those areas that have been invaded by other religions: Christianity, which arrived in North Africa during the first century and then permeated almost every part of the continent, particularly after the expansion of missionary Christianity, above all in the nineteenth and

Bloodthirsty imagery from the frescos painted on a Mayan tomb, c.790 CE, at Bonampak, Mexico. The battle was probably fought to capture victims for ritual human sacrifice.The jaguar pelts worn by the warriors indicate high social caste – one of them may be Chan Muan, the chief of the Bonampak people.

twentieth centuries; Islam, which displaced Christianity in North Africa from the sixth century and then spread to both East and West Africa in pursuit of trade and slaves (which are permitted in the Qur'ān); and Indian religions, notably Hinduism and Sikhism, in East and South Africa.

This immense variety across the continent means that there is no such thing as 'African religion'. Even so, attempts have been made to identify fundamental and recurrent themes – for example, a strong respect for ancestors, the importance of divination, magic, and witchcraft, and the creation of a context for individual lives in ritual, especially in rites of passage.

Another strongly recurrent theme, which was noticed by the earliest explorers and traders, was the recognition of a High God who delegates power and authority to lesser gods and spirits. William Bosman visited 'the Slave Coast' (that is, West Africa) in the late sixteenth century and wrote that Africans have a clear idea of 'the True God and ascribe to him the Attributes of Almighty and Omnipresent'. He went on, 'It is certain that...they believe he created the Universe, and therefore vastly prefer him before their Idol-Gods. But yet they do not pray to him, or offer any Sacrifices to him; for which they give the following Reasons. God, they say, is too high exalted above us, and too great to condescend so much as to trouble himself or think of Mankind; Wherefore he commits the Government of the World to their Idols; to whom, as the second, third and fourth Persons distant in degree from God, and our appointed lawful Governours, we are obliged to apply ourselves. And in firm Belief of this Opinion they quietly continue'.

This gave rise to the claim that Africa displays a 'diffused monotheism', a belief in One Supreme God that is characterized in various different ways. More recently this has been disputed on the grounds that it arises from the subconscious Christian assumptions of the early recorders of African religion. Our knowledge of early African religion is still too sparse for us to come to a definite conclusion on this point. However, in later African religion this feature becomes more visible, not least through the study of diaspora *(see box, page 20)* African religion.

AFRICAN-AMERICAN RELIGION

The African diaspora came about initially because of the Arab and European slave trades. From the sixteenth to the nineteenth century, at least ten million (perhaps as many as eighteen million) Africans were taken as slaves to North and South America. In South and Central America, this led to new (yet old) ways of worshipping God. Thus the Dahomey Fon people of West Africa named their god *Vodu* and believed that its spirit could be summoned to a local place or person; much Fon religion focused on rituals to summon *vodu* in the form of spirits and to bring their powers into effect. Taken by Africans to Haiti, the word was used first to speak of God, but was then applied to their religion in general, appearing in English as *Vodou* and *Voodoo*. Vodou began as the underground religion of plantation workers, but it rose to prominence during the slave revolt that led to Haiti's independence (1804) and became the indigenous religion of the only Black republic in the Americas. Vodou exemplifies the

'Diaspora'

The Greek word *diaspora* means 'a dispersion'. Among major religions, it was used originally of Judaism, since Jews were exiled or scattered from 'the promised land' *(see pages 192–193)*, establishing major communities in Egypt, Mesopotamia, and Rome (all before the first century CE), and subsequently in Europe and the United States. However, the term 'diaspora religion' now applies to many religions that are 'dispersed' throughout the world: to Christianity, because Christians are commanded to take the Gospel (good news) to the ends of the earth; to Islam, because Muslims are commanded to create a single people (*umma*) united in their allegiance (*islam*) to God; to Sikhs, because of pressure in the Sikh homeland; to Zoroastrians and Tibetans, because of persecution; and to virtually all religions now, because of the Internet.

pattern of a high God (known as *Bondye*, from the French *bon Dieu*, 'good God') made accessible through lesser spirits, who in turn are approached through ritual experts, the *hungans* (male) and *mambos* (female).

Diaspora Africans also took with them their way of worshipping God through drumming and dancing. In South America, especially in Brazil, Uruguay, and Argentina, African dancing was known by the European settlers as *macumba* and *candomblé*, but those were also the names of distinct religions in which the African understanding of God and gods remained alive; the word *candomblé* is thought by some people to be derived from *ka* (a custom or a dance) and *ndombe* (black). Here again the pattern persists of a high God (for Candomblé, *Olorun*) with powers that were delegated to lesser spirits.

Increasingly, the God and gods of Africa became associated with Christian beliefs and symbols. *Shango*, for example, was originally the protector of the Yoruba Oyo kings; taken to the Americas, he has become the protector of all who call on him, especially those who honour him with feasts and songs, and he has also been identified with St Barbara (despite the difference in gender) because they are both protectors against thunder.

The pattern of a high God acting through lesser gods became important for African Christians (and thus for the new religions) because they observed non-Protestant Christians addressing many devotions and prayers to the Virgin Mary and the saints, often with the help of images and pictures. The African gods seemed to resemble the saints in the services they performed, and in Mexico and the West Indies in particular, they were identified with one another. For example, *Eshu-Elegba* in Africa is a trickster who carries messages to heaven, so he was identified in Trinidad with the devil (the trickster) and in Cuba with St Peter (who carries the keys to the kingdom). In Cuba, this 'way of exchange' led to the religion of Santeria, which spread widely into the Caribbean countries and the United States.

The history of African religion in North America began in the slave communities, the 'invisible institution' of the South before the Civil War of 1861–1865, by which time the vast majority of slaves were American-born and Christianity had become, for most, part of their lives. The invisibility refers to the practice of Christianity (often forbidden by owners) outside the institutional churches.

The history of this form of African religion is well documented (see Albert J. Raboteau), and shows that African-Americans continued their own ways of understanding God, especially in dancing and drumming, and eventually in the songs of tribulation and hope that are known as Spirituals. Through these, they declared their freedom long before it was legally secured.

That inner freedom led also to an important independence in the development of their religion, first made publicly evident in the forming of the African Methodist Episcopalian Church in 1787, the first Church in North America to be made up entirely of African-Americans. This creativity has been exercised not only in relation to Christianity, but also to Judaism (Black Jewish movements began with William Crowdy, who established a congregation fused with Christianity in 1905, based on his belief that the original Jews were Black), to Islam (Black Muslim movements began before the First World War, but are more often associated with the Nation of Islam, derived from Wallace Fard in 1930 but better known in later forms under Malcolm X, 1926–65, and Louis Farrakhan, born 1933), and to African religions (of these, the best known is *Ras Tafari*, or Rastafarianism, which originated in the early twentieth century with the belief that Prince Ras Tafari Makonnen, who became Emperor Haile Selassie of Ethiopia in 1930 and who was believed to be descended from David and Solomon, would lead the exiled Africans back to their own country). The note of freedom from bondage and slavery is characteristic of African-American religion, reinforced as it is by the biblical story of the Exodus *(see page 186)*. It achieved its consummate expression in the leadership of the American civil rights movement by Martin Luther King (1929–1968) and in his speech at the end of the March on Washington on 28 August 1963, 'I have a dream' *(see pages 260–261)*.

NATIVE AMERICAN RELIGION

In North America, Africans and African religion soon came into contact with the very different beliefs and practices of Native Americans. Native Americans inhabited every part of North America, from the Arctic to the southern deserts, in many different tribes speaking many different languages, so it is unwise to generalize about 'Native American religion', especially since it also extends into Meso- and South America. Waldman and York's *Encyclopedia of Native American Tribes* (1998) begins with the wise warning, 'Keep in mind that each tribe has a detailed history to be further explored... Also keep in mind that each tribe has its own world view and ceremonials'. Each tribe (or First Nation as they are increasingly being called) had its own system of recording its history. The Algonquin, for example, developed the use of *wampum* belts in order to record important events and people; they made wampum from seashells ground into coloured beads, and used these as a way of marking important occasions such as the making of peace. Wampum belts were subsequently imitated by settlers, so that wampum became a form of money.

A Shoshone woman, from the nomadic nation that once lived in the midwestern deserts of North America, dances in a ceremonial costume. Dancing holds a paramount place in the rituals of all Native American peoples.

None of this, however, yields the kind of history that becomes possible once documents record the ways in which early settlers began to invade the territories of the Native Americans and to seize their land. The history then becomes one of increasing dispossession and destruction, in which Native American religion was frequently understood as a version of Tylor's 'unchanged savagery'. Reaction to this has often been expressed (in the past and still in the present) in religious terms, for example in the Ghost Dance (1890–1900, recently revived), and in an ecological emphasis on nature as spiritual.

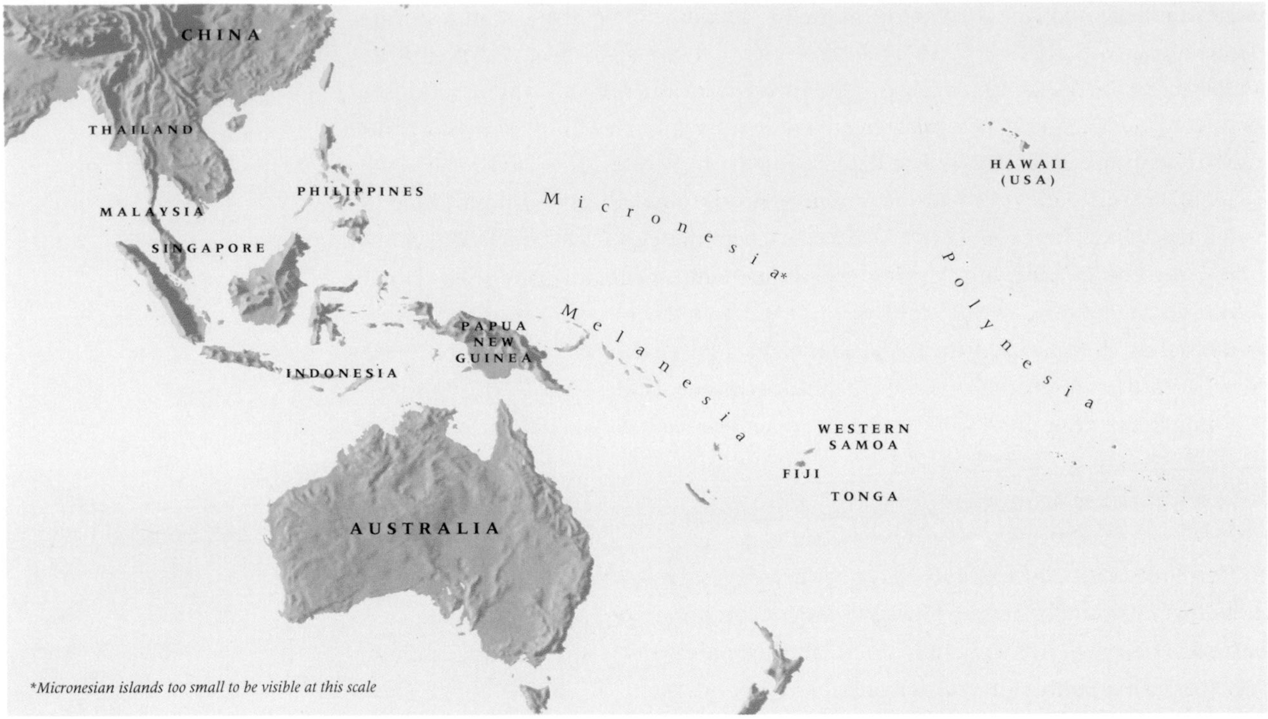

A map of the Pacific region, including the major island groups of Polynesia, Melanesia, and Micronesia.

OCEANIC RELIGION AND THE ABORIGINES

All the many problems, summarized above, involved in writing the early history of religions recur in the Pacific region. First, the area is vast (and for that reason was divided by early European explorers into three major areas: Polynesia, 'many islands', to the east; Micronesia, 'small islands', to the northwest; and Melanesia, 'black islands', to the southwest). Second, it contains many different territories, all with their own histories. Third, some of these came under the influence of traders, invaders, or missionaries who belonged to other religions so that indigenous beliefs were submerged – notably Hindus (in Bali, Sumatra, Java, and Fiji), Muslims (in Indonesia – which today has the largest Muslim population in the world at nearly two hundred million – Borneo, Brunei, Mindanao, and New Guinea), and Christians, throughout the region. Fourth, there are few written records (M. C. Ricklefs summarized the problem: 'It [the Islamization of Asia] is nearly as obscure as the indianization process of several centuries before... It is unlikely that there will ever be adequate evidence to describe, let alone explain, these processes in detail'). Fifth, there are many different religions; G. W. Trompf, following the view that different languages foster different understandings of the world, has pointed out that Melanesia is the home of about one-third of the world's languages, 'and that means – considering how languages are so crucial in defining discrete cultures – just as many religions'.

In these circumstances, the history of religions in this area cannot be written. However, as with Africa and the Americas, generalizations have been made, and the area thereby contributed terms to the study of religion that have passed into common usage. An early example is *mana*, identified by R. H. Codrington in his 1891 book *The Melanesians* as 'power *par excellence*, the genuine effectiveness of things which corroborates their practical actions without annihilating them: this is what causes the net to bring in a good catch, makes the house solid and keeps the canoe sailing smoothly: in the farms it is fertility, in medicine it is either health or death'. Passing into even wider currency was *taboo* or *tabu* (Polynesian *tapu*) – a power not unrelated to *mana,* which, if negative, marks people, places, or objects as dangerous. Outsiders used and understood *tabu* in ways far removed from the Polynesian application, not least due to the influence of the psychoanalyst Sigmund Freud (1856–1939) who, like J. G. Frazer, wrote his own history of early religion in which he imposed his opinions without much, if any, attention to evidence. Finding, for example, his Oedipal theory confirmed by the speculative account given by a biblical scholar, Ernst Sellin, of the death of Moses, Freud was not in the least dismayed when Sellin withdrew his account on the grounds that there was no evidence for it. Freud simply replied that even if the death of Moses had not happened in that way, it nevertheless *could* have.

It is thus a major problem for historians of religions to understand terms and concepts, like *tabu/tapu,* without imposing later (including their own) interpretations. The anthropologist Jean Smith wrote of how *tapu* is removed among the Maori of New Zealand, and observed that accounts of *tapu* fall into the error of assimilating all uses of the word to a single meaning or set of meanings. In contrast, she pointed out that 'the concept was involved in many different fields of practical concern (for example, status relations, the explanation of misfortune, the preservation of property), and it may be an unwarranted assumption that there was something significant in common between all the different uses of the concept apart from the ultrahuman sanction which was ultimately involved'. The creative genius of humans has been exercised in religion as much as in any other field. If, as a result, the meaning of concepts shifts greatly according to context, the history of early religions is going to be extremely difficult to write. If these meanings are then recorded by those who filter them through their own preconceptions, the problem is made worse.

These pitfalls led Tony Swain to observe of the earliest inhabitants of Australia that everything that is known of Aboriginal beliefs and practices has been *recorded* in a historical setting. His argument is that even the best-known concepts like 'dream-time' have been constructed according to the concepts of outside observers and interpreters, who happen to have had a strong Western sense of linear time. In contrast, Swain argues that 'dream-time' is not related to time at all, but to the space in which the life of all beings is lived in an interconnected and interrelated way.

The way in which preconceptions about time and causality have dominated the writing of the early history of religions has also been challenged by deconstructionists. Insofar as that challenge is confined to the question of perspective (on what grounds can we decide whose perspective, purpose, and method in writing history has validity or priority?), there would be support for it in the history of religions. Much of this book has been written from the perspective of those who value historiography as it has developed in and from the classical world of Greece and Rome. To write the history of religion from the perspective of historiography as it developed in and from the classical worlds of India, Africa, China, or the Americas would be to produce almost as many books as there are distinct religious cultures and histories.

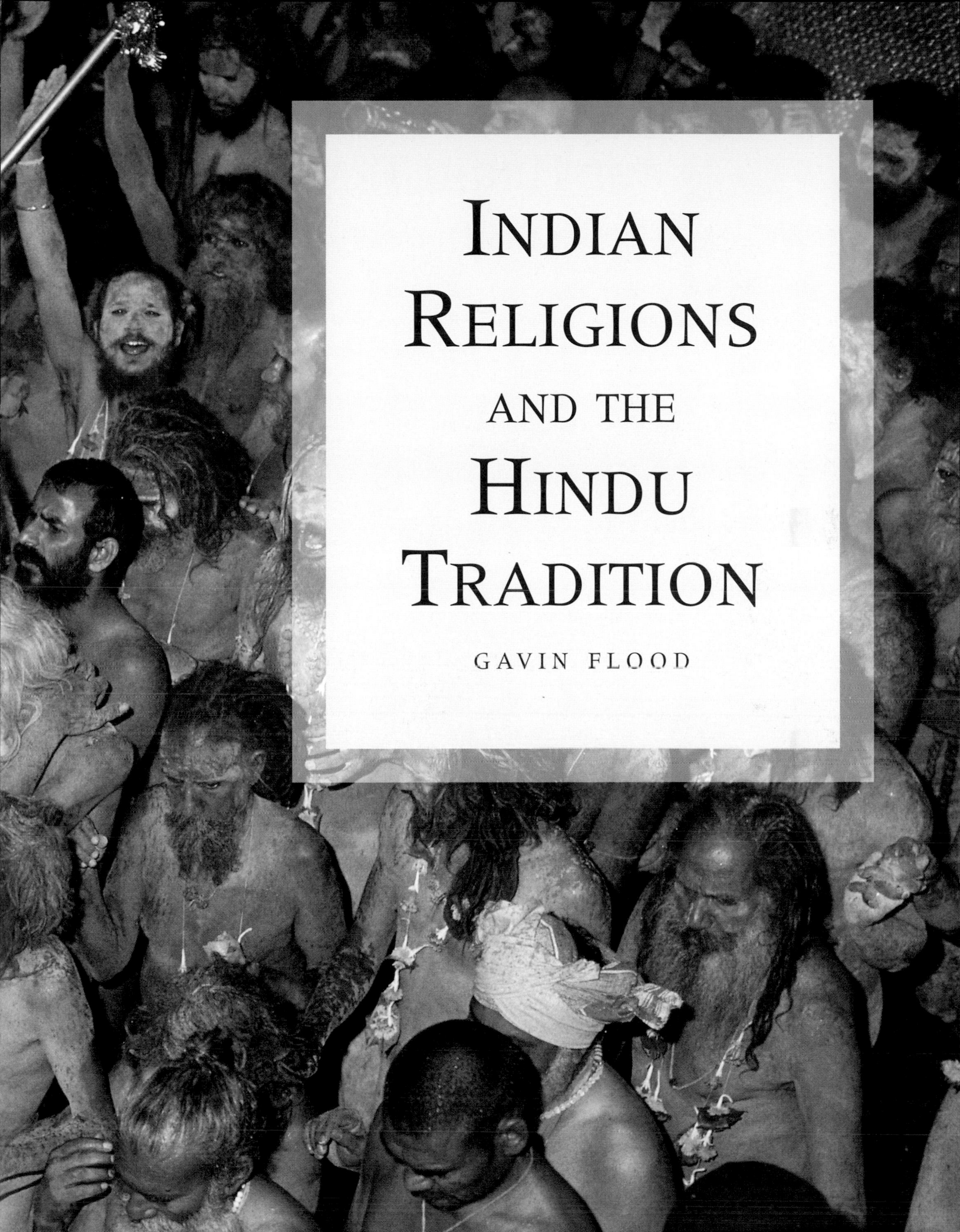

INDIAN RELIGIONS AND THE HINDU TRADITION

GAVIN FLOOD

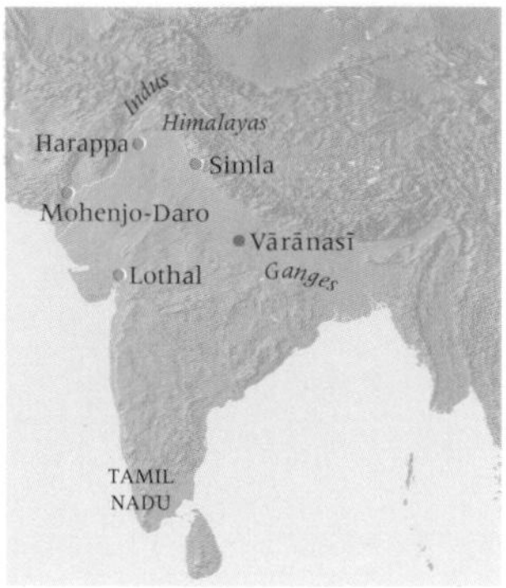

Indian Religions and the Hindu Tradition

The history of religion in early India is obscure and its interpretation has become increasingly politicized. The perception of the past has become an important element in the arguments put forward by Hindu political groups calling for greater Hindu self-awareness and assertiveness, partly as a reaction against the colonial history of the country. The debate about early India must be seen in the context of debates about the nature of history and about whether all history is constructed or based on a past that really happened in a specified way. But although dates are disputed and questions arise about the ancient cultures, through archeology and contemporary texts we know something about religion in those early times.

THE INDUS VALLEY CIVILIZATION

In 1921, the archeologists Sir John Marshall and R. D. Banerjea discovered the remains of an ancient civilization that had flourished along the banks of the great Indus River which flows through present-day Pakistan. Two cities were discovered at Harappa and Mohenjo-Daro that revealed a sophisticated urban culture. This Indus Valley civilization (also called the Harappan civilization) originated during the Neolithic period (7000–6000 BCE) and reached a high point around 2300–2000 BCE, but had declined by 1500 BCE. At its height, the civilization traded with Mesopotamia and extended over about 1,950,000 square kilometres (750,000 square miles) from Lothal in present-day Gujarat and Sutkagen Dor near the Iranian border up to the foothills of the Himalayas near Simla. Archeologists have found evidence of a continuity of culture from the earliest date, seen in the sequentiality of material remains such as pottery, architecture, and writing as early as the fourth millennium BCE. Large grain stores may indicate a system of tax-collecting which suggests that grain was probably the basis of the economy, as was also the case in contemporary civilizations in ancient Mesopotamia.

Our knowledge of religion in the Indus Valley is limited largely because we do not have access to the language of the time. There was a system of writing which has been found on soapstone seals and copper plates, but it has yet to be deciphered; to add to the challenge, we do not know what kind of language they spoke. There are two broad possibilities: one that it was from the Dravidian group of languages (now spoken in southern India), the other that it was from the Indo-Aryan group (now spoken in northern India). The script will probably remain undeciphered until either more samples are found to aid reconstruction or a bilingual inscription is discovered. Such an insight could tell us about daily transactions and possibly something about religion, although individual sacred texts may have only been preserved orally.

Evidence of religion in the Indus Valley can only be inferred from buildings that were probably temples, from soapstone seals, statues, and terracotta figurines. There may have been a state religion that focused on a cult of the king, and there was probably a concern with ritual purity. A great bath found in Mohenjo-Daro may indicate ritual bathing and is reminiscent of tanks found in later Hindu temples. Structures that could be altars have been found, so it is possible that animal sacrifice was performed, especially at the site of Kalibangan in the Punjab, about 320 kilometres (200 miles) from Harappa. The terracotta figurines and numerous seals depict what may be deities, and one very important seal shows a seated figure surrounded by animals. An interpretation of this horned figure is that he resembles the later Hindu god Śiva, with three faces and seated in a yoga posture. However, rather than being a proto-Śiva, the figure could represent a seated bull, for almost identical figures have been found on Elamite seals in Mesopotamia (c.3000–2750 BCE). Even so, iconographic elements represented here could have found their way into later representations of Śiva: while the relationship between Indus Valley religion and later Hindu traditions must remain speculative, it is tempting to think that there are such links.

THE ARYANS

The Indus Valley culture declined between 1800 and 1700 BCE, possibly due to the effects of flooding or conversely because of drought. Following this decline, the general consensus, unquestioned until recently, has been that groups of people calling themselves 'noble ones' (Aryans) migrated into or invaded southern Asia from the northwest and became the culturally dominant force. The most commonly accepted theory has been that some of these groups entered India through the northern passes from central Asia while others entered Iran. Indeed, there are close affinities between the Iranian Zoroastrian religion, with its scripture the *Avesta* *(see page 217)*, and the religion of the Veda, the sacred revelation of the Hindus. The Aryans spoke an

The ruins of the ancient city of Mohenjo-Daro, centre of what is now called the Indus Valley civilization. The city, which flourished in the third and second centuries BCE, was evidently a sophisticated construct with multi-storey houses, an efficient sewerage system, and a grid layout. It remains an enigma to scholars because the language found on stone tablets and artefacts has not yet been deciphered.

Indo-European language that developed into Sanskrit. This theory portrays the Aryans as being primarily concerned with worldly affairs and without the interest in transcendence that developed with later traditions. It presents the Aryans as subduing the local population over a period of time, and becoming the dominant culture in northern India, especially in the Ganges plain, which becomes known as the 'homeland of the Aryans' (*āryāvarta*). The theory further suggests that Aryan culture then slowly spread to southern India, becoming established there by the sixth century CE. This Aryan migration hypothesis sees the Indus Valley civilization as a Dravidian culture, speaking a Dravidian language, which became subordinated to the invading, or at least migrating, Aryans.

This view was challenged in the last two decades of the twentieth century by what might be called the cultural transformation hypothesis, which argues that Aryan culture was a development of the Indus Valley where the language belonged to the Indo-European group. The theory propounds that there was no Aryan incursion or invasion, this being a myth developed by colonial scholars who wished to claim that anything of value in India came from outside. There are even claims that Sanskrit was the language of the Indus Valley. This is a complex matter with evidence on both sides. But one piece of evidence against the view that the Indus Valley culture was Aryan is the absence of horse and chariot remains in the archaeological record; nor are horses depicted on the Indus Valley seals. The horse was important in Aryan culture; on a practical level horses pulled the Aryan war chariots, while on a religious they are represented in their sacred scriptures, the Veda, in which they are animals for sacrifice.

Our knowledge of the religion of the Aryans comes largely from the Veda, a collection of texts from around 1200 BCE (with a commentary possibly written into the early Common Era) in an early form of Sanskrit (Vedic Sanskrit). The Veda is central to Hindu beliefs and observances. These texts show the Aryans to have had a hierarchical society expressed in the Veda in terms of four classes: the priestly class or Brahmans, the warriors or nobility (*kṣatriya*), the commoners or merchants (*vaiśya*), and the serfs (*śūdra*). While this is a theoretical scheme, it probably reflects a hierarchical society that is the origin of the complex Hindu caste system. The first three classes were known as the 'twice-born' because the males underwent initiation into adulthood, and it is possible that the lowest group represented the indigenous population, if there is truth in the Aryan migration thesis (which there arguably is). The twice-born performed sacrifices, administered by the Brahmans, to various kinds of gods. These were classified as gods of the earth, atmosphere, and sky. In the earth realm lived the very important deities Agni, or fire, and the plant god Soma. In the atmosphere lived the warrior Indra, the storm gods, and the wind god Vāyu. In the sky-realm were the sky god Dyaus (comparable to the Greek Zeus, *see page 224*) and Varuṇa, the god of righteousness, among others. Agni conveyed the sacrifice from this world into the next while Soma (who may have represented a hallucinogenic mushroom or more probably a plant containing ephedrine, similar in effect to adrenaline/ epinephrine) conveyed the warrior into the divine realm. Over time, Vedic sacrifice became more elaborate and complex. Solemn Vedic rites are still performed in the present day, notably by some Brahman families in Kerala.

A Brahman priest prays on the banks of the Ganges at Vārānasī, one of India's most sacred cities and an important Hindu pilgrimage site. The Brahmans represent the highest caste in the Hindu tradition. All priests are Brahmans and have the right and responsibility to carry out rituals.

THE VEDIC PERIOD

Whatever the origins of the Aryans, during the first millennium BCE Vedic culture became firmly established, especially in the north of the subcontinent. Although a minority of the population, the Brahmans were the most important social group who performed rituals for the aristocracy and governed the religious ideology of the community. Their place is expressed well by hymn 10.90 in the *Ṛg Veda*, the oldest of the Vedic collections *(see page 30 and 34–35)*, which describes the origins of the world and of society in terms of a sacrifice. The gods created the world through the sacrifice and dismemberment of a giant man (*puruṣa*). From different parts of his body the cosmos, society, and even the Veda itself were formed. From his feet came the serfs, the lowest stratum of society; from his thighs the commoners or merchants, the support of society; from his arms came the society's strength in the nobility or warrior class; and the Brahmans came from his mouth as the speech of society.

The degree to which these divisions reflect social reality in Vedic times is difficult to determine, for this image presents an ideological model of a social hierarchy. There may in fact have been two dominant social elites, the Suris and the Aris, each served by their own priesthood, and there was probably more social flexibility than is reflected in this hymn. However, what is noticeable about the hymn is that the social hierarchy is continuous with the structure of the cosmos. The social order is an extension of the cosmic order and social law is part of eternal, cosmic law (*ṛta*). This cosmic law is articulated by the Brahmans, the speech of the social body.

BRAHMANICAL RITUAL

One of the most important functions of the Brahmans was the performance of ritual, particularly elaborate, public sacrifice. The central religious act of the Vedic Aryans was sacrifice and the sharing of the sacrificial meal with each other and with the gods (*devas*). Such sacrifices were initiated and paid for by a patron (*yajamāna*), as a consequence of which his social standing would be enhanced, the gods appeased, and prosperity secured for him and his family. Before the ritual, he would undergo preliminary rites involving some degree of asceticism (*tapas*) and initiation (*dīkṣā*). The term 'sacrifice' (*homa, yajñā*) indicated any offering placed within the sacred fires and included milk, clarified butter (*ghṛta*, or *ghee* as it is often known), curds, grains, and *soma*, as well as domestic animals. Two forms of ritual developed during the Vedic period: first the solemn, public rites (*śrauta*), and then the domestic and life-cycle rites (*gṛhya*). The solemn observances involved the use of three fires, the domestic the use of a single fire. The term *śrauta*, used to describe these ceremonies, is closely related to the word *śruti*, 'that which is heard', or the revelation of the Veda. These rites are described in texts called *Śrauta Sūtras* and other texts dealing with different branches of Vedic knowledge composed between the eighth and fourth centuries BCE. Although these writings are 500 years or more later than the composition of the *Ṛg Veda*, the *śrauta* rites were probably already established at that early period.

The *Ṛg Veda* mentions four classes of priest involved in the rites, each having a different sacrificial function and a different section of the Veda to recite. The chief priest (*hotṛ*) recited verses from the *Ṛg Veda*, a second priest (*udgātṛ*) would chant verses set to recitational patterns of the *Sāma Veda*, and a third priest (*adhvaryu*) would recite from the *Yajur Veda*. In time, a fourth priest (*brahman*) associated with the *Atharva Veda* came to oversee the proceedings and ensure that nothing was omitted. The recitation of the Veda in the ritual context would be entirely from memory. This is a good illustration of the fact that the sacred scriptures of the Hindus are primarily used in ritual; they are performed texts.

Carved horses in the Temple of Sri Raṅganāthaswami at Śrīraṅgam, near Tiruchirapalli, Tamil Nadu, at the southern tip of India. The only temple in India with seven enclosures (*prākāras*), it is the abode of Lord Raṅganātha and is dedicated to the cult of Viṣṇu, a minor god in Vedic terms, but one who went on to become a member of the Hindu trinity.

These sacrificial rites could be very complex and, presumably, very expensive, spreading over a number of days. One of these rites, the *agnicayana* or 'piling up of the fire,' involved the construction of an elaborate altar in the shape of a large bird. Two important rites were associated with kingship: the horse sacrifice (*aśvamedha*), and the consecration of the king (*rājasūya*). In the horse sacrifice, a stallion would wander freely for a year and was then ritually suffocated. The king's wife would symbolically sleep with the dead stallion, which was identified with the creator-father god Prajāpati, and the power of the god would enter the queen and through her the king and the people. The king's territory would be increased by the area covered by the roaming horse. The consecration of the king involved an elaborate process. For an entire year the king underwent an initiation, after which he performed a ceremony involving the application of unction and his symbolic rebirth from the sacrifice. These rites had multiple functions within early Vedic society. They increased the prestige of the patron, reinforced the power of the Brahmans, and expressed the social values of the community not only by who was included in the rites but by who was excluded.

The domestic rites that are incumbent upon a Brahman are described in texts called *Gṛhya Sūtras*. The Brahman must keep a domestic fire in his household, casting vegetarian offerings into it. These daily rites (*nitya-karma*) were supplemented by specific rituals (*naimittika-karma*) marking different stages of life, notably birth, initiation, marriage, and death. At initiation (*upanayana*), boys were endowed with a sacred thread, a symbol of high-caste males. This rite made the top three classes (Brahmans, nobles, and commoners) 'twice-born', being born a second time through initiation. Women did not undergo Vedic initiation, although the *Laws of Manu*, a Hindu law book composed between the second century BCE and the third century CE, says that marriage is a woman's Vedic initiation. In modern Hinduism there are women's rites of passage which are not based on Sanskrit texts but on oral, folk traditions; similar practices may have been present during the early period but we have no record of them.

Brahman Continuity

Brahmans still maintain ritual purity and observe the necessary ceremonies of their caste, and the solemn Vedic rites are still performed, albeit occasionally, by some Brahman families, especially in Kerala. This illustrates the continuity of ritual traditions in southern Asia. In spite of often radical political change, there is a level of observance that has survived such upheavals and may be linked to a certain equilibrium of social relations provided by the class and caste system.

Indian Philosophy

Philosophy in India has a long history, and philosophical debate has become a highly technical and refined practice. Many divergent schools developed whose positions regarding epistemological and ontological issues – that is, issues revolving around the study of the validity, approach, and scope of knowledge, and the first principles and nature of being – were gradually clarified through a process of dialogue. The different philosophical schools came to be known by the term *darśana*, 'view', which implies a critical world-view, although other terms such as *vāda* or 'discourse' are also used. These various schools flowered between the seventh and the seventeenth centuries.

Among the common concerns of Indian philosophical analysis are: the question of being, and whether there is truly a single primary reality or a plurality of realities; the meaning of human life; the nature of language and the relation of words to objects; and the nature of knowledge. While some of these concerns are close to the central debates of Western philosophy, the style of discourse in Indian philosophy is distinctive in so far as the debate in India about these issues took place over a number of centuries, mainly through commentaries on sacred texts, and subsequently through commentaries on commentaries. The history of Indian philosophy can be roughly divided into three broad periods: the pre-systematic thought of the Vedas, Upaniṣads, Epics, and early Buddhism; the classical systems of Hindu, Buddhist, and Jain thought, including the theologies of the theistic traditions; and modern Indian philosophy in the nineteenth and twentieth centuries.

From the seventh century CE onwards, traditions of commentary on sacred texts (or *sūtras)* proliferated. These *sūtras* were often so terse that they cannot be understood without a commentary, and – inevitably – different commentaries offered different interpretations. These systems of interpretation became codified by the medieval period into six systems of philosophy or six *darśanas,* namely Sāṁkhya, Yoga, Mīmaṁsā, Vedānta, Nyāya, and Vaiśeṣika, often grouped into three pairs: Sāṁkhya-Yoga, Mīmaṁsā-Vedānta, and Nyāya Vaiśeṣika. This scheme was an attempt by the proponents of Brahmanical orthodoxy to codify a divergence of views into those who accepted the Veda as revelation (*āstika*), and those who rejected this belief (*nāstika*), namely the Jains, Buddhists, and the materialists. The scheme also omitted the important philosophical speculations focused on the god Śiva, the Śaiva Siddhānta and non-Saiddhāntika traditions (the latter often referred to as Kashmir Śaivism).

While they shared a common terminology, the *āstika* schools differed widely in their views about the self, the process of reincarnation, and other metaphysical concepts. For example, the *Advaita* (meaning non-dual, or undifferentiated) Vedānta of Śaṅkara, a Brahman philosopher born in Kerala (788–820), argued that revelation reveals the single reality of Brahman with which the 'self' is identical, whereas the Vaiśeṣika maintained the existence of discrete, atomic entities. All of these schools regarded themselves as being traditions that afforded liberation (*mokṣa*) from the cycle of reincarnation. In contrast, Indian philosophy in the twentieth and twenty-first centuries does not have such salvationist concerns and has been strongly influenced by Western philosophy.

Contemporary scholarship about Indian philosophy has been particularly concerned with language and logic. Both philosophers and linguists have come to appreciate the sophistication of Indian grammarians and logicians.

A modern Indian philosopher applies himself to his text. Most of the books used in ancient Indian philosophy were commentaries designed to elucidate original religious and philosophical writings. Different interpretations led to the formation of different philososphical traditions. Modern Indian philosophers also examine ideas from the Western tradition.

HOLY AND INFLUENTIAL TEXTS AND TENETS

HINDUISM HAS A VAST BODY of sacred literature. While most of these texts are now available in book form, this was not always so, and Hindu revelation was passed down the generations orally for thousands of years. Hindu texts are divided into two broad classes: revealed texts (the Veda), and texts of human authorship. More accurately, perhaps, this literature may be treated as a secondary revelation, for these texts are treated with great reverence. Some Hindus have regarded other texts – called Tantra, composed between the seventh and the eleventh centuries CE – as revelation also.

Fragment from the *Atharva Veda*, a collection of hymns used for domestic rituals. Hymns and mantras for healing are mixed with hymns of praise and philosophical speculation. The *Atharva Veda* was added as a latecomer to the original threefold Vedic collections, the *Ṛg Veda*, *Sama Veda*, and *Yajur Veda*.

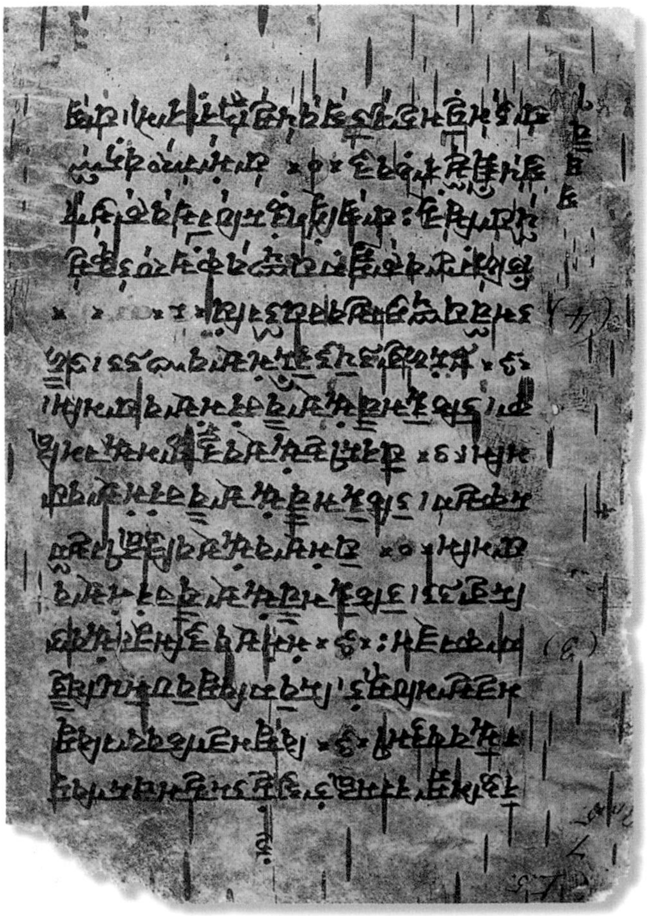

THE VEDA

The texts of the Aryans, the Veda, became regarded as a revelation or 'that which is heard' (*śruti*) by later traditions and became a defining feature of Indian traditions by the end of the first millennium BCE. The Veda is now regarded as central to Hinduism, although the term 'Hindu' does not appear in early scriptures and only occurs in texts from the sixteenth century CE onwards. *Veda* simply means 'knowledge' and many Hindus regard these scriptures as timeless revelation. For some, the Veda was created by a divine being, while for others it has neither a divine nor a human author but is eternal. The texts were received or 'seen' by ancient sages (*ṛṣi*) and were transferred to the human community. The Brahmans preserved the texts – and continue to do so – as oral traditions of recitation passed down through the generations. These texts are extremely important in Hindu self-representation and have had a significant influence on the various Hindu schools, providing a strong sense of continuity with the past.

The primary function of the Veda is ritualistic; the texts are recited during ceremonials and should be understood principally in terms of performance. It is the performance that is important, and which gives the writings meaning. There is a distinction between *mantra* or verses used in ritual, and *brāhmaṇa*, explanatory and interpretative texts. Whereas the *mantra* portions of the Veda are used ritually, especially during the Vedic sacrifice, the *brāhmaṇa* portions of the text have no practical or ritual use. One way of understanding the structure is to think of the Veda as comprising four traditions or streams (called the Ṛg, Yajur, Sāma, and Atharva). These four are called 'collections' (*saṃhitā*) and are made up of the mantras to the gods used in the sacrifice. Sometimes the term *Veda* simply refers to these four collections, which may have been composed around 1200 BCE. These four streams flow into three further classes of text: the Brāhmaṇas, which are commentaries on the meaning of the verses and explain how to perform sacrifice; the Āraṇyakas, or 'forest treatises'; and the Upaniṣads, the 'secret scriptures'. These three can be understood as commentaries on the ritual and as repositories for theological speculations. The 108 Upaniṣads are very important texts, for they were the inspiration behind many Hindu philosophical schools in later centuries. Although very difficult to date, the 11 major Upaniṣads were probably composed around 800 BCE, with some important texts such as the *Śvetāśvatara Upaniṣads* composed later (second century BCE–second century CE).

THE UPANIṢADS

Apart from the rituals of the Brahmans, other forms of religion also developed during the Vedic period. These forms reinterpreted the sacrifice, focused on the development of ideal inner states of being through meditation and yoga, and offered metaphysical speculation about the nature of the universe and the human condition within it. These ideas are found in the Upaniṣads, the 'end of the Veda' (*vedānta*). Like the Brāhmaṇas and the Āraṇyakas, these texts interpret the meaning of the sacrifice – but unlike the rest of the Veda, it is the resulting *understanding* of the ritual that is important rather than its actual performance. Knowledge of the correspondence between ritual and the cosmos lies at the heart of the Upaniṣads. The earliest Upaniṣads, the *Bṛhadāraṇyaka* for example, open by identifying the horse sacrifice with the world, the head with the dawn, the eye with the sun, and so on. This understanding is felt to give rise to a kind of power. In the Brāhmaṇas, the power of the ritual was called *brahman*; in the Upaniṣads, this idea comes to mean the energy underlying not only the ritual but the cosmos as well. It is also identified with the power that is the essence of the self (*ātman*), the highest truth of a person. In this way, the Upaniṣads internalize the ritual, and the power of the ritual becomes the innermost power of the self. Furthermore, this power is identified with bliss (*ānanda*) and with absolute consciousness (*cit*). This identification of absolute essence (*brahman*), the self (*ātman*), bliss, and truth (*satya*) became very important in later Hindu thought, particularly in the Advaita Vedānta tradition from the eighth century BCE and in modern neo-Hinduism.

Knowledge of this deeper, absolute truth of the self comes not through the performance of ritual nor through action but through the renunciation of action and through knowledge or wisdom (*jñāna*). To realize this absolute truth the believer must become a world renouncer and withdraw from social obligations and worldly transactions. The last stage of life, renunciation, becomes the ideal condition for enlightenment and awakening to a higher truth. The ascetics who followed this path, the world renouncers (*sannyāsin*), gave up the use of fire (both the ritual fires of the

Vedic householder and fire for cooking) and, clad in yellow robes or even naked, begged for their food. To realize or know the absolute within the self is to become detached from action (*karma*) and its consequences. While this originally meant ritual action, it came to refer to all action, the consequences of which are reaped not only in this but in future lives. The Upaniṣads are the first texts revered by Hindus that express the idea that the unchanging self passes from body to body, depending upon its actions. Thus good actions will reap good results, bad actions bad results in a future reincarnation. But knowledge of the absolute, which is ultimately the unchanging self, is beyond all good and bad action and beyond reincarnation. Liberation comes through knowledge, and to achieve this knowledge the Upaniṣads taught methods of detachment and concentration. Through *yoga*, the 'yoking' or control of the mind, breath, and body, the renouncer becomes one-pointed and can concentrate on the essence of the self. The texts describe various kinds of yogic practice. One important method is to focus on a sacred sound such as *oṃ* or sacred verses of the Veda. Through yoga, inner states of awareness are cultivated and the yogi realizes the true nature of the self to be *brahman*.

The tradition of the Upaniṣads is parallel to other renouncer traditions that developed at the same time or earlier. These were known as *śramaṇa* traditions and were characterized by an ideology of renunciation and the practice of asceticism. From about 800 to 400 BCE, texts bear witness to these beliefs and responses, teaching that life is suffering and liberation comes only through detachment from the material world. The most important of these traditions that have survived and thrived are Buddhism and Jainism (*see pages 54–63 and 72–109*).

DHARMA

Underlying the performance of Vedic ritual was a concept that was to become very important in the development of Hindu traditions. As we have seen, the caste system was regarded as sacred lore, and the structure of society as a continuation of the structure of the cosmos – part of the cosmic structure. The legitimization of power relations within the society was reinforced by the idea of *dharma*. This term has no direct English equivalent but might loosely be translated as 'law', 'virtue', 'duty', or even 'religion'. *Dharma* is the obligation to perform the ritual acts that are presented in the Veda and to fulfil duties owing to an individual's social group and family. The concept therefore encompasses not only ritual but moral behaviour as well. There came to be much speculation about *dharma* between the eighth and fourth centuries BCE, and one school of philosophy, the Mīmāṁsā, believed *dharma*, understood as the performance of ritual action, to be the most important human activity. *Dharma* should be performed not because it offers the prospect of a reward but primarily because the Veda declares that it should be done and its non-performance would be a sin (*pāpā*). *Dharma* as a Vedic obligation is eternal but is expressed through specific, ritual action. With law books such as the *Laws of Manu*, *dharma* came to have wider applications that focused particularly on caste duty and the maintenance of the status quo within society.

By the fifth century BCE, *dharma* had come to refer to two obligations: duty concerning an individual's caste or class (*varṇa*) and duty respecting his or her stage of life (*āśrama*). Indeed, one definition of a Hindu is a person born into an endogamous section of southern Asian society (marrying only within the group) who adheres to *varṇāśrama-dharma*, a standard sense of social obligation and respect for traditional modes of conduct. This concept became very important in the history of Hinduism. While the term *varṇa* refers to the four classes of the Vedic model of society, it can also refer to caste or *jati*, an endogamous division of Hindu society. Obligation to one's caste became paramount by the fifth century BCE, and the model of the *varṇāśrama-dharma* became the dominant ideology against which other religious groups defined themselves. Thus, later Tantric traditions rejected this social norm (*see pages 41–43*), as did Buddhism and Jainism to some degree.

Caste became central in the development of Hindu traditions. It reflected a hierarchy based on a polarity of purity and pollution, with the Brahmans at the top and groups called the *dalits* (oppressed) or 'untouchables' at the bottom, who, it was believed, would pollute the Brahman if they came into direct contact. These untouchable groups were placed below the fourth class of serfs in the social hierarchy. Alongside the ideology of caste there developed the idea of the stages of life by which each high-caste male lived through four phases: as a celibate student of the Veda after his initiation, married householder, hermit, and renouncer. This structure may have originated as four distinct options that became integrated into a coherent system. It represents an ordering of social relationships as well as an ordering of the high-caste individual's passage through life. Most people would probably simply have become householders, but some became hermits and world renouncers in order to seek a higher goal of world transcendence beyond social obligation.

Sādhus on the banks of the Ganges at Vārānasī. *Sādhus* are Hindu holy men who have renounced the ways of the world to seek *brahman* or God. They are sometimes known as *sant* (saint) and may belong to a formal order (*sampradāya*), or follow the ways and customs of Hinduism without undertaking initiation.

THE EPICS AND THE PURĀṆAS

The Sanskrit term *itihasā* incorporates the Western concepts of myth and history and refers to the narrative traditions that developed in India mostly between 500 BCE and 1000 CE. These traditions include the two great Sanskrit epics the *Mahābhārata* and the *Rāmāyaṇa,* and the Purāṇas. The *itihasā* are regarded as of human authorship (*smṛti*) rather than as revelations (*śruti*), although one may think of them as secondary revelations because they are believed to be divinely inspired. They contain a vast amount of material documenting political, social, ritual, and other religious concerns. They stem from popular, oral traditions performed in villages throughout India by specialists who reflect the interests of non-Brahman groups, most notably the Kṣatriya class. These texts document the rise of the great deities of Hinduism, Viṣṇu, Śiva, and the Goddess (Devī), and continue to be of importance in contemporary Hinduism, especially as mediated through television and cinema screens.

The *Mahābhārata* remains the longest epic poem in the world, comprising more than 100,000 verses. According to tradition, the author was Vyāsa, although scholarship has established the development of the epic over several centuries, reaching its present form around the first century CE. There were two major revisions of the poem in the north and the south, and there is a Tamil version of the southern rendering. The central theme of the poem is *dharma,* especially the *dharma* of kingship. The story is briefly as follows: the king of the lunar dynasty had two sons, Paṇḍu and Dhṛtarāṣṭra, the latter being born blind. Paṇḍu ruled a kingdom in north India and had five sons (Yudhiṣṭhira, Bhīma, Arjuna, Nakula, and Sahadeva). On Paṇḍu's death, the throne passed to his brother, so Paṇḍu's five sons, the Pānḍavas, grew up with their cousins, the Kauravas. The eldest Kaurava, Duryodhana, claimed the right to the throne and had his cousins and their mother banished. The plot is somewhat complicated at this point, but in the end the Pānḍavas spend many years exiled in the forest and eventually return to fight Duryodhana. All the Kauravas are killed in a fierce battle, the scene for the famous *Bhagavad Gītā* (second century BCE – third century CE), and Yudhiṣṭhira becomes king. He abdicates and, accompanied by his brothers and mother, leaves for the realm of Indra's heaven. Within this general narrative framework, many other stories are entwined.

The *Rāmāyaṇa* is not as long or complex as the *Mahābhārata*. It is the story of King Rāma, a prince of Ayodhya, who is forced to go into exile through the plotting of his stepmother. While there, his wife Sītā is abducted by the demon Rāvaṇa and taken to Sri Lanka. With the help of a monkey army, Rāma wins her back and becomes king again. This is the story of a heroic king who becomes deified and in the last book is referred to as an incarnation (*avatāra*) of Viṣṇu. As with the *Mahābhārata,* the *Rāmāyaṇa* is a tale about *dharma* and its triumph over *adharma,* of good over evil and order over chaos. It is very popular, and is retold in many different versions.

The Purāṇas, or 'stories of the ancient past', are a vast body of literature largely composed during the Gupta period (c.320–500 CE) incorporating complex narratives, the genealogies of kings up to the Guptas, cosmologies, law codes, and descriptions of ritual, temples, and pilgrimage. These texts were orally composed and recited by experts, who were traditionally thought to be the sons of Kṣatriya fathers and

Brahman mothers. They show a tendency towards sectarian affiliation, with texts, such as the *Viṣnu, Purāṇa,* and *Śiva Purāṇa,* reflecting the rise of the great religions of Viṣṇu, whose followers are Vaiṣṇavas, and Śiva, whose followers are Śaivas. This period saw the rise of the Vaiṣṇava doctrine of incarnations (*avatāras*), by which Viṣṇu incarnates into the world to restore *dharma*; the most important incarnations are Kṛṣṇa and Rāma. Other texts, such as the *Agni Purāṇa,* are not so clearly sectarian. Much of the material simply shows the popularity of Śiva and Viṣṇu and reflects how popular forms of religion were assimilated by the Brahmans. Such forms of religion focused not so much on ritual sacrifice as on devotion (*bhakti*) to different gods, expressed through the act of *pūjā,* making an offering to a god and receiving a blessing. *Pūjā,* undertaken by ordinary people as well as Brahmans, became the central act of Hinduism by the early medieval period. Gradually taking on varying degrees of complexity, it is performed simply in the home or in elaborate temple rituals.

The Purāṇas developed during a stable period that saw the rise of temple cities in the Gupta kingdom in the north and the Chalukya and Pallava kingdoms in the south. Later, from around 900 to 1200 CE, the southern kingdoms were replaced by the Pandeyas and, in the Tamil region, the Cholas. The great temple cities, such as Cidamabaram in Tamil Nadu, sacred to the god Śiva in his dancing form, remained undisturbed by power struggles and became centres of learning and pilgrimage.

THE MAURYAN AND GUPTA EMPIRES

During the first millennium BCE, Brahmanical religion developed, emphasizing the correct performance of ritual and the adherence to social obligation or *dharma*; the renouncer traditions, particularly Jainism and Buddhism, also developed. At this time, larger kingdoms replaced smaller ones and urban centres began to emerge as a result of an increase in both population and prosperity. This period also saw the rise of devotional movements and the ascent of the popular gods Viṣṇu and Śiva who became increasingly important in the development of Hinduism.

The Mauryan dynasty's territory (c.320–185 BCE) stretched from the Bay of Bengal to the Hindu Kush. Founded by Chandragupta (c.320–293 BCE), the dynasty became very powerful. Its capital, Pataliputra (modern Patna in Bihar), was a thriving, well organized city, protected by the River Ganges and an elaborate defence system. If accounts by the Greek ambassador Megasthenes are to be believed, it must have been the largest city in the ancient world. Chandragupta's chief adviser was the Brahman Kautilya who composed the important *Arthaśāstra*, the doctrine (*śāstra*) about the prosperity (*artha*) of the kingdom. The text describes how the king should develop alliances in order to win victory over the state's immediate neighbours, and how a successful economy ensured a prosperous kingdom. The text is also important in that it shows how Brahmanical religion and politics were intimately intertwined. *Artha,* prosperity or wealth, was regarded as one of the four purposes of life, the others being the performance of duty or *dharma,* the pursuit of pleasure (*kāma*), and finally liberation (*mokṣa*) from the cycle of reincarnation. After Chandragupta, the most important king was Aśoka (268–233 BCE) whose rule was characterized by tolerance.

Independent States

From 1192 to 1526 CE the north of India was ruled by the Muslim Sultanate of Delhi and then by the great Mughal empire (1526–c.1720, *see pages 66–67 and 294*). In southern India Hindu kingdoms continued, and in northern India *Rajputs* (princes) from ruling clans came to power. After initially fighting against the Mughals, they formed a much closer relationship with them during the sixteenth century. These bonds were further cemented by marriage. The Rajputs upheld the ideals of *dharma*, cultivated a Hindu culture which underlined caste distinctions, and declared the Brahmans to be of central importance in maintaining cosmic order. These traditions of heroic nobility were widely adopted, along with the controversial veneration of widow-burning (*satī*).

In the Punjab and western Gangetic plain, the counterpart of the Rajputs were the Jats, a caste of agriculturalists who became dominant in the development of the Sikh Panth. The Sikhs resisted Mughal rule and from 1799 to 1839 there was an independent Sikh ruler in the Punjab, Maharaja Rañjīt Siṅgh (1780–1839, *see page 69*). During his rule Sikhism flourished, but with his death the British annexed the Punjab and Sikhism was no longer linked to a particular polity.

SACRED KINGSHIP One of the most important ideas to develop under Mauryan rule was the concept of sacred kingship, with a political ideology that saw the king as the most important focus of the empire: its prosperity depended on the king who aspired to be a 'ruler of the universe' or *cakravārtin*. The king was identified with a deity. Just as the image of a deity was believed to mediate between the human and divine realms, so the king was thought to do likewise. This identification is reflected in a Sanskrit name for 'king': *deva*, or 'god'. Law books also testified to the divine nature of the king. The *Laws of Manu*, for example, described the king as being made from particles of the various gods, and even a child king was thought to be a deity in human form. The king was the centre from whom power flowed out to the polity and the people. However, the Hindu king was not simply an autocrat. Rather, the kingdoms that developed were segmentary, with a number of political groups forming a pyramid structure, each petty king paying allegiance to the higher king. The king of a large empire was therefore not so much the centre of a unified administration as the centre of a ritual structure and moral universe. The Hindu kingdom itself was embedded within a hierarchical cosmos in which purer, more refined worlds are located above the material world but which nevertheless incorporates this lower world, in a similar way to the Mauryan kingdom incorporating and being above lesser kingdoms. The functions of the king were to protect the people, ensure social order through maintaining caste boundaries, and administer justice or 'the stick' (*daṇḍa*). Just as other castes had their *dharma* to fulfil, so did the king.

The idea of sacred kingship can be found in the Veda. It developed along with the Mauryan dynasty, went on to evolve under the second large empire of importance – the Gupta empire (c.320–500 CE) – and is also found in the southern Indian kingdoms, such as the much later Vijayanagara empire (1346–1565 CE). The king was often identified with Viṣṇu, and the religion associated with this god developed during the Gupta period. The development of this tradition is rather complex; its early followers were called *bhāgavatas*, devotees of the Lord (*bhagavān*), the Lord being identified with a form of the god Kṛṣṇa. Generally, the Guptas supported the Bhāgavata religion and it became central to both state life and culture. The religion was not narrowly sectarian but was, rather, a general devotional movement that focused on the 'Lord', identified with Kṛṣṇa or some other incarnation of Viṣṇu who was linked to the idea of divine kingship. Indeed, the most famous Hindu work, the *Bhagavad Gītā*, is a text of the Bhāgavatas and reflects the non-sectarian and universal appeal of this tradition. In contrast to the monism of some Hindu traditions (which believe in the existence of only one indivisible substance, despite the apparent multiplicity of beings), the Bhāgavatas worshipped a personal, transcendent deity. Rather than identifying the soul with the absolute, they emphasized the soul's difference from the Lord and the concomitant necessity of love or devotion (*bhakti*). During the Gupta period, *bhakti* became the central religious orientation. It was also around this time that the Purāṇas were composed, along with much of the great epics the *Mahābhārata* and *Rāmāyana*. This was the classical age of Hinduism, with celebrated Sanskrit poets and dramatists such as Kālādāsa composing at the court of Chandragupta II (375–413/415 CE).

TANTRIC TRADITIONS

Alongside Purānic traditions, there developed esoteric movements that adhered to a distinct revelation embodied in texts known as Tantras (extensions). These texts were composed mostly between the seventh and the eleventh centuries CE within the written traditions of Śiva, Viṣṇu, and the Goddess, such as *Netra Tantra*, the *Jayākhya Saṁhitā*, and the *Kulārṇava Tantra*, yet they contain common material and often a common structure. Their main concerns are with standard and supererogatory rituals (the latter being non-obligatory but practically, morally, or spiritually beneficial) of the Brahman householder, depending upon the level of his initiation into a Tantric school. While there are Vaiṣṇava Tantras, it was mainly within the Śaiva fold that these traditions developed. The Śaiva Siddhānta ('teachings of Śiva') is an important tradition in which teachings are based on the revelation of the Śaiva Tantras, also called *Āgama* or 'that which has come down to us'. These texts are usually in the form of a dialogue between Śiva and the Goddess, Śiva's 'energy' (*śakti*), and are regarded as a revelation from Śiva that supersedes the Veda. These traditions originated around the seventh century CE with ascetics living in cremation grounds, although they were absorbed into mainstream, householder religion.

A statue of Nandi at the temple of Vaidyatt, a pilgrimage site for devotees of Śiva. Nandi was the god's sacred mount; statues of the animal guard the entrance of Śiva's temples, facing inwards so that they can see their Lord. One of the rituals dedicated to Nandi involves placing a drop of holy water on the forehead and at the feet of the bull statue.

The grand outlines of the Himalayas reflected in the calm waters of Lake Dal near the Kashmiri summer capital of Srinagar. Kashmir is the probable place of origin of the Tantric tradition of Śaiva Siddhānta.

The Śaiva Siddhānta originated in the north, probably in Kashmir, but virtually died out there after the Muslim incursions in the eleventh century, especially by Maḥmūd of Ghazni in 1014. However, the movement took root in southern India, particularly in Tamil Nadu, where large centres of learning and pilgrimage developed, such as the temple city of Cidambaram. Śaiva Siddhānta theology was 'dualistic', maintaining a distinction between the soul, the Lord Śiva, and the cosmos, which were regarded as three eternally distinct entities. Through Tantric initiation, a ritual process which involved symbolic re-creation of the initiate and allowed Brahman males to perform certain rituals at home and in the temple, the soul could eventually achieve liberation from the cycle of rebirth and become divine, although not identical with Śiva.

An alternative tradition developed in Kashmir in response to the Śaiva Siddhānta, a non-Saiddhāntika Śaivism which has become known as 'Kashmir' Śaivism, although its doctrines and practices spread beyond the borders of that region. This was a monistic school that, in contrast to the Śaiva Siddhānta, maintained that the soul, Lord Śiva, and the cosmos were in essence unified. This unity was understood by the tradition as pure consciousness, and the goal of ritual and yoga practice was to recognize the identification of the self with this pure consciousness. At the heart of this esoteric tradition – or more accurately group of traditions – the Goddess in one of her forms, especially the ferocious Kālī, was worshipped. There were Tantras devoted entirely to the Goddess, and these movements developed especially in the south. The Śrī Vidyā tradition, for example, worships the Goddess in the form of a particular mantra and a diagram of interpenetrating triangles. Although there are antinomian elements in the tradition, it has become absorbed into 'respectable' Hinduism.

From the earliest times, at least by the Mauryan period, the consumption of intoxicants and meat was prohibited to Brahmans in order to maintain spiritual and bodily purity, while sexual pleasure was recognized as an aspect of *kāma* but only within caste confines. A controversial aspect of some Tantras and traditions was the ritual use of wine, meat, and sex outside caste restrictions, which broke Brahmanical rules as laid down in texts such as the *Laws of Manu*. These traditions came to be known as 'left-hand' Tantras (acknowledging their contrary, taboo nature) and adherents claimed that liberation could be achieved in a single lifetime through initiation by a Tantric guru and taboo-breaking practices.

Although the more esoteric Tantric practices would have been the preserve of virtuosi, Tantric doctrine was nevertheless influential in the wider religious arena. Hindu kings were influenced by these traditions and playwrights in Kashmir mocked their effects at the court, suspicious of the moral degeneracy that Tantrism was thought to bring. The rulers of the medieval Vijayanagara empire in the south, where the king was ritually identified with the Goddess, the energy of Śiva, were probably influenced by Tantric traditions. While in the north Tantrism rapidly declined as a result of Muslim onslaughts and the establishment of the Delhi sultanate (1206–1526; *see page 293*), in the south Tantrism survived. Tantras are still used as temple texts in both Tamil Nadu and Kerala, where Tantris are high-caste Brahmans who install images in temples, a development that represents an orthodox, Brahmanical transformation of Tantric teachings.

SOUTHERN INDIA AND THE TAMILS

The sixth century CE saw the fragmentation of the Gupta empire in the north and a period of dynastic conflict. In the south, the Chalukya dynasty became important in the Deccan plateau, along with the Pallavas in northern Tamil Nadu and the Pandeyas in the far south. There were frequent clashes between these southern kingdoms, although religious traditions thrived, including that of Hindu temple architecture. The Rashrakuta dynasty, which briefly replaced the Chalukyas in the western Deccan plateau in the eighth century, saw the building of the great Kailash temple out of rock among the Ellora caves, and also the cave temples on the island of Elephanta. The Pallavas, from their capital of Kanchi, initially offered protection to Buddhists and Jains and the city was a centre of Buddhist pilgrimage, but Mahendravarman I (600–630) became a devotee of Śiva and Kanchi was turned into a Brahmanical sacred city. Rock-cut temples at Mahabalipuram on the east coast bear witness to the development of Hindu temples and their structure suggests a form of religion still recognizable today. However, it was under the Cholas (c. 870–1280), who overthrew the Pallavas, that Hindu culture truly developed in the south, as did a network of pilgrimage sites that was also a network of political power. In the late Middle Ages, the Vijayanagara empire became an important Hindu territory and bears witness to the significance of the ideology of sacred kingship and the identification of the king with a deity. On ritual occasions the king would receive homage and tribute from less powerful kings within his circle of influence.

DEVOTION TO ŚIVA AND VIṢṆU Of particular importance during the early medieval period was the rise of devotional or *bhakti* movements focused on Śiva and Viṣṇu. During the period from 600 to to the sixteenth century and later, they emphasized devotion to the Lord and the equality of devotees, an emphasis that can partly be seen as a reaction of lower-class groups against the heavy taxation imposed as a result of massive military expenditure. The belief was that every devotee was a slave of the Lord, conceived as Śiva or Viṣṇu, and each had a personal relationship with him. *Bhakti* was a very popular movement that can also be seen as a reaction against the ascetic and renunciatory traditions of Buddhism and Jainism. The Jains especially were subject to religious hostility, being accused of knowing no Tamil or Sanskrit, only Prakrit, and of being dirty and anti-social as well as atheistic. Buddhism and Jainism died out in the south and devotion to images of deities became the usual religious activity. *Pūjā*, customary Hindu worship involving the offering of incense and food to the image of a deity, became well established during this period.

Intense devotion to Śiva and Viṣṇu was expressed in the poetry or songs of the Nāyanārs and Alvārs in the 'sweet Tamil' language. These were peripatetic poet-saints who, between the sixth and ninth centuries, wandered from temple to temple singing the praises of their gods. There were 63 Nāyanārs whose poetry became absorbed into the canon of the Śaiva Siddhānta and under whose influence it became a strongly devotional tradition. Their poetry is about the loss of the limited self through an outpouring of love for the transcendent Lord. The *Tiruvacakam*, the sacred verses of Māṇikkavācakar (ninth century), speak of devotees being mad with the love of God. He, along with three other poets whose work forms part of the Śaiva canon, is regarded as one of the founders of the Śaiva Siddhānta in the south. The Alvārs were the Vaiṣṇava equivalent of the Nāyanārs. They composed devotional songs, helped to establish pilgrimage sites (most notably the great temple at Srirangam), and converted many people. There were 12 Alvārs who came from a wide spectrum of Tamil society. Nammālvār (c. 880–930), who came from a low-caste farming family, is the most famous, while Aṇṭāl (c. sixth–ninth century), the only female Alvār, was the daughter of a Brahman priest, himself one of the Alvārs. The male Alvārs came to be regarded as incarnations of Viṣṇu and Aṇṭāl as an incarnation of Viṣṇu's wife Śrī. Nammālvār's poetic text, the *Tiruvaymoli*, is regarded as the Tamil Veda and forms part of the canon of the Śrī Vaiṣṇava tradition.

MEDIEVAL DEVELOPMENTS IN HINDUISM

The medieval kingdoms of the south fostered the development of Hindu traditions and saw a popularization of Brahmanical religion. Rather than Sanskrit-learning and difficult ascetic practices, devotion to a personal deity became important, as did the composition of poetry in the vernacular languages, particularly Tamil which came to be regarded as equal to Sanskrit. Śaivism enjoyed royal patronage under the Cholas from the late ninth to the thirteenth centuries, and important centres developed at the enormous temple complexes of Cidambaram and Tanjavur. Vaiṣṇavism enjoyed similar royal approval at different times. Four main Vaiṣṇnava traditions developed, based on the teachings of the theologians Rāmānuja (c. 1017–1137), Madhva (thirteenth century), Vallabha (1479–1531), and Nimbarka (twelfth century). These traditions (*sampradāya*) each had their own teachings and lineage of gurus. The most important of them was the Śrī Vaiṣṇnava tradition, of which Rāmānuja was the head and whose centre was and remains at Srirangam. This tradition influenced the later Bengal Vaiṣṇavism and devotion to Kṛṣṇa expressed by Caitanya (1486–1533).

Lastly, mention should be made of the great philosopher Śaṅkara (788–820) who was born in Kerala. Śaṅkara taught, within the philosophical tradition of Vedānta, a philosophy of non-dualism (*advaita*), that the self (*ātman*) and the absolute reality (*brahman*) are identical. Liberation is the overcoming of spiritual ignorance or illusion (*māyā*) caused by the superimposition of what is not the self (a distinct entity) onto the self. He asserted that this truth is taught in the Veda and can be realized through renunciation. The later Vedānta theologians Rāmānuja and Madhva argued against Śaṅkara's philosophy and their position remains largely in the ascendant.

The temple at Srirangam, near Tiruchirapalli, Tamil Nadu. Established as a shrine during the Chola dynasty (ninth to thirteenth centuries CE), it has been undergoing constant embellishment and renovation ever since. It covers a huge (60-hectare [150-acre]) site, with a perimeter of 1.1 kilometres (⅔ mile). The highest pinnacles reach 71 metres (230ft).

THE GODS AND POPULAR DEVOTION

Popular Hinduism is characterized by the presence of many deities, from the great gods of the Hindu pantheon, such as Viṣṇu, to local gods and goddesses. Some Hindus claim that all these diverse divinities are aspects of a single, all-powerful divine being.

The historical development of Hindu deities is complex but, broadly speaking, three great traditions emerged, focused on Viṣṇu and his incarnations, Śiva, and the Goddess, although common themes and practices cut across the sectarian divides. Vaiṣṇavas worship Viṣṇu in one of his forms – such as the four-armed god holding various emblems of his divinity – or in an incarnation. While there are ten incarnations of Viṣṇu, Rāmā and Kṛṣṇa are the most popular and are associated with a rich body of literature, notably the great Epics and some of the Purāṇas. The popularity of these deities was attested in the 1987 televised version of the *Rāmāyaṇa*, which regularly attracted an estimated 80 million viewers in India. The focus of Śaivas is Śiva, the Lord of yogis, represented meditating in the Himalayas, with his hair piled up like an ascetic. Sometimes he is depicted as a family man with his wife Parvatī and their sons Skanda, god of war, and the popular elephant-headed god Gaṇeśa, Lord of beginnings and the remover of obstacles. The Goddess is worshipped as the consort of Śiva or Viṣṇu or in her own right as Durgā, the slayer of the buffalo-demon, or as the ferocious Kālī who demands blood offerings. Individuals and communities worship different gods depending on their allegiances, local traditions, and needs.

These great gods have been worshipped in large regional temples, such as the dancing Śiva at Cidambaram, for hundreds of years, but far more numerous are smaller temples to the major and local gods and simple wayside shrines. Caste plays an important role in Hindu worship, some temples being predominantly high caste, administered by Brahman priests, while others are low caste, such as the *teyyam* shrines of Kerala, in which local deities ritually possess a dancer and so are revealed to the community. The central act of worship or *pūjā* is making offerings to deities, represented by a temple image, or receiving a blessing, for example in the form of food offered to the deity or in the act of viewing the representation

(*darśana*). Pilgrimage is important in Hinduism and Indians will travel long distances to participate. A dramatic example is the Kumbha Mela, which is held every 12 years at the confluence of the sacred rivers Ganges and Yamuna and is famous for its procession of renouncers and many millions of participants.

The bright pantheon of Hindu gods and goddesses at Sri Murugan Temple, near Hampi, Tamil Nadu, in southern India. The worship of Śiva and Viṣṇu came to the south in the sixth century CE, after the fall of the Gupta Empire in the north. Śiva was associated with the local god Mudvalan, but Murugan remained an independent, yet integrated, Tamil deity.

MODERN INDIA

RELIGION IN MODERN INDIA has been formed not only by India's own rich heritage but also by colonialism, nationalism, and wider forces of modernity and globalization. The term 'Hinduism' was not used until the nineteenth century, and Hindu identity – developed partly as a response to colonization – became associated with Indian nationalism. Although modern India is a secular democracy with multiple religious, political, and ethnic viewpoints, there is some sense of a unified Hindu identity.

EUROPEANS IN INDIA

There is a long history of interaction between India and Europe. Alexander the Great and his armies went as far as India (327–325 BCE), and Greek kingdoms were established in Bactria (c. 250 BCE). There were trade links in the south with Rome, and there may have been mutual influence of religious ideas in the ancient world. But the European impact on southern Asia was not felt fully until the arrival of the Portuguese. Vasco da Gama landed on the Keralan coast in 1498, at a time when the Vijayanagara empire was at its height, and Portuguese settlement was soon established, especially in Goa. The Portuguese discovered an existing community of Syriac Christians in Kerala (who had come to India by the sixth century), but by the 1540s were pursuing a rigorous programme of proselytization among both them and the Hindus. Not all Catholic missionaries were hostile to Hindu traditions, and many learned the languages of the people they wished to convert. Roberto de Nobili (1577–1656), for example, was deeply interested in Hindu scriptures in which he sought an analogue for his own monotheism. The Dutch, the French, and the British followed the Portuguese, primarily as merchants rather than missionaries, and there was fierce rivalry over the spice trade. Particularly significant was the establishment of the British East India Company at the beginning of the seventeenth century.

Naga children at prayer in Imphal, Manipur, which borders the north-east of Myanmar. The Naga people never entirely assimilated the Hindu tradition, and there is a notable number of practicing Christians.

The Mughal empire *(see pages 68–69)* was the dominant power in the north, but it had collapsed by 1720 after the rule of Aurangzeb (ruled 1658–1707). The British stepped in to fill the power vacuum after the defeat of the Nawab of

Bengal by Robert Clive at the battle of Plassey (1757), and by the middle of the nineteenth century British power was firmly established. Queen Victoria became Empress of India in 1876. However, in 1857, the power of the British was threatened by what was referred to as the Sepoy or Indian Mutiny, described by Indian nationalists as the First National War of Independence. The causes of the uprising are complex, including discontent among the Rajputs (members of the Kṣatriya class from present-day Rajasthan) in the Bengal army about recruitment policy that required enlisted men to fight overseas, and a general sense of loss of status. However, the immediate cause of the revolt was religious in nature. A new rifle was introduced, the Lee Enfield, the cartridges of which were reputed to be greased with pig and cow fat. If true, this was repugnant and polluting to Muslims and Hindus. They refused to load the new cartridges, believing themselves to have been subject to extreme insensitivity on the part of the British rulers. The rebels were imprisoned and the mutiny was sparked; it was eventually crushed at great expense, both human and financial. Although the uprising had great political importance in the history of colonial India, it also had religious significance in that it showed the potential of Muslims and Hindus to unite in a common cause against the common enemy, European Christianity.

Sanskrit and German Philosophy

The first chair of Sanskrit at the University of Bonn was established in 1818 and was held by the philosopher Friedrich Schlegel (1772–1829). Hindu ideas were very important for German philosophers in the Romantic movement such as Friedrich Schelling (1775–1854), who regarded one form of Hindu philosophy, the Vedānta, as an idealism akin to his own thought. The Germanic philosophical interest in Hinduism continued into the twentieth century with novelists such as Hermann Hesse (1877–1962) and the Swiss psychologist Carl Jung (1875–1961).

WESTERN SCHOLARLY INTEREST IN HINDUISM

In spite of a certain rhetoric, colonial politicians were not, by and large, interested in the mass conversion of Hindus or Muslims (although certainly the Churches were); instead, a number of European scholars engaged in a deep study of Hindu traditions. With the arrival of the British, scholars began the systematic study of Sanskrit and the interpretation of Hindu and Buddhist traditions for the West. These were 'Orientalists', such as Sir William Jones (1746–1794), Charles Wilkins (1749–1836), and Thomas Colebrooke (1765–1837), whose work formed the foundation of the discipline of Indology, the philological study of Sanskrit texts. This discipline was, and remains, extremely important in understanding the history of Indian religions.

While there was great philosophical as well as philological interest in the field in Germany (*see box, right*), in Britain the interest in Sanskrit remained largely philological. H. H. Wilson (1789–1860) was the first Boden Professor of Sanskrit at Oxford University (1832–1860); he was succeeded by Monier Monier Williams (Boden Professor 1860–1888), whose work on Sanskrit texts was extremely important in furthering the Western understanding of Indian traditions. His dictionary, which is still in academic use today, was based on the massive scholarship of the Germans Otto Bothlingk and Rudolph Roth. For the Western understanding of Indian religions, of particular note is the work of Friedrich Max Müller (1823–1900) who edited a series of volumes called *The Sacred Books of the East* (1879–1894) and may be said to have virtually founded the academic discipline of comparative religions. At around the same time, a number of notable Sanskrit scholars emerged in the United States, including C. R. Lanman (1850–1941), while Hindu philosophy influenced the New England Transcendentalists Ralph Waldo Emerson (1803–1882) and Henry David Thoreau (1817–1862), author of *Walden* (1854).

THE HINDU RENAISSANCE

With British domination came intellectual interaction between Christianity and Hindu traditions, especially among the intellectual elite of Bengal in the nineteenth century. During this period, reform movements developed that sought to restore Hinduism to a perceived pre-colonial greatness, but which nonetheless absorbed a particular kind of rationalism derived from Christianity. This 'Hindu Renaissance' fed into the nationalist movement in the twentieth century.

The founder of the Hindu Renaissance was Ram Mohan Roy (1772–1833), sometimes called 'the Father of Modern India'. Roy was a very well educated Bengali Brahman who studied Arabic and Sanskrit and even Hebrew and Greek. He was employed by the East India Company. Influenced by the Upaniṣads, but also by Unitarianism (a Christian movement that looked for truth through human experience, not allegiance to doctrine), Roy believed that God is an ineffable, transcendent being who cannot be represented by images. Religion should be a rational, ethical system in which moral law is understood through reason. To this end, he condemned what he perceived to be immoral practices in Hinduism (a term which he was probably the first to use to describe these ancient and diverse traditions), such as child marriage and the burning of widows (*sātī*). Indeed, he was influential on the British government's eventual decision to ban *sātī* in 1829. Through the adoption of a rational, ethical religion purified of 'superstition' such as image worship and belief in *karma* and reincarnation, Hinduism could transform Indian society. In order to promote this end, Roy founded a movement called the Brahmo Samāj, modelled on Christian reform movements. He died in Bristol during a visit to Britain, but his work was continued by others such as Debendranath Tagore (1817–1905, the father of the famous poet Rabindranath Tagore, 1861–1941) and Keshab Chandra Sen (1838–1884) who were both opposed to image worship and the influence of the Purāṇas and Tantras, which they believed represented a corrupt form of Hinduism.

The Brahmo Samāj recruited from the educated Bengali classes but had little appeal at a popular level. A more popular movement that continued to develop the immanent nationalism of the Brahmo Samāj was the Ārya Samāj (Noble Society). This movement was founded in 1875 by Dayananda Sarasvati (1824–1883) who, influenced by Roy, advocated a return to a pure, Vedic form of Hinduism. This form rejected image worship and the later scriptures of Hinduism such as the Epics and Purāṇas, but nevertheless defended a 'purified' Hinduism against Christianity. The Ārya Samāj did much to foster a sense of national identity, including the establishment of schools (*gurukula*) to promote Vedic culture, and the teaching of both Hindi (advocated by Dayananda as a national language) and Sanskrit. The Ārya Samāj was particularly successful in the Punjab in re-converting low-caste people who had become Muslims or Christians in a ceremony called 'purification' (*śuddhi*): this converted 'untouchable' castes to high-caste or 'twice-born' status. After Dayananda's death, a split developed between those with conservative beliefs and those who wanted a 'progressive' education system and the abandonment of the Brahmanical diet, believing that it was an expression of a backward-looking belief system.

RĀMAKṚṢṆA AND VIVEKĀNANDA

The Ārya Samāj has been important in the development of Indian nationalist politics and has also influenced more recent Hindu nationalism in India (for example, Pandit Mohan Malaviya, a member of the Ārya Samāj and the first vice-chancellor of Benares Hindu University, founded the political party Hindu Mahāsabha in 1909). However, another movement that has emphasized universalism and tolerance has also been important. This movement was begun by Paramahamsa Rāmakṛṣṇa (1836–1886), a Bengali mystic who declared the unity of all religions. Although born into a Brahman Vaiṣṇava family, Rāmakṛṣṇa became a devotee of the ferocious Goddess, the Mother Kālī. He became a priest of a Kālī temple near Calcutta where he had numerous visions and experienced absorption into a different state of consciousness or *samādhi*. Through his experiences he claimed that the goals and sources of different religions in the world are the same, and that all religions are paths to the same eternal, undivided being experienced as knowledge and bliss.

Rāmakṛṣṇa attracted educated Bengalis, among whom was a young man who became a renouncer, taking the name Vivekānanda (1863–1902) and gaining the title *Swami* (master). A devoted disciple of Rāmakṛṣṇa and his theory of unity, Vivekānanda travelled the length of India, meditating upon a small island at its most southerly point off Cape Comorin (where a temple now stands), experienced the state of *samādhi*, and resolved to spread his vision of Hinduism, formalizing and building upon Rāmakṛṣṇa's beliefs. He promoted a new form of Vedānta, claiming that the essence of divinity is within each person and can be realized through practice of Hinduism. This recognition of the divine as the essence of oneself and of others would advance social harmony in the world. He went to the World's Parliament of Religions in Chicago in 1893 where he made a great impression, and was very influential in promoting Hinduism outside India and developing it into a 'world religion'. He founded the Vedānta Society in New York in 1895 and a monastic order, the Rāmakṛṣṇa Mission, on his return to India. This order has laid great emphasis on good works which it regards as the performance of *karma* yoga. Vivekānanda had a great impact on the West's perception of Hinduism and the idea that the East is somehow more 'spiritual'. His Hinduism has been largely accepted by the middle classes in India, although this Neo-Vedānta is very different from the medieval philosophical traditions or rigorous debate. Vivekānanda's teaching not only promoted Hinduism as a world religion but has also been influential in developing the idea of India as a single nation. This idea was to grip the imagination of many Indians.

Gandhi with Jawaharlal Nehru in 1946, a year before India gained her independence. Nehru went on to become the country's first prime minister; Gandhi was assassinated in 1948.

MAHATMA GANDHI AND THE INDEPENDENCE MOVEMENT

Vivekānanda's Neo-Vedānta has been and remains important in contemporary Hinduism, although its influence has been most significant in the development of Indian nationalism and in the teachings of Mahatma Gandhi (1869–1948). Gandhi was born into a merchant caste of Vaiṣṇavas and was strongly influenced by Vaiṣṇava teachings as well as being open to Jain, Christian, and Muslim principles. He studied law in London and worked as a lawyer for more than 20 years in South Africa, where he devised his philosophy of non-violence (*ahiṁsā*) and passive resistance to bring about change. Returning to India in 1915, he joined the nationalist movement and worked for Indian independence using non-violent means. In the *ashram* or religious community that he founded outside Ahmedabad, he promoted cottage industries and organized passive resistance to the British. This included resistance to the tax on salt, which inspired the famous march to the sea where he and his followers symbolically picked up grains of salt from the shore, thereby flouting British salt law. He became the leading voice in the Indian National Congress (the Congress Party, founded in 1885, becoming a nationwide political party in 1920) and in the nationalist struggle that resulted in Independence in 1947 and the inauguration of the Constitution of the Republic of India in 1950.

Following from Vivekānanda, Gandhi regarded truth (*satya*) as God, who is both the supreme being (*sat*) and the self (*ātman*). All creatures are united in a common spiritual essence that should be expressed through harmony and non-violence. Non-violence is a manifestation of truth, and passive resistance to political oppression is 'holding fast to the truth' (*satyāgraha*). This was the central idea that Gandhi identified with the struggle for Indian nationhood, a struggle founded on 'truth and love, or non-violence'. Non-violence lay at the heart of Gandhi's philosophy and he was distressed by the conflicts between Hindus, Muslims, and Sikhs generated by the partition of India to create Pakistan in 1947. Non-violence was the key, and its realization would be for the welfare of all (*sarvodaya*). However, non-violence is difficult and involves effort to control the senses and instincts, especially sexuality and anger, and to promote justice. Chastity or *brahmacārya* was of central importance to Gandhi, not only for himself but as a means of controlling the burgeoning population and as a way of finding God. Indeed, he was strongly influenced by the renouncer traditions which saw chastity as bestowing great spiritual power.

One of the most significant aspects of the 'welfare of all' was the emancipation of the 'untouchables'. These low-caste groups Gandhi called the 'children of God', a title they themselves tend now to reject in favour of the *dalits* or the 'oppressed'. The liberation of the untouchables, for Gandhi, would mean the transformation of Indian society, and his ideas have been influential on the abolition of untouchability in post-independence India, although discrimination against lower castes continues. Gandhi was not against caste as such and promoted a return to the ideals of the *varṇāśrama-dharma* of orthodox, Brahmanical Hinduism, which he saw as a means of organizing society into divisions according to occupation. The Hinduism that Gandhi promoted, like Roy and the other reformers, was an ethical one. Ritual and the worship of deities embodied in images were less important than universal ethics, non-violence, and holding fast to the eternal truth within all beings.

Gandhi was assassinated by a militant Hindu nationalist who was a member of the RSS (Rashtriya Svayam-Sevak Sangh, founded in 1925). Rather than the secularism of the Congress Party, the RSS promoted a nationalism that saw India as fundamentally a Hindu state. Although not a political party but a cultural organization, it has advanced the interests of Hindus over and above those of Muslims, Christians, and Communists, and has influenced Hindu political parties such as the BJP (Bharatiya Janata Party, founded in 1980) which has promoted Hindu nationalism. The BJP and the RSS have pan-Indian appeal while other nationalistic groups are regional. For example, the Shiv Sena in Maharashtra claims to promote the interests of Hindus against 'foreign influences' and has been responsible for violence against Muslims in Mumbai (formerly Bombay). Sectarian tension and clashes continue to be seen, dramatic examples from the end of the twentieth century being the assassination of the Prime Minister Indira Gandhi (1917–1984) by Sikh members of her bodyguard, and the demolition of an old mosque in Ayodhya in 1992, said to have been built on the birthplace of Rāmā, the incarnation of Viṣṇu. Much communal violence followed in the wake of both events.

Supporters rally for the pro-Hindu nationalist Bharatiya Janata Party (BJP) in Delhi, 1987.

Global Hinduism contrasts with Hindu nationalism. It lays emphasis on what it perceives to be common spiritual values such as social justice and peace. Very much in the spirit of the Hindu Renaissance and the teachings of Gandhi, this trend maintains that Hinduism contains the oldest revelation available to humans. There is, of course, interaction between global Hinduism and Hindu nationalism, particularly evident in the Hindu diaspora. Global Hinduism is important in the contemporary world because many elements of Hinduism have become widely available to those outside Hindu culture. Gurūs, meditation, yoga, and devotion have found their way into the West, which has in turn influenced Indian Hinduism through new interpretations and ideas. Similarly, Western ideas and movements have made their mark on Hinduism, of particular note being feminism and the development of a strong women's movement in India.

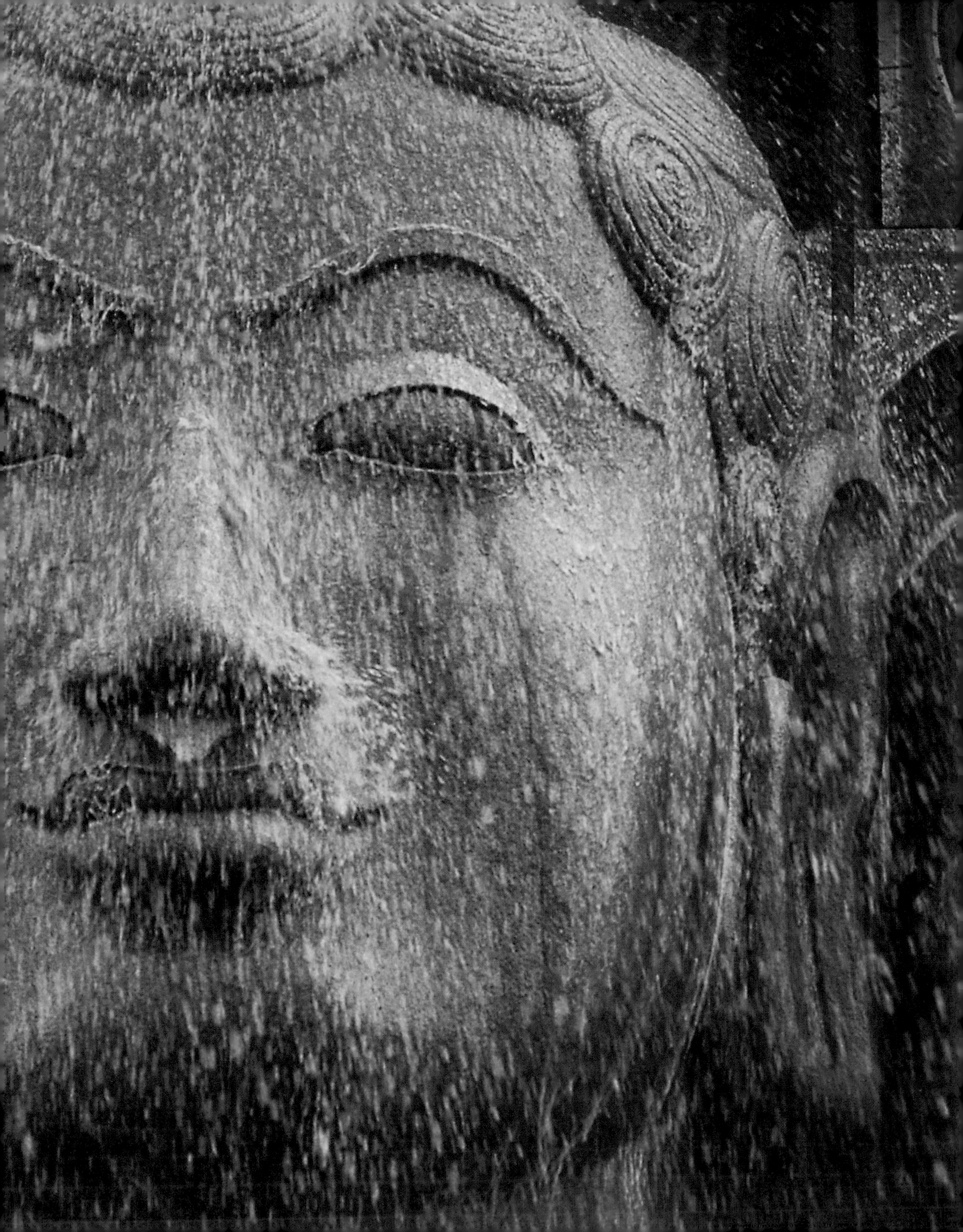

Jainism

Paul Dundas

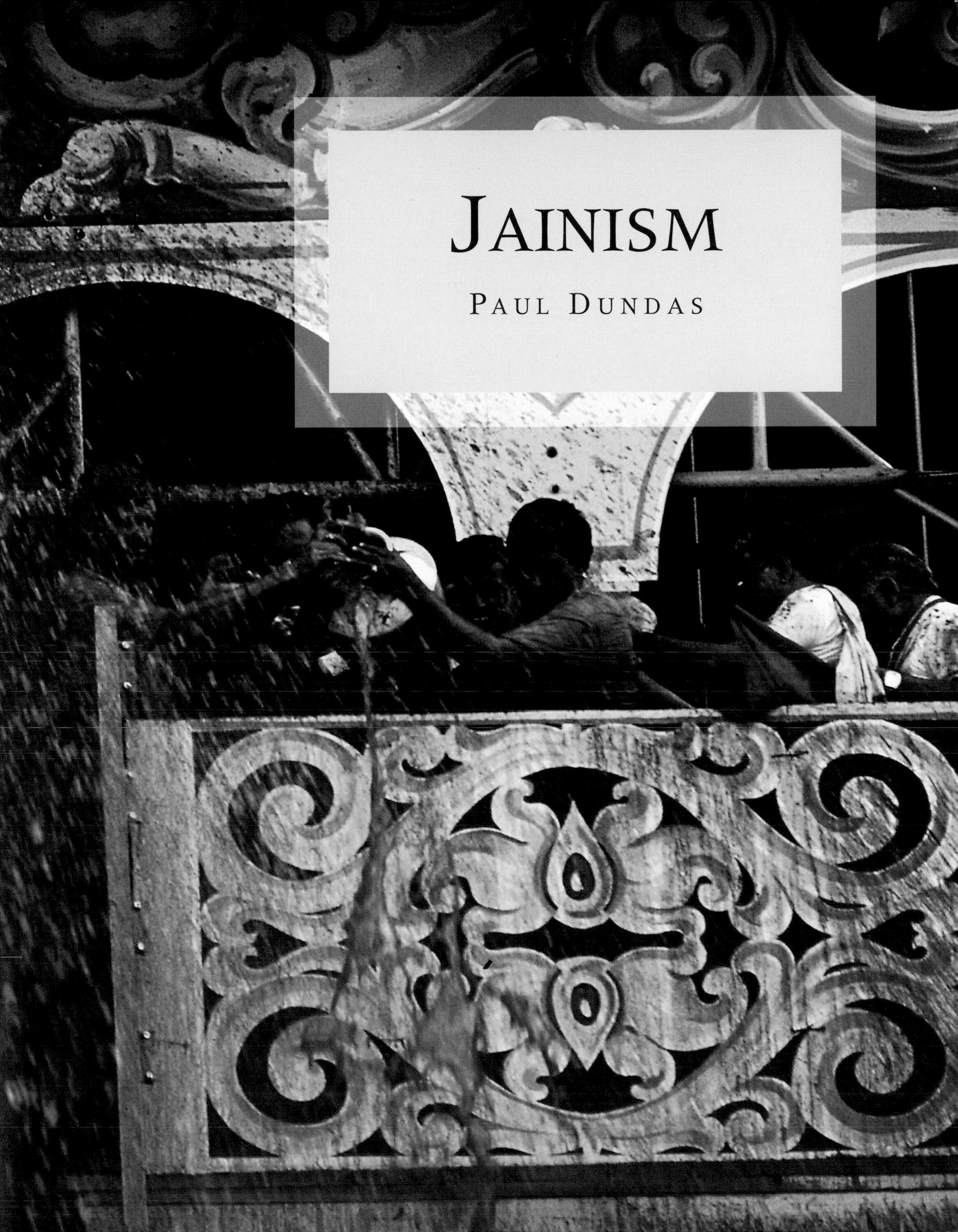

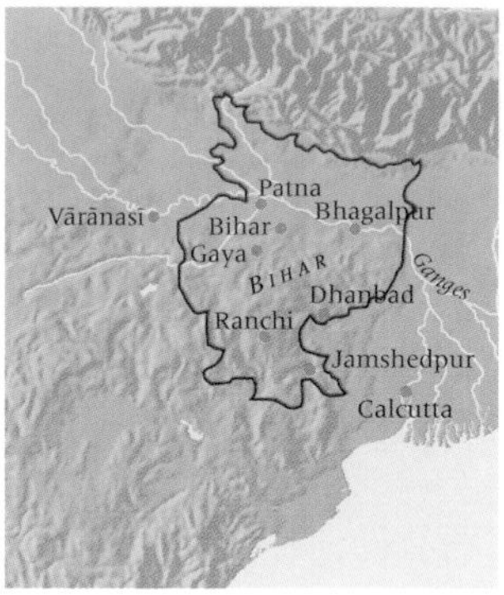

JAINISM

JAINISM ORIGINATED around the eighth–seventh centuries BCE in the basin of the River Ganges, an area roughly equivalent to the modern state of Bihar. *Jaina* (Westernized as Jain), from which Jainism derives its name, is a Sanskrit word describing the followers of the omniscient teachers called Jina, 'conqueror'. These teachers' conquering of the passions and the senses has enabled them to gain enlightenment and subsequent freedom from the cycle of rebirth, a liberation that is envisaged as a state of pure bliss, knowledge, and energy. Since during his lifetime each of these Jinas founds a community of monks, nuns, laymen, and laywomen, figuratively called the 'ford' (Sanskrit *tīrtha*) across the waters of rebirth, each is also commonly called *tīrthaṅkara*, 'builder of the ford'.

HISTORICAL BACKGROUND

Although Jainism holds that successions of 24 of these *tīrthaṅkaras* (each associated with an animal, auspicious object, or pattern) appear in every world age, envisaged as an upward or downward movement of a continually turning wheel, scholarship contends that only the last two of the current chain, Pārśva and Mahāvīra, were actual historical figures. Both lived during a period of significant sociopolitical realignment and religious speculation in North India. An ancient pastoral mode of life, which centred on the Indo-Aryan cult of sacrifice, described and interpreted in the

Worshippers offer a lamp at the feet of the monolithic sculpture of Bāhubali at the Jain shrine at Śravaṇa Belgolla. According to Digambara Jainism, Bāhubali was the first person in the age of Mahāvīra, the current *tīrthaṅkara*, to reach spiritual liberation. Traditionally, eight substances are offered: water, sandalwood, flowers, incense, a lamp, rice, sweets, and fruit.

scriptures collectively known as the Veda (c.1200–800 BCE, *see page 224*), and the authority of the Brahman priestly class, was gradually being replaced by urbanization and a complex new state system presided over by kings who enjoyed unprecedented power. The renunciatory way of life followed by Pārśva and Mahāvīra was a common response to the social and intellectual uncertainty of this time.

No firsthand record of Pārśva survives and our picture of him has to be constructed from later sources. Most likely he lived in the eighth or seventh centuries BCE. He is portrayed as a prince, like all the *tīrthaṅkaras*, who renounces the world in the prime of life and, after living as a wandering ascetic and practicing a course of austerities, gains enlightenment, a state that eventually culminates in deliverance from rebirth. His teachings seem to have involved a cosmology and a moral code centring on non-violence, non-lying, not taking anything that has not been given, and non-possession. This moral code, with the addition of the renunciation of sexual activity, represents the five great vows advocated by Mahāvīra for all Jain ascetics and still followed by them to this day.

Mahāvīra is usually understood to have been the founder of Jainism, but more reasonably he might be viewed as an expander of Pārśva's teachings. His traditional dating is 599–527 BCE, although this may well be a century too early. The biography of Mahāvīra was developed over a considerable period of time in the Jain scriptures, albeit based on a solid historical core.

After having his royal consecration ceremony celebrated by the god Indra, an Indo-Aryan divinity whom the Jains accepted as ruling other gods, Mahāvīra was born to King Siddhārtha (not to be confused with Buddha) and Queen Triśālā, the latter having seen in a dream the various auspicious objects – such as an elephant and a parasol – that according to Indian tradition presage the appearance of a great monarch or religious leader. The boy was given the name Vardhamāna (Increasing) because the wealth of his family grew after his appearance in his mother's womb.

At the age of 30, Vardhamāna became convinced of the worthlessness of human existence and renounced the world to become a mendicant wanderer. From this moment he was Mahāvīra, 'Great Hero'. For 12 years he led a life of intense asceticism, early abandoning clothes and going naked for the rest of his life. Eventually, in accord with his destiny, earned through meritorious and compassionate actions of non-violence carried out in innumerable previous existences, Mahāvīra gained enlightenment, which in Jainism is envisaged as full knowledge of the past, present, and future with regard to all beings in all quarters of the universe. After this, Mahāvīra set about founding the Jain community. The most important event in this respect was his conversion of 11 Brahmans who were to be the heads of the Jain ascetic order and mediators of the eternal scriptures, which are composed in the Ardhamāgadhī language (a form of language different from the Sanskrit of the priestly Brahmans), based on Mahāvīra's preaching. Finally, after a career of some 30 years of mendicancy, punctuated by periods of retreat during the rainy season, Mahāvīra eliminated his karma (in Jainism, the matter that weighs down the soul, *jīva*, thus attaining the final state of emancipation called *mokṣa*) and died in meditation at the town of Pāvā in the present-day state of Bihar.

Teachings

Mahāvīra's fundamental teachings derived from his understanding that the suffering of the world is caused by violence inflicted on souls, which live in embodied form at all levels of existence, and that this impedes each individual entity's innate spiritual potential. The means to minimize this violence and ultimately achieve release from rebirth is to quieten the senses of the body and withdraw from action as much as possible through renunciation of the social world and its material concerns. Jain teachings therefore highlight the importance of non-violence (*ahimsa*) to all creatures and have a marked ascetic idiom. Vegetarianism has been an important index throughout Jain history.

Essential Features of Jainism

Jainism is a religious tradition that puts human beings and their concerns at its very centre. It teaches that the universe is eternal, and that it does not have a creator. While gods do exist in a system of heavens above the human world, they have no influence on mortal affairs and will themselves eventually cease to be gods, and so will be reborn.

Jain teachings describe reality as consisting of two categories: the *jīva* – that is, the soul (which, in its pristine form, is characterized by qualities of total knowledge, energy, and bliss); and the non-*jīva* – atoms, the qualities of motion and rest, and ether, which together constitute the material world in which *jīva* is located. Jainism teaches a spiritual path that enables the soul to escape from the influence of *karma* (which is attracted to the soul by violent action), and that also frees the soul from rebirth, enabling it to regain its pristine qualities in the world of the liberated at the top of the universe.

The observance most common to all the denominations of Jains is the *sāmāyika*, a 48-minute period of reflection and withdrawal from all activity. On significant religious occasions all Jains utilize the 'Five Homages' mantra, which salutes the liberated souls and the *tīrthaṅkaras*, along with the teachers, preceptors, and monks.

The inner recesses of temples provide locations for the images of the *tīrthaṅkaras* which, as symbols of the fruition of the Jain path, can be worshipped mentally or with physical offerings.

The festival that unites all Jains is Mahāvīr Jayantī, the birthday of Mahāvīra, which is celebrated around the end of March or the beginning of April.

Carved figures at the temple of Mount Shatrunjaya. Jain temples usually house an image of the *tīrthaṅkara* to whom they are dedicated as well as figures of gods. Image worship is thought to aid meditation, although some sects reject it.

DEVELOPMENTS IN THE EARLY COMMON ERA

Jainism may have started as an ascetic-based means of spiritual salvation revolving around monks and nuns, but it quickly encompassed a laity and turned into a developed religious culture. It then spread beyond its original confines in eastern India along well established trade routes to the west and south of the subcontinent.

The most important early evidence for Jainism in the west is to be found at the city of Mathurā, to the south of Delhi, a major staging-post at the junction of the main caravan routes used in ancient times. Archeological evidence from Mathurā from as early as the first century BCE suggests a devotionally-oriented iconic cult of the *tīrthaṅkaras*, while inscriptions point to the presence of lay devotees and patrons of the religion who came from a largely bourgeois background.

For almost a millennium after Mahāvīra, Jainism was a relatively unified phenomenon, which was most clearly evinced in *Tattvārtha Sūtra*, the codification of doctrine and practice provided by the teacher Umāsvāti (c. fourth–fifth centuries CE). In this work Umāsvāti expounds his teachings on the Three Jewels – right belief, knowledge, and conduct – that mark the way to liberation. However, potential areas of disagreement were present from an early period, and these ultimately led to the emergence of sectarianism and the development of two contentious groups: namely Śvetāmbara and Digambara Jainism.

The main area of contention related to the clothing of ascetics. The ancient texts had been ambivalent as to whether monks should go naked in token of their total renunciation of worldliness or wear robes. Eventually, by around the fifth century CE, there can be identified the beginnings of the two groups that continue to exist in Jainism to this day: the Śvetāmbaras, the 'White-clad', who hold that monks can wear robes, and the Digambaras, the 'Sky-clad', who insist that the true monk must be naked. Among other differences, the Digambaras deny the possibility of spiritual liberation for women. They still have nuns, who accept that they have to be reborn as men to gain spiritual improvement. Men can also be reborn as women.

This sectarian split confirmed what had gradually become the geographical reality of Jainism during the early medieval period. The naked monks and their lay supporters predominated in the south of the continent; the white-robed monks together with an attendant lay community were located in the north and west. The Digambaras went further in their split with the Śvetāmbaras: they rejected the authority of the scriptural corpus established, sometime in the fifth century, by the Śvetāmbara in conclave at the city of Valabhī in what is now the western state of Gujarat. Instead, they developed their own scriptural tradition, avowedly based on the genuine ancient transmission of texts and composed in a vernacular dialect known as Śaurasenī. For a millennium great teachers such as Kundakunda (early common era?), Samantabhadra (fifth century CE), and Akalaṅka (eighth century CE) continued to develop and defend Digambara Jainism as a spiritual and intellectual system. The most noteworthy of the Śvetāmbara teachers was Haribhadra (c. eighth century) who produced still authoritative works in a wide range of intellectual areas. (The Digambara Samantabhadra and the Śvetāmbara Haribhadra are different figures from the Buddhist teachers of the same names.)

ROYAL SUPPORT IN MEDIEVAL SOUTH INDIA During the medieval period, Digambara Jainism was frequently patronized by royal families in South India. They were perhaps attracted by the spiritualization of martial activities which characterizes the imagery of much Jain teaching, for example in the repeated references to the heroic conquest of the passions carried out by Jain ascetics. Digambara monks often served as the preceptors of prominent kings. The most noteworthy example of this was Amoghavarṣa (ninth century), a monarch of the powerful Rāṣṭrakūṭa dynasty which ruled in Karṇāṭaka. His adviser was the monk Jinasena, who produced one of the most important literary works of Digambara Jainism, entitled *Ādipurāṇa*, or The Lorebook of the Beginning. This work is both a legendary history of Jainism from the beginning of this world-age and a practical manual of kingship for a Jain ruler.

Digambara Jainism was unable to sustain its connections with political power in the far south, and it gradually gave ground under the impact of devotional Hinduism. By the twelfth century it had been displaced to the fringes of society, where it has remained. Similarly, in the region of Karṇāṭaka, the Digambara Jains slowly lost royal patronage and suffered badly at the hands of the militant Hindu Vīraśaiva movement which began in the twelfth century. Many Digambaras converted to Hinduism, and although never marginalized to the same extent as the Jains in the far south of the continent (in what is now Tamil Nadu), those that remained faithful to their ancestral religion were influential only in a few areas, such as the coastal region of south Karṇāṭaka.

Hemacandra and Kumārapāla

The Śvetāmbaras in the north and west did not involve themselves quite so closely with ruling dynasties as did the Digambaras in the south. However, their leading teachers also on occasion forged close relationships with kings who showed themselves to be sympathetic to Jainism. Most famous of these is the celebrated monk Hemacandra (1089–1172) who was court scholar and preceptor to Siddharāja and his nephew Kumārapāla, two rulers of the Caulukya dynasty in Gujarat. Hemacandra's great summary of Jainism, the *Yogaśāstra*, or Treatise on Behaviour, was intended to show Kumārapāla how to lead the pious life of a Jain layman, and tradition has it that the monk actually helped the young prince gain the throne on his uncle Siddharāja's death.

Śvetāmbara nuns on pilgrimage in Rājasthān, distinctive in their white robes. Each carries a whisk, one of the few traditional possessions allowed to them. The whisks are to remove to safety any insects on the ground before the nun sits down. Śvetāmbara nuns outnumber monks three to one.

DEVELOPMENTS IN MODERN JAINISM

The broad tenor of Jainism throughout its history has been devotional, centring on the worship of images of the Jinas and temple ritual. Yet there has also been dissatisfaction with the image cult, partly on the grounds that the oldest scriptures say nothing of it and also because prominent Jain teachers have often emphasized the more mystical elements of the religion. These anti-iconic tendencies have exerted a particular impact on the Śvetāmbaras, among whom two significant reforming sects have emerged in recent centuries.

In the fifteenth century, a Gujarati layman called Lonkā concluded that temples and images should not play any role in Jainism and that the monastic practice of his day was corrupt. Lonkā and his followers were the forerunners of the anti-iconic Sthānakvāsī sect which emerged in the seventeenth century. It was so called because its monastic members, in the course of their ascetic wanderings, sought temporary lodgings in halls (*sthānak*) and disused buildings rather than the temples frequented by other Śvetāmbara sects.

As well as rejecting the image cult and portions of the scriptures, the Sthānakvāsīs also insisted on the wearing of a cloth mouth-shield (*muhpatti*) by monks and nuns at all times. This is indicative of total adherence to the principle of non-violence, since Jainism teaches that unguarded breathing can injure minute organisms in the air. The Sthānakvāsīs have remained a minority sect within Jainism, but they are to be found in all parts of India, with important centres in Punjab and Gujarat.

The Sthānakvāsīs in turn gave rise to another reforming anti-image sect, the Terāpanthīs. The originator of this was Bhīkhanjī, later called Ācārya Bhikṣu (1726–1803), who came from the desert region of Marwār in what is now Rājasthān

Jain temple complex on Mount Shatrunjaya, at Palitana, in south-eastern Gujarat. Jain temples are often very elaborately designed, and are considered to be replicas of the *samasvasaraṇa*, the divinely-constructed assembly halls of the 24 ford-builders. Temple building and maintenance is funded by donations from Jain lay people, many of whom are very successful merchants and traders.

and from whom all leaders of the sect trace their line of succession. Originally a Sthānakvāsī monk, Bhīkhanjī reacted against what he saw as the laxity of his fellow sectarians and, taking a fundamentalist stance on the basis of scripture, advocated an intensely ascetic brand of Jainism. Like the Sthānakvāsīs, Terāpanthī monks and nuns always wear a mouth-shield, but of a more oblong design. The name Terāpanth (*panth* means 'path') which came to be used of the sect derives – according to varying explanations – either from the fact that Bhīkhanjī's followers originally consisted of 13 (*terā*) monks and 13 laymen, or because the sect could be regarded as following the 13 major precepts of Jainism.

Although the Terāpanthī Jains are a relatively small sect in terms of actual numbers, their leaders have sometimes attained a high public profile, and in particular have attempted to inspire participants in post-Independence Indian political and business life to act in a more morally responsible manner.

Both the Śvetāmbara and Digambara image-worshipping ascetic communities experienced a severe contraction of numbers in the eighteenth and much of the nineteenth centuries, when very few received ordination as monks. However, a revival of what might be styled 'traditional' Jainism took place in the twentieth century, with ascetic numbers rising among the Śvetāmbaras and, to a much lesser extent, the Digambaras. Alternative modes of religiosity, focusing on Jainism's mystical concerns, have also appeared. Most notable are followers of the largely Digambara-derived, innermost-self-oriented teachings of the Śvetāmbara layman Śrīmad Rājacandra (1867–1901), who had – for a short time – a degree of influence upon the young Mohandas (later Mahatma) Gandhi. Another interesting component of modern Jainism is the Kānjī Svāmī Panth, whose founder Kānjī Svāmī (1889–1981), an ex-Sthānakvāsī monk, promulgated a neo-Digambara brand of the religion stemming from the mystical writings of the teacher Kundakunda.

THE JAIN DIASPORA Many Jains from western India migrated in the wake of age-old trading links to East Africa and then, as a result of political instability in the 1960s, to the United Kingdom (at the end of the twentieth century, numbers stood at around 30,000). Jains are now also to be found increasingly in the professional sector in North America (around 100,000). A substantial number of Jains from this background, especially the younger generation, see no difficulty in calling on the ancient resources of Jainism to promote what are, in the West, the largely secular stances of vegetarianism and environmentalism as a means of confirming both their religious identity and their modernity.

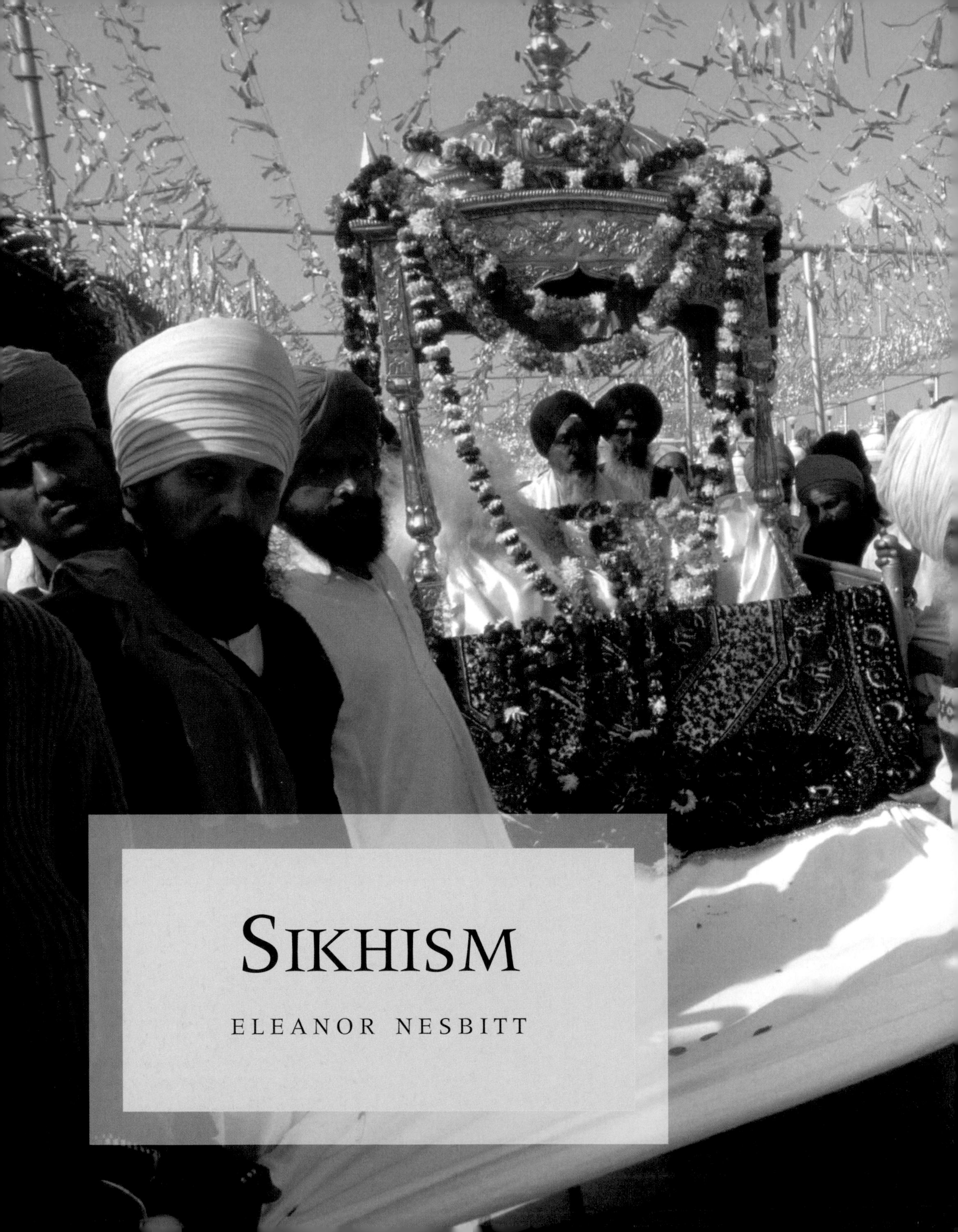

SIKHISM

ELEANOR NESBITT

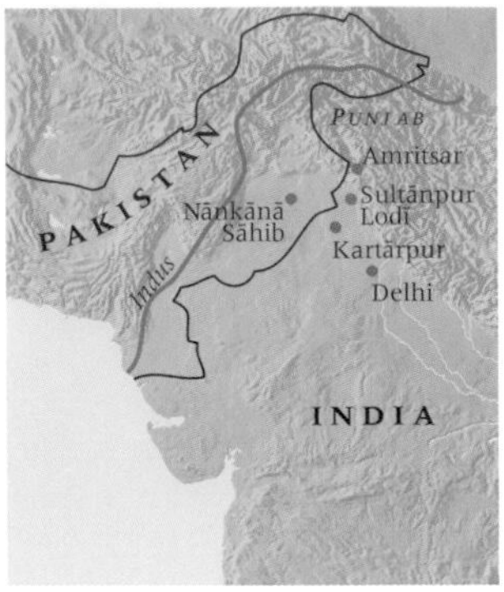

Sikhism

Sikhism is a religious tradition that originated in the late fifteenth century in the Punjab (Pañjāb) in northern India and whose followers (called Sikhs) also speak of it as *Gurmat* (the Gurūs' doctrine) or *Sikhī* (Discipleship). Sikhism is based on the religious teachings of ten spiritual leaders. To understand the Gurūs' teaching it is necessary to turn to the insights contained in the hymns of Gurū Nānak (1469–1539), the founder of Sikhism, and the nine Gurūs who followed him.

GURU NANAK AND HIS SUCCESSORS

On either side of the border separating India and Pakistan are two largely agricultural states called Punjab that, before partition in 1947, formed a single region. Information about Gurū Nānak's life is limited, but it is known that he was born in the Punjab in a place now called Nānkānā Sāhib in Pakistan. In about 1499, after a seminal religious experience, he renounced his former life, announcing that 'There is neither Hindu nor Muslim'. The *janam sākhīs* (birth witnesses) are stories of Gurū Nānak's life which include his experience of being called into God's presence and reveal how he gave up everything in order to share his vision and to challenge hypocrisy and misguided convention.

A traditional image portraying the first of the ten Sikh Gurūs, Gurū Nānak (1469–1539). He was called by God while working at Sultānpur Lodī.

Gurū Nānak travelled widely for many years, communicating his insights mostly through singing his poetry, before settling and establishing a community in Kartārpur (now in India). His poetic genius, spiritual stature, and practically-based leadership – including the announcement of his successor, Gurū Aṅgad, before he died – combined to launch what has become a distinct and enduring religion, which has its own scriptures, ceremonies, calendar of festivals (including Gurū Nānak's birthday and Vaisākhī, *see page 68–69*), and place of communal worship, the *dharamsālā* (later called the *gurdwārā*).

Gurū Nānak's life coincided with the advent of the Muslim Mughal emperors in northern India; indeed, in four of his hymns he refers to the Mughal emperor Bābur's devastating invasion of the area (*see page 294*), which resulted in the capture of the Punjab region and of the town of Delhi (1520–1526). The fluctuating relationship between successive Gurūs and their rulers was extremely significant. Bābur's successor Humāyuṅ consulted the second Gurū, Aṅgad (1504–1552), while the emperor Akbar visited the third Gurū, Amar Dās (1479–1574).

Gurū Nānak's message is contained in 974 hymns included in the scriptures which are known as both *Ādi Granth* and (since the death of the tenth Gurū) as *Gurū Granth Sāhib* (*see below and page 69*). His compositions include the *Japjī, Āsā Kī Vār, Sodar, Ārati,* and *Sohilā,* which devout Sikhs recite daily. Their message is that true religion transcends an outward preoccupation with ritual and dress. God is one, single, and indivisible. The formula *'ik oaṅkār'* (God is one) reiterates this throughout the *Gurū Granth Sāhib.* Adherents should combine constant remembrance of *nām* (not just the name but the nature and being of God) with involvement in family life as a married person. Ultimate attainment of *mukti* (union with God after repeated rebirths) depends on one's service to others and on the Gurū's grace, and in this respect an individual's gender and caste are irrelevant. This contrasts with the pervasive Hindu model of society as a hierarchy, and of individual life as a progression towards spiritual detachment. People who succumb to the natural inclination to be preoccupied by the ego also succumb to the five tendencies of lust, anger, greed, materialism, and pride. By contrast, the true Sikh's life should be directed towards the Gurū. In accordance with their Gurū's insights, Sikhs regard God as the ultimate preceptor; one of the names which they use for God is *Satgurū* (True Teacher).

The question of how far Gurū Nānak was influenced by Hindu and Muslim principles has been energetically debated. There are resonances between Gurū Nānak's compositions and those of Kabīr (c. 1440–1518), Ravidās (c.1500), and other fifteenth- and sixteenth-century North Indian *bhagats* (poets whose influence transcended religious boundaries, and whose songs of yearning for God are still popular).

AMRITSAR AND THE SCRIPTURES

The religion, its scriptures, and its holy centres continued to develop under subsequent Gurūs. Gurū Amar Dās collected his own hymns together with those of Gurū Nānak and Gurū Aṅgad Dev, along with compositions by some of the *bhagats,* in volumes known as the *Mohan Pothīs.* His son-in-law, the fourth Gurū, Rām Dās (1534–81), founded the town that became Amritsar and was responsible for excavating further the natural pool there, already reputed for its healing qualities (*Amritsar* means 'pool of sacred water'). In the centre of the pool Gurū Rām Dās began the construction of what was later to become the Harimandir Sāhib, now widely known as the Golden Temple. The building was completed by the fifth Gurū, Arjan Dev (1563–1606), and it was here that in 1604 he installed a sacred volume, the *Ādi Granth* (Original Book), comprising the contents of the *Mohan Pothīs* plus his own and Gurū Rām Dās's compositions. Gurū Arjan Dev arranged these according to their *rāg* (melody evoking a mood or time) and they constitute a major part of the *Gurū Granth Sāhib.* Gurū Arjan Dev's 2,216 hymns are the longest contribution to the *Ādi Granth,* and his greatest work is the *Sukhmanī* (Hymn of Peace). His death at the hands of Muslim captors in 1606 marks the beginning of a new period of Sikh history (*see page 68*).

(Left to right) Top: Gurū Rām Dās, Gurū Amar Dās, Gurū Aṅgad, Gurū Nānak (the natural canopy of the tree is a traditional device for showing respect), Bhāī Bālā (attendant with peacock-tail fan), Gurū Har Rāi, Gurū Har Krishan. Bottom: Gurū Arjan Dev, Gurū Hargobind (with weapons and hawk), Bhāī Mardānā (musical accompanist for Gurū Nānak's hymns), Gurū Gobind Siṅgh (with weapons and hawk), Gurū Tegh Bahādur.

MARTYRDOMS

In 1605, the Mughal emperor Akbar died and Jahāngīr succeeded him (*see page 294*). Angered by Gurū Arjan Dev's evident popularity and by his sympathy for the rebel prince Khusro, Jahāngir had the Gurū tortured to death. Sikh militarization followed, as Gurū Arjan Dev's son, the sixth Gurū, Hargobind (1595–1644), declared his temporal power over all Sikhs everywhere (*mīrī*) in addition to the spiritual authority (*pīrī*) of previous Gurūs. He also established, on a site facing the Golden Temple in Amritsar, a platform known as *Akāl Takht* (Timeless Throne) from which edicts affecting the *Panth* (Sikh community) would be issued.

Later interactions between Mughal emperors and Sikh Gurūs included Jahāngīr's detention of Gurū Hargobind in Gwalior fort and his subsequent release, and Aurangzeb's summons to the seventh Gurū, Har Rāi (1630–1661), to explain his support for the emperor's rival brother. In the event, the Gurū sent his son, Rām Rāi, to represent him in Delhi, and Rām Rāi's readiness to alter a line of the scriptures to please the emperor disqualified him from succeeding his father as Gurū. Instead, though still a child, Rām Rāi's younger brother Har Krishan (1656–1664) succeeded briefly as the eighth Gurū, and, with a cryptic pronouncement, nominated his great-uncle Tegh Bahādur (1621–1675) to follow him. Gurū Tegh Bahādur's execution in Delhi is believed to have followed his pleading on behalf of a group of Kashmiri Brahmans who had refused Mughal orders to convert to Islam, and is indicative of his preference to give up his head rather than his faith.

The idea of the saint-soldier (*sant sipāhī*) encapsulates the Sikh ideal of maintaining a meditative focus on God together with a readiness to confront oppression and defend the vulnerable. The lasting legacy of the violent deaths of two Gurūs was a certain wariness of Islam and the creation by Gurū Gobind Siṅgh of a visually distinctive Sikh community, the *Khālsā*.

DOCTRINAL DEVELOPMENTS

As with Gurū Arjan Dev's martyrdom, there were formative repercussions for the Panth following Gurū Tegh Bahādur's execution. Tegh Bahādur's son, Gurū Gobind Rāi (subsequently Gobind Siṅgh, 1666–1708), grew up to be a military commander and poet. In 1699, on the Vaisākhī festival day (the Hindu spring festival, from this date onwards also celebrated by Sikhs for its historical significance), he rallied his followers, dramatically challenged volunteers to come forward, and then proceeded to initiate the first five, known as *pañj piāre* (five beloved ones), with *amrit* (sweetened water stirred with a double-edged sword). By so doing he inaugurated a community with its own distinctive code of discipline and appearance into which he asked the *pañj piāre* to initiate him. As a sign of equality, all men would replace their family names with *Siṅgh* (lion), and women would take the title *Kaur* (princess).

Gurū Gobind Siṅgh's *rahit* (code of discipline) involved a demarcation from Muslim society through such means as a ban on smoking, eating *halal* meat, or having intercourse with Muslim women. For these devoted Sikhs he used the term *Khālsā*, a word which at that time had a double meaning of 'pure' and 'land that directly belongs to the emperor himself rather than to his lords'.

According to Sikh tradition, it was from the day of the Vaisākhī festival day in 1699 that Gurū Gobind Siṅgh required his followers of both sexes to adopt the five Ks (*pañj kakke*) as outward signifiers of their commitment to Khālsā Sikh. These are *kesh* (uncut hair), *kaṅghā* (comb), *kirpān* (sword), *kachhā/kachahīrā* (cotton breeches), and *kaṛā* (steel or iron bangle).

Gurū Gobind Siṅgh composed poetic works, such as his autobiographical *Bachitar Nātak*, that are included in the *Dasam Granth* (Book of the Tenth [Gurū]), and he also completed the *Ādi Granth* by incorporating his father's hymns into the collection. Gurū Gobind Siṅgh's four sons met early deaths. Perhaps in view of this and of the repeated tendency for each Gurū's death to be followed by competitive claims from would-be successors, he is believed to have announced that after his death Gurūship would be embodied by the Panth (Sikh community) and the scriptures. The volume is known respectfully as *Gurū Grānth Sāhib* since Gurū Gobind Siṅgh instructed his followers to regard it as their Gurū. The presence of the Gurū-scriptures makes a space a *gurdwārā*.

Eighteenth-century Sikh history was particularly turbulent. In 1716, one of Gurū Gobind Siṅgh's converts, Bandā Bahādur, was tortured to death after rallying an army and challenging the Mughal rulers of Punjab. Between 1747 and 1767 Sikh forces (*misls*) repeatedly drove the invading Afghan ruler, Ahmad Shāh Abdālī, out of Punjab. As the Afghan threat waned, the *misls* increasingly fought one another until Rañjīt Siṅgh (1780–1839, *see box, page 40*), leader of the Shukerchakīā *misl*, unified them. As Maharaja, he governed Punjab from 1799 to 1839, and Sikhs remember him as their greatest ruler. By gilding the upper two stories of Amritsar's holy Harimandir Sāhib he transformed it into the Golden Temple. The violent upheavals following his death enabled the British to annex Punjab to British India in 1849.

Vāisakhī day, 1699: Mātā Sāhib Kaur adds sugar sweets to the water her husband Gurū Gobind Siṅgh is preparing, with which he will initiate his followers. This event is recalled in all Sikh initiation ceremonies.

BRITISH RULE AND THE SIKH DIASPORA

Identity, and in particular an identity distinct from the Hindu society in which the Sikh community evolved, has been a recurrent concern of Sikhs, whether during the British Raj or in independent India, or even when living overseas. There have been many milestones. For example, in 1925 Sikhs gained full control of their *gurdwārās* in India, while a definitive code of Khālsā discipline, known as the *Rahit Maryādā*, was issued in 1950. During the 1980s and 1990s, some Sikhs campaigned violently for greater autonomy from the Indian state.

In 1849, Maharaja Rañjīt Siṅgh's son, Dalīp (Duleep) Siṅgh (1838–1893), was deposed by the British, and the Punjab was annexed to British India. Under British rule many Sikhs moved further afield, either as army recruits or as farmers resettled in the newly developed 'canal colonies' in the west of the Punjab. Their British officers required soldiers in the Sikh regiments to maintain Khālsā discipline, including the five Ks. Nevertheless, nineteenth-century observers (including Max Arthur Macauliffe who, in 1909, published his influential six-volume work, *The Sikh Religion*) feared that Sikhism was declining.

Macauliffe's account reflects the reformist thinking of the *Siṅgh Sabhā* (Siṅgh Society). The first Siṅgh Sabhā was founded in Amritsar in 1873 with the aim of alerting Sikhs to the risk of indiscriminately merging with Hindu culture or being converted to Christianity. The Lahore Siṅgh Sabhā (established 1879) was even more strongly committed to repudiating the view that Sikhs were just one of many kinds of Hindu.

In 1909, as a result of this concern, the *Anand Marriage Act* was passed, so recognizing a distinctively Sikh rite, solemnized with the verses of Gurū Rām Dās in the presence of the *Gurū Granth Sāhib*, in lieu of the Hindu fire-centred Sanskrit rite that Sikhs had used hitherto. Rites marking other stages of life – birth and naming, initiation (*amrit pāhul*), death and funerals – were also formulated to distinguish Sikh from Hindu practice. Meanwhile, Sikhs' historic *gurdwārās*, including the Golden Temple at Amritsar, continued to be in the control of custodians who allowed Hindu worship to take place within them.

In 1920, the Akālī Party was established in India in order to free *gurdwārās* from corrupt management (*Akālī* means 'follower of the timeless one [God]'). Following intense agitation from 1920 to 1925, the *Sikh Gurdwārās Act* (1925) conferred control of the *gurdwārās* on the Shiromanī Gurdwārā Parbandhak Committee (SGPC), which had also been founded in 1920. The SGPC continues to be Sikhs' most powerful elected body.

After partition (*see page 294*), the Sikhs' homeland, Punjab, was divided between India and the new state of Pakistan. Sikhs and Hindus fled to the Indian side of the border, but although geographically concentrated as never before, Sikhs still did not form a majority in the Indian Punjab. Under Akālī leadership they campaigned for a new state of Punjabi-speakers to be created from the existing Punjab. State boundaries were redrawn in 1966 and the resultant smaller state of Punjab became India's only majority Sikh state. The Indian government did not accept the Akālīs' religious and economic demands as issued in the 1973 Anandpur Sāhib resolution. A militant Sikh preacher, Jarnail Siṅgh Bhindrānwāle (1947–1984), inspired escalating violence as followers campaigned for Sikh autonomy. He died when the Indian army stormed the Golden Temple, a crisis that led to the assassination of prime minister Indira Gandhi and stirred many nominal Sikhs worldwide to active commitment (*see page 53*).

EMIGRATION AND DIASPORA In the 1890s, Sikhs went to East Africa as indentured labourers to construct railway lines, and by 1960 over 20,000 Sikhs lived in Kenya alone. At the end of the nineteenth century Sikhs also began migrating to the Far East (including Hong Kong), Canada (especially British Columbia), and the United States (notably California). The first British *gurdwārā* dates from 1911, but Sikh numbers remained low in the United Kingdom until, following India's independence in 1947, increasing numbers of Sikhs, especially from the Jullundur/Jalandhar district of Punjab, emigrated there. Hong Kong's Happy Valley *gurdwārā* opened in 1902, and by the 1980s Sikhs in the territory numbered about 5,000. By the year 2000 there were approximately 500,000 Sikhs in the United Kingdom, and the Sikh population of Canada and the United States has risen significantly following the liberalization of immigration legislation in the 1960s; around 195,000 Sikhs were estimated to be living in Canada by 1991, and in the United States the Sikh population reached 180,000 during the 1980s. Diaspora Sikhs in the United Kingdom and North America have repeatedly campaigned for the recognition (by government, employers, head teachers, and so on) of Sikhs' rights to wear turbans and *kirpāns* (swords).

In 1999, Sikhs worldwide celebrated the tercentenary of Gurū Gobind Singh's inauguration in 1699 of the Khālsā, the distinctive community of saint-soldiers.

Girls studying Punjabi in the open air (Jullundur/Jalandhar, Punjab). Since 1966 Punjabi (in the Gurmukhī alphabet of the Sikh scriptures) has been the official language of the Punjab.

BUDDHISM

INDIA AND SOUTHEAST ASIA
DAVID L. GOSLING

TIBET
ADRIAN ABBOTTS

CHINA
ROGER CORLESS

JAPAN
PAUL INGRAM

KOREA
YOUNGSOOK PAK

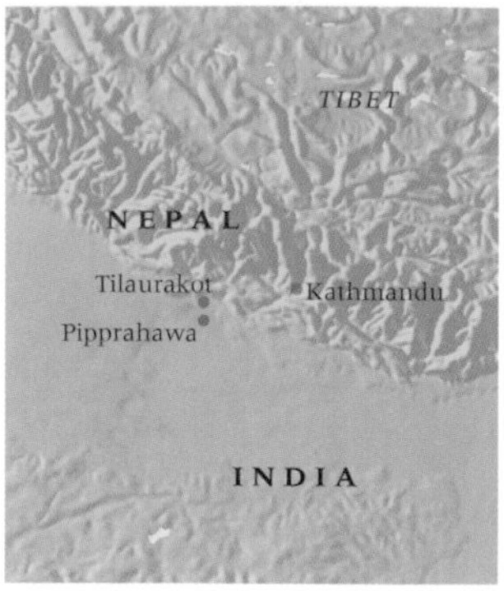

India and Southeast Asia

The most recent scholarship suggests that the Buddha was born in 480 BCE in Kapilavastu, currently Tilaurakot, just inside the border of Nepal. He left his aristocratic family at an early age, and after trying various Hindu techniques for attaining enlightenment, eventually achieved it in an animal sanctuary in what is now Bihar in India. He travelled and preached extensively in northern India and died when he was 80 (or possibly older).

This much is reasonably accurate history. Further details can be obtained only by comparing a wide range of texts which must be set against the background of events in the region at the turn of the fifth century BCE. Archeological evidence relating to early Buddhism in India is scanty; however, a major determinant in using other sources is the separation between the life of the Buddha and that of the Mauryan emperor, Aśoka (ruled 272–232 BCE) (*see page 80*). It is possible that the Buddha died as late as 370 BCE which, separated from Aśoka's reign by a mere century, increases the value of the relatively abundant Aśokan and post-Aśokan data and artefacts in understanding early Buddhism.

The birth of Siddhārtha Gautama as Buddha Śakyamuni, the Wise One of the Śakya clan.

At the Buddha's birth, the Magadhan kings ruled the region including Kapilavastu. Their province would have covered an area little larger than what is now Bihar – possibly much less. The best-known of these Hindu kings was Bimbisāra (ruled during the fifth century BCE), who became an acquaintance of the Buddha. The Śakya people, with whom the Buddha's family were associated, were an autonomous group in Nepal. They were prosperous, and their increasing prosperity and that of their neighbours was reflected in the progressive peaceful integration of the various regions of the northern plains which paved the way for the eventual assimilation of the Gangetic states into the Mauryan empire. Within the Hindu caste system the Śakyas are described as warriors.

A Buddhist monk meditates at a stone altar at Sarnath. He wears the yellow robes of a mendicant, similar to those worn by Buddha himself when he took up his search for nirvāṇa.

THE LIFE OF THE BUDDHA

The Buddha, whose Sanskrit name was Siddhārtha Gautama (or Siddhatta Gotama in the Pāli language, which derives from Sanskrit and is the language of the Buddhist scriptures), was born in a sacred grove of *sal* (*Shorea robusta*) trees. His early childhood was comfortable and uneventful. He married Yaśodharā who bore him a son named Rahūla. Scriptural references to the Buddha's departure from home to seek an enlightened state, *nirvāṇa* (*nibbāna* in Pāli), in which he would be free from old age, sickness, and death, are presented as largely incidental to the events leading up to and including his enlightenment. Head shaved and wearing the yellowish robes of a religious mendicant, he sought the assistance of Hindu teachers in order to attain the mental states of absorption known as *jhānas* which would lead to *samādhi*, the ultimate level of concentration. Wandering in the Magadhan countryside, he was accepted into the company of five ascetics who initiated him into severe physical austerities designed to achieve enlightenment. But nothing came of these, so the ascetics left him and he began to resume a normal, if frugal diet. It was in this intermediate state, between the austerities of Hindu asceticism and the comparative affluence of his upbringing, that he became enlightened – hence the designation of Buddhism as the Middle Way between two extreme lifestyles.

Details of these events may be gleaned mainly from the *Mahāvastu*, the 'Great Event', which is in Sanskrit, and the three Pāli narratives (*suttas*, Sanskrit *sūtras*) known as the *Ariyapariyesana Sutta* (the Discourse on the Noble Quest), the *Mahāsacceka Sutta* (the Greater Discourse to Sacceca), and the *Mahāvagga*, which analyses the Buddha's enlightenment. This literature, which is of an uncertain date, is based on even earlier traditions. Much of it eventually became part of the Pāli Canon (or Tripiṭaka, the Theravāda text collection), which was probably completed in Sri Lanka by the end of the first century BCE. The words of the Buddha and commentaries form the Buddhist scriptures; there is no 'Bible' as such.

The Buddha's later life was taken up with teaching, ordaining, and travelling extensively in north India. He died (that is, entered a state of *parinibbāna*, or nirvāṇa-beyond-rebirth) uttering the words, 'Subject to decay are all compounded things; with mindfulness, strive on.' According to legend, his death was accompanied by both thunder and an earthquake, and the *sal* trees on each side of him bloomed out of season.

THE BUDDHA'S ENLIGHTENMENT

The Buddha's enlightenment and first sermon (*see pages 78–79*) took place early in the second half of the fifth century BCE. The accounts of these events illuminate important Buddhist beliefs. According to the *Ariyapariyesana Sutta*, he was seated in a pleasant location at Uruvela, near what is now Bodh Gaya in Bihar, when he achieved his sublime goal. In this account there is no Bo (*bodhi, Ficus religiosa*) tree and no struggle with Māra, the tempter. The *Mahāsacceka Sutta* takes up the story of the Buddha's return to relative normality – the scripture is careful to stress that his nourishment remained frugal – as he continued to meditate.

Statues of the Buddha at the restored Mahābodhi Temple, Bodh Gaya, Bihar. A major place of pilgrimage, this is the legendary site of the Bo tree under which the Buddha gained enlightenment.

The first stage of the Buddha's enlightenment was the attainment of the four *jhānas*. (The Sanskrit form of this term is *dhyāna*, which became *chan* in the Chinese languages and *zen* in Japanese.) The first *jhāna* consisted of reasoned thought accompanied by a sense of elation. The second allowed thought to subside through concentrating the mind. The third encouraged elation and the effort of concentration to subside into equanimity, and the fourth permitted the equanimity so attained to be applied retrospectively to all previous experiences. In this fourth *jhāna*, the Buddha is described as feeling purified by a combination of equanimity and mindfulness. He is in full control of his faculties and completely aware of his surroundings.

Relief carving of Gautama Buddha. He is shown experiencing *bodhi*, or awakening, the perfect clarity of mind that allows one to see things as they are. One who has achieved *bodhi* is called a buddha. All beings are potential buddhas.

The *Mahāsacceka Sutta* continues by describing the Buddha's three kinds of knowledge. The first of these is his recollection of all his previous existences – some pleasant, some painful – which he was clearly able to see as though illuminated by a powerful searchlight. The second knowledge, achieved during the second part of the night of his enlightenment, enabled him to see all beings in their true state. Thus he could see all the inhabitants of the universe in their various conditions of pleasure and pain, well-being and misery, depending on their balance of *karma*. The Buddha's third and final knowledge, achieved as his historic night drew to a close, was that he himself was free from the limitations and impurities of karmic existence and was released into his final birth. His physical body needed to run its course, but this would no longer generate karmic consequences; when his life ended, his body would dissolve into nirvāṇa.

The *Mahāvagga* account of the enlightenment begins with the Buddha seated beneath a Bo tree. However, it is presented not in terms of a nocturnal sequence but as an ancient, pre-existing meditational formula known in Pāli as *paṭicca samuppāda*. This is translated by many scholars as 'causal arising', but a better definition is 'interdependent co-arising'. This difficult but cardinal Buddhist belief is significant for Buddhist ethics, and binds together human and non-human life and the physical world in an elaborate sequence of cause and effect. Following these experiences, the Buddha (enlightened one) travelled to the holy Hindu city of Vārānasī on the River Ganges and sought out the ascetics who had been his earlier companions. He found them in an animal (not necessarily deer) sanctuary where he preached to them his first sermon; this contains the essence of Buddhist teaching. In the sermon, he claims the title of Tathāgata, which implies that he has reached the deathless state of Buddhahood.

The Buddha's First Sermon

The essence of Buddhist teaching is contained in the various different accounts of the Buddha's enlightenment and his first sermon, which was delivered to a group of Hindu ascetics. These events mark a decisive break between the Buddhist and Hindu traditions. Although Buddhism eventually developed into two major streams, Mahāyāna and Theravāda, there is a common core which distinguishes the tradition as a whole from Hindu beliefs.

The exposition of the Four Noble Truths and the Noble Eightfold Path contained in this first sermon represents the core of early Buddhism. *Dukkha*, translated here as 'sorrow', represents the unsatisfactoriness of our humanity or personhood, which Buddhists describe in terms of five *khandhas* or components. There is, therefore, no need for the existence of a soul or self, as in the Hindu tradition.

A Buddhist monk meditates at Sarnath, near Vārānasī. The stūpa before which he is seated is thought to mark the site where the Buddha gave his first sermon.

The Buddha's first sermon was given to five of his followers at the animal sanctuary. Objects symbolizing the event are kept at Jokhang Temple, Lhasa, Tibet.

Once the Lord was at Vārānasī, at the deer [animal] park called Isipatana. There he addressed the five monks. 'There are two ends not to be served by a wanderer. What are these two? The pursuit of desires and of the pleasure which springs from desire, which is base, common, leading to rebirth, ignoble, and unprofitable; and the pursuit of pain and hardship, which is grievous, ignoble, and unprofitable. The Middle Way of the Tathāgata [he who has thus attained] *avoids both these ends. It is enlightened, it brings clear vision, it makes for wisdom, and leads to peace, insight, enlightenment, and Nirvāṇa...*

'This is the Noble Truth of Sorrow. Birth is sorrow, age is sorrow, disease is sorrow, death is sorrow; contact with the unpleasant is sorrow, separation from the pleasant is sorrow, every wish unfulfilled is sorrow – in short, all the five components of individuality are sorrow.

'And this is the Noble Truth of the Arising of Sorrow. It arises from craving, which leads to rebirth, which brings delight and passion, and seeks pleasure now here, now there – the craving for sensual pleasure, the craving for continued life, the craving for power.

'And this is the Noble Truth of the Stopping of Sorrow. It is the complete stopping of that craving, so that no passion remains, leaving it, being emancipated from it, being released from it, giving no place to it.

'And this is the Noble Truth of the Way which Leads to the Stopping of Sorrow. It is the Noble Eightfold Path – Right Views, Right Resolve, Right Speech, Right Conduct, Right Livelihood, Right Effort, Right Mindfulness, and Right Concentration.'

Samyutta Nikāya, quoted in *Sources of Indian Tradition*,
DE BARY, W.T., MOTILAL BANSARIDASS, DELHI, 1963

ORGANIZATION OF BUDDHISM

The Buddha's new disciples were formally called upon to renounce ordinary life with the words: 'Come, monk! Well taught is *dhamma*; follow the supreme way for making a complete end to suffering.' (*Dhamma* is the Pāli form of *dharma*, *see pages 36–37*). Initially there was no organized monastic community, and women were included among those ordained. The chosen followers were described as *arahats*, a term that originally applied to all ascetics but came to refer to those who have attained the penultimate state of perfection.

EARLY MONASTICISM As time went by, the initial informal association between the Buddha and his followers became more structured. This was evident at the first Buddhist Council (c. 370 BCE). Monks were sent out alone to teach the dhamma and were permitted to ordain disciples according to a defined pattern. Candidates for the monkhood were to have their heads shaved and wear yellowish robes with the upper robe across one shoulder. They should pay respect at the feet of the presiding monks and declare three times that they take refuge in the Buddha, the dhamma, and the *saṅgha* (monastic community). By this time it appears that monastic buildings (*vihāras*) had been constructed to accommodate monks on their journeys, and were particularly important during the rainy season. It is possible that the problems associated with accommodation and travel under hazardous conditions made it necessary to discontinue the ordination of women; it is not known when this practice stopped.

Within 100 years of its foundation, Buddhism was able to claim no less a personage than the Mauryan emperor Aśoka among its adherents. By the time of Aśoka's accession (272 BCE), the Mauryan empire had expanded to such an extent that it included most of the subcontinent, providing Buddhism with easy access to a vast area. The religion's straightforward analysis of the human condition, its egalitarianism, and the respectability afforded by the emperor's conversion, gave it a considerable advantage over other Indian belief systems.

The rules governing the behaviour of new monks were initially as follows: no taking of life, no stealing, no sexual intercourse, no lying, no taking of intoxicants, no eating at the wrong time (usually after midday), no dancing or music, no decorations or ointments on the body, no sleeping on raised beds, and no acceptance of money. Of these, the first five are incumbent on all Buddhists and are known as the *pañcaśīla*.

The ten original rules of Buddhist monasticism were eventually supplemented by others, creating what became an integral part of the Pāli canon, the *Paṭimokkha*, which is recited regularly in all monastic communities. This contains 227 injunctions about a combination of issues relating to communal living, personal hygiene, and respect for all living creatures. Thus: 'Should any *bhikkhu* [monk] dig the earth or have the earth dug, this entails expiation; in damaging plants, this entails expiation; should any *bhikkhu* knowingly pour water with living things in it onto grass or clay, or have it so poured, it entails expiation.' The *Paṭimokkha* is an early part of the Vinaya (Conduct), one of the three 'containers' of the Pāli canon, or Tripiṭaka, the others being the Sutta (Discourses) and the Abhidhamma (Further Dhamma/Dharma).

THE BUDDHIST COUNCILS The first Buddhist Council was held at Rajagriha in the year of the Buddha's death (c. 370 BCE). Although the intention was to systematize the Buddha's teaching, its deliberations had little influence on the eventual shape of the Tripiṭaka. The second Council at Vaisali was held several decades later and concentrated almost completely on monastic rules and practices, such as the handling of money by monks.

The third Council at Pataliputra was held in 250 BCE and was presided over by the emperor Aśoka. It was the most important of the three and resulted in the Great Schism between the *theras* or elders (who became the Theravādins) and the 'Great Assembly' or Mahāsāṅghikas, who paved the way for Mahāyāna Buddhism. The theras were concerned about the preservation of the exact teaching of the Buddha, monasticism, and the personal quest for liberation. The Mahāsāṅghikas were more open to doctrinal innovation and the involvement of lay Buddhists in their activities.

Stūpas at Sarnath, the Buddhist centre in the middle of a sacred Hindu area. The great Buddhist emperor Aśoka erected the stūpas. A Buddhist monastery flourished on the site until the Muslims came.

BUDDHIST SCHOOLS

At an early stage of its development, Buddhism embraced the notion of the Three Jewels, according to which all true Buddhists take refuge in the Buddha, the dhamma (teaching), and the saṅgha (the monastic community). This emphasis on teaching and community presupposed a lineage of authoritative teachers who could be traced back to the Buddha, and controversies then began to arise over the authenticity of both the teachers themselves and their teaching. These disputes form the basis of the various 'lineage groups' – usually known as schools – which developed during and after the three Councils.

There are two major streams of Buddhism, the Theravāda and the Mahāyāna. Both of these emerged from earlier traditions, and it is difficult to assign precise dates to either. At one time, it was imagined that the former was based on scriptures which reflected fairly accurately the original teaching of the Buddha, while the latter was derived from much later material. We now know that this is far from being the case. Vajrayāna Buddhism, which offers swift enlightenment in the present lifetime (like a thunderbolt or *vajra*, hence the name), is sometimes counted as a third grouping and at other times viewed as part of the Mahāyāna tradition. The Mahāyāna developed as a family of schools under two main cultural and linguistic headings: Tibeto-Mongol and Sino-Japanese. Theravāda Buddhism was more consistent; it spread without significant major changes from India to Sri Lanka and from there to Southeast Asia.

According to tradition, early Buddhism divided into 18 schools based on scholarly disputes about the Three Jewels. In reality it seems more probable that the main schools derived their characteristics from a wider range of influences. Thus, the Mahāsāṅghikas parted company with the theras (the early Theravādins) because they wanted to include the full range of aspirations of the laity, whereas the theras wanted to revert to the earliest monastic teaching.

THERAVĀDA BUDDHISM Theravāda Buddhists base their beliefs and practices on the Pāli canon, which sets out the essential features of Buddhist monasticism. The central figure of Theravāda Buddhism is the *arahat*, a term which originally referred to any ascetic worthy of reverence on account of his spiritual achievements – the Jains also used the term. Later, it came to signify one who, like the Buddha, achieves the penultimate state of perfection that is possible in this existence. Chinese, Japanese and Korean Buddhism all contain a comparable notion (Chinese, *alohan*; Japanese, *arakan*; Korean, *arahan*). In Theravāda Buddhism there are also *pratyekabuddhas*, which differ from arahats in that they do not belong to any monastic order or attempt to communicate their beliefs to anyone else – one early text compares the pratyekabuddha to a lonely rhinoceros! The Buddha himself is described as a supreme pratyekabuddha, or *samyaksambuddha*.

Theravāda Buddhism grew in influence in Sri Lanka during the centuries immediately prior to the beginning of the Common Era, and a legend grew up that the Buddha had actually visited the country. Sri Lankan Theravādins began to incorporate certain Hindu beliefs into their tradition (for example, the building of shrines to gods inside temples, and the use of statues of the Buddha), and public festivals such as Vesak, the full moon in May, were used to celebrate the Buddha's birth, enlightenment, and departure. Monks and nuns 'made merit' for the laity and statues of the Buddha became objects of personal piety. In the fourth century CE a relic purporting to be one of the Buddha's teeth was brought to Sri Lanka; it is currently housed in the Tooth Relic Temple in Kandy, from where it is carried in procession every year. When Sinhala Buddhism was eventually transmitted to Southeast Asia, the meritorious and pietistic elements which it had absorbed were reinforced by existing animist and brahmanistic Hindu practices (for example the veneration of *nats* in Burma). But the saṅgha itself continued to be regulated by the detailed Vinaya rules of the Pāli canon, with the result that the monastic and popular Buddhism continued to co-exist without any apparent contradiction between them. Theravāda Buddhism is currently to be found in almost all parts of the world, although the vast majority of its members are in Asia. It is estimated that of the global population of 324 million Buddhists, 38 per cent are Theravādin, while the remainder are either Mahāyāna (56 per cent), or Tantric or Tibetan (6 per cent).

MAHĀYĀNA BUDDHISM Mahāyāna Buddhism regards itself as a more complete expression of the dhamma than the 'lesser' Theravāda. Its distinctive teaching is centred on compassion for all sentient beings to such an extent that the ideal Mahāyānist will delay his or her entry into nirvāṇa-beyond-rebirth until they are all able to do the same. A key concept which played a major role in the development of Mahāyāna Buddhism is *śūnyatā*, emptiness or voidness. Just as the no-soul doctrine denies the existence of an enduring soul, so *śūnyatā* stipulates that the whole of reality is empty. In the earliest stages of Buddhism, the ideal Buddhist was known as an arahat, essentially one who practiced insight into various attributes such as loving-kindness. The Mahāyāna replaced this notion with the *bodhisattva*, who was characterized by transcendental wisdom (an ability to see reality from the perspective of emptiness) and compassion for all living beings. The term *bodhisattva* is pre-Mahāyānist and popular early Buddhist literature contains many references to the concept. Transcendental wisdom is *prajñā-pāramitā*, which expresses a level of compassion so strong that some bodhisattvas refuse to enter nirvaṇa-beyond-rebirth unaccompanied.

A person becomes a bodhisattva on making a vow to work for enlightenment for all creatures. He or she then progresses through six stages, known as perfections, after which he or she is in a position to understand the significance of *śūnyatā* and the true nature of reality (stage seven). At this point the bodhisattva cannot fall back to the earlier stages and progresses through the remaining perfections to full Buddhahood, the step beyond stage ten. Bodhisattvas have names; thus Avalokiteśvara is a bodhisattva at the ninth stage – the Heart Sutra expatiates on his goodness and generosity, and Mahāyāna temples are full of illustrations of his aspects. The Lotus Sutra is another important Mahāyāna text which sets out the paths of bodhisattvas. The Mahāsānghikas had diminished the role of the historical Buddha and elevated the long-enlightened Buddha, whom they conceived as perfect, infinite, and permanently withdrawn into a trance. Some Mahāyāna schools took over this 'Buddhology'.

The Temple of the Tooth, also known as the Dalada Maligawa, in Kandy, Sri Lanka. The last of a series of shrines, it houses the relic of the Buddha's tooth, brought to Sri Lanka in the fourth century CE. Once a year the relic is brought out to be displayed in a devotional procession.

OTHER BUDDHIST SCHOOLS

The Mādhyamakas, an influential school of the early centuries CE, claimed that *śūnyatā* is in between (*madhyama*) conflicting positions. They emphasized the idea of instantaneous continuity whereby phenomena constantly reproduce themselves in a moment-to-moment sequence of change. Mādhyamaka philosophy played an important part in the development of Chinese Buddhism.

The idealistic Vijñānavādins, also known as Yogācārins, were influential in the fourth century CE. Their main thesis was that consciousness is the only reality, and that the diversity of empirical phenomena derives from mental projections which are misinterpreted. This school paved the way for the Tantric synthesis of the Vajrayāna and played a large part in the development of Tibetan and Far Eastern Buddhism (*see pages 90–109*).

DEVELOPMENT OF BUDDHISM IN INDIA

Buddhism declined in India following Aśoka's death, and the advent of the Muslim invaders progressively weakened it (*see pages 293–294*). Buddhist monks lived in monasteries, which were easy targets for the Sultans and the Mughals who raided India from the twelfth century onwards. By contrast, Hindu beliefs were embedded in social structures such as caste, community, and family, and could not be eliminated so easily. Major Buddhist sites remain in India – the temple at Bodh Gaya in Bihar where the Buddha is alleged to have attained enlightenment is a potent example – but the total population of Buddhists in India at the 1991 census was estimated to be less than 1 per cent. However, in some respects the influence of Buddhism in India remains strong; Jawaharlal Nehru was strongly influenced by Buddhism, as was B. R. Ambedkar, the leader of India's untouchables at the time of Independence. The official emblem of the Republic of India, the Sarnath Lion Capital, is Buddhist.

THE SPREAD OF BUDDHISM IN SOUTH ASIA

SRI LANKA Buddhism arrived in Sri Lanka during the reign of Aśoka. The Sri Lankan king was reconsecrated according to the instructions of Aśoka, four monks having first been despatched to establish dhamma on the island. The cult of *stūpas* (mound-shaped monuments that often contained sacred relics and became important Buddhist symbols), sacred trees, and temples for Hindu gods became popular and were accepted by orthodox Buddhists. The famous Tooth Relic became associated with the royal court. Sri Lankan Theravāda Buddhism played a substantial part in the eventual development of Southeast Asian Buddhism.

SOUTHEAST ASIA The first Buddhist emissaries to Southeast Asia were sent by Aśoka in the third century BCE. They followed familiar trade routes to the 'Land of Gold', which was probably the west coast of Indonesia. However, the religion only began to have an impact from the beginning of the first century CE, by which time many Indians had settled in the region.

Mahāyāna Buddhism began to arrive in Indonesia in the seventh century and became influential in Sumatra under the patronage of the Srivijaya kings. Indonesian students travelled to Nalanda in Bihar where they became acquainted with Vajrayāna teaching. The magnificent Borobudur centre in Java, dating from the ninth century CE, combines the form of the early Buddhist stūpa with a more exotic style of Vajrayāna architecture.

The Tibeto-Burmese who have inhabited Myanmar (formerly Burma) since the eleventh century were preceded by the Pyu, who were of Tibetan stock, and the Mon, who are thought to have come from the east coast of India. The Pyu of Central Burma had adopted Theravada Buddhism – possibly exported from southern India – by the sixth century, and the Mon, further south, were also Theravādin. Mahāyāna Buddhism may have arrived overland from Bengal and Assam even earlier. During the eleventh century, the king of Pagan (the capital of the first Burmese state) attempted to remove Tantric influences from Burmese monasteries and restore Buddhist monasticism to its original Theravādin form as preserved by the Mon. Mahāyāna Buddhism declined and Pāli superseded Sanskrit as the official language of the scriptures (although vernacular translations have always been widely used), which were revised with the assistance of monks from Sri Lanka. The unification of Burma as a great centre of Buddhist culture and learning during this period resulted in the suppression of many cults of *nats* or indigenous spirits, though both these and certain elements of brahmanism remain a significant feature of Burmese Buddhism.

The Khmer, who came from the Mekong Valley, assumed control of what later became Siam and Cambodia during the ninth century. They were Hindus who readily combined the worship of their gods with Mahāyāna bodhisattvas and indigenous spirits and ancestors. Khmer cosmology played a central part in the belief systems of both Buddhists and Hindus in Southeast Asia.

The Khmer kingdom was overthrown in the fifteenth century by the Thai, who were Theravāda Buddhists living at that time in the vicinity of the Chao Phraya river. Under their influence, Theravāda Buddhism became the dominant religion in

Cambodia. Theravāda Buddhism was also introduced into Laos when the kingdom was founded in the fourteenth century. The Laotians were similar to the Thai and their culture exhibited a variety of popular elements such as astrology, which Buddhism had no difficulty in retaining. The Thai, like the Burmese, were less influenced by Hindu beliefs than Cambodians and Indonesians. This was primarily because the Mon peoples embraced Theravāda Buddhism comparatively early.

In Burma, Thailand, Cambodia, and Laos, Mahāyāna Buddhism has diminished, and whatever Tantric elements may have been present at an early stage have been largely suppressed. Theravāda Buddhism has grown in all four countries to such an extent that monks can move from monastery to monastery between them without hindrance (other than political constraints), using the same Pāli scriptures and adhering to the same monastic discipline. Over the centuries they have consolidated earlier links with Sri Lanka, and many of them continue to study at the centres of Buddhist learning in India.

THAI BUDDHISM Thai Buddhism is addressed in detail here because it is much more accessible than the Buddhism of surrounding countries like Burma, Laos, and Cambodia. Also, Thailand has never been formally colonized, which means that its Buddhist institutions – the monarchy and the saṅgha – retain an unbroken connection with the past. Thai Buddhism essentially derives from two sources: the Theravāda tradition of India and Sri Lanka, and the elements that have shaped the religion's history since it first reached Southeast Asia in the first and second centuries CE. The oldest and largest Buddhist site in Thailand at Nakhon Pathom dates from the sixth century CE, but there is evidence of Buddhist activity in the region before then.

The Thai kingdom of Sukhodaya lasted from the early twelfth century to 1350, when the centre of power moved south to Ayutthaya. This kingdom was subjected to defeat at the hands of the Burmese on two occasions and lasted until 1767, after which the twin cities of Thonburi and Bangkok became the national capital. During this extended period, the various kings saw themselves as protectors of the saṅgha against external enemies and rarely interfered in internal monastic affairs.

The kings of the Bangkok period, which ran from approximately the end of the eighteenth century until the present day, are known collectively as the Chakri dynasty, and several of them made significant monastic reforms. Prince Mongkut, who became King Rama IV in 1851 (ruling until 1868), had been ordained as a monk in 1824, and it is therefore not surprising that he made a number of major changes to the saṅgha. Dissatisfied with the way of life of the forest-dwelling monks, he insisted that primacy be given to learning rather than to meditation (*vipassanā*) or ascetic practices. He inspired and led the movement known as *dhammayuttika*, meaning 'those adhering to the law [scripture]'. Dhammayuttika monks wear their robes across both shoulders and generally observe the letter of the monastic Vinaya rules more closely than unreformed *maha nikai* (large assembly) monks.

King Chulalongkorn (Rama V, ruled 1868–1910) continued Mongkut's policies for promoting education and in 1898 entrusted the monks with a national programme of primary education. In 1902 he passed the first of three *Saṅgha Acts*, which set out the obligation of monks to obey 'three types of laws: the laws of the land, the Vinaya, and custom'. The Act set out the duties of various monastic authorities and standardized saṅgha administration. Following the replacement of absolute by constitutional monarchy in 1932, the second *Saṅgha Act* of 1941 was a move in the direction of ecclesiastical democracy, while the third in 1963 reflected the authoritarian policies of Prime Minister Sarit Thanarat (in office 1958–1963). It concentrated power in the supreme patriarch and replaced the various saṅgha committees with a single council of elders. This council, known as the Mahatherasamakhom, is made up of senior monks from both the dhammayuttika and maha nikai branches of Thai Buddhism. It relates closely to the Department of Religious Affairs of the Ministry of Education (which is staffed largely by ex-monks) and to the higher reaches of the monarchy. Its outlook is extremely conservative, but it is so unwieldy that the more progressive monks are able to avoid confrontation.

Young Buddhist monks study in Lamphun, Thailand. Novices and monks are not allowed to attend state schools or colleges, because they would then come into too much contact with women.

CONTEMPORARY THAI BUDDHISM

In spite of the control that the Thai secular authorities exercise over the Buddhist saṅgha today, there is still considerable variety among its members and between different monastic communities. There is the Dhammayuttika movement which broke away from the older (and much larger) Maha Nikai, and many monks from both have been strongly influenced by the scholar and reformist monk Buddhadāsa (known as Putatāt in Thai), 'servant of the Buddha' (1905–1983), who reinterpreted cardinal Buddhist doctrines to give them a 'this-world' emphasis. This in turn has stimulated ecclesiastical missionary and community development programmes ranging from politically motivated attempts to propagate Buddhism among tribal groups in the north to sophisticated courses to train monks as paramedics. The latter was the brainchild of Dr Prawase Wasi, a distinguished haematologist, who has also been instrumental in persuading some monasteries to act as hospices for people with AIDS. Such activities are legitimized from a Buddhist perspective by references to expositions by distinguished monks such as Phra Rajavaramuni, Phra Paññānanda, and Phra Payom Kallayano, a student of Buddhadāsa who spices his sermons with street-level slang and is very popular with young Thai.

Extreme right-wing Buddhism is represented by Phra Kittiwuddho, director of Chittapawan College near Bangkok, who has been accused of everything from gun running to illegally importing Volvo cars. Leftist monks have to air their views carefully; they tend to be associated with Sulak Sivaraksa, a social critic and distinguished Buddhist scholar.

Despite historical evidence that women were once ordained in Thailand, the practice has died out, although a few have been fully ordained in Taiwan. However, there is an increasing number of women who are initiated as lay nuns and live in communities similar and often adjacent to monasteries. They are known as *mae chii*. *Mae* means 'mother' and *chii* or *ji* in Thai can refer to Buddhist monks, certain non-Buddhists such as Jains, and also to Buddhist women who shave their heads and wear white robes. Mae chii resemble nuns in various religious traditions in some respects, such as the wearing of special robes, while the complete disregard shown for them by many monks and lay people sets them apart from these orders.

BUDDHISM IN THE WESTERN WORLD

The spread of Buddhism in its Theravāda form into south and Southeast Asia and in its Mahāyānist form into the regions to the north and east of India was only the beginning of a process by which Buddhism has become an acknowledged world religion. Buddhist centres, many accommodating monks following a variety of monastic disciplines, are to be found throughout Asia and the Western world, although less so in Africa where Islam is strong, and South America where Roman Catholicism is dominant.

British interest in Buddhism began in the late nineteenth century with the work of the Pāli Text Society, founded in 1881 by T. W. Rhys Davids (1843–1922), who became the first chairman. On his death, his wife C. A. F. Rhys Davids (1857–1942)

Western Buddhists in the Shrine Room of the Buddhist Temple in London. According to the *Journal for Buddhist Ethics*, there were about 800,000 American Buddhists and 362,000 European Buddhists (including Russia) in the mid-1990s. However, the immigration of Asian Buddhists of various traditions into North America and Europe over the last 30 years means that the overall number of Buddhists of all kinds is much higher.

was made president. The society encouraged translation work and historical and philological studies. Various European scholars also did important translation work, such as Edward Conze, and several became Buddhist monks, remaining in Asia for many years. The first Buddhist centre in the United Kingdom was founded in 1908 by an English monk who had been ordained in Burma.

There are currently well over 100 Buddhist centres and societies in the United Kingdom and many more in the United States. Some are primarily centres for Buddhist immigrants from Asia (for example, the Thai temple in Wimbledon, London, and the Khmer temple near New York); others cater mainly for Westerners who want to learn meditation or live according to a Buddhist way of life. The Friends of the Western Buddhist Order, established in London in 1967 by the Venerable Sangharakshita, has members across Europe and North America, most of whom are Mahāyāna Buddhists. There are currently estimated to be 100,000 Buddhists in the United Kingdom, making it the fourth-largest religion after Christianity, Islam, and Judaism.

Tibet

The emergence of Buddhism in Tibet coincides with our first historical awareness of Tibet as a nation. The king at the time, Songsten Gampo (c.609–650), although the thirty-third king by Tibetan tradition, is the first monarch we know of with certainty. He was a powerful man, and the story of Tibetan Buddhism begins with two wives he received as tributes from weaker foreign powers: Princess Wencheng from China, and Princess Bhrikūti Devī from Nepal. It is unclear whether the king personally converted to Buddhism, but his two wives were fervent believers and he seems happy to have pleased them by building two temples, the Jokhang and the Ramoché, to house the two Buddha statues they brought as dowries. Of these, the image of Jowo Rinpoché (Precious Lord), originally housed in Ramoché but later switched to the Jokhang, remains the holiest image in Tibet. Songsten Gampo must have appreciated the value of Buddhism because he not only made it the national faith but he also dispatched a translator, Thonmi Sambhota, to India to create a Tibetan alphabet suitable for the translation of Sanskrit texts. The translator did the job so well that Tibetan texts can be used today to recreate, word for word, lost Sanskrit works.

A perfectly restored replica of what is believed to be the oldest building in the country, the fortress palace Yumbulagang, in the Yarlung valley in central Tibet. Legend tells that when King Latotori lived there, Buddhist writings fell from the sky onto the palace roof. Although the king could not read them (they were written in Sanskrit), he worshipped them as sacred objects, as did his son who was thereby miraculously cured of his blindness.

The adoption of Buddhism as the national religion in Tibet was not, however, without opposition. There was already a religion in Tibet – Bön – and its adherents had no desire to see it supplanted. Probably animistic and without a sophisticated cosmology or formulated ethics, Bon evolved as a pseudo-Buddhism far removed from its original form. Yet early Bön had its power-base, and several centuries of political in-fighting followed. This is most apparent during the reign of Trisong Detsen (c. 755–797). A great military leader, he conquered both the Chinese capital Chang'an (present-day Xi'an) and Samarkand (now in Uzbekistan), forcing the Caliph of Baghdad, Haron ar-Rashid (*see page 281*), into an alliance with the Chinese emperor to counter the Tibetan threat. For such a king to choose peace-loving Buddhism as his faith may seem strange, and the idea that he was using it as a tool to defeat certain nobles (including his wife) who had associated with Bön, must be a possibility.

Trisong Detsen sought to create a monastic community based on the philosophy and practices of Indian Mahāyāna Buddhism (*see page 83*). (Chinese Buddhism, already well developed at this time, was pointedly excluded from his plans.) To this end, in c. 775 he established a monastery at Samyé and invited two Indian teachers to oversee it: Śāntarakṣita (c. 705–788), a professor from Nālanda in Bihar, and Padmasambhava (eighth century), a yogi from the Buddhist stronghold of Swat (now situated in modern Pakistan), with a reputation for supernatural powers and the slaying of demons. It took 12 years for these great men to train a handful of monks to the required standards, after which Trisong Detsen rewarded Padmasambhava by offering him his most recent wife. Shortly after this a number of Chinese Buddhists appeared at Samyé to challenge Indian Buddhism's right to govern the faith in Tibet. There followed the Great Samyé Debate (c. 792–794), in which the Chinese monk Hua Shang Mahāyāna was defeated by Śāntarakṣita's leading pupil, the Indian scholar Kamalaśīla, whose arguments included the thesis that enlightenment came gradually rather than suddenly. The Chinese were expelled from Tibet, and Indian Mahāyāna Buddhism seemed all set to inform the identity of a religiously transformed land.

It was not to be – at least, not yet. When the Bön-supporting King Langdarma (c. 803–842) usurped the throne by having his own brother assassinated in 836, a drive against Buddhism followed. With utter ruthlessness, all monasteries were destroyed and thousands of monks and lay adherents murdered. Langdarma was himself killed by an opportunistic monk, Lhalung Palgyé Dorjé, but Buddhism, although it was well-seeded on the fringes of the empire thanks to the arrival of fleeing monks, was not seen again in central Tibet for another three centuries. How it reappeared – in what is now called the 'second diffusion' – through the kidnapping of Yeshe Öd and is a story worthy of theatre.

The Second Diffusion

Yesh Öd, a pious regional ruler, was kidnapped by a tribe of Muslim brigands. The ransom demanded was his weight in gold. His nephew arrived with the gold in sacks, only to find he was short by the weight of his uncle's head. 'Don't worry about it,' said his uncle. 'Let them kill me, and spend the money on inviting the Buddhist teacher Atiśa from India instead.' And so it was. Atiśa (c. 982–1054) – himself a king who had exchanged his throne for a monk's robes – arrived in 1042 and was overwhelmed by the quality of the Buddhist literature preserved in monasteries on the edges of Tibet. With his disciple Dromdon he inspired a renaissance of the faith, while Bön seemed to have lost all strength and influence.

The revival was opportune. Within a century, Buddhism in India would be virtually wiped out by invading Muslim armies, who had already erased it across central Asia. The great universities such as Vikramaśīla and Nālandā, with reportedly 10,000 students each, three-storey libraries, and a hundred lectures a day, would be razed to the ground. Indian Mahāyāna had nowhere to go except Tibet, which offered itself in humility as an empty page to be inscribed.

FORMS OF TIBETAN BUDDHISM

Gelukpa monks hold an alfresco discussion of Buddhist texts. The Geluk (Virtuous Way) school, founded in 1409 by Tsong Kha pa when he established his Riwo Ganden (Joyous Mountain) monastery, is the last of the four principal Tibetan schools and currently the largest. Monks take a vow of celibacy and undergo a rigorous intellectual and religious education that lasts for 24 years. The Dalai Lama belongs to the Geluk school.

Tibetan Buddhism is often called Tantric Buddhism, from a verb meaning 'to weave'. The 'tantras' are texts that originated within Indian Mahāyāna Buddhism around 500 CE (*see pages 41–43*) and consist of meditational practices designed to transmute everyday awareness into 'enlightened mind'. Since Buddhism teaches that desire causes suffering, it is desire that the tantras seek to transform. The acceptance of sexuality as a religious issue was one of the factors separating Indian Mahāyāna from Theravāda, and the tantras treat it as an obstacle on the path to enlightenment. Yet when Atiśa arrived in Tibet, he found that however well these texts had been preserved, they were not well understood, and a certain moral looseness prevailed among the monks. Atiśa emphasized the need for graduated study so that the tantras were only practiced after many years of studying *vinaya*, *sūtra*, and *abhidhamma*, and then only under the guidance of a teacher. When Dromdon asked him which was more important, the text or the teacher, he replied: 'Without the teacher, the text and the man will go separate ways.' It is thus to Atiśa that the most salient feature of Tibetan Buddhism, the relationship with the teacher or lama (*bla.ma*, 'higher one'), a 'spiritual friend' in whom the faithful should see the inspiration of the Buddha, can be traced. Since becoming a lama traditionally involves prowess in areas such as visiting people in dreams and controlling rebirth, and a belief that the mind and the world are not entirely separate, it is not surprising that Tibetan Buddhism has acquired a reputation in the West for magic and mystery.

Tibet today has four principal schools. First, the Nyingma, which derives from the time of Padmasambhava and the 'first diffusion' and has the oldest texts. One such is the *Tibetan Book of the Dead* (*bar.do'i.thos.grol*), one of a class of 'treasure texts' (*gter.ma*) said to have been buried in the hills by Padmasambhava, to await discovery at a time when Tibet would be more ready for the teachings held within. Another school, the Sakya, dates from Khon Konchog's establishment of the Sakya ('grey earth') monastery in 1073. It allows its teachers to marry and transmits leadership through the male line of a ruling family. The Kagyü school was founded by Gampopa (1079–1153), and its later leaders, the Gyalwa Karmapas, were the first to institute the practice of reincarnating lamas or tulkus (*sprul.sku*, 'transformation body') in the thirteenth century. The

Geluk is the largest school; it emphasizes morality and was founded in 1409 with the establishment of the Riwo Ganden monastery by Tibet's foremost intellectual figure, Tsong Kha pa (1357–1419), whose *Great Graduated Path to Enlightenment* (*lam.rim.chen.mo*) owed much to Atiśa. Each school differs in philosophical presentation, although all would sit happily within Indian Mahāyāna as exemplified by the supreme Buddhist philosopher, Nāgārjuna (c. 150–250). They all emphasize the voidness of *dharmas* (existent things), the need for compassion as the starting point on the *bodhisattva* path, the practice of meditation to control the mind, and the importance of training the *saṅgha* (monastic communities) along a rigorously intellectual passage to Buddhahood, with textual debate as a key measure of progress.

After Atiśa, Buddhism in Tibet bloomed unhindered. In 1240, the Mongolians, threatening invasion, stopped short of Lhasa and requested 'spiritual advice'. The Tibetan leader at the time, Sakya Paṇḍiṭa (1182–1251), sent his nephew, Pakpa (c. 1235–1280), who so won over Kublai Khan that the latter prostrated himself before Pakpa as his teacher, beginning a priest–patron relationship and thus safeguarding Tibetan political autonomy. And so Tibetan Buddhism became the dominant religion throughout Mongolia and beyond into eastern and central Asia (where it is now resurgent following the fall of the USSR). China's current claims to Tibet take no account of Tibet's autonomy at this time, whereas China recognizes Mongolia as an independent country.

Tibet is well known today through the office of the Dalai Lama, a title (from the Mongolian *Ta Le*, 'Ocean') bestowed on Sonam Gyatso (1543–1588) by the Mongolian leader Altan Khan in 1578. Sonam Gyatso retrospectively applied this honour to his two previous incarnations, thus making Gendun Drub (1391–1475) the 'first' Dalai Lama. The current, fourteenth Dalai Lama, Tenzin Gyatso (born 1935), who received the Nobel Peace Prize in 1989, is seen by Tibetan Buddhists as a bodhisattva of compassion and is respected on the world stage as a statesman and spiritual leader. He was selected by a process that combines the predictions of his previous incarnation regarding the place of his rebirth with confirmation of a search party's choice of infant by both the state Oracle (a spirit medium) and the Kashag (governmental cabinet). Historically, rule by a single reincarnating lama inevitably creates periods of national weakness during the leader's childhoods, and many of Tibet's problems have occurred at such times.

Chinese Suppression

Following the invasion by China in 1950 and his permanent exile in India since 1959, the Dalai Lama has watched from outside as 1.2 million Tibetans – more than one in six of the population – have died, many of them monks and nuns in labour camps, others through starvation. Of some 6,000 destroyed temples and monasteries, only a handful have been rebuilt, and these are run by police committees who grant 'religious practice licences' to specially selected monks with 'politically correct' backgrounds. In 1996, possession of a picture of the Dalai Lama was declared illegal. By contrast, outside Tibet, Tibetan Buddhism grows rapidly around the world, with reincarnate lamas identified in Western children: the faith will survive. Inside Tibet, the prognosis for both culture – by the end of the twentieth century, Tibetans were outnumbered in their own land by Chinese soldiers and workers – and religion is grave. There is the question of who will speak for Tibet in the years before a future Dalai Lama's majority. The Panchen Lama (from *paṇḍiṭa.chen.po*, 'Great Teacher'), head of the Tashilhunpo monastery in Shigatsé, is the second most important figure in Tibet. The seventh Panchen Lama, Chokyi Gyaltsen (1938–1989), was actually chosen by the Chinese after the 1950 invasion, but he suffered years of imprisonment following one pro-Tibet speech, and many believe that he was murdered following another. In 1995, the eighth Panchen Lama was identified by the Dalai Lama as a six-year-old boy, Gedhun Choekyi Nyima. The Panchen Lama historically has no say in the selection of a future Dalai Lama (although he may advise the Kashag), but control over the Panchen is an important political tool, and following his identification, Gedhun Choekyi Nyima and his family were immediately abducted by the state, making him the world's youngest political prisoner if he remained alive. A child selected by the Communist Party was placed on his monastic throne. In January 2000, however, the seventeenth Gyalwa Karmapa, Urgyen Thinley (born 1984) escaped to India. Before the Dalai Lamas, the Karmapas had ruled Tibet; Urgyen Thinley, in exile, may prove to be a future voice for his threatened nation.

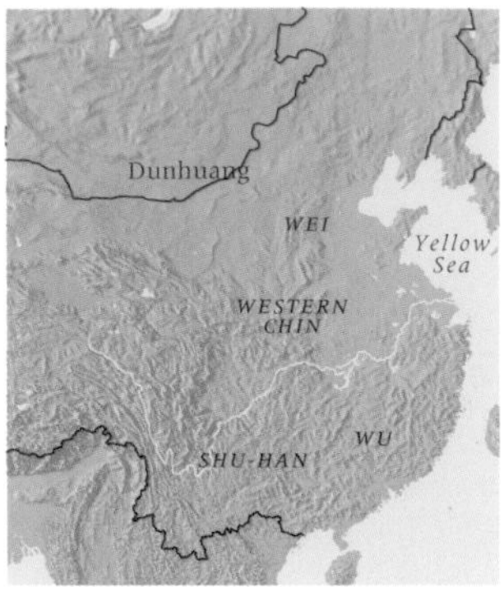

CHINA

BUDDHISM ENTERED CHINA from the Indian subcontinent via Central Asia around the beginning of the Common Era. Extensive cave temples were established at Dunhuang, the main entry point, now a rich source of texts, art, and other archeological artefacts. There are usually six historical periods recognized in Chinese Buddhism. *(See also pages 110–143 for Chinese religions.)*

The introductory phase (to the end of the Han dynasty, 219 CE) saw the arrival of texts, beginning with Hīnayāna material on meditation and followed by Mahāyāna material from the Perfection of Wisdom corpus (*see page 83*). Adaptation followed during the periods of Three Kingdoms and Two Jin (220–419), bringing 'Buddho-Daoism', when an attempt was made to express Buddhism in Daoist terms. This was criticized as misleading and was abandoned.

The third period marks differentiation and occurred during the Northern and Southern dynasties (420–588). Authentically Buddhist lineages and schools of thought emerged, some being adaptations of Indian forms, others being new developments. Tiantai and Huayan were comprehensive scholarly systems, while Chan (Zen) and Jingtu (Pure Land Buddhism) were more accessible to the common people. Consolidation followed (Sui period, 589–617); commentaries on the deep meaning or hidden significance (*xuanyi*) of texts were composed and lists of patriarchs drawn up to establish the authenticity of the lineages. The fifth phase saw dominance and decline (Tang, 618–906), as Buddhism became the victim of its own success. It drew men and women away from family and bureaucratic obligations, and established large monasteries with considerable land holdings. In 845 an alarmed Emperor Wuzong suppressed Buddhism. The suppression was short-lived, but the great monastic institutions were slow to recover. Chan and Jingtu, less dependent on property, revived more readily. Tantric Buddhism was introduced as the Zhenyan (Mantra) lineage. Although the lineage itself quickly died out, elements of Tantric Buddhism became an enduring part of Chinese Buddhism.

The final period marks survival and renewal (907 to the present). Division into lineages and schools – a prominent feature of Tang dynasty Buddhism – decreased, and Chinese Buddhism developed as a variety of syntheses of doctrines and practices, usually with a strong Jingtu base. A reform movement led by Taixu (1890–1947) was followed by suppression and regulation by the Communist government from 1949. After the death of Mao Zedong in 1976 there were indications of a revival of Buddhism on the mainland. In Taiwan (ROC), Buddhism has remained strong and innovative.

Detail of a temple hanging depicting the Pure Land of Amitābha Buddha, showing a bodhisattva being born out of a lotus in the lake in front of Amitābha. According to Pure Land (Jingtu) Buddhism, persons who have faith in and chant the Name of Amitābha Buddha in this life will be born in his Land (called Pure because it has none of the pollution of cyclic existence, *saṃsāra*) as advanced bodhisattvas.

BUDDHISM AND CHINESE RELIGIONS When Buddhism arrived in China it found a culture that already possessed sophisticated religious and philosophical systems. It could not, therefore, become the leading ideology, supplanting the native systems and reducing them to secondary importance, as it had elsewhere. Buddhism and Chinese culture quickly developed a love–hate relationship, which has lasted to this day.

The Chinese regarded Buddhism with some suspicion as a 'barbarous' religion from the mysterious and semi-mythological West, yet, at the same time, they were fascinated by it. One scholar was so impressed by Buddhism that he likened its teachings to a great ocean in comparison with the lakes and puddles of Confucianism and Daoism. Eventually, Buddhism was accepted as the equal of Confucianism and Daoism. All three were called *jiao* (teaching or tradition) and, by the Song dynasty (960–1127), the phrase *'sanjiao heyi'* (the three traditions are harmoniously one) became a popular saying. Nevertheless, Buddhism has often been regarded in China as a joyless tradition, forbidding as it does the consumption of meat and alcohol and recommending celibacy, and its foreign origin has given it a vaguely anti-patriotic aura.

Chinese Buddhism had the most creative interaction with Daoism. Its meditation practices and ideas of liberation from death encouraged comparisons with Daoist techniques aimed at gaining immortality. Perhaps, it was thought, Buddhism was another form of Daoism. Since it was believed that Laozi (*see page 116*) had departed to the West, it could be argued that he met the Buddha, who became his disciple, and so Buddhism could be an expansion of Daoism. Buddhists countered that the similarities were due to the Buddha's having taught Laozi. Although the differences gradually, over a period of about 400 years, became clearer due to increasingly accurate translations and repeated contacts with authentic sources in the Indian subcontinent, the feeling of similarity between Buddhism and Daoism did not go away and Chinese Buddhism, especially Chan, contains many doctrinal and artistic features that resonate with Daoism.

Confucian interaction with Chinese Buddhism was more social than doctrinal. Although its ethical base was praised, its recommendation of celibacy struck at the heart of the Confucian family system, because monks had no issue, and the Buddhist teaching of rebirth made it unclear as to who or what was being worshipped in the ancestor rites. On the other hand, unwanted daughters might be conveniently disposed of as nuns. Confucian principles of family etiquette were gradually adapted to fit the 'family' of the monastery.

Laozi, the traditional founder of Daoism, from a sixteenth-century painting by Qing Gu. Said to have been a contemporary of Confucius, and sometimes claimed by Chinese Buddhists to have been a disciple of the Buddha, he is credited with writing the *Daode Jing (Tao-te Ching)*.

CHINESE BUDDHISM IN PRACTICE

Inevitably, Chinese Buddhism saw distinctive doctrinal developments which marked it out from the way the religion was followed in other countries and regions. Both esoteric and popular forms developed.

HUAYAN Huayan is a philosophical school, founded by Du Shun (557–640 CE), based on a sūtra of the same name (*Huayan Jing*, Garland Sūtra). The teachings of the sūtra are literally of cosmic significance; they are so profound that they are addressed mostly to deities rather than humans. In essence they describe a cosmology of the interpenetration of ordinary reality by the realm of the Buddhas and the realm of the Buddhas by ordinary reality. The teachings were encapsulated by Fa Zang (643–712 CE) in *The Essay on the Golden Lion*.

Adapting a classical Chinese distinction between *li* (essence) and *shi* (manifestation), Fa Zang described the realm of liberation (nirvāṇa, *Dharmadhātu*) as *li* and the realm of suffering (*saṃsāra*) as *shi*. *Li* and *shi* interpenetrate in every possible way. Using the analogy of a golden statue of a lion, he compared the gold to *li* and the lion form to *shi*, and pointed out that every aspect of the statue is simultaneously gold and lion-shaped, elements which are distinguishable in theory but not in practice. Thus, *saṃsāra* and nirvāṇa are different but not separate. This is a version of the Mahāyāna teaching that appealed to the Chinese sense of the value of ordinary reality, mitigating the notion of world denial while not rejecting its teachings on liberation from *saṃsāra*. Everything could be seen as Buddha but not without the development of meditative insight.

Śhakyamuni Buddha preaching the Diamond Sūtra. Detail from a Chinese translation on a 5m (16ft) scroll dated 868 CE, claimed as the oldest extant printed work in the world. The Diamond Sūtra is one of the shorter texts of the extensive Perfection of Wisdom corpus. It teaches emptiness (*śūnyata*) in short, apparently contradictory, phrases.

TIANTAI Tiantai is a practice lineage named after the sacred mountain Tiantai Shan on which Zhi Yi (538–597 CE) meditated and, according to tradition, systematized the school founded by Hui Si (515–576 CE). He was said to have organized the texts, doctrines, and meditative practices, which had arrived in China in disarray, according to a graded system based upon what was presumed to be the order in which they were taught by the Buddha.

After his enlightenment, the Buddha gave exalted teachings to deities and later gave simpler teachings to humans. In this way the *Huayan Jing* was said to have been taught first, followed by the Hīnayāna teachings on the Fourfold Truth, then the Mahāyāna teachings on emptiness (in two sections, elementary and intermediate). Finally, the Buddha revealed the most profound teachings of the Mahāyāna, the Round or Perfect Teachings, in the Lotus and Nirvāṇa Sutras (*see page 83*). The consummate vision is '*yi nian san qian*', 'the three thousand realms in one thought' (literally, 'one thought, three thousand'). The three thousand realms are the sum of reality: ten mutually interpenetrating realms of rebirth (100 realms), each with ten features (1,000 realms) and three aspects (3,000 realms). One thought is the timeless meditative present of the practitioner's mind. The system was elaborated by linking different meditative practices to each level of doctrine and distinguishing between Four Teaching Methods (Sudden, Gradual, Secret, and Variable) and Four Teaching Types (Hīnayāna, shared Hīnayāna and Mahāyāna, Bodhisattva, and Perfect), providing a full programme of doctrine and practice.

The Western Paradise of the Pure Land, with Amida Buddha – also known as Amitābha (Immeasurable Light) or Amitayus (Immeasurable Life) – presiding over it. Beings are born into the Pure Land if they recite his name. The invocation of Amida's name (*Nian Fo*) is one of the most common practices of Chinese Buddhism.

CHAN Chan-na, abbreviated to Chan (the Chinese transliteration of the word *dhyāna*, 'meditation') was brought to China by Bodhidharma (c. 470–520 CE). It claims a direct mind-to-mind transmission of the 'lamp' of enlightenment from the Buddha. Its distinctive practices are *zuo-chan* and *gong-an*. In *zuo-chan* (sitting meditation), the mind is simply held in the present moment, alert and aware. *Gong-an*, better known in English in the Japanese form *koan*, is a mode of dialogue between teacher and disciple intended to uncover the Buddha Mind by posing a question that is a riddle to the ordinary mind. Focusing on the experience of enlightenment unencumbered by the vessels of text and doctrines, there is a strong iconoclastic rhetoric associated with the school (for example, 'If you meet the Buddha, kill him!'), but in practice Chan is doctrinally conservative. The lineage passed to Korea as Son, Vietnam as Thien, and Japan as Zen.

JINGTU (Pure Land Buddhism) The *Nian Fo* (Invocation of Buddha) – '*Nan-mo A-mi-tuo Fo*' ('Hail, Amita Buddha!') – is perhaps the most common phrase used in Chinese Buddhism. It is based on the sutras that tell the legend of Dharmakara Bodhisattva, now Amita (or Amitābha) Buddha, who vowed that when he became a Buddha he would preside over a Pure Land (Jingtu) which would be a realm outside *saṃsāra* (hence 'pure'); humans could be born there simply by calling on his name. Progress to nirvāṇa would then be easy and assured. Since Nian Fo can be practiced in everyday life, Pure Land Buddhism is as popular with lay people as it is with those living within monastic orders.

Tantric Elements in Chinese Buddhism

Tantric Buddhism in China had only a brief existence as a separate lineage but it has survived in elements of the syncretic mix of post-Tang Buddhism.

Like Daoists, many Buddhist teachers are renowned for their proficiency in super-normal powers, and they may sometimes be asked to perform ceremonies which, for example, influence the weather.

JAPAN

BUDDHISM ENTERED JAPAN from Korea in the mid-sixth century, perhaps as early as 538 and possibly as late as 552. The eighth-century *Nihongi* (Chronicles of Japan, *see page 157*) records the first Japanese reference to Buddhism when, in 552, the Korean king of Paekche, Song, sent tribute to Kinmei, the Japanese emperor, which included an image of the Buddha and Chinese translations of some Buddhist scriptures. This early encounter with Buddhism provoked a conflict with the indigenous religious traditions which the Buddhists called Shintô, or 'the way of the gods,' as distinct from *bukkyō*, or 'teachings of the Buddha'. While the Korean Buddhists largely adopted the veneration of the Buddha in place of the worship of Shintô *kami* (deities), Japanese clans and priests of the Shintô tradition organized strong opposition to the presence of Buddhism, especially in the imperial court. However, by the seventh century, Buddhism was in the ascendant in court circles.

EARLY BUDDHISM AND THE NARA SCHOOLS

Buddhism's early history in Japan is a story of the battle for acceptance by clan leaders, the imperial court, and the state, as a consequence of which Buddhism was at the centre of the political and cultural struggles of the newly forming imperial court. For six centuries Buddhism served as the vehicle by which Chinese culture was gradually imported into Japan, adapted to Japanese conditions and needs, and transformed into distinctively Japanese forms (*see pages 150–179 for Japanese religions*).

Japanese Buddhists revere Prince Shôtoku (574–622) as the 'founder' of Japanese Buddhism. He saw the religion as a foundation for the imperial household's political status and power. He wrote several commentaries on difficult Buddhist texts and gave Buddhism its first legal recognition. He also sent Buddhist monks to China to study not only Chinese Buddhism but also Chinese art, politics, and technology, Confucianism and Daoism (*see pages 114 and 116*). What the monks learned was brought back to Japan and adapted to meet the needs of the Japanese. In other words, Buddhism served as a vehicle by which Chinese culture in general – art, political philosophy, technology, medicine, and writing – was brought to Japan. Chinese culture became the foundation on which the Japanese built their own distinctive culture.

In the Nara period (710–784), Buddhism became a state religion. In 741, Emperor Shômu ordered 'provincial temples' to be built in every province, the resident monks and nuns reciting Buddhist texts for the protection of the state as part of their daily practice. The general picture of Nara Buddhism suggests an aristocratic religion with monks and nuns largely confined to monasteries and the imperial court. Six Nara schools were transmitted from China by Japanese monks (in Japanese Buddhism, two dates can be applied to each school, depending on the criteria used to determine their foundation. Some scholars use the year a doctrine was brought over from China, while others base the date on the formal establishment of the school in Japan. Where appropriate, both dates are given here): Jôjitsu (625), Sanron (625), Kegon (736, 740), Ritsu (738, 754), Hossô (654, 661), and Kusha (658, 736). Nara Buddhism is famous for its philosophy, since all the Mahāyāna forms of Buddhist philosophy that existed in the Chinese and Korean traditions were cultivated in these schools. The Nara school is also famed for its temple art and architecture. The last was a primary factor in the decision to move the imperial capital in 784 from Nara to Heian-kyô (present-day Kyoto). This briefly freed the imperial court from Buddhist interference. The move also triggered the renewal of Buddhism in the ninth century, initiated by the establishment of the Tendai and Shingon schools (*see pages 158–159*).

Shôtoku Daishi (574–622 CE, Prince Shôtoku) with his two wives, both of whom encouraged his interest in Buddhism, the philosophy that had been brought by Chinese monks from Japan via Korea in the sixth century. The prince gave Buddhism legal status, studied and lectured on important Buddhist texts and, in 607 CE, founded the temple complex of Hōryū-ji, situated 12 kilometres (7½ miles) from the imperial capital of Nara. During the eighth century, Buddhism became the state religion of Nara Japan.

THE HEIAN PERIOD: THE TENDAI AND SHINGON SCHOOLS

By the end of the eighth century, the major traditions of Japanese Buddhism were taking shape. An important aspect was the continued importation of Buddhism from China. Most of the religious innovations in Japan during the Heian period (794–1185) were directly related to Buddhist currents. For example, both Daoism and Neo-Confucianism were reintroduced to Japan in the wake of the importation of Buddhism from China and Korea. Religiously, the period is noted for the introduction from China of two new Buddhist schools, each established by a powerful Japanese monk: the Tendai School of Saicho (767–822) – posthumously honoured as Dengyô Daishi – and the Shingon school of Kûkai (774–835), posthumously honoured as Kôbô Daishi.

The Shingon school encompasses esoteric Buddhist doctrines and practices that have their origin in Indian Buddhist tantra. Shingon doctrine divides Buddhism into exoteric (or public) and esoteric (or secret) teachings. Exoteric teachings are common to most forms of Buddhism and are regarded as incomplete versions of the complete truth of esoteric teachings. Accordingly, Shingon doctrine is highly symbolic and is perhaps the most complex in Japanese Buddhism.

The central text of the Tendai tradition (called Tiantai in China, *see page 97*) is the Lotus Sūtra (*see page 83*), which Tendai masters in both China and Japan held to be the supreme teaching of the Buddha. Saichô regarded all interpretations of this text other than his own as false. After the Heian period, the Tendai school became increasingly more significant than the Shingon school because of its influence on the creation of distinctively Japanese forms of Buddhism, since the creators of the Kamakura schools were Tendai monks. For Saichô, the Tendai school was superior to all other forms of Buddhism, and one of his dreams was to establish a Tendai ordination altar in Japan modelled after the Tiantai tradition he studied in China. Because of the objections of the Nara schools, the state did not grant permission for the erection of such an altar until several years after Saichô's death.

THE KAMAKURA SCHOOLS

The shift of political power from Heian-kyô to Kamakura had two immediate consequences for Japanese Buddhism: first, the political and economic decline of the court nobility severely limited the imperial court's patronage of the Tendai and Shingon schools; and, second, the violence and uncertainties of life during these times energized Buddhists – mostly from the Tendai tradition – to establish forms of teaching and practice relevant to the political climate and the needs of ordinary people and which were not, therefore, merely copies of the previously prevalent Chinese Buddhist traditions.

A Buddhist theory that underlies these shifts was the 'decline of the *dharma*', one textual source of which is the Lotus Sūtra. This theory presupposed three stages of degeneration of the Buddha's *dharma*: the age of 'True Dharma' (*shōbō*), when people followed the teaching of the Buddha and attained awakening; the age of 'Counterfeit Dharma' (*zōbō*), when people practiced Buddhism but very few attained awakening; and the present age called the 'End of the Dharma' (*mappō*), when no one achieves awakening through the practice of Buddhism. The people who lived through the frequent wars and social upheaval and disintegration of the Kamakura period saw a parallel between their experience and the theoretical doctrine of the 'decline of the *dharma*', although its message about the present age would have brought very little, if any, real comfort.

Some Tendai monks developed alternative forms of Buddhism which they believed could help beings achieve awakening during the age of *mappō*. These developments are the Rinzai and Sôtô Zen schools founded by Eisai (1141–1215) and Dôgen (1200–1253), Jôdo Shu or the Pure Land school founded by Hônen (1133–1212), Jôdo Shinshû or the True Pure Land school founded by Shinran (1173–1262), and Nichiren Shu or the Nichiren school founded by Nichiren (1222–1282, *see pages 160–161*). All of these reformers held two assumptions in common: since in the age of *mappō* all institutions, including Buddhism, exist in a corrupted form and are therefore incapable of helping any person achieve awakening, and since human nature itself is now governed by egoism and passion, the complexity of Buddhist doctrine and practice must be simplified to help and meet the needs of people reborn in this degenerate period of

Buddhism in an Age of Instability

One of the ironies of Japanese Buddhist history is the speed with which the Tendai and Shingon schools degenerated into the wealthy decadence of the Nara schools against which they had revolted. Shingon especially became an elaborate ritual system for the wealthy, focusing on ceremonies to mark death and funerals, while Tendai alternated between mountain meditation and political interference in the capital, Heian-kyô, at the foot of Mount Hiei – the centre of the Tendai movement. If the Heian period was a time of relative peace, the Kamakura period (1185–1333) was a time of violence that was initiated by the removal of the political capital from Heian-kyô to Kamakura by a newly evolving warrior class (the samurai), led by feudal landowners called *daimyō*. The strongest *daimyō* – Minamoto Yoritomo – emerged as the winner of a 20-year civil war known as the Onnin War. He forced the emperor to declare him *Shōgun* (literally, barbarian-quelling general). From this time until 1868, Japan was ruled by a series of shōguns, hereditary military rulers, who wielded supreme military and political power in Japan while the emperor and his court were maintained in powerless seclusion in the imperial palaces in Heian-kyô.

history. Accordingly, Eisai taught that the practice of *kôan* meditation was the best method to achieve awakening while ignoring the 'words and letters' of Buddhist doctrine and ritual, whereas Dogen reduced Buddhism to the practice of *zazen* or 'seated meditation' in which the conscious flow of the mind's content is observed without 'stopping' on any particular item until the mind is calmed and centred and experiences no external distraction. In this state, awakening can be experienced.

For Honen, practicing Buddhism in the age of *mappō* meant taking refuge in Amida (the Japanese form of Amita) Buddha *(see page 97)* and seeking rebirth into the Pure Land through the practice of *nembutsu* or Buddha reflection, which in Jôdo Shu teaching means constantly repeating *'namu amida butsu'* ('I take refuge in Amida Buddha') in order to inspire a moment of undoubting faith in Amida Buddha's 'original vow', and so bring all sentient beings to the Pure Land. Hônen believed that this was the 'easy path' and that it was our only option in this age. For Shinran, Buddhism meant 'faith' or 'trust' in Amida Buddha's vow or 'other-power' to bring all beings into the Pure Land, and distrust of one's own 'self-powered' efforts to achieve awakening through traditional Buddhist forms of meditation. Like Honen, Shinran believed that only his teachings were suitable for beings who were reborn in the age of *mappō*. Finally, Nichiren reduced Buddhism to the practice of faith as trust in the Lotus Sūtra, which he regarded as the final wisdom of the Buddha. Since the Buddha's wisdom is incarnate in this text, followers need only trust it as they chant *'namu myōhō renge kyō'* ('I take refuge in the Lotus of the Good Law Sūtra').

A modern Buddhist monk from the Kamakura region practices meditation. During the unrest that characterized the rise of the Kamakura shōgunate, many Buddhist schools were founded.

For the first time in Japanese history, these reform movements saw Buddhism capture the attention of vast numbers of Japanese people, and today they claim the majority of Buddhist temples and adherents within Japan. No significant new schools arose in Japan until the Tokugawa period, except for the Obaku school of Zen imported from China in the seventeenth century. Obaku Zen was founded by Inen Zehiji in the sixteenth century. It combines *kôan* meditation with the practice of Pure Land *nembutsu*. But unlike Jôdo Shu teaching, Amida Buddha is not regarded as a transcendent bodhisattva. There exists no Amida outside of one's own mind. Like *kôan* meditation, chanting *nembutsu* is a practice aimed at helping one to see into one's own nature and so achieve awakening.

TOKUGAWA BUDDHISM

The Tokugawa period (1603–1868, *see pages 166–167*) was a time of peace and order thanks to the unification of the country by Tokugawa Ieyasu, who became shōgun in 1603. Most of the period was characterized by stability and conservatism rather than innovation and creativity. A fundamental element of Tokugawa policy was the final elimination of Buddhism's political and military power, a force that had helped to divide the country into warring factions for two-and-a-half centuries. However, as a religion, Buddhism was patronized by the Tokugawa government as a means of unifying the country – and it was also used as a method of persecuting Christianity. Christianity was introduced to Japan by Jesuit missionaries in 1549. From 1612 it was a proscribed religion and Buddhism became an arm of the government in order to enforce this proscription. Every family was required to register at a Buddhist temple, to record births and deaths there, and to undergo periodic examination by a temple priest. State money flowed freely into the temples, at the cost of their autonomy and vitality, and Buddhist clergy became little more than government bureaucrats. (Christians continued to worship in Japan, in secrecy and great peril.)

Student monks at the Shingon temple complex on Mount Koya, Wakayama Prefecture. The Shingon (True Word) sect was founded by Kukai and established on Mount Koya in 816. Today there are over 110 temples on the site.

JAPANESE BUDDHISM FROM 1868 TO THE PRESENT DAY

The Meiji Restoration (*see pages 168–169*), which saw the Emperor restored to symbolic importance, caused a crisis in Japanese Buddhism. Centuries of patronage by the Tokugawa government had resulted in priests and temple authorities taking for granted their status and wealth. They were so entrenched that financial corruption and spiritual laziness characterized the leadership of most Buddhist institutions. When the last Tokugawa shōgun abdicated in 1868, government patronage ended and an important source of Buddhism's wealth and residual political influence abruptly disappeared. Not only did the Meiji government withdraw support from Buddhism, it disestablished Buddhism and established Shintô as the state religion, calling it *kokka shintô* (State Shintô). In its zeal to restore Shintô to the centre of national life, the Meiji government sought to limit the influence of Buddhism among the people.

Buddhism accepted the challenges of Western learning by sending scholars to Europe and America. On the whole, Buddhist monks were much more in touch with Western culture than were laypersons. With the establishment of Western-style universities in Japan in the nineteenth century, Buddhist monks and occasionally nuns and laypeople enrolled for training in Buddhist philosophy and the classical Buddhist languages, Pāli, Sanskrit, Chinese, and Tibetan. In 1876, Nanjo Bunyu went to England to study Sanskrit with Max Müller, the pioneer of the comparative study of religions in Europe. Nanjo was the first Japanese Buddhist to adopt Western methods of historical and philological scholarship. Because of his work, interest in the academic study of early Indian Buddhism and Buddhist texts through the lenses of Western methods of critical scholarship became part of contemporary Buddhist thought. Anesaki Masaharu continued Nanjo's work in 1905 as the first occupant of the chair of the science of religion at the University of Tokyo. However, Buddhist scholarship had little effect on the lives of most ordinary Japanese people, nor does it have much influence on the lives of Buddhist and non-Buddhist Japanese people today, who continue to study and practice Buddhism in a more traditional light.

Although Buddhism supported Japan during the Second World War, it did not experience the stigma of defeat as did the Shintô tradition, which had been used to create a political ideology justifying the war. Nevertheless, in the postwar period, when the Allied occupation removed restrictions on religious practice and there was complete religious freedom, Buddhism was hard-pressed because of institutional disorganization. After 1945 temple affiliation became more flexible and Buddhist temples and monasteries suffered acute financial problems. Monks and temples continued to function in funeral and memorial services for most Japanese, but often without inspiring great religious feeling. Some renewal of Buddhism took place in the late twentieth century through the increasing participation of laypeople and the greater public awareness of Buddhism as a worldwide religion. Zen Buddhism gained increasing influence outside Japan, particularly through D. T. Suzuki (1870–1966) and popular works such as Robert M. Pirsig's *Zen and the Art of Motorcycle Maintenance* (1974), but perhaps the most influential forms of Japanese Buddhism today are Buddhist-inspired 'new religions' (*shinshukyo*) such as Sôka Gakkai (*see page 173*) and Rissho Koseikai, lay Buddhist movements which centre on devotion to the Lotus Sūtra.

Women as Transmitters of Japanese Buddhism

According to the *Kojiki* ('record of ancient events'), in 584 CE, some 30 years after Buddhism was introduced to Japan from Korea, a young woman named Zenshin-ni was moved by the Dharma to seek ordination as a nun. Ordination for both monks and nuns could only be performed in the presence of ten fully ordained monks, but because no such quorum existed in Japan in 587, Zenshin-ni was granted permission from her parents to go to Korea and receive full ordination there. Two other young women accompanied her for the same purpose: the daughter of Ayabito no Yaho, who took the Buddhist name Zenzō-ni, and Ishime, daughter of Nishikori Tsubu, who took the Buddhist name Ezen-ni. These three women were the first Buddhists in Japan to receive full monastic ordination. The Buddhism these women studied in Korea was probably a form of Southern Sung Chinese Buddhism.

They returned to Japan in 590, after receiving full ordination, and took up residence in a temple called Sakura-ji in the present-day Nara prefecture as the first ordained Buddhist monastics in Japan. From this time on, nuns were instrumental in the establishment of Buddhism in Japan, predating the involvement of Prince Shôtoku (574–622) in promoting the religion. In 623, little more than 30 years after Zenshin-ni and her sisters inaugurated monastic Buddhism, there were 569 nuns and 816 monks; 50 years later (674), records indicate that Emperor Temmu (ruled 673–686) gathered some 2,400 nuns for a ceremony. While it is not certain why so many women became Buddhist nuns, many did so for the sake of the nation, the country's health and its protection from natural disasters such as fire, earthquakes, and droughts being their primary concerns.

Women have always played a key role in the development of Buddhism in its Japanese form. Here a modern Japanese Buddhist ties paper prayers to the fence surrounding the ancient Hōryū-ji temple complex in Nara, founded by Shôtoku Taishi in 607CE.

Women not only led the way in the establishment of Japanese Buddhism, they also received early support for their work from prominent male members of Japanese society, most notably Prince Shôtoku. In his efforts to establish Buddhism in Japan, he relied on nuns. Of the seven temples he is said to have built, five were *amedera* (nuns' temples). The most famous of these was Chugu-ji, which still stands in Nara beside Hōryū-ji, the equivalent monks' temple. Others include Tachibana-dera and Ike-shiri-ji, and he also built Katsuragi nunnery. From the first ordained Japanese Buddhists in the sixth century to leaders of educational and monastic reforms in contemporary Japan, Buddhist nuns have made a significant contribution to the shaping and preservation of Japanese Buddhist teachings, practices, and institutions.

The history of Japanese Buddhist nuns helps to bring to the surface the continuing role of women in Japanese Buddhism. Because Buddhist nuns, more so than their male counterparts, continue to uphold Buddhist monastic training and practice in all its ascetic rigour, and focus on the self-disciplined practice of meditation, they are the primary role models of committed Buddhist practice for Japanese men and women. Alongside their commitment to the monastic life, nuns continue to follow the Buddhist tradition of awakened social engagement with the community of lay persons as spiritual advisors, social workers, carers for the elderly and the sick, advocates for the poor, and teachers of Buddhist ethical values.

The history of Buddhist nuns in Japan is still in the process of being written; however, what is gradually becoming clear is that women have played defining roles equal to their male counterparts in the history of Japanese Buddhism. The traditional paradigm of Buddhist monastic life is not a thing of the past in contemporary Japan; it is alive and well in the communities of the nuns.

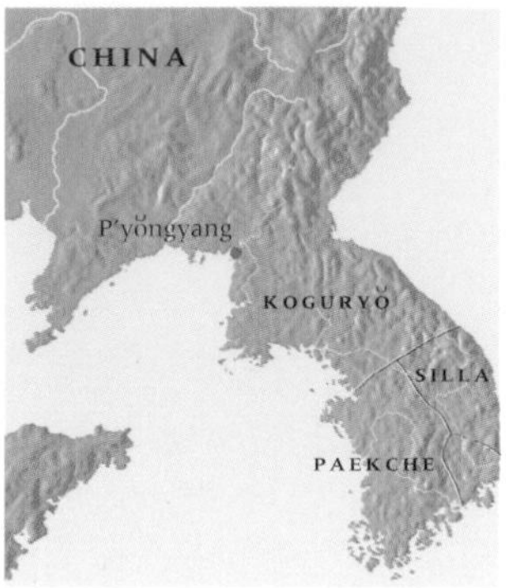

KOREA

THE IMPACT OF BUDDHISM on Korean culture is incalculable. It is manifested in architecture, art, craft, and literature. Through Buddhism, Korea joined the league of civilized East Asian nations. The introduction of the Chinese alphabet and written culture was essential in this transformation, because it facilitated the introduction of Chinese Buddhist and Confucian texts to the Korean context. *(See pages 144–149 for Korean religions.)*

THE EARLY HISTORY OF KOREAN BUDDHISM

Mahāyāna Buddhism was introduced to Korea in the fourth century CE during the Three Kingdoms period (Koguryo 37 BCE–668 CE; Paekche 18 BCE–660 CE; Silla 57 BCE–668 CE, according to *Samguk Sagi,* a Korean historical source). The new religion was soon recognized by the royal houses and the aristocracy and until the fourteenth century it was firmly established as the state religion. Buddhism has had a momentous importance from that day to the present.

In 372, the Chinese monks Sundao and Adao from the Qin dynasty brought Buddhist images and sutras to Koguryo and built monasteries there. In 384, the Paekche court received an Indian monk, Marananta, from Eastern Jin, who started to propagate Buddhism. In 527 (according to the legend as related in the Korean source *Samguk Yusa*), during the reign of King Puphung, Silla became the last of the Three Kingdoms to accept Buddhism. This occurred only after the martyrdom of the courtier Ich'adon, who offered to be executed in the hope that miraculous events stemming from his death would persuade ministers to look favourably on Buddhism; the religion was immediately recognized on his death. Buddhism rapidly changed Silla society; its ideological role, including politics, diplomacy, and living style, was considerable.

Buddhist studies in this period were concentrated on the teachings of the *Three Treatises* (texts which had originally been written by Indian Buddhist masters considering the total negation of existence), *Ch'ont'ae* (in Chinese, Tiantai), and the Nirvāṇa Sūtra. The Paekche monk Kyomik brought five versions of the *Vinaya* (rules for monastic life) from India in 526 and became the founder of the Korean Vinaya school. Koguryo and Paekche monks were instrumental in the transmission of Buddhism and Buddhist art and architecture to Japan, making an important contribution to the development of Japanese culture.

In Korea, Buddhism flourished under the patronage and protection of the royal houses and their associated aristocrats. The Buddhist teachings of reincarnation and rebirth, based on the concept of *karma,* justified their position as rulers. Until the end of the fourteenth century, Korean monarchs were without exception devout Buddhists. The religion offered a sense of well-being for the state and, by extension, for the ordinary individual.

SILLA'S STATE-PROTECTING RELIGION

The syncretic role of Buddhism as *hoguk pulgyo*, the state-protecting religion, was established in 668 when Buddhism acted as the central spiritual force behind the unification of the Korean peninsula under Silla rule. During the reign of King Chinp'yong (579–632), the eminent Silla monk Won'gwang set out the precepts of loyalty, filial piety, sincerity, courage, and benevolence as the Five Commandments for Laymen. These were followed by the youthful warrior elite, *hwarang do*, some of whom were regarded as incarnations of Maitreya, the saviour Buddha of the Future. Buddhist ceremonies, such as *Inwanghoe*, 'the Assemblies of Benevolent Kings', or *P'algwanhoe*, 'the Eight Prohibitory Commands for Laymen', served to protect the nation. The Vinaya master Chajang, on his return in 645 from Mount Wutai (in Shanxi Province, China), oversaw the building of the famous nine-storey pagoda of Hwangnyong Monastery in the centre of the Silla capital, Kyongju, that would reinforce Silla's hegemony among the Three Kingdoms. Buddhism became the spiritual foundation for the Silla kingdom.

During the Unified Silla period (668–935), Buddhism experienced an unprecedented flowering. Silla monks were from aristocratic families and were both celebrated scholars and religious leaders of the nation. They travelled not only to Tang China but also to India to bring back the latest Buddhist teachings. Hyech'o wrote of his pilgrimage through Central Asia and in northeast India in 726 in his *Wang o ch'onch'ukguk chon* (*Travels to Five Indian Countries*). The eminent monks Uisang (625–702) and Wonhyo (617–686) are regarded as the founders of *Haedong Hwaom*, the Korean Avatamsaka school. Towards the end of the Silla dynasty there emerged the Son (Chinese, Chan; Japanese, Zen) or Meditation school which became the mainstream of the Chogye Sect in Korean Buddhism and developed into Nine Mountains of Son.

The gilt-bronze image of Maitreya (seventh century, now in Puyo National Museum) and the sublime Buddha group in Sokkuram (an artificial granite cave of the mid-eighth century), coupled with elegant stone pagodas that have yielded exquisite gold and crystal reliquaries, are seminal expressions of Korean Buddhist sentiments.

A granite, three metre- (13 feet-) high Buddha sculpture at Sokkuram, Kyongju. It dates from the unified Silla Kingdom.

BUDDHISM UNDER THE KORYŎ DYNASTY

The first monarch of the Koryŏ dynasty (918–1392), T'aejo (ruled 918–??), was a devout Buddhist who built ten great monasteries in the capital Kaekyong, also known as Song'ak (present-day Kaesong). Geomancy was used to select an auspicious location for these temples, typifying the syncretic character of Korean Buddhism. He instituted the Ten Injunctions which formed the moral constitution for his descendants, upholding Buddhist teaching being one of the first of these.

The system of *wangsa*, Royal Preceptor, or *kuksa*, National Preceptor, titles that had been granted to distinguished monks acting as state advisers since the Unified Silla dynasty, continued during the Koryŏ period. It also became customary for one of the members of the royal family to become a monk. *Taegak kuksa*, the National Preceptor of Great Awakening, Uich'on (1055–1101), was one of the most prominent royal princes, the fourth son of Munjong (ruled 1046–83). He studied Huayan (Avatamsaka) and Tiantai in Song, China, from 1086 and on his return became the abbot of Hungwang Temple. There he established the *Kyojang Togam* (Directorate for Buddhist Scriptures) to publish the texts he had collected in Song. He is generally regarded as the Korean founder of the Tiantai school, whose principal teaching is based on the Lotus Sūtra. The Avatamsaka school also flourished, and Uich'on initiated the synthesis of the opposing Buddhist schools of Kyo (doctrinal) and Son (meditation).

This unique synthesis of the two schools was accomplished by *Pojo kuksa*, the National Preceptor of Broad Radiance, Chinul (1158–1210). His teaching, that an individual's own awakening should come first, in order to rescue the multitude, fostered self-discipline and total concentration or meditation. To achieve this goal he relied on *chong* (*samadhi*, 'composing of the mind') and *hye* (*prajña*, 'wisdom'). He founded the Suson Monastery in Chogye Mountain and his followers are known as the Chogye school, thereafter the mainstream of Korean Buddhism. Chinul's efforts saw the restoration of the Son school, which had steadily degenerated, by harmonizing doctrinal and meditation traditions.

KORYŎ SCRIPTURES AND ART

The collecting and printing of the Buddhist canon, *Taejanggyong*, were the main tasks of the Koryŏ dynasty. The merit accumulated by such devout action is well documented in editions of the scriptures. The first Koryŏ edition of 5,048 volumes in woodblock print was produced under Hyonjong (ruled 1009–1031) when the Khitans (Liao kingdom) invaded Koryŏ in 1010. The royal court had faith that Buddha's power would help drive out their enemies and demonstrate the cultural superiority of Koryŏ to the 'northern barbarians'. The completed edition was stored in Puin Temple. Uich'on also collected more than 4,700 volumes of canonical scriptures between 1073 and 1090 (*Sokjanggyong*, the additional concessional *Tripiṭaka*) and stored them in Hunghwang Monastery in the Koryo capital, Kaekyong.

Both the first Koryŏ edition and Sokjanggyong were destroyed during the Mongol invasion (1231–59) of Yuan Chinese. This disastrous event initiated the second edition of the Koryŏ Tripiṭaka. In 1236, Directorate of Tripiṭaka, *Taejang Togam*, was established. The carving and printing of the entire canon was completed in 1251. It took 81,137 woodblocks which are known as *P'alman taejanggyong* or Koryŏ Tripiṭaka and are preserved in Haein Temple. The accuracy of the text and the quality of the printing were acclaimed and it became the basis of the modern version of Taisho Shinshu Daizokyo of Japan, the canonical text widely used by scholars today. The printing of the vast Buddhist canon epitomizes the idea of *hoguk pulgyo* (state-protecting Buddhism).

Numerous Dharma meetings, ceremonies, prayers, and offerings combined to bring about a flourishing period in Buddhist art. Splendid illuminated manuscripts of scriptures, written in gold and silver on indigo blue paper, and hanging silk scrolls of sumptuous Buddhist paintings, were commissioned by royal or aristocratic devotees. The most frequently copied Buddhist texts were the Lotus Sūtra, Avatamsaka Sūtra, and Amitābha Sūtra, while paintings for private offerings and prayers often depicted Amitābha Buddha and other bodhisattvas related to the Pure Land, the Buddhist paradise. However, the gradual accumulation of wealth by the monasteries, the illegal endowment of lands, and the excessive power of the monastic communities in the later Koryŏ period all resulted in a drastic deterioration in the spirituality of Koryŏ Buddhism.

Contemporary Korean Buddhism

Korean Buddhism in the twentieth century experienced turbulence during the Japanese colonial period (1910–45). Buddhist monasteries were divided into 31 main temples and more than 1,200 sub-temples as a consequence, and there were divisions and conflicts between unmarried *(vikshuni)* and married monks. The monk-poet Han Yong-un (1879–1944) was a key figure during this period. He not only thwarted the aim of the colonial rulers to eliminate the essence of Korean Buddhism, he also laboured tirelessly to reform the religion, organizing the young devotee group Chosŏn Pulgyo Ch'ongnyonhoe in 1924 and establishing a monthly magazine, *Pulgyo (Buddhism)*. He was one of the 33 prominent figures who signed the Independence Declaration against Japanese rule in 1919.

Since 1945, the Buddhist community has had a central office in Seoul supported by provincial offices. Their tasks are promulgation of the faith, education (Buddhist universities have been founded), restoration of temple buildings, and involvement in social works such as running orphanages.

CHOSŎN DYNASTY

When Neo-Confucian scholar-bureaucrats held political power in the early Chosŏn period (1392–1910), the privileges enjoyed by the members of the Buddhist community were radically reduced, reform of monastic estates was carried out, and new strict rules were imposed on Buddhist monks. For example, in order to enter a monastery, postulants had to pass state examinations (*sunggwa*).

Buddhism continued to be supported by the royal family, including the female members. Among the Chosŏn monarchs, even the great king Sejong (ruled 1418–50), under whose direction the Korean alphabet, *hangul*, was invented, was a devout practitioner of Buddhism. His nephew, King Sejo (ruled 1455–68), established the *Kankyong Togam*, Royal Superintendency for Sutra Publication, in 1461 for the purpose of translating Chinese Buddhist scriptures into *hangul* text.

Although significantly restricted in their activities, monasteries during the Chosŏn period still produced outstanding spiritual leaders. The Great Son master Sosan (Western Mountain) Hyujong (1520–1604) and his disciple Samyong Yujong (1544–1610) were national heroes when the Japanese under Hideyoshi invaded the Chosŏn kingdom in 1592–98. Sosan was appointed Commander of the Eight Provinces' monks' army while Samyong later became the emissary of the Chosŏn king, meeting Tokugawa Ieyasu in Edo in 1604. Sosan continued the Koryŏ tradition of the harmonization between Son and Kyo, teaching that '*kyon song song bul*' – that penetrating the mind is to become a Buddha – the essence of Meditation practice.

Chinese Religion

Xinzhong Yao

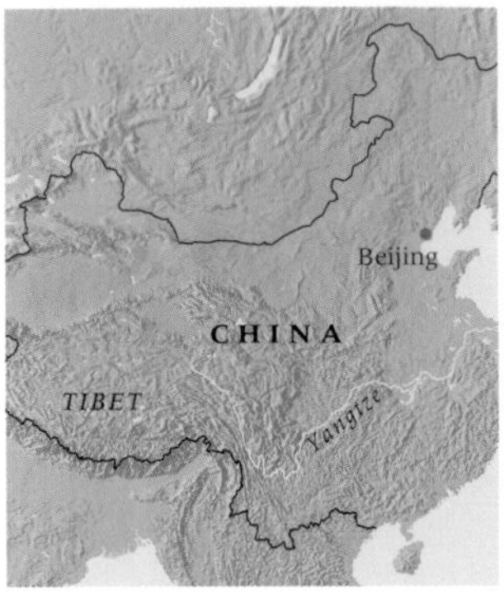

CHINESE RELIGION

IT IS IMPOSSIBLE TO KNOW when religion began in China. Periodically, archeological excavations supply new evidence of religious practices from an age predating surviving written texts. However, it is traditionally believed (and is supported by archeological evidence) that by the time of the Shang (or Yin) dynasty (1600?–1046 BCE), systematic beliefs and practices relating to the 'otherness' of life had been developed in China. These practices further evolved during the Zhou dynasty (1046–256 BCE), becoming the foundation of religious beliefs in early China. *(For Chinese Buddhism, see pages 94–97.)*

EARLY SPIRITUAL BELIEFS

Oracle bones were a key element of early religious practices in China – discovered by chance in the late nineteenth century. In 1898, the Chancellor of the Imperial University (*Guozi jian*), Wang Yirong (1845–1900), was given a prescription for curing his ague which required the use of 'dragon bones' (actually tortoise shells and cattle bones). When the 'dragon bones' were purchased from a pharmacy, Wang discovered that some carried strange inscriptions, which, being a renowned scholar of ancient Chinese culture, he realized related to inscriptions in the then earliest known Chinese writing system found on bronze artefacts. He ordered that all bones of this kind be collected and, together with more recent discoveries, some 155,000 pieces of tortoise shell and ox shoulder-bone have been amassed. There are several million characters on these bones of which 4,500 to 5,000 different characters have been identified, although less than half of these have been deciphered.

However, enough can be understood to know that most of these oracle bone inscriptions are the records of state divinations, including rituals, questions, and interpretations of oracle messages. They shed light on the religious life of the Shang dynasty and give an insight into the spiritual pursuits and beliefs that form the fountainhead of later Chinese religions. Oracle bone inscriptions provide evidence to support what is recorded in the Confucian classics, such as *The Book of History* (a collection of historical documents regarding important religious and political events in early China, traditionally believed to have been edited by Confucius, 551–479 BCE), with regard to early religious beliefs, rituals, practices, and customs.

OMNIPOTENT GODS AND ANCESTRAL POWERS The spiritual convictions of the Shang people centred on their belief in Di or Shang Di, the Lord or the Lord on High, who presided over the world and administered spiritual and human matters. Di was regarded as the ultimate authority over all natural and human affairs, issuing orders and having a sense of good and evil. The Shang people believed that all matters concerning natural events, such as wind and rain and calamities and disasters, and all human affairs, such as good and bad fortune, harvest and famine, victory and defeat in wars, occurred according to the will of Di. Di executed his power through his agents or messengers, the lesser spiritual powers or beings, including the gods of wind, rain, thunder, mountains, rivers, and the four directions. The association of Di with other deities is believed to have taken place at an early stage of the Shang dynasty when consolidation of the empire included the incorporation of the religious beliefs of conquered neighbouring tribes and the assimilation of various gods into the pantheon of Di who received sacrifices either with Di or in their own shrines.

Belief in the supreme authority who was high above, infinite, all-encompassing, overwhelming, all-knowing, and universal, became the centre of religious life in early China. It was manifested not only in belief in the Lord on High of the Shang dynasty but also in the worship of Tian, or Heaven, by the Zhou and subsequent dynasties right up to the early twentieth century. Tian, originally simply meaning 'sky', became equivalent to the Lord on High by the beginning of the Zhou dynasty and, as the highest authority, was the focus of religious beliefs and was closely associated with human authority on earth. The people of the Zhou believed that Tian determined their fate, that the Mandate of Heaven (*Tian ming*) was the foundation of the dynasty, and that Tian would withdraw its mandate if the ruler behaved in an evil way. These ideas are found in bronze inscriptions on ritual vessels dating from the early years of the Zhou dynasty, as well as in the Confucian classics such as *The Book of History* and *The Book of Poetry* (a collection of 305 poems of the Shang and early Zhou dynasties), both traditionally believed to have been edited by Confucius.

As well as the lesser spiritual beings, the Supreme Power or Lord, either in the name of Di or Tian, was also assisted by royal ancestors who were particularly concerned with the performance of their descendants on earth. Therefore worship of ancestors, including making sacrifices to them and invoking their names in divination, was essential for the continuity of the royal house. Equally, it was believed that the support and blessing of ancestors

A nineteenth-century incense burner outside the Temple of Heaven in Beijing. The Temple dates from the Ming dynasty (1368–1661) and is also known as the Hall of Annual Prayers. Chinese emperors, or 'Sons of Heaven', offered annual burnt sacrifices here at the winter solstice.

would not be bestowed unless their descendants provided the dead with proper sacrifices and with the assurance that the royal lineage would be strengthened and continued. This mutual support between the commemorated dead and the conscientious living remains the central thread of religious beliefs in China.

Archeological discoveries made since the 1970s, such as ritual jades and ceramic vessels which coincide with the Xia dynasty (c. 2070 – c.1600 BCE), have shown that diverse neolithic societies had occupied the landmass of present-day China before they were gradually brought together to become a culture we recognize as Chinese. These, together with the discovery of various cult artefacts contemporary with the Shang at Sanxingdui in Southwest China in the 1980s, suggest that religious life in early China was diverse and that in other parts outside the Shang domain in North China people were more inclined to pantheistic practices. It is therefore too simplistic to assume that all religious beliefs accorded with the recorded monistic system.

CONFUCIUS AND HIS TEACHINGS The close relationship perceived to exist between the Supreme Lord on High and human authority on earth would backfire if the worldly affairs of political struggles weakened rather than strengthened people's faith in the power of the Lord. This was exactly the situation towards the end of the Western Zhou dynasty (1046–771 BCE), when communities were devastated by natural disasters and state cruelty, and prayers and pleas met with no response. Where was the Mandate of Heaven? A group of new thinkers emerged who began to search for different interpretations that might lead to an understanding of the deep meaning of life. Among them, Confucius pioneered a fresh way forwards.

Confucius laden with his scrolls, from an eighteenth-century painting. A self-educated and ambitious man, Confucius worked to 'justify the ways of god to man' in a manner that people from all stations in life could readily understand.

Confucius is the Latin transliteration of Kong Fuzi or Master Kong, who was born in 551 BCE to a family of the lower rank of the nobility in the small state of Lu, near the modern city of Qufu. According to his biography in the *Records of the Historian* by Sima Qian (145?–86? BCE), his ancestors came from a branch of the royal Shang house and his father died when Confucius was young. Confucius regarded himself as a person who 'set his mind upon learning at 15 years old', and who 'had established himself by 30' (*Analects* 2:4). He became one of the most admired teachers and many people, rich and poor, came to him to study ritual, poetry, music, and other humanistic arts. His public career reached its peak in his fifties when he was successively appointed Minister of Works, Minister of Justice, and even reputedly acting Prime Minister for a short period. However, disappointed with the Duke of Lu and alienated by the powerful families, Confucius left the state and wandered for 13 years among neighbouring states in search of an 'enlightened' ruler who would put his ideas into practice. Failing to find one, Confucius returned to his home state, devoting the rest of his life to editing the classics and educating his students. He died at the age of 73.

The most reliable source on Confucius and his teaching is a short collection, probably compiled by the second generation of his disciples, which became known as *Lunyu* (*The Analects*) during the latter stage of the Warring States period (475–221 BCE). It records some 500 remarks and conversations of Confucius and his disciples. It is clear from the records that Confucius retained the traditional belief in the power and the Mandate of Heaven, believing that his mission to transmit ancient culture was from Heaven, and arguing that if a person offended against Heaven, there was nowhere to turn to in prayer. When asked why few people understood him, Confucius replied, 'I do not complain against Heaven, nor do I blame humans. In my studies, I start from below and get through to what is up above. If I am understood at all, it is, perhaps, by Heaven' (*Analects* 14:35).

With his interest in human problems and desire to find solutions, Confucius turned much of his attention from the worship of deities to the exploration of the Universal Way which could guide and prescribe human activities. He introduced humanistic elements into ancient culture and transformed spiritual beliefs into humanistic practices. When one of his disciples asked what wisdom was, Confucius said that it was to 'devote yourself earnestly to human duties, and respect spiritual beings [*gui* and *shen*], but keep them at a distance' (*Analects* 6:21). This explanation can be interpreted either as evidence of a moderate attitude to spirits or as the propagation of a humanistic understanding of eternity. When asked about the meaning and value of death and spirits, Confucius replied that 'if we are not yet able to understand life and to serve humanity, how can we understand death and serve spirits?' (*Analects* 11:12). Concerning sacrifices to the spirits of the dead, he emphasized that it was important to be sincere when conducting such rituals. For Confucius, the word 'sacrifice' encompassed the idea of 'presence': 'one should sacrifice to the spirits as though these spirits were present' (*Analects* 3:12). This illustrates the way in which he thought of religious sacrifices and gives us a clue to why Confucius said that the sacrifices of his disciples are not simply formalities of ritual, and that their value lies in sincere human attendance. For him, humans should gain an experience in their beliefs and in carrying out what they believe. Thus, the Confucan requirement that serving the dead as if they were alive should not be understood only literally, but more as a humanistic moral training, was expressed by Zengzi (born 506? BCE), a disciple of Confucius: 'When proper respect towards the dead is shown at the end of their life and continued after they are far away, the virtues of the people will have reached their highest point' (*Analects* 1:9).

Concentrating on improving the quality of human life, Confucius called for universal education, which for the first time was extended to the poor and the lower part of society, although it was not yet available to women. Confucius strongly contended that in education there should not be classes, and he would admit anyone who was willing to learn, for a nominal tuition fee. He believed that by studying the Way, students would be able to transform their characters. For him, if a person did not learn, then he could not be, act, speak, or live in a proper way. Central to Confucius' curriculum is the set of ritual formulas known as *li*, which includes rites, moral codes, and rules of propriety. Teaching on rituals, Confucius did not intend to train his students simply to strictly follow rules but inspired them to become virtuous people, the most important virtue being *ren* (humaneness, benevolence, or humanity). A person of *ren* was called by Confucius a Junzi, translated as 'gentleman' or 'authoritative person', who would be the only legitimate person to govern because he had a heart of love and acted in accordance with rules of propriety. By this means Confucius hoped that the world would return to the harmonious state of ancient times.

A worshipper burns incense sticks at Shi Jing Temple at Chengdu, Sichuan Province. Incense (*hsiang*) is used in general to ward off disease and evil spirits, but Daoists consider that it sharpens and focuses the senses and so helps worshippers to follow the Dao.

'A HUNDRED SCHOOLS'

The age of Confucius and the subsequent period were war-torn. Many rulers saw that to survive they would benefit from the advice of learned counsellors, so they sponsored scholars who aided the government, the states in turn supporting the religious or philosophical groups to which their advisors adhered. These groups developed into 'a hundred schools', of which four had a lasting impact on religious life.

DAOISM Daoism (*dao* meaning the 'Way') takes many, often interacting, forms, the main two being philosophical (*dao jia*) and religious (*dao jiao*) Daoism (*see page 122*). As the term derives from a work attributed to a possibly mythical figurehead, it is debatable whether Daoism is appropriate to denote the beliefs of the group of people who claimed to have found the right way for life during the Spring and Autumn period (771–476 BCE, a name taken from the *Chunqiu* – the *Spring and Autumn Annals* – believed to have been edited by Confucius). Laozi was the most renowned sage, said to be an elder contemporary of Confucius and the author of a book of 5,000 characters, either called the *Laozi* after him, or entitled *Daode Jing, The Book of the Way and its Power*. However, modern scholars tend to think that the book, which collected the sayings of individuals who lived in harmony with nature, was compiled by an unknown scholar or scholars early in the Warring States period (475–221 BCE). For Laozi, Dao is the beginning of the universe, the law of the world, and the source of life (*Daode Jing*, 25). Dao is given different names in the *Daode Jing*, including 'the ancestor', 'the mystical female', 'the spirit of the valley', and 'the One'. It is claimed that, to gain eternity, humans must become one with Dao by following the path of *wu wei*, non-action, and withdrawing from the world. Daoist ideas were further developed by Zhuangzi (399?–295? BCE) who believed that civilization had corrupted human hearts and destroyed the harmonious relation between people and the cosmos. Zhuangzi, like many early Daoists such as Guan Yin (dates unknown) and Yang Zhu (fourth century BCE), preferred to lead a life in harmony with nature to a life that was glorious for a moment but was soon destroyed. Like Laozi, Zhuangzi advocated that the ideal life is one of union with Dao. This cannot be achieved except through the emptiness of the heart, which Zhuangzi called 'the fasting of the heart'. Zhuangzi strongly believed that life and death were nothing but different stages of cosmic transformation, and that we should not enjoy life or fear death but simply accept them as being different forms of the great Dao (Zhuangzi, 6:4).

MOISM Moism originated from the teachings of Mozi or Modi (active 479–438 BCE) and was one of the most influential schools during the Warring States period. Confucius and his followers introduced humanistic elements into the traditional concepts of Heaven and the Mandate of Heaven (*tianming*) while Mozi emphasized spiritual interpretations of them. He strongly opposed the Confucian use of ritual, music, and poetry in finding solutions to human problems, and he condemned Confucianists for their overemphasis on humaneness as the only way to peace and harmony. Instead, he argued that the moral criteria of behaviour and action must lie in prosperity and the benefits this can bring. Love need not begin with filial piety; rather, it should be universal, given equally to all families and states. To practice this kind of love, Mozi and his followers travelled from state to state to dissuade a king from making war or to advise a weak state how to defend itself. Influential as it was, Moism soon declined and its teaching became unknown after the third century BCE.

CONFUCIANISM Confucianism, as it is called in the West, was not a unified school during this period. After the death of the master, his disciples spread to various states, finding employment in government, education, or the editing of ancient texts. Different understandings of Confucius' teaching led to different presentations of the Confucian way. By the time of the Warring States period, eight distinctive schools had emerged which claimed to be truly Confucian. Among these, two pioneered different interpretations of the world view of Confucius, one led by Mengzi (372?–289? BCE) and the other by Xunzi (313?–238? BCE). The Mengzi school championed an idealistic way in which all humans are said to be born with a good nature; by cultivating one's nature, anyone can become a sage, the paragon of virtue. The Xunzi school presented the opposite argument, that humans are born with an evil nature and must be disciplined through the teachings of the sages and restricted by *li*. In so doing, people would be able to overcome their selfish desires and eventually reach the highest ideal. During the Qin and Han dynasties (221 BCE–220 CE), Xunzi's interpretation of Confucianism was in the ascendant, but his position declined rapidly and by the Song dynasty (960–1279) Mengzi was regarded as the Second Sage after Confucius.

GODS AND GODDESSES

Diversity among gods and goddesses is one of the most distinctive features of communal religion in China. The religion practiced by ordinary people in local communities developed its doctrinal framework by drawing not only upon the theological and ethical concepts of Confucianism, Daoism, and Buddhism, but also upon orally transmitted traditions and legends.

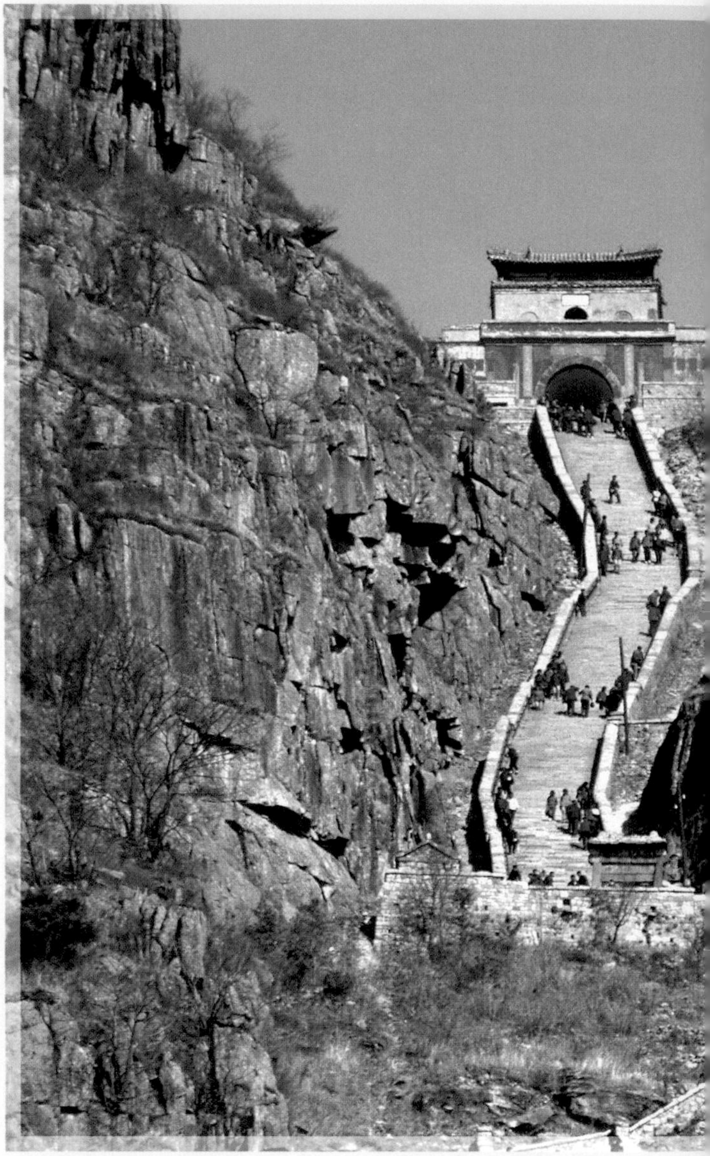

Through a combination of syncretism, localization, and imagination, communal religion generated a host of gods and goddesses who were closely associated with narrative history, local customs, and the natural environment; such traditional beliefs and observances remain alive in rural China. The worship of the gods and goddesses varies in terms of its geographical scope and their perceived function, and many of the deities were historical figures. Some are worshipped throughout China and are universal deities: Guan Yu (died 220), who was a noble and courageous general and was later worshipped as Guandi (Lord Guan), is God of Wealth and Righteousness who protects communities and brings blessings and good fortune to the people; Guan Yin, originally a Buddhist bodhisattva, is worshipped as Goddess of Compassion who looks after people's spiritual journeys and helps both individuals and communities. Some deities are venerated by specific trades or professions, such as Wenchang Di, a scholar of the fourth century according to certain legends, who became the God of Literature and Literary Success and blessed men taking civil service examinations, and Lu Ban, a skilful carpenter from around the fifth century BCE and patron God of Carpentry and Construction. However, most gods and goddesses are of a local character. The goddess Mazu, the Wife of Heaven (*tian hou*), is celebrated as the chief protective goddess in southeast China and Taiwan, and Huang Daxian, a great immortal, is known for his ability to predict the future and to protect worshippers in Hong Kong.

In communal religion, there is a strong belief that people's spiritual and material lives can be both improved and protected by such gods as the God of the Sea (Hai Shen, who controls tidal waves for the benefit of fishermen), the God of the Mountain (Shan Shen, overseer of all matters related to mountainous areas), Cheng Huang (god of cities and towns and the ruler of the spirits of the dead), Tu Di (the virtually omnipresent god of the earth in rural areas), and King Dragon (a god

The temple of the Jade Emperor, Mount Tai in Shandong Province. In Chinese myth, Mount Tai is the body of Pangu, the ancestor of all things. Emperors from many dynasties made sacrifices to Heaven and other deities at the top of the mountain, and built temples and steles on it in homage.

who controls rainfall). The family unit and the domestic setting together form the fabric of communal religion wherein ancestors, the spirits of the dead, immortals, bodhisattvas, and gods and goddesses of the door, the kitchen, the bedroom, the well, and even the lavatory are celebrated, worshipped, and respected. Deities of various kinds are invoked through such communal activities as festival celebrations (*miao hui*) and rites of passage (particularly marriage, birth, and death). All of these activities constitute an essential part of communal life and together they create a powerful environment in which each individual leads his or her life, religious as well as moral and social.

THE YIN-YANG AND THE FIVE AGENTS SCHOOL There is evidence that the concepts of *yin* and *yang* went back to antiquity and were used widely in all schools. Yin and yang are two basic forces of the cosmos and in their complementary nature they underlie all phenomena: yin (pictographically meaning clouds shadowing the sun) represents the negative force of the universe, manifested, among others, as earth, the feminine, the moon, and water, while yang (the sun shining) represents the positive power such as heaven, the masculine, the sun, and fire. It was Zou Yan (305?–204? BCE), however, who organized these ideas alongside those of the Five Agents (water, fire, earth, wood, and metal) into a systematic doctrine that was used to interpret human history and natural occurrences. Although Zou Yan's school did not last long, the concepts of yin-yang and the Five Agents become fundamental to all Chinese traditions, religious or non-religious, that upheld the Chinese way of life.

STATE ORTHODOXY AND RELIGIOUS DEVELOPMENT

When the Qin conquered all states and established a unified empire in 221 BCE, the king (Ying Zheng, 259–210 BCE) became the first August Emperor of Qin (*Qin Shihuangdi*). The war was ended by brutal killings, and the rule and unity of the empire was maintained through severe laws. Attempts to bring various teachings and schools to obedience prompted the Emperor to burn books and execute scholars who failed to pay homage to his authority. Despite this, the Qin collapsed soon after the death of the first Emperor and was eventually replaced by the Han (206 BCE–220 CE).

The Qin mobilized maximum force to impose their empire by adopting Legalism, draconian policies and punishments for the disobedient, and by giving handsome rewards to those who performed their duties well. But why was the empire so short lived? With the victory of the Han, people analyzed the reasons for the Qin's failure to maintain their rule and it was gradually realized that recourse to the strict rule of law might be useful in times of war but was not suitable as the basis of permanent government. The concept of an ordered government, demanding conformity with its will and obedience to its orders, ran counter to the beliefs of the intellectuals who were absorbed in the mystics and the teachings of *Dao*, the Way, as exemplified in the devotion that was still paid to Huangdi (the Yellow Emperor, a mythic figure and ancient sage–king for Confucians, who became a Daoist advocate) and Laozi, the alleged founder of Daoism. Defined values of right and wrong were seen by such scholars as merely subjective judgements. Huang-Lao thought was the basis of a more naturalistic mode of government, and it continued to hold sway during the early decades of the Han empire. The death of the formidable Grand Empress Dou in 135 BCE marked the turning point. It was suggested that Confucianism, embedded in traditional culture, should be adopted by the empire in place of Legalism and Huang-Lao doctrines as it would provide a unifying universal focus. Official steps were taken accordingly to promote the ethical ideals advocated by Confucius and his followers, and encouraged by famous Confucian scholars such as Dong Zhonshu (179?–104? BCE), Han Wudi (r. 141–87 BCE) finally elevated Confucianism to the position of state orthodoxy against which all other schools and doctrines were judged and measured.

SYNCRETIC STATE RELIGION Han culture comprised an eclectic range of elements. The Way of Taoism, the political ideas of Legalism, the theories of Yin-yang and the Five Agents, shamanistic practices, traditional beliefs in spirits, and rituals and music preserved in Confucianism were all composite parts. Sacrifices to natural deities, such as the Five Lords (*Wu di*), namely those of white, green, yellow, red, and black, were an integral part of the state religion, and the first few emperors of the Han dynasty, such as Han Wendi (r. 180–157 BCE) and Han Jingdi (r. 175–141 BCE), frequently offered artificial services to the Five Lords and to the Lord of the Earth (*Hou tu*). Han Wudi carried out the first act of worship by an emperor to Grand Unity (*Tai yi*), at the winter solstice of 113 BCE. However, due to the increased influence of Confucianism, which assigns primary importance to Heaven (*Tian*) and its decrees, these sacrifices were gradually replaced by those offered to Heaven, Earth, and royal ancestors, either in temples or in open space such as the Eastern Spiritual Peak of Mount Tai. Just as the kings of the Zhou had seen themselves as the Sons of Heaven, so the Han emperors saw their own rule as a gift from heaven, with its consequent obligations and privileges. As such, the Emperor's rule formed an integral part of the cosmic system which comprised the three interdependent states of heaven, earth, and humans, operating in a harmonious way according to the cycles of yin and yang.

The yin-yang symbol (above) graphically represents the concept of opposing cosmic forces in balance, each containing a germ of its opposite. Balance in action (below) is demonstrated by a worshipper ascending the 'stairway to heaven' that leads to the peak of Mount Tai.

Confucians were instrumental in the establishment of a new type of state religio-politics by adding a moral dimension to the religious and political realms, believing that if government was to acquire the respect it both deserved and needed it required something more than mere obedience to an emperor's will or to the law. The government must be seen to rest on an orderly conduct of its affairs, an appreciation of civil as well as military merit, and an accepted system of social distinctions which determined an individual's relationship with his kin and his neighbours and his superiors and inferiors. To meet this need officials enforced respect for *li*, codes of conduct and rites that originated with ancient sage-kings and were recorded in the classics that Confucius edited and in the commentaries compiled by his followers.

Alongside the recognition of the supreme value of Confucius' teaching, Confucius himself became the object of worship. A tradition ranking the life of Confucius among the highest of human achievements was revitalized by the followers of the New Text School (*jin wen*), who took Confucius to be the saviour of humankind and treated the Confucian classics as a means to obtain the revelation of secret messages. In this way, worship of Confucius was firmly established to assist the political and religious needs of the Han empire. It is said that the founding emperor, Han Gaozu (ruled 202–195 BCE), paid homage at the grave of Confucius and offered large sacrifices (*tai lao*) of an ox, a pig, and a sheep. Confucius was considered the Uncrowned King (*su wang*) whose mission was to bring order and peace to a chaotic world. By the beginning of the Common Era, worship of Confucius had become compulsory in all schools and government institutions. Offering sacrifices to the Supreme Sage and Ancient Teacher (*zhisheng xianshi*) remained part of official duties at all levels of society until 1912.

THE EVOLUTION OF RELIGIOUS DAOISM There had been a long tradition in China of distinguishing state religion, practiced at the court and by government officials, from popular religion among the family and local communities. While this distinction was maintained during the Han dynasty, beliefs in Dao (the Way) and a longing for immortality were widespread among all classes and were the inspiration behind a new religion that became an essential part of Chinese life.

Religious Daoism is both related to and in contrast with philosophical Daoism, and it is early Daoist texts, primarily the *Daode Jing* and the *Zhuangzi*, a work probably compiled by the disciples of Zhuangzi, that provide much of the theoretical foundation for Daoist religion. Whether or not this claim is accepted, it is clear that religious Daoism was like a cauldron in which useful elements of various practices, religious and non-religious alike, were integrated into one system. These 'ingredients' included teachings of earlier Taoist masters, a mixture of yin-yang and the Five Agents ideas, Huang-Lao mysticism, Confucian moral codes, the metaphysical deliberations of Mystical Learning (*xuan xue*) scholars, and practical methods adopted by 'prescription practitioners' (*fangshi*) who had been acting as medical doctors and spiritual masters since the time of the Warring States. The search for longevity was of primary significance to early Daoist religion, in pursuit of which numerous practices were followed: alchemy, dietary rules, gymnastic, respiratory, and sexual exercises, searching for 'magical herbs' or an 'immortality elixir', as well as praying to gods or spirits.

Daoism evolved through a gradual and slow process until, by the Later Han dynasty (25–220 CE), leaders of various messianic movements (often with a political agenda) claimed to have had the Supreme Way revealed to them either by Laozi or some other mighty power who commissioned them to lead the people to the realization of eternal peace on earth. The leaders of Yellow Turbans, Zhang Jue (died 184) and his brothers, organized a military movement in eastern and central China based on religious Daoism, calling for the confession of sins and the practice of meditation. They preached the Great Peace (*taiping*), a Daoist utopia of harmony, wisdom, and social equality. Slightly earlier than the Yellow Turbans, a Daoist named Zhang Ling or Zhang Daoling (dates unknown) claimed that Laozi appeared to him in a dream in 142 CE, telling him that the Mandate of Heaven had been removed from the Han emperor and he was now entrusted with the Heavenly Master who was responsible for the chosen people. On the divine command, Zhang went from eastern China to the west to preach Daoist teachings and establish Daoist communities, which led to a movement called the Way of the Five Bushels of Rice (its name drawn from the fact that each member was obliged to give five bushels of grain to provide for the community and relief of the poor). Zhang Daoling's mission was inherited by his son, Zhang Heng (dates unknown) and grandson, Zhang Lu (active 155–220), who developed Zhang Daoling's teaching and organized communities into controlled religious 'churches'. The lineage developed into what was later known as Daoism of Heavenly Masters, a religious community centred on Heavenly masters who act as mediators between the unfathomable Dao and believers. It is clear that these so-called Daoist movements were threatening the establishment of the Han, and the government and social elites which had been under the influence of Confucian doctrines fought jointly against them. Although the movements were suppressed or died out, their ideas and practices paved the way for a powerful Daoist religion.

There were clearly moral elements in Daoist religion, and Confucian virtues such as humaneness, righteousness, loyalty, and filial piety were adopted as part of its practices. But the highest virtues were those called for by Laozi: flexibility, femininity, humility, non-action, and tranquillity. Gods, Goddesses, or spirits were said to be recording all misdeeds, and human wrongdoings must be expiated by reciting sacred texts, notably Laozi's *Daode Jing*, confession, and penance that consisted of community service. The requirements on believers were redoubled by the demands of spiritual powers or beings. For example, in Heavenly Master Daoism, the three Gods or Officials of Administration (*san guan*), Heaven, Earth, and Water, were said to be in charge of checking on human behaviour and sanctioning human actions. Early Daoism also developed a set of practices typical of all later Daoist sects, such as 'nourishing one's vital power' (*yang qi*), 'avoiding cereals' (*pi gu*), 'preserving the One' (*shou yi*), and carrying out breathing, meditational, and physical exercises.

Daoist Texts

A number of early religious texts played an important role in arming Chinese religious movements with the Daoist view of the world, the most influential of which were *Taiping jing* (dating from the Former Han dynasty, 206 BCE – 8 CE), a book illustrating how grand peace can be achieved internally and externally, and *Zhouyi Cantong qi*, a collection of commentaries supposedly on the *Book of Changes*, which is generally considered to be the earliest work on alchemical techniques. The doctrines and speculations in these texts were further developed by a number of significant Daoist theorists and practitioners. Ge Hong (283–363) formulated his understanding of Daoist immortality and its related practices in a book entitled *Baopuzi (The Master who has Embraced Simplicity*, c. 320), in which how to become an immortal is discussed in detail. Kou Qianzhi (365–448) claimed to be entrusted by Laozi, the Supreme Lord, to reform Daoism and institute disciplines and rituals, and he revived the Heavenly Master tradition in the north, while, in the south, Lu Xiujing (406–477) brought classification to Daoist texts and have a theoretical illustration of the established *Lingbao* school, which had developed under the influence of Buddhist devotion to bodhisattvas, and emphasized the ritual and worship of heavenly deities. Tao Hongjing (456–536) consolidated the newly developed *Shangqing* tradition, the scriptures of which concentrate on meditative and visionary techniques. These sects constituted different aspects of religious Daoism, and pushed it into intensive interaction with Confucianism and Buddhism.

RELIGION, POLITICS, AND INTERNATIONAL RELATIONS

After the Han dynasty, China suffered more than three centuries of disunity and conflict. This ended with the establishment of the Sui dynasty (589–618) which was soon replaced by the Tang dynasty (618–906), a much better organized regime. Based on an economically richer and more civil society, organized religions flourished during this period and were to dominate the spiritual life of the people over and above folk and localized traditions. More religions of foreign origin were also becoming established. Religion, domestic politics, and international relations, and their interaction, became essential, vibrant characteristics of this period and played significant roles in promoting the quality of life in China. Buddhism, which was introduced during the Han period and gradually became extensively sinologized *(see pages 94–97)*, came to play a particularly important part.

RELIGION AND POLITICS As major religious and secular forces, Daoism and Buddhism penetrated all levels of society and became deeply involved in state politics; their priests were frequently summoned to court to give lectures and to serve as the Emperor's personal spiritual masters. With the surname of Li, the same as that of Laozi, the imperial clan claimed to be descendants of the traditional founder of Daoism and took Daoism as the royal family religion. This prompted the first Tang ruler, Gaozu (ruled 618–626), to erect a splendid ancestral temple at the supposed birthplace of Laozi. However, Buddhism also enjoyed the patronage of emperors and empresses, some of whom were devoted believers. Donations and privileges from the royal family and officials of central and local government were showered upon Buddhist temples and priests. Daoists and Buddhists competed for the patronage of the royal families and their positions fluctuated according to the favour of the current emperor or empress. For example, Taizong (ruled 626–649) issued an edict in 637 that the stability of the empire rested on the merits of *wu-wei* or non-action, a Daoist concept, and that henceforth in all ceremonial affairs and discussions Daoists were to take precedence over Buddhists. However, in 691, a devotee of Buddhism, Empress Wu (ruled 684–705), issued a decree reversing the policy of the previous Tang emperors, giving priority to Buddhism over Daoism, and ordered that Buddhist chapels be established within the imperial precincts in the eastern and western capitals (Luoyang and Chang'an). Buddhist palace chapels already existed under previous dynasties but not on such a large scale as under the Empress and the succeeding Tang emperors. With the accession of Xuanzong (ruled 712–756), Daoism regained imperial favour and was again given priority over Buddhism. Daoist temples were established in the two capitals and in all the prefectures and the populace was urged to study Daoist classics, such as the *Daode Jing* and *The Book of Zhuangzi*, which were even included in civil service examinations. The unequivocal triumph of Daoism finally came in 845 when Emperor Wu-zong (ruled 840–846) enforced the persecution of Buddhism which marked the beginning of Buddhist decline in China. During this time, Confucianism gradually consolidated its position in government and education, and the bureaucrats who stepped up through civil service examinations exerted more and more influence over political and religious matters.

RELIGION AND INTERNATIONAL RELATIONS Flourishing trade between China and the Arab world, Syria, Iran, India, and other central-Asian states made Tang China a dynamic focus of a wealth of civilizations, promoting intercultural communication and exchange. In the wake of merchants came religious missionaries, priests, and devotees, who not only spread Chinese civilization to other parts of the world but also brought to China new customs, technologies, and ideas, as well as different faiths, rituals, and ways of life. Multifaith communities thus coexisted in a number of northern cities and southern ports in China and religions became closely associated with international relations.

The central authorities of Tang China pursued a policy of religious tolerance as the Tang emperors regarded themselves as rulers of all the peoples under heaven. Nestorian Christianity arrived in the Chang'an in 635 when a Persian named Aloben was received at the court, and several years later an imperial decree permitted Christians to build churches and preach their gospels. Manicheism, an essentially gnostic and dualistic faith of Iranian origin known as the 'Religion of Light' (*ming jiao*) in China, was evident during the early years of the dynasty and in 694 its practices were legalized. Manichean priests influenced the Chinese understanding of astrology and astronomy and introduced the week of seven days associated with the sun, the moon, and the five planets (only five had been discovered by this date). Another religion from Iran, Zoroastrianism (*see pages 216–219*), penetrated China during the Southern and Northern dynasties and by the seventh century was firmly established in a number of cities, with its magician-priests performing rituals in temples and in the streets. Advances of Muslim armies and counter-offensives by the Chinese in the seventh and eighth centuries marked the first contact between Islam and the Chinese in the north, and the maritime trade extended the link between southern China and the Arab world. Most foreign religions were seriously undermined by the persecution of 845, and such influence as they had over China's religious life was confined to a very small area.

A Zen Buddhist monk from the Hongfu Monastery at the top of Mount Quianling, the 'first mountain of Southern China', in Guiyang. Buddhism was just one of the many traditions established in seventh-century China.

Feminine Features of Chinese Religion

Chinese religion originated and developed in a patriarchal society in which men dominated the social, moral, and spiritual spheres. However, oracle bone inscriptions from the Shang period (1600?–1046 BCE) include references to women, and mentions of a deceased mother (*bi*) are more numerous than those made of a father or male ruler. It has been suggested that the predominance of female names points to a matriarchal society in early Chinese history. The concept of yin and yang polarization gave rise to the belief that the two dimensions of the cosmic power – yin representing receptiveness and femininity, and yang manifested as activeness and masculinity – rely on and supplement each other, and that both men and women are of importance in maintaining social stability and spiritual soundness. This underlying idea is expressed differently in the different streams of Chinese religion.

Closely associated with the patriarchal tradition, Confucius held a low opinion of women (Analects 17:25), and Confucians defined the primary virtues of a young woman as filial piety to her parents or parents-in-law, obedience to her husband, and dedication to the education and service of her children. However, there are elements in Confucian doctrines which promote the

position of women. For example, Confucian filial piety asserts that mothers and grandmothers must be held in respect and admiration, while Confucian guidance on the division of labour within the household gives female members of a family a clear range of responsibilities that allow them to exercise their wisdom and apply their feminine virtues. More feminine features of Chinese religion are manifested in Daoism. In contrast to Confucianism, which emphasizes yang and masculinity, Daoism enshrines the other side of the cosmic power, yin and femininity. For this reason the Mysterious Female (*xuan pin*) is said in the *Daode Jing* to be the mother of the myriad aspects of the universe, and qualities that are considered to be feminine, such as flexibility, softness, and humility, are regarded as part of the character of Dao. On such a theoretical foundation, religious Daoism nurtured an empathy with the feminine which inspired an attachment to the Queen Mother of the West (who was first mentioned as the Goddess of the West in the literatures of the second century BCE), and produced a number of female pioneers, such as Wei Huacun (251–334), the first 'patriarch' of the Shangqing sect. The Daoist understanding of femininity was also partly responsible for the transformation of Mahāyāna bodhisattvas in Chinese Buddhism. The replacement of the masculine Avalokitesvara by the Goddess of Compassion (Guan Yin), and the Eternal Mother venerated by various messianic movements, coupled with the great popularity of numerous goddesses (*niang niang*) in communal religion, bear witness to a strong conviction that femininity was, and remains, an inalienable part of religious life in China.

A procession of the gods and goddesses of the heavenly constellations – in this case the Great Bear – from one of two great Dao frescoes that once adorned the east and west walls of the Daoist temple in Ping Yang, South Shanxi. It was painted c.1325 CE. The feminine principle is essential to Daoist thought, and is expressed in the concept of yin, the universe's counterbalance to the masculine yang.

FURTHER DEVELOPMENT OF THE 'THREE RELIGIONS' In spite of the presence and relative success of foreign religions, the 'Three Religions' (*san jiao*) of China still dominated the arena of religious life: Confucianism, Daoism, and the well-absorbed Buddhism. Each consolidated its position during the Tang era while a syncretic view of the three religions gained ground among intellectuals, monks, and priests. Confucian scholars strove to reconstruct the religion's doctrinal structure and to strengthen its influence over education and community and personal life. Indeed, the decline in the standing of Confucian institutions – national schools and colleges for training officials, civil service examinations, the cult of Confucian temples – was gradually reversed, which prepared for the religion's full revival in the Song dynasty. Daoist priests built upon the achievements of earlier ages, namely, editing and publishing the Daoist canon, improving Daoist rituals, and developing technologies for making immortality pills (*wai dan* or 'external alchemy') and producing inner powers (*nei dan* or 'internal alchemy') by circulating and nourishing *qi*, the vital life energy; they also made great efforts to serve the spiritual needs of the ordinary people. Buddhism reached its high point in China during the Tang dynasty. Buddhist schools achieved maturity and Buddhist visions of the world, its spiritual longings and metaphysical views of life, inspired art, architecture, and literature.

THE CONFUCIAN REVIVAL AND ITS SPREAD IN EAST ASIA

During the Tang dynasty, Confucian scholars began to look at their tradition for a new perception of the world. This trend continued in the Song dynasty (960–1279) when leading intellectuals engaged in reconstructing Confucian cosmological, epistemological, ethical, political, and religious doctrines, challenging Buddhist and Daoist theories and practices. An intellectual revolution took place which eventually drove all other traditions, Chinese and foreign, into a subordinate sphere of religious and ideological influence. This revolution is termed 'Neo-Confucianism' in the West.

The Garden of Confucius at Qufu, near the sage's birthplace. Statues of heads of state stand guard over a tomb in the Garden's cemetery. Confucius spent much of his life trying to reconcile the Heavenly powers with the earthly.

THE RISE OF NEO-CONFUCIANISM Han Yu (768–824), a man of letters, was at the forefront of a movement that wanted to return to the ancient sources of the Chinese tradition and to rid China of foreign influences; the primary target was Buddhism. In his attempt to re-establish the transmission of the orthodox Confucian tradition, Han insisted that the promulgation of ancient wisdom had been disrupted after Mengzi until his era. The themes Han Yu and others started to explore were those of *xin* (heart/mind), *xing* (nature, specifically human nature), and *sheng* (sagehood), which were believed to have been the central topics of classical Confucianism. These themes were developed by Confucian scholars of the Song era, leading to a renaissance of humanistic and rationalistic Confucianism which differed from the Han understanding of Confucian doctrines and presented a new approach to cosmological, ethical, and personal issues, challenging Buddhist and Daoist spirituality.

This was a monumental period in the history of Chinese religion. Great Confucian scholars such as Zhou Dunyi (1017–1073), Zhang Zai (1020–1077), Cheng Yi (1033–1107), Zhu Xi (1130–1200), Lu Xiangshan (1139–1193), and Wang Yangming (1472–1529) were stimulated by Buddhist and Daoist teachings and by disagreements among themselves and sought to answer systematically the questions raised by Buddhism and Daoism. They successfully traced the sources of their answers to ancient classics and found an ideal and a vision in The Four Books – the *Analects of Confucius, The Book of Mengzi*, the *Great Learning* (date unknown), and the *Doctrine of the Mean* (date unknown) – and in the metaphysical views explored in *The Book of Changes*. The real value of Neo-Confucianism is not only in its 'return' to classical Confucianism but in the fundamental transformation of Confucian doctrines, which enabled scholars to construct a comprehensive and complicated doctrinal system that satisfied the spiritual and social needs of the age.

RATIONALISM, IDEALISM, AND PRACTICAL CONFUCIANISM In the development of philosophical and religious discourses, Neo-Confucians followed one of two ways: rationalistic, which was represented by Cheng Yi and Zhu Xi, and idealistic, which was represented by Lu Xiangshan and Wang Yangming. Rationalism (*li xue*, Learning of the Principle) pursued an interpretation of the world and life by means of *li* (Principle). True knowledge was simply the knowledge of Principle; in order to know universal Principle, the believer had to investigate the principle of particular things, including not only the observation of phenomena but also the study of Confucian classics. The doctrines of the Idealistic school (*xin xue*, the Learning of the Heart/Mind) supplemented as well as opposed those of Rationalism, holding that the heart/mind was the Supreme Ultimate (*tai ji*), the Way (*dao*), and Heaven (*tian*) and contained the whole universe and all principles as well as all virtues. In opposition to the rationalistic interpretation of Principle, the heart/mind, and sagehood, Idealists argued for different theses: that the heart/mind was Principle, that the heart/mind was endowed in humans by heaven, and that the heart/mind of the sages was the same as the heart/mind of an ordinary person, which in itself was complete and holistic. By looking at the heart/mind and by appreciating their own sage-nature, anyone could become a sage.

Neo-Confucians were not simply scholars who indulged themselves in theoretical deliberation and philosophical debate. They were also very practical, applying their understanding to society at large and attempting to solve serious problems which they believed prevented society from developing in the right way. Some Neo-Confucians emphasized that family rituals were of great importance in cultivating a good character, while others gave more weight to an individual's spiritual cultivation. Zhu Xi wrote on the codes of family conduct and rituals (*zhuzi jiali*) for the members of his clan; he also believed that learning could help overcome obstacles such as personal desires and feelings caused by the faulty functioning of qi in the mind and body. Wang Yangming propagated the idea of the unity of knowledge and action, insisting that as soon as an evil idea appeared, a person had done wrong. These ideas and practices became the foundation of spiritual and moral training in later ages.

THE SPREAD OF NEO-CONFUCIANISM IN EAST ASIA Cultural exchanges between China and its East Asian neighbours had been intensively pursued since the Han era and the strong influence of Chinese politics, ethics, education, and religions (as well as art) was evident in Vietnam, Korea, and Japan during the Tang era. However, it was Neo-Confucianism that had the greatest influence and turned all East Asian societies into virtually Confucian states. In Korea, the Choson dynasty (1392–1910) adopted it as the state ideology in order to create a model Confucian society. Korea became the most thoroughly Confucian state, culture, and society in East Asia, leading to the suppression of Buddhism and folk religion. Two famous philosophers from this period, Yi Hwang (1501–1570) and Yi I (1536–1584), were widely recognized in China. In Japan, both the Learning of the Principle and the Learning of the Heart/Mind were introduced and developed, which, in the hands of Hayashi Razan (1583–1657) and Kaibara Ekken (1630–1714) among others, were transformed into Japanese ideology supporting political regimes. Confucian ethics had a fundamental influence on the indigenous Japanese ideas and practices of Shintô, the quintessential Japanese religion and the symbol of Japanese culture (*see pages 155ff*).

CHRISTIANITY IN CHINA

The presence of Christianity in China began with the Nestorians in the seventh century and Catholic missionaries in Beijing, the capital of the Mongolian Yuan dynasty (1260–1368), but a serious dialogue was not entered into until the arrival of the Jesuits towards the end of the sixteenth century. This marked the start of yet another new era in which Christianity and Chinese traditions became enmeshed, and the interaction between them had a significant impact on religious life.

THE JESUITS: MATTEO RICCI AND CONFUCIAN ALLIES One September morning in 1583, two Italian Jesuits, Michael Ruggieri (1543–1607) and Matteo Ricci (1552–1610), landed in southern China: their arrival would lead to one of the most important events in interfaith dialogue in the religious history of China. Ricci in particular absorbed himself in the study of Chinese language, ancient classics, and local customs. He and his fellow missionaries (others soon followed) adopted a strategy of accommodation, adapting their preaching to the culture of the land and concentrating their attention on highly educated Confucians. They soon allied their mission with Confucian orthodoxy in the fight against Buddhism, Daoism, and popular beliefs, which they branded as utterly superstitious. Ricci found analogies with Christian faith and practices in the Confucian tradition and he successfully turned himself into a well respected 'Scholar from the West', which paved the way for him to settle in Beijing and successfully convert a number of literati into Confucian Christians. The best known of these converts were Xu Guangqi (1562–1633), Yang Tingyun (1557–1627), and Li Zhizao (?–1630), who were convinced that there existed a special spiritual relationship between ancient Confucianism and Christianity.

Most of the early Christian missionaries were remarkably learned men whose knowledge of science and technology and whose talents in painting and music impressed the Chinese elites enormously. Besides performing their religious duties, the missionaries occupied themselves with learning Chinese, making astronomical observations, working on geographical and cartographic projects, and engaging in mathematical calculations. In many senses, they functioned well as the intermediaries between the European and Chinese civilizations, introducing the learning of the Christian West to China and Chinese classics and knowledge to Europe, which made the communication and dialogue between the West and the East a lively two-way affair for the first time in history. Their command of classical Chinese enabled them to write, with the help of their Chinese friends and associates, moral essays clarifying ethical points and refuting 'evil thoughts', thereby gaining the trust, respect, and friendship of Confucian scholars.

Taking advantage of this, Christian missionaries spread their message about God, the commandments, the good news, and broader Christian doctrine and produced such works as Ricci's *Tianzhu Shiyi* (*The True Meaning of the Lord of Heaven*, 1603), which specifically targeted the misunderstandings of the Chinese about the Christian faith and propagated Christian teaching in a manner that was adapted to Chinese thinking. The moral stand and hostile attitude adopted by Christian missionaries towards Buddhism and Daoism were much appreciated by the Confucians who, by the late sixteenth/early seventeenth century, had become deeply unsatisfied with Neo-Confucianism, which they felt was tainted by the influence of foreign Buddhism; they became determined to revive the true spirit of early Confucianism. In exchanges between Confucian scholars and Christian missionaries at this stage we find an example of genuine dialogue and communication.

Controversies and Disputes

Ricci's success did not mean that everybody agreed with him and his approach, and differences were soon noticed between Christian teaching and Chinese culture, not only by other Christian missionaries but also by Chinese scholars. The superficial similarities between Confucian principles and Christian ethics gave way to an awareness of the deeper contradiction between theism and the secular-based moral tradition, and the rapidly developed Christian communities were seen as evidence by many Chinese of the evil purpose of Christians who came to destroy rather than strengthen Confucian ideals. On the other side, the 'Ricci way' caused strong reaction from other missionaries who appealed to Rome in the so-called Chinese Rites Controversy: should the term Tian (Heaven) be used to represent the God of Christianity? Should Chinese Christians be allowed to participate in ceremonies in honour of their ancestors and pay homage to ancient sages, especially Confucius? Ricci died in the midst of these debates and reactions. The conciliatory attitude adopted by Ricci's followers towards ancient classics and Confucian rites were strongly supported by the newly established Manchu Qing dynasty (1644–1911) but they were condemned by Rome many times. This interference in Chinese affairs by the Catholic Church was in turn furiously condemned by the Chinese court, which issued counter decrees to expel all the missionaries who did not wish to follow the 'Ricci way'.

PROTESTANTISM AND THE CLASH OF CULTURES European and American Protestant missionaries arrived in China in the early nineteenth century. To facilitate the translation of the Bible they had to study the Confucian classics, and some of the missionaries took Confucian terminology as a frame of reference to introduce the Christian gospels. The Christian message heavily influenced a generation of Chinese that sought a revolutionary solution to the problems of the day. Hong Xiuquan (1813–1864), a candidate who had failed the civil service examinations, adopted some ideas from Christianity and launched a peasants' revolution which aimed to establish the eternal heavenly peace on earth. He founded the Heavenly Kingdom of Great Peace in 1851 and proclaimed himself the King of Heaven, the second son of the Heavenly Father and a younger brother of Jesus. Ironically, the Heavenly Kingdom movement was crushed by the joint force of Western powers and local armies under the leadership of Confucian scholars. The expansion of Christian missions in China caused great tensions between Christians, who were backed by Western powers, and the Chinese, ordinary people as well as intellectuals, and this soon moved from religious disputes to political confrontation, leading to violent protests and retaliations which frequently broke out in the second half of the nineteenth century *(see also page 259)*.

RELIGIOUS DIVERSITY AND SYNCRETISM

The co-existence of the 'three religions', Confucianism, Buddhism, and Daoism, made it possible for each to gain something from the others, which cultivated a syncretic spirit among religious people. At the same time, within the three traditions, diversified versions evolved which developed into different sects.

No religion in China is a unified system in the sense of a single institution that binds all branches together. Rather, there are loose connections between different interpretations of the core doctrine, and from these diverse approaches new schools or sects are formed. Confucianism was such a tradition. The debates between the Old Text School and the New Text School lasted for around 2,000 years, and within Neo-Confucianism not only were there the two main streams of Rationalism and Idealism, but new paths opened up within these, such as the numerous sects formed by the followers of Wang Yangming in the later Ming (1368–1644) and early Qing dynasties.

The same was true of Buddhism, which was characterized by diverse approaches pioneered by prominent masters; for example, in Chan Buddhism (*see page 97*), 'Five Schools and Seven Sects' developed after the Song dynasty. Religious diversity also manifested itself in Daoism. Different ideas explored by early Daoist masters were used to justify new systems which led to the creation of new sects. Among these, the most important from the Song to the Ming era were *Taiyi* (Supreme Unity), based on ethical rules of conduct and magical techniques to fight disease; *Zhenda Dao* (True and Great Way), known for its teachings on ethics and practical morality; *Zhengyi* (Orthodox Unity or Orthodox One), a direct successor of the Heavenly Master sect which also took in the theories of the Maoshan and Lingbao sects as all three emphasized the value of charms, spells, and rituals; and *Quanzhen* (Perfect Truth), which came to prevail in the north, focusing on the cultivation of inner strength and altruistic practices while simplifying rituals and encouraging non-reliance on scriptures. This Daoist school advocated asceticism and the rejection of magical customs while drawing on the main scriptural and liturgical traditions of early Daoism.

RELIGIOUS SYNCRETISM On the one hand religions in China diversified into sects competing with and even opposing each other, while on the other they demonstrated a strong tendency towards syncretism. From as early as the fourth century, religious syncretism was attempted at three levels. On the first, the so-called 'three religions' or 'three teachings' (*san jiao*) adapted themselves to each other and strict demarcation between them had almost disappeared by the time of the Ming. On the second level, within each of the religions, different sects gradually entered into de facto mergers through sharing practices that used to sharply distinguish one from the other. For example, two major branches of Buddhism, Chan and Pure Land, borrowed from and penetrated each other. Chan was interpreted as the way to the Pure Land which represented the enlightened mind. Buddhist practices such as contemplation, prayer, and visualization, and strict observance of monastic codes, were skilfully combined. In Daoism, Zhengyi and Quanzhen became the major Daoist traditions after the end of the thirteenth century, having absorbed useful elements from early Daoist traditions, at which point the distinction between the rituals and ceremonies of Zhengyi and the inner cultivation of Quanzhen were considered to be no more than formalities. Simultaneously, the main trends of Daoist philosophical thought were adapted to become key tenets of Neo-Confucianism. On the third level, all the sources of religious theories and practices were absorbed into popular religions where elements were combined to form the basis of daily worship and customs.

With reference to the first level of syncretism, the early desire to reconcile Buddhism (a foreign religion) with Chinese culture and indigenous traditions seems to have been the first step in moulding the 'three teachings' into one unity; then, by degrees, a significant number of Daoists and Confucians looked for common ground among the triumvirate. By the Tang Dynasty, the belief was fairly widely held that the Buddha, Confucius, and Laozi were identical and that their teachings were essentially the same, supplementing rather than contradicting each other. The three-in-one consciousness was further cultivated in exchanges of Daoists and Buddhists during the Ming period, manifested in such popular novels as *Journey to the West* by Wu Cheng'en (c. 1500–1582), and culminating in a religious organization called Three-in-One Religion (*san yi jiao*), founded by Lin Zhaoen (1517–1598). In 1584, a temple of the Three-in-One Religion (*sanjiao si*) was established in which four statues were worshipped: Confucius, the Founder of the Sage Religion (*sheng jiao*), Laozi, the Founder of Mysterious Religion (*xuan jiao*), the Buddha, the Founder of the Ch'an Buddhist Religion (*chan jiao*), and Lin himself, the Founder of the Three-in-One Religion. This concept had a great impact on Chinese religious life during the latter part of the Ming dynasty, and although during the Qing period its adherents were persecuted, its influence remained. In many temples tablets or statues of Confucius, Laozi, and the Buddha were either worshipped together or in different halls.

STATE CONTROL OF RELIGION AND SECRET SOCIETIES

The relationship between religion and politics is a constant factor in the history of Chinese religion. Religions relied on the state for protection and for opportunities of expansion, while the state made use of them for the purposes of control and legitimization and closely watched them for any signs of heresy or wayward practice. Thus, the state's control of religion and secret religious societies became necessary and unavoidable parts of religious life in China.

In theory, there was a tendency towards state tolerance of religions based on the Daoist idea that the less the government interfered the better it was, and religious beliefs and activities were regarded as the internal affairs of individuals, the family, community, or different sects. However, this inclination was not always realized in practice because the need to direct religions in the direction in which the state wanted them to go was a constant pressure.

The Confucian concern for the stability and effective use of legitimate governing power was clearly one of the motives for the state's control, and this was particularly seen during the Ming and Qing dynasties when Neo-Confucianism penetrated all

Flags of the Manchu (Qing) dynasty blow freely on the Great Wall of China. Under Manchu rule, China's various religions became political tools, used to back up imperial power but discredited when they became ideologically inconvenient.

layers of society, which precluded any possibility of religions being independent of political influence. The growth or decline of a religion or sect came to depend on the political vision of the ruler as the control of religion took such forms as the regulation of numbers of temples, the appointment or dismissal of chief priests, promotion or demotion of gods, and the approval or rejection of the establishment of temples and churches. Rulers also tried to make use of religions, and the Manchu Qing emperors, like their Mongolian predecessors (Yuan dynasty, 1260–1368) (*see page 126*), extended special honours and privileges to Lama Buddhism on the assumption that the Tibetan religion would provide spiritual support to Manchus who were a ruling minority among the Han Chinese. In its control over religions, the imperial government tended to manipulate one religion or sect against the others, so that one developed at the expense of many others.

SECRET SOCIETIES Under a powerful government, new religious movements frequently began as secret societies and their religious ideals were mixed up with political ambitions that were often aimed at changing the established order. Towards the end of the Yuan dynasty, revolutionary movements made use of millennarian beliefs in Maitreya (the Buddha of the future, expected to come at the end of the age), and the followers of the White Lotus Religion (*bailian jiao*) developed into the army of the Red Turbans, whose leader was regarded as a reincarnation of Maitreya. Rebellion became religiously motivated by the message that the reincarnation of Maitreya signalled the change of dynasties. Further, the founder of the next dynasty, Zhu Yuanzhang (ruled 1368–1398), who rose from the Red Turbans movement, named his dynasty the Ming (Light) to align himself with the widespread Manicheism (*Ming Jiao*, 'Religion of Light').

Established after the anti-Yuan rebellions, rulers of the Ming dynasty (1368–1644) were clearly aware that secret religions represented a double-edged sword and so, as soon as they had consolidated their ruling position, they decreed the disbandment of all societies which bore the names White Lotus or Maitreya. However, secret societies continued to demonstrate their power and threatened the order of the state throughout the Ming era. For example, the insurrection led by Tang Saier (date unknown) in 1420, who claimed to be the 'Mother of the Buddha' (*fo mu*); the revolutionary movement of 1489 which asserted that 'Maitreya descending from Heaven will rule the world'; and the Wu-Wei (Non-Action) Religion which was founded by Luo Qing (1424–1527), all began as secret societies, bearing the hallmarks of millennarian movements.

When the Manchus became the new rulers of China, secret societies and religions combined forces and began to initiate rebellions against 'barbarian rule', the Manchu Qing, aiming to restore the Ming. As many as 72 such revolts are believed to have occurred during this period. After the first Opium War (1840–1842), most secret societies and religions additionally directed their attacks against foreign invaders and missionaries, culminating in the massive movement known in the West as the Boxer Rebellion or Boxer Rising (1898–1900), *ye he tuan* in Chinese, the Righteous Harmonious Fists secret society.

Besides their rebellious and millennarian nature, new religious movements of the Qing era were made distinctive by the following common characteristics. First, most of them worshipped a supreme god or goddess which was named either as Maitreya or the Eternal Mother (*wusheng laomu*). Secondly, the majority of the new religions transformed Buddhist kalpas (immense tracts of time) to various doctrines of the cycle of cosmic birth and death. Some of them, for example, propagated the idea that there was the kalpa of the past in which Buddha Dipamkara resided, the kalpa of the present over which Sakyamuni presides, and the kalpa of the future when Buddha Maitreya will be in charge. Others of a more Daoist nature would call these three kalpas three periods of Green Yang, Red Yang, and White Yang (the colours denoting the significant stages of the evolution of cosmic power). Thirdly, they declared that, by converting to their religion, a person could take sanctuary during the catastrophe at the end of the kalpa and rise to the heavenly paradise. Fourthly, the founders of the religions claimed to be the reincarnation of Maitreya or the Eternal Mother who had descended to save the good and punish the evil. And lastly, the doctrines and practices of the new religions were in fact of a strongly syncretic nature, with the worship of Sakyamuni the Buddha, Laozi, and Confucius as major deities, together with the pursuit of Buddhist and Daoist spiritual practices such as calming the heart, reducing desires, contemplation, and visualization of the god or goddess, and the use of Confucian moral codes as religious disciplines.

In 1911, the Manchu Qing dynasty was finally brought to an end by the combination of republican and nationalist forces led by Sun Zhongshan (Sun Yat-sen, 1866–1925). This was followed by wars: first among warlords; then between nationalists and communists; and finally between China and Japanese invaders. During this period, all traditional religions were subjected to close rational scrutiny and struggled to survive. Some successfully went through the transformation that was necessary for a revival, while others rapidly declined and disappeared altogether from the Chinese world.

RELIGION UNDER FIRE

Revolutions and wars destroyed the economy of China and tore apart the traditional society. Fundamental questions urgently needed to be answered: why did China fail to protect itself from the onslaught of foreign powers? How could China be revived in order to stand equally with other countries? Liberal and rational intellectuals ascribed the weakness of China to the traditional structure of the state and to traditional ideology and religions. For them, the country needed not only a new political structure but also new ideas and thinking that would transform the society. The search bore its first fruit in the New Culture Movement that culminated in the Fourth of May Movement (1919), in which science and democracy were seen as two powerful weapons in the fight against 'old culture'. Inspired by these weapons and Western rationalism, intellectuals such as Chen Duxiu (1879–1942), Hu Shi (1891–1962), and Lu Xun (1881–1936) became increasingly hostile to all traditional beliefs and practices. It was argued that China's path to modernization and rebirth was blocked by the old guard of feudalism and its cultural furnishings, such as codes of conduct, loyalty, filial piety, chastity, and righteousness. There were two criteria for judging traditional culture: whether it was attached to the old systems of the past dynasties (anti-democracy) and whether it was 'superstitious' (anti-science). As traditional ideologies, religions were believed to have failed to bring any benefit to society and therefore should be thrown away and replaced by new ideas and ideals.

Of the three established religions, Confucianism was the first target of revolutionary forces. Having just established itself in Nanjing in 1912, the republican government issued decrees to separate the learning of Confucian classics (*jingxue*) from moral education and to abolish the cult of Confucius in public schools. While efforts were made to revitalize Confucian learning and Confucian religion – Confucian values were used to launch the New Life Movement promoted by the Nationalist Party of Jiang Jieshi (Chiang Kai-shek, 1887–1975) in the 1930s, and Confucian learning was advanced by a number of Modern New Confucians (*xiandai xin rujia*) – Confucianism was more and more confined to the sphere of pure philosophical study and historical research. Buddhism had a bright but brief glory in the 1920s and 1930s when a number of distinguished monk-philosophers explored the modern values of Buddhist doctrines and led Buddhism in the direction of a universal faith that would bring material benefits to the people and society. Daoism followed a slightly different route. Facing a rapidly changing society, Daoists became aware of their weaknesses in protecting themselves and preaching their message. The Central Association of Daoism was set up in the White Clouds Temple in Beijing as the national organization of Perfect Truth Daoism in 1912, while the sixty-second Heavenly Master attempted to have the national organization for Orthodox One Daoism established in Shanghai. But these measures did not save Buddhism and Daoism from further decline, and in 1928 the nationalist government issued decrees to seize or dismantle temples dedicated to Guandi (Lord Guan, a deified general of the Three Kingdoms period, 220–265), Yue Fei (a deified general of the Song dynasty), the God of Soil, God of Hearth, Kings of Dragon, goddesses, and many others, most of which were then reused as schools, government offices, and military camps.

Revolutionary leader Sun Yat-sen (1867–1925) and staff inspect Ming dynasty tombs. Sun Yat-sen led the uprising against the Manchu Qing dynasty, and after some years in exile became the first President of the Chinese Republic in 1912.

RESILIENT RELIGIONS Comparatively speaking, the religions of the common people were less influenced by the rationalism and atheism that dominated social elites, and so secret societies and communal religions continued to flourish in the countryside and cities alike during the first half of the twentieth century. Among the new religions that had been founded under the Qing, some, like the Way of True Emptiness (*zhen kong dao*), aligned themselves with the nationalist government; others, like the Pervading Way (*yi guan dao*), made an alliance with the Japanese invaders; while others, such as the Society of Red Spears (*hong qiang hui*), eventually joined the communists. For the majority of people, who were neither members of secret societies nor dedicated followers of the three institutionalized religions, communal rituals and practices were parts of their daily lives which had remained largely unchanged for centuries, regardless of the government or religious powerplay. This situation changed dramatically in the 1950s, when the communists took power and abolished all superstitions and all societies that had a connection with the nationalist government or any opposing parties.

The Chairman of the Communist Party, Mao Zedong, at a mass rally in Beijing, 1971. Under Mao, traditional religions were banned, while Maoism took on cult status and the man himself was venerated as a kind of god.

COMMUNIST SUPPRESSION AND THE CULT OF MAO

When the communist army made their passage through northwestern China in 1934–1935 during the Long March, few people realized that this mission would change the course of Chinese history more fundamentally than any other event. In less than 15 years, the communists had won a decisive victory over the nationalists and a new China was born in which, among many other radical changes, religion was turned definitively in a new direction. All this was associated, directly or indirectly, with one person – Mao Zedong (1893–1976).

Humiliations experienced by China during the modern era made the Chinese long for a new age of lasting peace, equality, and prosperity. The surrender of the Japanese (who had invaded northeast China in 1931 and the whole of China in 1937) in 1945 did not turn this longing into reality and the corruption of the nationalist government provoked further discontent. Supported by peasants and workers, the communist army drove the nationalists to the island of Taiwan, and the People's Republic of China was declared on 1 October 1949, with Mao as both Chairman of the Chinese Communist Party and President of the Republic.

CONTROL OF RELIGION While nationalists had appeared to be relatively tolerant of religious organizations and in some sense even supported religions, largely because a number of the leaders were themselves Buddhists or Christians, communists regarded all religions as superstitious and potentially anti-revolutionary. Communist policymakers in 1950s 'New China' adopted a system of watching, restraining, and controlling religious activities. They believed that religion, as Marx's 'opiate of the people', weakened an individual's will to fight against abuse and repression; that traditional religions were closely related to feudalism and the nationalist government and were used to suppress people and exploit the working classes; that Buddhists and Daoists were parasites because they relied on the working people for food and clothing while they did no useful work themselves; and that Christianity was a tool in the hands of imperialist countries that intended to invade China and exploit her people. These attitudes resulted in a series of policies that aimed to bring all religious organizations and activities under control. Under such directives, a religion or religious organization was allowed to exist only if it accepted and acknowledged the leadership of the Communist Party and if its adherents were patriotic in the face of foreign interference and were willing to serve the people and the socialist cause.

THE CULT AND DEIFICATION OF MAO By contrast, fervour was building around Mao. Since the 1940s, he had been celebrated as the cultural hero and saviour who rescued the Chinese from suppression and exploitation. Although during the first decade of the republic he somewhat restrained the development of the cult forming about him, his efforts were not firm enough to prevent the spread of a national wave of veneration which eventually elevated Mao to the position of the greatest hero in Chinese history and the greatest Marxist in the world. The movement was initiated by Lin Biao (1907–1971) in the People's Liberation Army, where a model soldier was

Chinese Religion

defined as one who 'reads the works of Mao, follows the words of Mao, acts according to Mao's instruction, and does everything to be a good soldier of Mao'. Ironically, the revolutionary movement that aimed to rid China of all religious influences created a devotion that resembled that of a religion. The personal cult of Mao reached its peak during the Cultural Revolution (1966–1976) when Mao was worshipped as a 'revolutionary god' who alone steered the ship of China away from disasters to the utopian Communist society. When Mao died in 1976, he was mourned sincerely by most people who feared that China would be crushed again without the great helmsman.

Children wave flags at a Cultural Revolution rally in Washi. After Maoism removed religion and traditional ritual from Chinese daily life, revolutionary fervour rushed in to fill the vacuum.

Mao was impatient with the slow progress of economic development. He launched the so-called Great Leap Forward in 1958, which not only destroyed the Chinese economy but also provoked criticism within the Communist Party. Dissatisfied with his own position in the second line of leadership, frustrated that the old traditions in art, literature, and the way of life were still popular, and deeply worried about the prospect of more moderate 'revisionism' in China, Mao started criticizing 'old' culture in 1965, a stand that became a revolution in the summer of 1966. While the establishment in the Communist Party tried to rein in the movement, high-school and university students reacted fervently to the appeal of Mao and turned themselves into Red Guards who, in their eagerness for emancipation from the trammels of 'old ideas, old culture, old customs, and old habits', smashed their cultural heritage and attacked the establishment represented by education, the arts, literature, the government, and eventually the Communist Party. With scarlet bands on their arms, badges with Mao's portrait on their chests, and little red books of Mao's sayings in their hands, Red Guards brought to every corner of China not only the latest instructions of the chairman but also their devotion for him. In the name of Mao, they persecuted thousands who were branded as 'black gangs' or 'sinister gangs' (*hei bang*). They also repeatedly proclaimed that they would happily die to protect Mao's thoughts.

While they were hostile to religions and 'old culture', the Red Guards demonstrated, if unconsciously, practices and attitudes reminiscent of the religious enthusiasms and behaviour of traditional China. Their faith in Mao was like the traditional belief in the 'Son of Heaven', their trust in Mao's words was similar to the worship of Confucius and his wisdom, and their demonstrations and propaganda were like religious processions to celebrate the festival of a god or goddess. The Red Guards ceased to be the main force behind the Cultural Revolution in 1969, and when the revolution was formally ended in 1976 (following Mao's death), any attempt to deify Mao was seriously criticized and then forbidden.

But traditional religious impulses again found expression through Mao in the 1980s, and the revival of traditional faiths has also influenced people's view of him. Some twenty years after his death, Chairman Mao is again revered by millions in China. His portrait is thought to ward off evil spirits and to help make a fortune (many taxi drivers have his picture in their cars and there are dozens of 'Mao's Restaurants' in Beijing). Some people no longer regard him simply as the leader of the Communist Party but as a semi-god who can bring protection and blessings. Temples dedicated to Mao have appeared in many places and miracles have been credited to him. The Communist Party and the government have felt it necessary to curtail such worship.

RELIGION TODAY

This section covers all religious organizations, activities, and relationships in contemporary China, mainly on the mainland but also overseas. While the traditional Buddhism, Daoism, and Confucianism, popular religions, and 'imported' faiths such as Christianity and Islam are practiced in Taiwan, Hong Kong, and overseas Chinese communities, religion in mainland China is much more complicated.

'OFFICIAL' AND 'UNDERGROUND' RELIGIONS In mainland China, there is a systematic structure of religious organizations, derived from the direct involvement of the government in religion. The 'Five Religions' (*wu da zongjiao*) recognized by the government are Protestant Christianity, Catholic Christianity, Buddhism, Daoism, and Islam. Each religion has its own national and local monitoring bodies which work with the United Front Work Department of the Communist Party and the State Council's Religious Affairs Bureau in supervising religious activities and managing the relationship between religion and the government. By law, religious people must register with a recognized faith in order to take part in religious activities, and the places of worship and the priests and officials must also be sanctioned and approved by the authorities.

While the authorities overseeing religions and their adherents are powerful and broadly achieve their ends, some people do not want to register with officially recognized institutions or do not want to have to proclaim their faith publicly. The tension between 'official' and 'private' religion is especially high in Catholicism and Tibetan Buddhism. In Catholicism, many believers are still faithful to the Vatican, but this attachment is discouraged or forbidden in official churches, while in Tibetan Buddhism, loyalty to the Dalai Lama and participation in Buddhist ceremonies pose a serious risk to Tibetans (*see page 93*). Tensions also exist in other religions; for example, in Protestantism, there is a distinction between churchgoers and the participants in (private) house-meetings, while in Islam, contacts with some foreign Muslim countries can pose a serious challenge to the status quo among Muslims in northwestern China. Thus there are two arenas of religion in contemporary China, official and underground, and statistics supplied by the two do not always concur. This tension is gradually reducing with the relaxation of controls on religion and with the expansion of religious consciousness and activities among the people.

'NORMAL' AND 'SUPERSTITIOUS' RELIGIONS Since the end of the Cultural Revolution, religious tolerance has gradually increased in China and religious observances and beliefs have become increasingly important to ordinary people. Ancestral worship is practiced widely, and most families offer sacrifices to the dead during festivals or on birthdays. The siting of family graves in rural areas are again chosen according to the advice of masters of yin-yang and *fengshui* (geomancy). Local shrines and temples, where gods or goddesses are regularly offered food and incense, have become popular again, while revolutionary heroes are neglected. Buddhist monasteries and Daoist temples are attracting growing numbers of people, and alms-giving is common among pilgrims. Implicit religions are developing their doctrines by means of syncretizing certain aspects of Buddhism, Daoism, and Christianity, especially in the name of exercising qi through practices such as *qi gong* (or chi kung).

However, popular or communal religions have also met with problems. The government stipulates that, while all 'normal' religions are protected and allowed, 'abnormal' or 'superstitious' religions and cults will be persecuted and suppressed. The question is where the line between the normal and the abnormal should be drawn. Religious practitioners such as wandering Daoists and shamans and religious activities such as the study of physiognomy, fortune-telling, and geomancy were traditionally part of popular religion but are now regarded as reactionary and superstitious. Various forms of *qi gong* which were extremely popular during the 1980s and 1990s have now been defined as 'cults', the 'evil religions', seen in the recent suppression of Falun Gong, or the Practices of the Wheel of Dharma, a successfully developed part-religious, part-psychophysiotherapeutic, part-commercial organization which claims that its practices and beliefs are able to cure all diseases. It was banned by the government in 1999, primarily because of the darker side of its practices and its involvement in political matters.

MARXISM AND THE FUTURE OF CHINESE RELIGION From the second half of the twentieth century, Marxism was the major ideological tool in dealing with religious affairs in mainland China, but the case of Falun Gong shows that it is far from being able to control the religious life of the people as effectively as it did before. Marxism's position is threatened by rapidly growing commercialism and is seriously weakened by religious competitors, such as Buddhism and Christianity. The question arises whether a different ideological system will replace Marxism. Some suggest that a traditional religion such as Daoism or Buddhism, or a combination of the two, is a natural candidate, but there are doubts about the religions' capacity to lead the Chinese in their spiritual pursuits. Others look to Christianity and predict that it will become the dominant religion in China during the twenty-first century, although there is the fact that, in the eyes of the majority of Chinese people, Christianity remains a foreign religion. Confucianism was the dominant system for 2,000 years and aspects of its ideology have become part of the very fabric of Chinese society, partly in the modern age through certain shared values with Marxism; this ancient tradition could be a candidate for predominance, had it not been debased and attacked for so long.

Thus it seems unlikely that there will be a single system dominating religious life in mainland China in the near future. Instead, a truce between Marxism, Confucian values, indigenous religions, traditional spirituality, Christianity, and Islam seems to be inevitable, and the gap between religion on the mainland and religious practices in Chinese communities in other parts of the world will quickly narrow.

Marxism is challenged by an alliance of religion and capitalism. The 500-year old Buddhist temple on Little Putuo Island, Yunnan Province, is a popular venue for tourists, who have their earthly needs met by a busy market.

KOREAN RELIGION

JAMES HUNTLEY GRAYSON

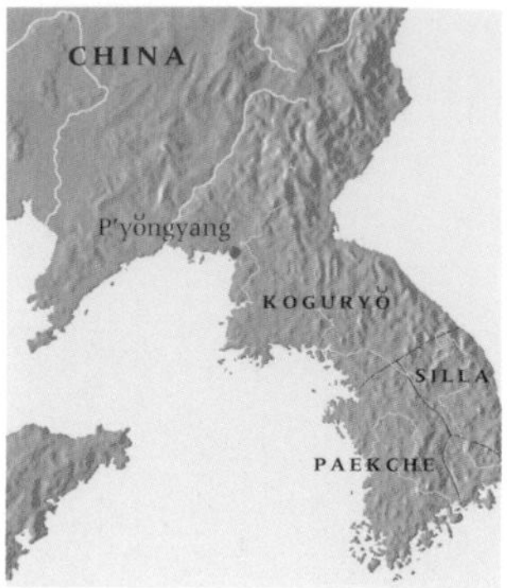

KOREAN RELIGION

Korean primal religion, with roots going deep into the nation's ancient past, is often referred to as 'shamanism', which is incorrect. Shamanism is a key feature of indigenous Korean religious practices, but it does not encompass them all. Like other folk religions – the customary religious practices of a people – there is no name for this tradition. In the twentieth century Korean scholars have coined terms for it, such as *musok* (shamanistic customs) or *musok-kyo* (religion of shamanistic customs), but there is no Korean name by which the followers of this tradition actually refer to it.

CLAN ANCESTORS

Prior to the advent of Buddhism in the fourth century *(see pages 106–107)*, Koreans worshipped a range of spirits related to agriculture and had a well-developed cult of clan ancestors. The founding ancestors were depicted in the clans' foundation myths as descending from heaven to the tops of mountains. Each clan had its own sacred grove, called a *sodo*, in which resided the clan shaman, who interceded with the spiritual realm on behalf of the clan members. In the state of Silla (from the fifth century up to 927) the rulership originally rotated among the heads of the chief clans, who were referred to by titles such as *ch'ach'a'ung*, which suggest that they were grand shamans, or by Chinese terms such *ch'ŏn-gun* (heavenly prince), which suggest that they claimed divine descent. Thus, in the ancient period, shamans intereceded with spirits on behalf of the nation or of a clan. This system lost its national prominence with the widespread acceptance of Chinese civilization and the Buddhist religion. However, many ancient religious practices, but not the state cult, survived or became syncretized with Buddhism. Throughout the succeeding Koryŏ (918–1392) and Chosŏn (1392–1910) dynasties, records indicate the continued survival of these traditions. In the Chosŏn period there are frequent references to attempts made by Confucian magistrates to suppress all forms of superstition or heterodoxy.

A modern female shaman, or *mudang*, performing a *kut* (ritual). There are an estimated 10,000 practicing shamans in Korea, most of them female. Their work focuses on healing the sick and interceding between humanity and the spirit world. Many *mudangs* now perform rituals and tell fortunes for the tourist trade.

SHAMANISTIC RITUAL Contemporary Korean folk religion is composed of two major strands, the shamanistic strand and the non-shamanistic strand. A wide variety of spirits is worshipped or propitiated, including the ruler of Heaven, called *Hanŭllim* (August Heaven); the rulers of the five cardinal points of the Universe, including the centre; the Mountain God (*San-shin*); the Dragon King, Ruler of the Sea (*Yong-wang*); various spirits of nature and agriculture; household spirits (including the spirits of the house site, the kitchen, and the toilet); specialized spirits such as the Smallpox Spirit and the Birth Grandmother; spirits of the ancestors; and nameless, restless spirits.

Although there are both male shamans (*paksu*) and female shamans (*mudang*), the vast majority of shamans are female. Korean shamans wear the clothing of the opposite sex during the *kut,* or shamanic ritual, and they are possessed by their familiar spirits, who speak through them. Their principal roles lie in curing disease, obtaining blessings or benefits for an individual or a family, and conducting funerals in which the deceased's soul is led to the next world. Spiritual healing is their primary work. Other sets of rituals are conducted by temporary ritual leaders who are known as *chegwan;* these are usually village men who are selected on an annual basis in order to perform *tongje,* or village rites, which are addressed either to the founding ancestor of the village, or to the village tutelary spirit. In addition, household rituals, including ancestral rites, are conducted by members of the family. There are a number of different types of ancestral rite, including indigenous, non-shamanistic rites, shamanistic rites (*ogu-gut*), and Confucian ancestral rites (*chesa*). Among the *chesa* rites are special rituals that are addressed to the ancestors of the royal family, as well as to Confucius and his principal disciples. Reverence for ancestral spirits has been such an important component of Korean culture that there are both Buddhist rituals for the ancestors and Christian ones (*ch'udo yebae*).

Mudangs on Cheju Island perform a rite to the Dragon King, Ruler of the Sea, to implore for blessings for a client. The Dragon King is considered to be particularly powerful and beneficent spirit. Offerings of food are thought to placate 'hungry' spirits.

OTHER INFLUENCES Over the years there has been a considerable amalgamation of Korean folk religion with world religions. In the rear of virtually every temple in Korea is a *Sansin-gak,* or shrine, to the Mountain God, who is not a local god, but the ruler of all mountains. He is also a guise of Tan'gun, divine founder of Chosŏn, the first Korean kingdom. Sometimes such shrines are dedicated to the Pole Star Spirit (*Ch'ilsŏng,* the Seven Star Spirit, or *Samsŏng,* the Three Star Spirit). There has also been a form of reverse syncretism in which the indigenous traditions have absorbed the outward forms of a world religion such as Buddhism. Around the central shamanistic shrine in Sŏul, the Kuksa-dang, are a number of 'temples' with all the paraphernalia of a Buddhist temple, but at which shamanistic rites are performed.

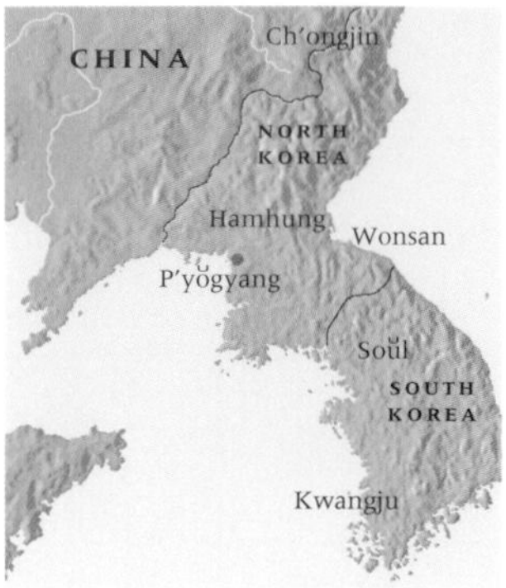

Christianity in Korea

Although Korean Confucian scholars from the seventeenth century onwards were aware of Christianity *(see pages 230–269)* through the writings of Jesuit missionaries in China, there were no Christians in Korea until the end of the eighteenth century. Young Confucian scholars wrestling with ethical and spiritual concerns in the late eighteenth century read the Jesuits' tracts and sent to Beijing one of their number, who was baptised there. Upon returning to Korea, he evangelized among his friends. Within a decade of his conversion there were several thousand believers.

THE ARRIVAL OF CATHOLIC MISSIONARIES

The first missionary to Korea was Father Chou Wên-mu (1752–1801), a Chinese priest who arrived in 1795. As the Roman Catholic Church in China forbade its followers to take part in *chesa*, or ancestral rites, because they were idolatrous, Korean Catholics refused to do so. The Korean government therefore persecuted the Catholic community for undermining social morality, because the *chesa* rites were seen to be the outward sign of filial piety, the chief Confucian virtue. From 1801 until 1871 thousands of people were martyred, including the French priests who entered Korea from 1836. The persecutions had three effects. First, the initial aristocratic believers fled into hiding in remote mountainous areas in the east of the country, or shed their class attributes and became members of the lowest class of society, selling cheap household pottery. Second, these educated Catholics spread Catholic teaching among the underclass of society, demonstrating hope for the future, a sense of dignity, and the ability to bear up under suffering. Third, the persecutions were so violent that the Church developed a 'ghetto' mentality from which it did not break free until the 1960s. Since then, the Catholic Church has grown rapidly, developing both a strong evangelical attitude and a prophetic social and political critique, a reflection of the historical social sense of the Church. In 1984 Pope John Paul II visited Korea for the bicentennial of the Church and canonized 103 of the nineteenth-century martyrs, the largest number of martyrs to be canonized up to that point, and the first time that such a service had been held outside Rome.

Catholics venerate the Virgin Mary in Sŏul. The first Catholic missionaries arrived in Korea in the late eighteenth century and by the 1860s there were 17,500 Roman Catholics. Protestant missionaries arrived in the 1880s, with the Methodists and Presbyterians being especially successful. Today around 25 per cent of the population of South Korea describe themselves as Christian.

THE SPREAD OF PROTESTANTISM John Ross (1842–1915), a Scottish missionary in Manchuria, translated the New Testament into Korean in 1882 in the indigenous alphabet, *Han'gŭl*. Through this translation Protestantism spread throughout northern Korea and in communities in Manchuria. Like Roman Catholicism, Protestantism was spread initially by Koreans themselves. The first missionaries, largely American Presbyterians and Methodists, arrived from 1884 and began by conducting institutional evangelism in hospitals and schools. At a time of dynastic decay, Protestant Christianity appealed to the young members of the elite sector of society because of its ethics, its emphasis on education, and the hope that it offered of personal and national salvation. When Japan annexed Korea in 1910 *(see page 169)*, Christians constituted a significant part of the nationalist movement. Unlike other areas of the world, Korean Christianity has never had associations with Western imperialism. Half of those who signed the 1919 Declaration of Independence from Japan were Christians. Accommodation to Korean culture took place from the 1920s, and when an independent Korean Methodist Church was created in 1930, a Korean Creed was also adopted, which was later accepted by the American Church as an alternative creed. In deference to sensibilities about deceased relatives, Christians also began to hold *ch'udo yebae*, a ritual to give thanks for their lives.

PERSECUTION AND REVIVAL Like Korean Catholics, Protestants have also had their martyrs. During the late 1930s and the early 1940s, the Japanese colonial government required attendance at Shintô shrines. Thousands of Protestants were tortured and at least 50 died for their refusal to participate in idolatrous rituals. After the Second World War and the division of Korea into communist and non-communist halves, more than 320 Protestants were killed by the communists for their beliefs. In the 1960s, in a rapidly urbanizing and industrializing state, the Church grew quickly among factory workers in the cities, as well as among the educated elite. For three decades not only did Protestant denominations grow in number, creating some of the world's largest congregations, but the laity provided leadership in the movements for social equity and for a more representative democracy. Currently one-quarter of the population of the Republic of Korea (South Korea) is Christian, with more than two million Roman Catholics, five million Presbyterians, and two million Methodists. We know virtually nothing about Christians in North Korea, however, although it was the traditional heartland of Protestantism prior to 1945.

PROTESTANT INFLUENCE Protestantism has had an immense impact on Korean religious culture. It provided an example to Catholicism to break free of its 'ghetto' mentality in the 1960s; and it acted as a competitive stimulus to Buddhism, which by the end of the nineteenth century had become enfeebled after centuries of persecution. Protestant evangelical success, its use of lay and student societies, its hymn tunes, and other outward features of Protestantism all provided a model for the Buddhist revival in the twentieth century. Protestant impact on new religious movements has likewise been extensive. The first modern Korean syncretic religion, Ch'ŏndo-gyo (Religion of the Heavenly Way), was by the 1920s borrowing Protestant models for religious buildings and for the style of its services. The majority of new religions, such as the Unification Church *(see page 308)*, are – from a scholarly point of view – simply traditional Korean folk religion wrapped up in many of the external forms of Christianity.

JAPANESE RELIGIONS

JAY SAKASHITA

Early Evidence and its Problems

Little is known about the religious beliefs and practices of prehistorical Japan. There is debate in a number of areas, including where the Japanese people came from, how the language was formed, and the cultural relationship with the Ainu (people who once occupied much of the main island of Honshû, *see map*, but were driven east and northward from 300 BCE). The Japanese word *kami*, for example, which is central to the character of Japanese religion (*see page 155*), seems to be related to the Ainu term *kamui*, meaning 'gods' or 'deities'. Yet most Japanese share physical traits more akin to modern Koreans than to the Ainu, who are racially Caucasian. An influential but much debated theory developed by the cultural anthropologist Oka Masao in 1933 suggests that Japanese religion, language, and social structures were influenced by five major cultural components: Melanesian, Austroasian, northeast Asian, southeast Asian, and Altaic.

THE THREE PERIODS OF JAPANESE PREHISTORY

Archeologists divide the prehistory of Japan into three periods. The Jômon period (6000–300 BCE), named after the distinctive cord patterns impressed on pottery surfaces, was characterized by a hunter-gatherer existence. Objects dating from this period, such as large stone clubs and clay figurines representing female genitalia (*dogû*), suggest a connection between religion and fertility, while human remains found in burial sites often have folded limbs reminiscent of the fetal position. The dead may have been buried in an embryonic posture to assure rebirth or to lessen the chance of their haunting the living. Skeletons also indicate that tooth extractions were performed, perhaps as initiatory or puberty rites.

The Yayoi period (300 BCE–300 CE), named after the district in Tokyo where the pottery of this period was unearthed, is marked by the development of rice cultivation and the introduction of metals such as bronze and iron from the Asian continent. Although rice cultivation may have begun early in the first millennium BCE, during the Yayoi period there was an increased emphasis on religious rituals that linked the growing and harvesting of rice to fertility. Burial customs varied at the time, including interment in large urns or stone cists (chest-like burial chambers), wooden coffins, and jars. Burying the dead in jars is a custom that originated in Korea. A variety of tools and accessories were also buried with the dead, although the function and meaning of their inclusion with the body is a matter of speculation. Evidence, including bones burned to aid fortune-telling, shell ornaments, sacred jewels, and bronze bells, suggests the presence of shamans and mediums. Indeed, one of the few written references to prehistorical Japan concerns a shaman. The Chinese Wei dynasty chronicles (220–265 CE) describe the reclusive Queen Himiko (or Pimiko) of Yamatai (or Yamai) as a shaman who ruled from a heavily guarded palace and who used her brother to transmit and interpret her messages.

The third period of prehistorical Japan is called the Kofun era (300–645 CE), after the large earthen tombs or mausolea built during this time. Some of the largest and most elaborate mausolea, built for the ruling class, occupied several hectares/acres. A characteristic of this period was the arrangement of small clay figurines, or *haniwa*, in and around the burial tombs. Representing people, animals, and artefacts, *haniwa* seem to have been intended to accompany the deceased into the next life. The construction of the large tombs and the existence of *haniwa* suggest that a structured society with nobility, peasants, and artisans was in the process of emerging. Archeologists have also unearthed stone boats buried in several tombs, which suggest that people of this period may have believed that the souls of the dead were transported to another land. The discovery of stone horses at sacred compounds could indicate that the belief that the *kami* came by horse was already current during the Kofun period. And the three sacred symbols of imperial authority – the sword, jewel, and mirror – can also be traced to this era as stone images of the three have been found buried with the dead.

A shrine to Jizo at Kumano, Japan. Jizo was a bodhisattva (enlightened being) believed to help children, particularly dead infants and aborted fetuses. Shrines and statues were placed in graveyards, and offerings were made to them by parents to ensure that dead children would enjoy a better reincarnation.

Japanese religion was not a unified system during the prehistoric period. Scholars theorize that a number of ethnic groups from the Asiatic continent, South Pacific, and other regions began to migrate to Japan, bringing with them various customs. Contact with Korean and Chinese kingdoms increased during the Kofun period, which resulted in the introduction of Buddhist, Confucian, and Daoist beliefs and observances. That there is evidence of Ainu, Korean, Chinese, and several other traditions in Japanese religious practices indicates that there is no single source of Japanese religion. Even during the prehistoric period, different ethnic and cultural streams began to merge and influence one another – and this process has continued to inform the religious beliefs and practices of Japan and is one of the major themes underpinning Japanese religion. Because of this, Japanese Buddhism, which is discussed in the context of Buddhism as a whole (*see pages 98–105*), is also considered here, so indivisible is it from the evolution of Japanese religion.

THE ARRIVAL OF BUDDHISM

Buddhism was officially introduced to Japan in 552 CE (according to the *Nihongi*, an eighth-century semi-mythological history of Japan and its emperors, *see page 98*) or 538 CE (according to the *Jôgû Shôtoku hô'ô teisetsu*, the oldest biography of Shôtoku Daishi, written during the eighth century). The religion may have arrived in Japan earlier, however, with the coming of Chinese and Korean settlers. The formal introduction of Buddhism in Japan was occasioned by the competition between three Korean kingdoms: Silla, Paekche, and Koguryo *(see page 106)*. The King of Paekche sought the alliance and support of the Emperor of Japan and sent him a Buddhist statue, Buddhist scriptures, and ceremonial ornaments as gifts, with a letter explaining that the image represented a powerful new religion that could provide the emperor with material and spiritual benefits. Buddhism was not immediately accepted, however, as it encountered resistance from the Mononobe clan, an influential family in the imperial court who were anti-Buddhist, anti-Paekche, and supporters of the native religious tradition. Buddhism overcame these objections thanks to the patronage of the Soga clan, another powerful family in the Yamato (an old designation of Japan) court of the sixth and seventh centuries. The two clans

A modern Shugendô Buddhist monk performs a daily ritual in the temple precinct on Mount Haguro, in Yamagata Province. Shugendô is a very ascetic form of Buddhism peculiar to Japan and is based on the worship of mountains. Adepts are known as *yamabushi*. The Haguro order was founded 1,400 years ago.

struggled for imperial control, both sides invoking the deities of the religious traditions they supported. The pro-Buddhist Soga was victorious and secured the Yamato court's approval to worship the image of the Buddha as an experiment. The victory of the Soga clan appeared to show that the new religion had triumphed. However, the experiment seemed to bring bad fortune as a plague broke out, which was interpreted as being the result of the wrath of the native gods. The anti-Buddhist factions then won the court's approval to thow the image of the Buddha into a canal.

However, with the accession of a pro-Buddhist emperor (Yômei, ruled 585–587) from the Soga clan, the seeds of Buddhism were planted in Japan. Buddhism was promoted as the primary religion of the Japanese state, a position it was to hold for much of the following 1,200 years. The Soga clan also supported the imperial Prince Shôtoku (574–622), who is credited with establishing a strong central government and creating Japan's first constitution. He played an important role in helping Buddhism to flourish in Japan and is regarded as the 'father of Buddhism' there. Chinese culture was also held in esteem and Prince Shôtoku sent scholars, officials, and Buddhist priests to China to facilitate the absorption of Chinese culture. Yet he also recognized the significance of the native tradition of Japan and in 607 proclaimed the importance of venerating the native gods of Shintô.

The Influence of Chinese Religion

Although Confucianism and Daoism did not formally establish themselves as separate organized institutions, both had an impact on Japanese religious culture. It is not known precisely when the two ideologies were introduced into Japan, although it is thought that they were present in the country by the sixth century when other elements of Chinese culture, including Chinese script, art and architecture, and government models, were imported.

At this time, attention shifted from the Korean states to Chinese dynasties as a model for government reform, and Confucian influence is apparent in the religious and ethical foundations of the reformed Japanese state system. Confucianism is not so much a religion as a moral philosophy. Its main theme is the harmonization of an individual's desire to live in peace and goodness with the style of state government that may engender the appropriate conditions to realize that desire. Confucian thought informed a number of important official documents and also apparently provided a source of inspiration for the Taika reform (645), essentially a land reform that nationalized agricultural land and rendered the people direct subjects of the throne.

Daoism had its strongest impact on popular religious beliefs. Although there have been instances when Daoism was organized by the government, such as the Bureau of Divination, or Onmyôryô, of the Nara period (*see page 157*), for the most part the influence of Daoism on Japanese religion was either indirect or implicit, a number of Daoist tenets and practices permeating and shaping it. Methods of prediction and divination, astrology and the interpretation of nature and time, and ideas of lucky and unlucky days and directions, are some of the religious ideas to be found in modern Japan that can be traced to Daoism.

SHINTÔ

Scholars have said that the term Shintô (the way of the gods) was devised after the arrival of Buddhism in Japan so that the native religious tradition could distinguish itself from the new religion. In fact the term was first used in the *Nihongi*. Before the arrival of Buddhism, the native religion was local in nature. It centred on the veneration and worship of *kami*, a term that refers to what is sacred, pure, and powerful. *Kami* were not only the divinities found in sacred texts, but could also be people, animals, trees, plants, rocks, mountains, and seas – anything that appeared impressive, inspired a sense of awe, or exhibited a life-force. Before the construction of wooden shrines for the performance of formalized ceremonies, *kami* were worshipped at ritual sites in natural surroundings. Shintô beliefs and practices became more standardized partly as a reaction to the introduction of Buddhism and Chinese culture. Indeed, the relationship and interaction between Shintô and Buddhism largely underpins Japanese religion.

NARA PERIOD

Located on the southern part of Honshû, Nara was modelled on the Tang Chinese capital, Chang-an, and served as Japan's first permanent capital as well as the country's religious, political, and cultural centre. The Nara period (710–784/794) represents the high point of Japan's effort to learn from China.

BUDDHISM AND SHINTÔ UNDER NARA During the Nara period, six schools of Buddhism were introduced to Japan from China – Jôjitsu, Kusha, Ritsu, Sanron, Hossô, and Kegon – and gained the support of the imperial government *(see pages 98–99)*. The Jôjitsu, Kusha, and Ritsu schools belonged to the Theravāda tradition while the Sanron, Hossô, and Kegon schools were from the Mahāyāna *(see pages 82–83)*. The six schools represented all the major currents of Buddhist thought, and priests and scholars received their training at more than one school. The Nara schools were later regarded as narrow, academic, and cloistered traditions because they were mostly associated with monks and the ruling elite, yet they served as important intellectual and religious foundations for the future development of Buddhism in Japan. Three of the schools still exist today (Hossô, Kegon, and Ritsu).

In 741, the Emperor Shômu (ruled 724–749) instituted a national network of state-supported provincial temples (*kokubunji*) and nunneries (*kokubuniji*) charged with bringing divine blessing and protection to the nation through spiritual practices. Connecting the temples was Tôdaiji, the great Buddhist centre that houses the Daibutsu (Great Buddha) and the temple built by the order of the Emperor in 745. Tôdaiji served as the geographical and administrative centre for the *kokubunji* system and as the religious focus of the country. Although the Nara government promoted Buddhism, the state exercised tight control over the status of priests and nuns according to an administrative and penal code known as the *ritsuryô* system.

The Great Buddha Hall, or Daibutsu-den, at the Tôdaiji temple complex in Nara City, Japan. Rebuilt in 1709 after a disastrous fire, the hall is 48 metres (157 feet) high and 58 metres (187 feet) wide; it is the largest wooden building in the world, although one-third smaller than the original. Inside sits Daibutsu, the world's largest gilded Buddha, a cast bronze statue over 15 metres (50 feet) in height.

Although Buddhism spread rapidly among the nobility and became influential thanks to the support of the government, Shintô continued to play an important role in the legitimization of the imperial household and promotion of national myths. For example, the *Kojiki* (712) and *Nihongi* (720), texts that contain a collection of myths and legends as well as an imperial chronicle of Japan, were compiled during the Nara period. They were initiated by Emperor Temmu (ruled 673–686), who wanted to attribute divine origins to the imperial family. Thus the texts served several functions, including the endorsement of the country's line of sovereigns and the spiritual elevation of Japan and its people as descendants of the *kami*. Such ideas helped to shape the national ideology. The texts also reveal a clash between the imperial family (represented by the sun goddess Amaterasu) and a rival family based in Izumo (represented by Amaterasu's brother, the storm god Susano-o), which ended in victory for the imperial family. Many stories in the *Kojiki* and *Nihongi* tell of a world marked by violence and death, yet what is distinctive about the Japanese myths is the avoidance of moral judgement and sermonizing. Behaviour is accepted or rejected based on specific circumstances, not on set moral or ethical codes.

CHINESE AND POPULAR RELIGION UNDER NARA The Nara government modelled itself on Chinese patterns. The Bureau of Divination, or Onmyôryô, based on the Chinese bureaucratic system, was the official means of incorporating Daoist practices into the Japanese government and was adopted in the eighth century. Confucianism also influenced the development of the Nara government. The Seventeen-Article Constitution (604), a pre-Nara document issued by Prince Shôtoku as a set of guidelines to court officials, contains Buddhist and Shintô ideas, but the primary inspiration is Confucian political and ethical thought. Confucian influence can also be seen in the Taihô Code of 702, perhaps the first written law of Japan to provide a political, administrative, and juridical framework for the state. Both the Constitution and the Code influenced the form of the Nara government.

Ascetics, healers, and other popular religious figures incorporated a variety of Buddhist, Daoist, and Shintô influences into their practices. These holy men began to assemble religious communities in the mountains during the Nara period, in defiance of the established Buddhist sects. Mountains were seen as distant, inaccessible, and dangerous places, where various spiritual entities, including the souls of the dead, resided. They were thus fitting places for religious observance, where magical powers could be acquired by undergoing austere disciplines. A part of this tradition would later take the form of Shugendô (*see page 159*), a distinctive movement of asceticism and religious life on sacred mountains. En-no gyôja, the legendary founder of Shugendô who is the focus of numerous miracle stories and legends, is considered the ideal ascetic whose spiritual powers could prevail over the local *kami* and demons.

After initial objections by Shintô supporters, Buddhism received official support during the Nara period. However, corruption and growing secularism characterized the latter half of the era. The Buddhist monk Dôkyô, for example, plotted to ascend the throne through his influence on Empress Shôtoku. Such interference led the Emperor Kammu to move the capital from Nara to Heian-kyô (*see page 99*) in 784.

HEIAN PERIOD

Emperor Kammu (ruled 781–806) moved the capital from Nara to present-day Kyoto (then known as Heian-kyô), initiating the Heian period (794–1185, *see pages 99–100*). This may have been an attempt to end a recent succession of disasters, or the Emperor may have been wary of the growing number of powerful Buddhist temples in Nara.

BUDDHISM AND SHINTÔ UNDER HEIAN The Heian period saw the emergence of two influential Buddhist sects, Shingon and Tendai, which helped transform Buddhism in Japan from an institution supported by nobility into a religion with popular appeal. Shingon Buddhism was founded in Japan by Kûkai, known by his posthumous title, Kôbô Daishi. Central to Shingon Buddhism are esoteric practices that enable people to attain enlightenment or Buddhahood within the physical body of ordinary existence. Kûkai travelled to China in 804 to study and practice the esoteric tradition and Shingon Buddhism developed in Japan based on the knowledge he gained. The central deity in Shingon is Dainichi (Mahavairochana, the Great Sun Buddha), who is considered by the Shingon tradition to be the *dharmakaya* (Buddha Body of Truth) and essence of all Buddhas.

Saichô (also known by his posthumous title, Dengyô Daishi) established the Tendai Buddhist sect in Japan after his return from China, where he studied the Chinese Tiantai tradition *(see page 97)*. Tendai incorporated diverse Buddhist ideas and rituals, including esoteric rites, although it gave new interpretations to these teachings. Although it was eclectic in nature, particular value was attached to the Lotus Sūtra as the supreme Buddhist scripture. Centred at Mount Hiei, Tendai Buddhism played an important role in shaping Japanese Buddhism because it produced the founders of the Kamakura Buddhist sects of Zen, Jôdo, Jôdo Shinshû, and Nichiren *(see page 100)*.

Shingon and Tendai Buddhism developed systems of thought that accommodated various points of view, Buddhist and non-Buddhist alike, in an all-embracing synthesis. Kûkai, for example, created a scheme of the ten stages of spiritual development in which teachings from all the major schools of Buddhism and from Hinduism, Confucianism, and Daoism were ranked. Not surprisingly, Shingon Buddhism was held in the highest regard. Tendai and Shingon thus differed from earlier schools of Buddhism in Japan which emphasized particular aspects of Buddhist thought.

One of the central characteristics of Japanese religion is the affirmation of the everyday world. Various beliefs and practices express this theme, including the idea of *hongaku* (innate enlightenment). This concept referred to the quality that enabled all beings to realize enlightenment. The development and interpretation of *hongaku* discourse within Shingon and Tendai Buddhism helped to shape the beliefs and practices of the Buddhist sects that emerged during the Kamakura period, while *hongaku* thought was also an essential part of the worldviews that were found in Shintô and folk religion.

Shintô rituals and prayers developed into distinctive forms during this period. The earliest compilation of *norito*, forms of prayer used to address the *kami* during rituals, is found in the *Engishiki*, court records compiled between 905 and 927. The flowing robes that Shintô priests usually wear are based on the dress of Heian court nobles.

In an effort to produce a harmonious fusion between the two religions, the Japanese assimilated Shintô with Buddhism (*shinbutsu shûgô*). For example, local *kami* were incorporated as patron deities of Buddhist temples and monasteries, and so Kûkai adopted Inari as a protector of the Buddhist temple Tôji. Construction of shrine-temples in the vicinity of Shintô shrines allowed Buddhist priests to chant sutras and perform Buddhist rites for the enlightenment of the *kami*. The Buddhist-Shintô syncretism culminated in the elaborate theory of *honji suijaku*, where *kami* were identified with various Buddhas and bodhisattvas. In the Ryôbu Shintô system, for example, the sun goddess Amaterasu was identified with the Buddha Dainichi, who was traditionally associated with the sun.

CHINESE AND POPULAR RELIGION UNDER HEIAN Chinese religious beliefs and practices continued to influence the development of Japanese religion. Practices based on Chinese astrology and divination were utilized to interpret human activity and fate. Abe Seimei (921–1005), an adviser to the imperial court, became one of the leading figures of Onmyôdô (beliefs and practices based on notions of yin-yang cosmology, *see page 120*) and was famous for predicting natural catastrophes.

Magico-religious beliefs and practices of both indigenous and Chinese origins continued during the Heian period, especially among the lower strata of society. Various cults of the dead or ominous spirits (*goryô shinkô*) proliferated in Japan, especially during the ninth and tenth centuries. The focus of the cults mostly centred on court officials who had died in disgrace. Esoteric rituals were used to pacify the spirits and help transform them into benevolent and heroic souls. Chanting the name of Amida Buddha (*nembutsu*) was used for such purposes, showing how Buddhist practices had permeated all aspects of Japanese religion.

Shugendô developed into organized forms during the Heian period. The aim of its practitioners (*yamabushi*) was to achieve enlightenment in this life, gain magical powers through ascetic practices undertaken in the mountains, and to use those powers to help people. Although the religion would later be forced to affiliate with the Tendai and Shingon Buddhist sects, Shugendô retained its Shintô, Daoist, and folk religious elements.

The Heian period came to a close in the late twelfth century with a series of bloody battles involving warriors and courtiers. The result was a new age dominated by warrior rulers – the Kamakura period.

A massive statue of Amida Buddha (better known as Daibutsu, or Great Buddha) sits on the ground of the Pure Land Buddhist Kotokuin Temple at Kamakura. Kamakura is also the site of Shintô shrines, and other temples and monasteries of various Buddhist schools.

KAMAKURA PERIOD

The shift of the capital to Kamakura and the establishment of military rule under a shōgun mark the Kamakura period (1185–1333). At this time, a combination of natural disasters, civil wars, and the notion that the *dharma* was in a state of decline (*mappō*) coloured the beliefs and practices of Japanese religion *(see pages 100–101)*.

BUDDHISM AND SHINTÔ UNDER KAMAKURA For Buddhism, the Kamakura period is best known for the new sects that emerged during the era. However, Kamakura Buddhism was a complex phenomenon, a mixture of religious itinerants, traditional monks, lay followers, and innovative founders of new schools.

The Pure Land sects of Jôdo (founded by Hônen, 1133–1212) and Jôdo Shinshû (Shinran, 1173–1262), emphasized devotion to Amida Buddha and reliance on Amida's power to lead followers to the Pure Land. Consequently, there was little need for celibate priests or monasteries in Pure Land Buddhism because the believer was saved by the 'other power' of Amida and not through self-effort. For Hônen, calling on the name of Amida (*nembutsu*) was the only means available for attaining enlightenment during *mappō*. In Shinran's view, Amida's compassion and saving power were so complete and absolute that all people, regardless of their spiritual condition, were already saved. Recitation of the *nembutsu* was performed instead as an expression of sincere gratitude to Amida. There were other interpretations of the Pure Land sect, including the Jishû movement founded by Ippen (1239–1289). Ippen taught that every moment that the *nembutsu* was recited was a moment of salvation, and so chanting the *nembutsu* transformed this world into the Pure Land.

A Tendai temple named Enryakuji. Located on the eastern slope of Mount Hiei, Enryakuji is the main headquarters of the Tendai sect.

The Zen schools of Rinzai (Eisai, 1141–1215) and Sôtô (Dôgen, 1200–1253) began as monastic meditative disciplines but came to have an influence on Japanese culture and the arts. The Rinzai sect emphasized the possibility of sudden enlightenment within everyday life and the use of *kôan* (Zen riddles) to help achieve this end. The Sôtô sect focused on *shikan-taza* (just sitting) meditation, and enlightenment was achieved more gradually. The development of Sôtô Zen into a major Buddhist denomination in Japan, however, was mainly the work of Keizan Jôkin (1268–1325). Keizan blended Zen with other ritual practices, including Indian Tantrism, Daoism, and folk religion. The Buddhist priest Nichiren

(1222–1282) sought to restore what he considered to be the true teaching of the historical Buddha, and towards this end preached a simple act of faith in the Lotus Sūtra, the chanting of the Daimoku, a sacred incantation that gives praise to the sūtra. Nichiren viewed this as the only means of achieving enlightenment during *mappō* and harshly denounced other Buddhist denominations that taught otherwise, even condemning to hell government rulers who did not embrace his message.

Although much has been made of the new Buddhist sects that emerged in the Kamakura period, the major sects of the Heian period continued to develop and play important roles. The Tendai priest Jien and the Shingon priest Kakuban, for example, made important contributions to the development of Buddhism. In fact, Shingon experienced a revival during the Kamakura period, attracting followers from all parts of society. Even schools from the earlier Nara period continued to evolve, as is shown by the attempt of the Kegon priest Myôe to synthesize Kegon and esotericism.

There were other religious movements during the Kamakura period that transcended sectarian boundaries and influenced the development of religion in Japan. The *hijiri* were popular but unorthodox religious figures who practiced asceticism outside the auspices of monastic institutions. Their itinerant nature helped Buddhist temples raise funds as the *hijiri* travelled through the countryside preaching and distributing talismans while soliciting donations.

Japanese Buddhists had long believed Shintô to be subservient, its *kami* regarded as local manifestations of higher Buddhist deities. During the Kamakura period, movements emerged that sought to assert the Shintô tradition over Buddhism. One such developed into Watarai Shintô (or Ise Shintô), a system that highlighted purity and honesty as the highest Shintô virtues and emphasized rites of purification.

Established by priests of the Watarai family, who served at the Outer Shrine of the Ise Shrine, Watarai Shintô was an attempt to emancipate the faith from the domination of Buddhist thought. For example, it reversed the ignominious Buddhist teaching of the period and declared that the Buddhas and bodhisattvas were manifestations of Shintô *kami*.

POPULAR RELIGION UNDER KAMAKURA By the twelfth century, Shugendô had developed great centres of ascetic practice and pilgrimage in various mountain regions, complete with a strict hierarchy of rank and division of labour among its adherents. The most influential of these mountain centres was at Kumano in the present-day Wakayama prefecture. The *yamabushi* travelled extensively around Japan, expanding their areas of influence to remote places, advertising their holy mountains, and distributing amulets and charms. In addition to their spiritual abilities, Shugendô practitioners gained worldly powers during this period. Because they were well acquainted with hidden mountain paths, they were recruited as spies and became involved in the military actions of feudal lords.

The Kamakura period came to an end when the emperor Go-Daigo, with the help of the Ashikaga and other powerful families, overthrew the warrior government and established direct imperial rule. This lasted only three years, however, for the emperor was soon forced to flee Kyoto, leaving Ashikaga Takauji as the new shōgun.

Pilgrimage

Pilgrimage, the act of travelling to and visiting sacred sites and engaging in acts of worship there, is one of the main forms of religious activity in Japan. It transcends sectarian and institutional boundaries, and is widely practiced by followers of traditional and established faiths as well as by members of new religions. Journeying through and to religious centres is also an integral part of folk religious customs. There are no limits to the number of pilgrimages a person can make, and even today, many Japanese people will make at least one during their lives.

On one level, pilgrimage represents the physical, mental, and spiritual attempt to establish or re-establish a bond between the pilgrim and a deity, saint, or sacred tradition. This distinguishes pilgrims and pilgrimage from tourists and tourism, who do not necessarily seek to create such religious ties. Pilgrimages may also be undertaken for other reasons, such as the search for cultural identity, the practice of austerities, and the securing of practical benefits.

There are numerous types of pilgrimage in Japan and a variety of terms is used to describe them. There are pilgrimages that are limited to a few participants, such as the intensely arduous *Sennichi Kaihôgyô* (thousand-day mountain pilgrimage) on Mount Hiei, which is restricted to ascetic Tendai monks, and pilgrimages that are open to all, such as the popular *Shikoku henro*, the 88-stage pilgrimage around the island of Shikoku, dedicated to the founder of Shingon Buddhism, Kôbô Daishi. There are also pilgrimages that focus on a single site, such as the *Ise mairi* (pilgrimage to the Ise Shrine), and pilgrimages such as *Saikoku junrei* (a circuit pilgrimage in the western part of Japan dedicated to the bodhisattva Kannon) that incorporate multiple sites, each considered integral to the pilgrimage.

It is customary to see pilgrims carrying a notebook or scroll in order to take an impression of each temple's seal, while some pilgrims, regardless of their religious tradition, also don special coats or hats, and carry a staff along with the rest of their travel equipment. When they are dressed in this fashion, pilgrims are no longer tied to the usual social norms that they observe, and the expectations of everyday life; the act of pilgrimage can be understood as an attempt to be apart from one world and a part of another, more spiritual existence. It

Modern pilgrims on Mount Haguro, one of the three sacred mountains of Dewa. It is the smallest mountain, home to the Shugendô sect, a tradition combining Buddhism and Shintô. Every autumn the *yamabushi*, followers of the sect, make a week-long pilgrimage around all three mountains. Deprived of food and sleep, they undergo rituals and perform sacred purification ceremonies.

is also common for pilgrims to place stickers bearing their own names and those of their home towns on temple pillars, walls, or beams. One reason for doing this is to establish a personal connection with the sacred site, and consequently the stickers are usually placed in inaccessible spots so that the priests cannot remove them easily.

ASHIKAGA PERIOD

The Ashikaga period (1336–1537) was characterized by power struggles within the *bakufu* (military government), famines and epidemics, peasant and religious uprisings, and the devastating Ônin War (1467–1478). Not surprisingly, this chaos and strife affected the religious landscape.

BUDDHISM AND SHINTÔ UNDER ASHIKAGA While no major new Buddhist sect emerged in this period, the existing sects struggled with issues of power and reform, including armed combat. Nichiren followers staged an armed rebellion to defend themselves against an oppressive government, while followers of Jôdo Shinshû revolted in the Kaga region in 1487 and temporarily established a self-ruling government. Jôdo Shinshû had degenerated into a moribund state and had split into several groups until Rennyo (1415–1499) initiated measures of reform. Rennyo was the eighth head of the Honganji branch of Jôdo Shinshû and was successful in strengthening the sect by systematizing its liturgy and eliminating heresies.

In 1571, Oda Nobunaga (1534–1582), a feudal lord, destroyed the Enryakuji temple complex at Mount Hiei. Enryakuji, the power-base of the Tendai Buddhist sect, had political influence because of the number of nobility among its patrons, its major landholdings, and its warrior-monks. Buddhist monasteries and priests at Mount Hiei and Mount Kôya further resisted Oda's attempts at national unification and so suffered persecution. At the same time, Christianity was encouraged as a means of counteracting Buddhist influence. In spite of this suppression, the Ashikaga period is noted for religious and cultural developments related to Buddhism. The combination of Zen and Pure Land traditions, coupled with Chinese aesthetics, contributed to the growth of flower arranging, the tea ceremony, calligraphy, and *nô* drama.

In 1484, Yoshida Kanetomo (1435–1511) established Yoshida Shintô at Yamashiro, Kyoto. Yoshida Shintô is noted for its insistence that the Buddhas and bodhisattvas were manifestations of the *kami* and not vice versa, as the *honji suijaku* theory had stated.

The tea ceremony, or *cha-no-yu*, is a Zen meditation ritual. Tea-drinking, thought to keep the mind alert during meditation, was introduced from China by the monk Eisai (1141–1215). The elaborate ceremony, formalized by Sen no Rikyu (1521–1591), lasts several hours, takes place in a hut designed to mimic an isolated retreat, and is governed by 100 rules.

CHRISTIANITY UNDER ASHIKAGA Christianity formally began in Japan when the Jesuit missionary Francis Xavier arrived in Kagoshima in 1549. Initially Christianity enjoyed a period of success, with some 300,000 converts by 1614. During the latter part of the Ashikaga period, Japan suffered civil wars which not only resulted in great bloodshed but also in swings of loyalty to the competing feudal lords. Christianity offered a new value system that helped people at this time of strife. The perception of Christianity as a foreign religion has been both an asset and a detriment to the religion during its history in Japan. In periods of conflict, the foreign character of the religion worked in its favour as people turned to it precisely because it represented something new. For this reason intervals of rapid social change and upheaval in traditional values, such as the civil wars (1482–1558), the early Meiji era (1868–1891), and the postwar occupation (1945–1952), saw Christianity make significant progress in Japan. By contrast, during periods of stability or when issues of national identity come to the forefront, Christianity has suffered for its alien status.

The Jesuit missionaries, who were mostly Portuguese, advocated accommodation to Japanese culture. For example, the name for the Great Sun Buddha of the Shingon sect, Dainichi, was initially adopted as the designation for God, while the Buddhist term *jôdo* (pure land) was used for heaven. The Jesuits also largely focused on the nobility in their evangelizing efforts. This contrasted sharply with the mostly Spanish Franciscans who arrived in 1593 and emphasized work among the poor while adopting a more confrontational approach to evangelism.

The early success of the Jesuit missionaries was also due in part to the gifts that they brought with them for people in high positions. Books, clocks, muskets, and other items were attractive to feudal lords interested in importing Western products and using the technological and cultural knowledge of the West to their benefit. In this context, that Christianity was associated with the West was to the advantage of the religion. However, the intense rivalry between the Portuguese Jesuits and the Spanish Franciscans played a part in arousing the suspicion of military rulers against the foreigners and their countries, and hindered missionary work. Fears of Japan becoming embroiled in European conflicts and concerns about the links between Japanese Christians and powerful Christian countries such as Spain and Portugal resulted in a ban on the religion in 1612.

CHINESE RELIGION UNDER ASHIKAGA The continued introduction and proliferation of Chinese learning and culture was facilitated by the Gozan temples, a system of Zen monasteries that became religiously and politically powerful during the Ashikaga era. Ryôan Keigo (1425–1514) introduced Wang Yang-ming Neo-Confucianism during the latter part of the period, but Confucianism as a whole was to have a greater impact on Japanese political thought in the Tokugawa era *(see page 130)*.

The civil wars of this period ended and reunification of Japan was achieved through the accomplishments of three successive military leaders: Oda Nobunaga, Toyotomi Hideyoshi (1537–1598), and Tokugawa Ieyasu (1542–1616). Their struggles and their rise to power initiated a period of relative stability and a new milieu for Japanese religion.

Toshugu shrine with its stone lanterns at Nikko National Park. The shrine is dedicated to Tokugawa Ieyasu, the first leader of the new shōgunate that ruled Japan from the seventeenth to the nineteenth centuries. Tokugawa instituted Buddhism as the unifying state religion of Japan.

TOKUGAWA PERIOD

Tokugawa Ieyasu and his successors during the Tokugawa period (1603–1868) completed the unification process begun in the sixteenth century and revitalized the shōgunate *(see page 102)*. The policies of the dynasty aimed to keep Japan in a stable state of controlled orthodoxy by removing foreign political and religious threats. This included banning Christianity and effectively closing Japan to the rest of the world.

BUDDHISM UNDER TOKUGAWA Buddhism came under the control of the government and the number of Buddhist temples rose from 13,037 during the Kamakura period to 469,934 under the Tokugawa shōgunate, yet the only major new group to emerge during this period was the Ôbaku Zen sect. In 1635, a system of temple support was instituted that tied the Japanese to Buddhism and largely reduced Buddhism to being an arm of the government. Regulations were implemented in part to ensure that the Japanese were not Christian. Under the *danka* system, extended families had to register as parishioners with Buddhist temples and annually obtain certificates stating that they were innocent of association with Christianity, and funerals and memorial services had to be performed at Buddhist temples. People had little say about which temple they belonged to and could not easily move their affiliation. The *danka* system was abolished in the late nineteenth century but remained influential well into the twentieth.

Pilgrimages became very popular during the Tokugawa period, the Ise Shrine being considered particularly efficacious in procuring blessings for the pilgrims. There were four mass pilgrimages during the Tokugawa era (1650, 1705, 1771, and 1830), when millions made the journey to the shrine.

A Shintô restoration movement gained considerably in influence during the second half of the relevant period. Pro-Shintô supporters, including such people as Kamo Mabuchi (1697–1769), Motoori Norinaga (1730–1801), and Hirata Atsutane (1776–1843), were attempting to return the country to an idealized past, a pure Japan that had been untouched both by foreign culture and by religion, and efforts were made to separate Shintô from Buddhism, Confucianism, and Christianity. *Honji suijaku* and other theories that sought to fuse Buddhism with Shintô were rejected by this movement, and special emphasis was placed on the *Kojiki*, *Nihongi*, and *Manyôshû* (a collection of early Japanese poetry written between 600 and 759) as repositories of the native tradition.

CHRISTIANITY AND POPULAR RELIGION UNDER TOKUGAWA Pressures to ban Christianity and close Japan to the West came to a head with the Shimabara revolt of 1637–1638, seen by the government as being partly inspired by Christianity. Christianity was condemned as a subversive religion, and the official ban lasted for almost 230 years. Persecution had begun years earlier, however. In 1597, Toyotomi Hideyoshi crucified 26 Christians, including nine Europeans, at Nagasaki. The in-fighting between the Jesuits and Franciscans had probably aroused the suspicion that missionaries were the precursors of an invasion. Now, suspected Christians had to demonstrate their rejection of Christianity by performing *fumie*, stepping on a copper tablet that bore the image of a crucifix or other Christian symbol. Some remained steadfast in their faith despite horrific tortures. The ban on Christianity did not eradicate the religion from Japan but forced practicing Christians to conceal their faith. The Kakure Kirishitan (hidden Christians) transmitted their beliefs from generation to generation, camouflaging them with Shintô and Buddhist symbols. In 1865, some 20,000 Kakure Kirishitan were discovered in Nagasaki. Persecution of Christians was renewed and only came to an end in 1873, after intense diplomatic pressure from Western nations.

In its efforts to control religion, the Tokugawa government attempted to limit the influence of Shugendô and its centres of practice by discouraging the *yamabushi* from wandering freely. Instead, they were restricted to local villages where they became religious leaders and teachers. There were others, however, who resisted government control, such as the *gannin*, or religious performers, who attracted audiences with performances of songs and dances and sales of charms and amulets. The weakening of the shōgunate's control in social and political affairs towards the end of the period allowed for the development of new religions such as Kurozumikyô, Konkôkyô, and Tenrikyô, which drew upon the charisma and spiritual powers of its founders.

CHINESE RELIGION UNDER TOKUGAWA The Tokugawa shōguns supported the reorganization of society and values based on Confucian ideals. Although Confucianism had been a factor in the shaping of Japanese culture for centuries, it received its greatest support at this time: a form of Confucianism was adopted as the official ethical philosophy of Japan. The family was recognized as the basic social unit, loyalty to one's superiors was considered the highest virtue, and the subordination of individual interests to the collective good was emphasized. Tokugawa Ieyasu employed a Confucian adviser, Hayashi Razan (1583–1657). Hayashi worked for the Tokugawa shōgunate for more than 50 years, drafting legal codes, editing Japanese history, and establishing a school and shrine to Confucius. Readily interpreted to recommend a hierarchical order, Confucian learning was considered a formal preparation for government service.

The combination of corruption and incompetence that weakened the shōgunate, along with the return of Western powers during the latter part of the nineteenth century, opened the way for an effective coup. The last shōgun was forced to step down in 1868 and a teenage emperor was then restored to power, heralding a new period in Japan's history.

MEIJI PERIOD

The modern period in Japanese history begins with the establishment of the Meiji regime in 1868. During this period (1868–1912), Japan adopted Western styles and institutions such as the solar calendar, Western dress, a postal service, and the railway. Eating habits too were affected as beef became part of the Japanese diet. Yet the new Meiji regime also sought to establish a theocratic state with the restoration of the ancient principle of unity between religion and state. Religion was influenced by this dual theme of modernization and a return to an idealized past.

Court musicians accompany a ceremony at the shrine of Emperor Meiji in Tokyo. Under Meiji's rule, Shintô ousted Buddhism as the official religion of the state. A version known as Fukko Shintô (Restoration Shintô) advocated a return to a mythical way thought to exist before Chinese and Indian ideas came to Japan, encouraged emperor-worship, and emphasized nationalism.

BUDDHISM AND SHINTÔ UNDER MEIJI Buddhism not only lost the state patronage it had enjoyed during the Tokugawa period but suffered persecution as the new government set about reviving and recreating Shintô as the state religion *(see page 103)*. Buddhist temples, images, and other priceless treasures were destroyed and the religion lost much of its land holdings. Moreover, some Buddhist priests were made to renounce their ordination and were forced to become Shintô priests.

Buddhism responded to the new social and religious environment in a number of ways, including redefining and repositioning itself so as to support the new government. Doctrines and arguments were presented that contributed to the legitimization of the imperial system and its ideology. The change in the social climate also stimulated Buddhism in a more positive direction. Buddhist monks studied at Western universities and were exposed to European Buddhist scholarship. Buddhists responded to the influx of new technology and science by producing studies that demonstrated the compatibility of Buddhist thought and science. And they also engaged in socially beneficial work, building schools and hospitals, partly in response to Christian activity in this area.

Building upon the restoration movement in the latter part of the Tokugawa era, Shintô became a cornerstone for the new Meiji regime. The government created State Shintô to help implement an ideology that fostered veneration of the emperor and heightened nationalism. State Shintô was declared a non-religious institution by the government, and its priests became civil servants and its shrines instruments of the state. To preserve the secular status of State Shintô and prevent it from becoming involved in overtly religious or sectarian activities, the government created a new category, which was known as *Kyôha* (Sect) Shintô, which officially recognized thirteen religious Shintô groups.

Efforts to find and separate a pure form of Shintô after centuries of amalgamation with Buddhism resulted in the proscription and persecution of religious traditions that blended elements of the two religions. Shrines and temples that contained mixed deities were destroyed or had the images replaced with pure, albeit unfamiliar, *kami*.

Japanese nationalism during this period can be understood in part as an attempt to swiftly become a modern nation on the one hand, while simultaneously striving to return to an idealized past on the other hand. This can be clearly seen in the promulgation of the Meiji constitution on 11 February 1889. The constitution was patterned after Western models yet it was adopted on the traditional date, according to the *Nihongi*, of the founding of the Japanese state in 660 BCE.

Extension of Japanese Religion

The expansion of Japanese religion to lands that lay beyond the confines of theJapanese archipelago began during the late nineteenth century. The power struggles that accompanied the end of the Tokugawa shōgunate and the formation of the Meiji government were factors in carrying Japanese emigrants – and as a consequence Japanese religion – abroad. Priests and missionaries of the various different religions were soon being sent to minister and aid Japanese emigrants who had settled in Hawaii, on the United States mainland, in Brazil, and in Korea.

The Meiji period came to an end in 1912 with the death of Emperor Meiji. Japan was still largely an agricultural economy, but it had adopted Western-style institutions and had also developed military strength. The country was now a regional force to be reckoned with. Indeed, the treaty signed at Portsmouth, New Hampshire, in 1905 following Japan's naval defeat of Russia proved that the balance of power in the Far East had changed. In 1910, Japan formally annexed Korea.

CHRISTIANITY UNDER MEIJI The opening up of the country to contact with the West saw an influx of Christian groups into Japan. Indigenous Christians were also discovered. The Kakure Kirishitans, for example, had successfully practiced their faith in secret for more than two centuries. What emerged after the ban on Christianity was lifted in 1873 was an indigenous faith that had merged Christianity with local beliefs and customs. After contact with the Catholic Church was renewed, a number of the 'hidden' Christians returned to the Catholic fold. However, a significant number of Kakure Kirishitans were unwilling to make changes to their faith in order to align themselves with the Catholic Church and to this day they remain a separate religion.

CHINESE AND POPULAR RELIGION UNDER MEIJI Confucian ethical and moral values were incorporated into the imperial system so as to encourage and support loyalty and filial piety. These values were promulgated in the influential Imperial Rescript on Education (1890). This document combined Confucian ideals with Shintô mythology and emphasized social harmony with loyalty to the emperor. It served as the basis for moral education not only for students but for society at large.

In 1872, the Meiji government outlawed Shugendô and its syncretic system of fusing Shintô and Buddhism when an official decree forced the separation of the two religions (*shinbutsu bunri*). Shugendô centres and temples had to become either Shintô shrines or Buddhist temples, the *yamabushi* were stripped of their status, and its members were imprisoned.

TAISHÔ PERIOD

During the era of the weak emperor Taishô, political power gradually shifted from the dominance of elder statesmen (*genrô*) to parliament and the democratic parties. The Taishô period (1912–1926) saw Japan continue to rise as a world power and experiment with new technologies, economic systems, and political philosophies.

Laws promulgated during the Taishô period had an impact not only in the area of religious practice but in religious education. In 1918, private universities received official recognition under the *University Act* (*Daigaku rei*). This allowed educational institutions founded for religious reasons to gain university status, and many religious groups made the most of this opportunity. In the Buddhist lineage, for example, Ryûkoku University and Ôtani University (Jôdo Shinshû), Risshô University (Nichiren), Komazawa University (Sôtô), Mount Kôya University (Shingon) and Taishô University (Jôdo, Shingon, and Tendai) emerged. Shintô institutions included Kokugakuin University and Jingû Kôgakkan University. In Christianity were Protestant universities such as Dôshisha University, Rikkyô University, and Kansei Gakuin University, while Catholic foundations included Sophia University.

SHINTÔ AND CHRISTIANITY UNDER TAISHÔ During the Meiji period, Shintô had undergone a number of transformations, being established as the state faith with precedence over other religions, and later being adopted as a non-religious state ideology. The Taishô era saw the continuation of this dual identity, and Shintô was defined as a unique, patriotic practice for the purpose of which priests became government officials who oversaw nationalistic rituals. Accompanying this was a shift in emphasis from the worship of physical nature to the worship of ancestors. This change meant that Shintô as practiced in colonial territories could be controlled from Japan, the home of all forefathers, who would be worshipped at shrines dedicated to Amaterasu (the sun goddess, maintaining a connection with the veneration of nature).

Despite the beginning of participatory democracy in Japan, a heightened sense of nationalism continued to have an effect on religious practices during the Taishô era. Religious groups seen as being outside the state and thus independent of official ideology were viewed with suspicion. In such an environment, followers of religions other than Shintô were at times subjected to persecution; Buddhists, Christians, and adherents of numerous new religions suffered under state intimidation. In particular, devotees of Ômoto (founded in 1892) suffered intense persecution due to its criticism of State Shintô. Its leaders were jailed in 1921 and its headquarters destroyed in 1935.

A number of socialist and trade union movements was founded during this period to help resolve pressing social problems caused by industrialization, and Japanese Christians were closely involved in this. Many of the founding members of the Social Democratic Party were active Christians, including Suzuki Bunji who, in 1912, founded the Yuikai or Friendship Foundation, which later developed into the Nihon Rôdô Sôdômei or Japan Federation of Labour. The Nihon Nômin Kumiai (Japan Farmers Union) was co-founded in 1922 by Kagawa Toyohiko, a famous Christian socialist who worked in the slums of Kôbe. However, many of these movements were subsequently split by disputes and much of the initial Christian influence was lost.

The *torii*, or Shintô gateway, marks the presence of *kami* and separates the Shintô shrine from the ordinary world.

POPULAR AND CHINESE RELIGION UNDER TAISHÔ The arrival of Western thought and culture during the Meiji period created a changing social environment that had an impact on popular religion. Western cultural fads for seances, telekinesis, clairvoyance, and hypnosis, for example, found their way into Japanese spiritualism during the Taishô era and gained popular appeal. Efforts were made to stem the upheavals caused by Western influences. In 1918, several Confucian organizations were established or re-established and, with support from the government and business sector, endeavoured to combat what was seen as the materialistic spirit of the West, social unrest, and the decline of public morals.

NEW RELIGIONS UNDER TAISHÔ In 1925, Kubo Kakutarô (1892–1944) and Kotani Kimi (1901–1971) founded one of the largest new religions in Japan, Reiyûkai, which combined Kotani's shamanistic and charismatic qualities with Kubo's organizational skills and priestly functions. This pattern of priestly male and shamanistic female co-founders is a theme common to a number of new Japanese religions. Reiyûkai bases its teachings on interpretations of the Lotus Sūtra. Fundamental to its beliefs is the idea that all problems are the result of a person's own shortcomings, among which one of the most serious is the neglect of ancestral spirits. Reiyûkai is important not only for its own observances but for the impact it had on other religious movements in Japan. A number of groups broke away and developed into other new religions, including Risshô Kôseikai (founded by Naganuma Myôkô and Niwano Nikkyô in 1938), which went on to become larger than Reiyûkai.

The Taishô era was a transitional period for Japan, helping to develop democracy while introducing the problems of a modern industrial nation. Taishô democracy succumbed to repression and authoritarianism in the 1930s.

SHÔWA PERIOD

The`Shôwa era (1926–1989) can be divided into two important parts: from Emperor Hirohito's enthronement in 1926 to the end of the Second World War, a period of intense nationalism; and the postwar era, characterized by Japan's rapid modernization. The end of the war brought an end to government restrictions on religion and the implementation of a new constitution that guaranteed complete religious freedom. The transition between the two periods has had a marked effect on religion in Japan.

BUDDHISM AND SHINTÔ UNDER SHÔWA Two legal developments during the Shôwa period had an impact on Buddhism and its financial resources. The first was the promulgation of the land reform of 1945–1946 which denied to Buddhist temples lands formerly owned by them. This eliminated a major source of temple income. The second was the Civil Code of 1947 which recognized the nuclear family over the traditional system of interlocked households. This weakened the *danka* system which tied households to particular Buddhist temples and ensured their financial support. Buddhist temples responded in a number of ways, opening their doors to tourists, starting property and land management and other businesses, and in general becoming more diversified in their activities. Buddhist temples also established K-12 schools (primary and secondary schools for five- to eight-year-olds), homes for orphans and the elderly, and other social institutions that helped strengthen ties with the community.

Memorial tablets in one of the temples on Mount Haguro. The tablets are inscribed with the names of worshippers' ancestors so that they may feel honoured and respected. It is thought that neglected ancestors become restless ghosts who punish their families with misfortune.

The Shôwa period saw the transformation of Shintô from a state-sponsored ideology, which sought to create a heightened sense of nationalism through veneration of the emperor as divine, to a religion deprived of government support. With the Shintô Directive, issued by the occupation authorities in December 1945, state sponsorship of Shintô officially came to an end. School trips to shrines were forbidden, altars enshrining the imperial portrait and the Imperial Rescript on Education were removed, and Shintô doctrines that promoted a nationalistic ideology were removed from school textbooks. The emperor formally renounced his divinity in a broadcast in 1946 and Shintô was completely disassociated from the state. Shintô thus began a separate existence as an explicitly religious entity.

Controversies associated with Shintô have, however, continued into the present. There remains a lobby of right-wing and conservative nationalists that wants to restore the links between Shintô and the state. On several occasions, the state has introduced bills to again give Yasukuni Shrine (a war memorial in Tokyo) government support. Although the bills have failed to pass, politicians have continued to fan the flames of controversy, as when the prime minister Nakasone Yasuhiro and his cabinet paid formal tribute at Yasukuni Shrine in August 1985, creating an uproar both in Japan and abroad. Disputes over state endorsement of Shintô ground-blessing purification ceremonies have also raised strong emotions and have had to be settled in Japan's Supreme Court. In 2000, comments made during a speech by Prime Minister Mori Yoshiro sparked public and international outrage when he referred to Japan as 'a land of the gods with the emperor as its heart'.

CHRISTIANITY UNDER SHÔWA In 1941, the United Church of Christ in Japan was formed. This was a number of Protestant denominations that united partly as a result of government pressure and partly from the wish to establish a Church free from administrative and economic dependence on foreign Churches. With the end of the war and the restoration of religious freedom, several groups seceded from the United Church of Christ in Japan, but it remains the single largest Protestant body in the country.

The call to develop an indigenous Christian Church that is self-governing, self-supporting, and self-propagating stems from the fact that Japan has been the focus of concentrated missionary efforts by foreign Churches. However, the major denominations of Christianity in Japan continue to be dependent on foreign help, reflected in the fact that in 1979, less than 40 per cent of clerical income came from the offerings of Japanese congregations.

POPULAR AND NEW RELIGIONS UNDER SHÔWA The new decree guaranteeing freedom of religion allowed Shugendô practices to be revived in former centres like Mount Haguro and Mount Ômine, but the religion never recovered the influence and prominence it enjoyed during the medieval period.

The Shôwa period produced some of the largest and most influential new Japanese religions, including Seichô no Ie (1929), Sôka Gakkai (1930), and Shinnyoen (1936). Such religions provided their followers with practices that allowed access to the spiritual world and thus the possibility of influencing their spiritual and material fate. The postwar years saw new religions begin aggressive proselytizing campaigns, both within Japan and abroad, especially in Hawaii, California, and Brazil where large Japanese communities existed. In 1955, Sôka Gakkai began to advance its religious and social goals through active participation in the Japanese political arena, and in 1964 it formed its own political party, Kômeitô. This was the first time that a religious organization had formalized its political ambitions in Japan. Kômeitô took a centralist position on a number of issues and became the third largest political party in Japan.

By the end of the Shôwa period, Japan had become an economic superpower. Partly as a result of this newly found status, Japanese culture and practice became a topic of increased international interest. The tension between preserving tradition, however defined, and cultivating international influence characterized religion in Japan at the end of the last millennium.

Temples and Altars

Japan's landscape is filled with markers indicating the presence of the spiritual world, from the *shimenawa* (sacred straw rope) around trees or rocks that, following Shintô rites, announces the presence of the sacred in natural objects, to small wayside shrines and altars, to massive Buddhist and Shintô compounds that enshrine numerous *kami* or Buddhist deities.

Two of the most prominent symbols of sacred space in Japan are the Buddhist temple (*tera* or *jiin*) and the Shintô shrine (*jinja* or *jingû*). The presence of Shintô shrines is marked by the *torii*, a gateway consisting of two posts with two crossbeams that usually extend beyond the posts. The torii represents the demarcation between the outer secular world and the inner sacred world of the shrine. Buddhist temples may be marked by pagodas and a gateway, the *sanmon* or *niômon*. *Niômon* have niches on either side of the entrance, each containing a carved figure of a celestial guardian (*niô*), and, like their Shintô counterparts, denote the passage into the realm of the holy. The sacredness of a particular Buddhist temple to a family is enhanced by the presence of the ashes of ancestors that are kept there.

Many Japanese visit temples and shrines and their reasons are diverse, including the pursuit of practical benefits. There are temples and shrines dedicated to helping individuals sever a relationship or obtain a divorce, such as the Enkiri Fudô temple at Machida, the Oiwa Inari shrine in Shinjuku, and Kamakura's 'Divorce Temple', Tôkeiji. The practical and logical aspects of Japanese religion also manifest themselves in a willing response to pressing social issues. With the Japanese living longer and the elderly population increasing, it is now possible to visit temples that offer protection against senility (*boke fûji*) or even to pray for a quick and easy death at *pokkuri-dera* (sudden-death temples). Kanayama temple in Kawasaki is known for its sexually related benefits, including AIDS-related protective charms and amulets.

As well as their religious significance, temples and shrines in Japan are often important cultural sites. The blend of diverse motifs can be readily seen in the activities at some of the more popular shrines and temples, with schoolchildren enjoying guided field trips, tourists buying trinkets at souvenir stalls, and worshippers engaging in prayer, chanting, and other acts of devotion, all mingling in and around the same site. The annual number of visitors to some of the better-known shrines reaches into the millions. The temple of Hōryū-ji *(see page 105)* in the Nara prefecture, for example, is particularly famous for its collection of Buddhist art treasures. It houses valuable paintings and Buddhist sculptures, while the temple structure itself is an example of carpentry as an art form, as the buildings on the compound have been put together without nails.

Buddhist and Shintô symbols of the spiritual world are prevalent not only in large public areas but also in smaller private spaces. The home may be considered sacred due to the presence of Buddhist or Shintô altars and the deities or spirits enshrined therein. *Kamidana* are household Shintô altars dedicated to guardian *kami*, while *butsudan* are box-shaped household altars dedicated to Buddhist deities and ancestral spirits that protect the family. The *butsudan* often contain a memorial tablet or *ihai*, which represents the spirit of the ancestor. This tablet is a symbol of family solidarity and a standard part of domestic life, prayers and offerings being directed to it. The religious world is an intrinsic and significant part of the general, ordinary flow of Japanese life, reflected in the presence of abundant sacred symbols both indoors and out.

Shintô priest at a shrine in Kazahinominomiya, Naiku, Japan. Shintô priests *(shinshoku)* do not lead formal worship but chant special prayers *(norito)* on behalf of worshippers. *Norito* give praise to the presiding spirit *(kami)* of the shrine. They can be standard prayers or chants devised by the priests to suit specific occasions or particular worshippers' requests.

RELIGION IN MODERN JAPAN

Japan's rapid modernization and the shift to a more industrial and urban lifestyle have brought a host of social issues and problems that have had an impact on Japanese religion and practice. Traffic safety amulets, car blessings, spiritual counselling, and temples dedicated to starting or ending love affairs are some examples of the innovations seen in modern Japanese religion.

BUDDHISM AND SHINTÔ The major Buddhist sects that emerged centuries ago still exist today, with many adopting new forms and emphases so as to maintain vitality and relevance in modern society. There are nearly 40 religious bodies belonging to the Nichiren sect, including some of the largest new religions in Japan. In its effort to remain an integral part of Japanese society, Buddhism has developed responses to social issues that are of increasing importance in contemporary Japan. Trends and movements within Buddhism, such as *boke fûji* (prevention of senility), *pokkuri* (sudden death) temples, and *mizuko kuyô* (memorial rites for terminated fetuses), are popular and controversial responses to the pressing issues of aging and senility, birth control, and termination.

Shintô priests (*shinshoku*) perform a purification ritual at a shrine in Kyoto. Purification from defilement is an important aspect of Shintô worship, which is based on rites, rituals, and festivals conducted in the sacred space surrounding a shrine.

Shintô remains a social and religious force in contemporary Japan through festivals, popular prayer rituals, and life-cycle and community ceremonials. Shintô deities also continue to have devoted followings. The most widely venerated Shintô deity in modern Japan is Inari. Originally a deity of the rice harvest, Inari is now respected as a god of business and is consecrated at more than 30,000 shrines throughout Japan. Inari's continued popularity may be partly due to the deity's malleable nature. Besides this capacity to modernize, Inari may be considered either female or male, depending on the location. In fact, centres of Inari worship may be either Shintô or Buddhist.

CHRISTIANITY One of the more interesting aspects of Christian development in Japan is the attempt to produce an indigenous Church. Towards this end, certain Christian groups have blended Confucian, Shintô, Buddhist, and folk elements into the religion, forming an indigenous brand of Christianity that will hopefully appeal to a larger audience. Many Churches have instituted a wide range of post-funerary rites to accommodate Japanese folk-religious customs, while founders of Japanese Christian groups are often accorded the type of veneration reserved for founders of other forms of Japanese religion. Moreover, some Christian groups have adopted the practice of calling on the name of Christ (*nembutsu kirisutokyô*) which closely resembles the sound and rhythm of the Buddhist practice of reciting the *nembutsu*. Other attempts to give a local character to Christianity include baptizing ancestral spirits and the incorporation of ascetic disciplines into spiritual training, such as *misogi* water purification rituals and walking across beds of hot coals.

Christianity is also making an impact at a popular level. Christian weddings are popular in Japan even though the number of Christians remains small. Many Japanese women want to have wedding dresses and rice showers, and even though they may not be Christian, they often take Bible study classes so that they can get married in a church.

POPULAR AND CHINESE RELIGION Although many of its customs have changed over time, Shugendô continues to be a part of the religious landscape of Japan. Despite the decline in the numbers of its purest practitioners, Shugendô has translated itself in some places into a performing art that perpetuates its worldview through the medium of dance.

Interest in the New Age movement *(see page 307)* has increased and so religions that place an emphasis on individual experience and mysticism rather than traditional religious and social structures have gained in popularity. Instead of belonging to a tight-knit cell within a particular religion, individuals have the option of practicing on their own using books and magazines or via the Internet. Those seeking spiritual insight can customize their own religious practice by picking and choosing elements from a variety of religions and religious styles.

Although Daoism has never established itself as a separate religious entity in Japan, its influence continues to be present in various different religious and cultural activities. From street-corner fortune tellers who use Daoist divination practices, to home-builders and buyers who are guided by Daoist principles of geomancy to create and ensure a safe and prosperous dwelling, Daoism has contributed to the character of Japanese religion and culture.

Today, Confucianism is rarely discussed or studied except by scholars, but its influence remains apparent in innumerable ways that are inherent in both the etiquette and the customs of Japanese society. Filial piety, loyalty, hierarchy, and harmony are basic Confucian principles that continue to colour education, politics, and social life in modern-day Japan.

OTHER RELIGIOUS TRADITIONS Other religious traditions can be found in Japan, including Islam. The religion probably entered Japan during the Meiji period but became widely known in the 1970s after the oil crisis in 1973. There is no reliable estimate of the Japanese Muslim population, but claims range from a few hundred to as many as 30,000.

As Japan has become a more affluent and cosmopolitan country, so it has become a more prominent player in the international community. The interaction between its numerous religious traditions and the dialogue they foster with the nation's path of progress will continue to play a significant part in the shaping of Japan's political, social, and cultural landscape.

NEW RELIGIONS

A large number of new Japanese religions has emerged since the beginning of the nineteenth century. These groups are eclectic and syncretistic, often incorporating Buddhist, Christian, Shintô, and folk religious elements along with features from spiritualism, the occult, and science fiction. Although new Japanese religions display a diverse array of characteristics, as they cross a significant span of time and trends, scholars have identified certain themes and traits that run through many of them.

New Japanese religions offer a new paradigm in which the uncertainties of the world can be influenced and interpreted, if not controlled, by the accumulation of spiritual merit and the acquisition of supernatural power. Reiyûkai and Agonshû, for example, see a link between misfortune and incorrect veneration of the ancestors. Such a worldview is appealing to those who are dissatisfied with the apparent spiritual desolation of modern society, or who view the demands of modernity as overly stressful and empty of meaning. There are also apocalyptic leanings in the worldview of an increasing number of new religions, stemming from the growing recognition of the problems of modern industrial society. In such groups, members believe they can help the world avoid a cataclysmic end by their devoted practice.

New religions often centre on the powerful personality and charisma of founders and leaders. Their teachings and interpretations of tradition and spiritual practice are viewed as vital for salvation, and followers turn to them in person or in prayer for guidance and remedies when faced with problems. The religious insights and powers founders are believed to possess were won through their own devoted and arduous spiritual practice. Nakayama Miki (Tenrikyô) and Kitamura Sayo (Tenshô Kôtai Jingukyô) are examples of such founders. Not surprisingly, many founders of new religions are highly venerated, believed by their adherents to be the manifestation or expression of a new or traditional *kami* or god.

Proselytism

Proselytism is a prominent feature among many of the new religions. The ability of followers to successfully bring in converts is linked to their spiritual development, and successful proselytism is viewed as clear evidence of the legitimacy and significance of the group within contemporary society. Many new Japanese religions also seek to spread their teachings beyond Japan, establishing branches abroad and attaining an international presence that lends support to their perceived universal relevance. Sôka Gakkai, Mahikari, and Seichô no Ie are among a number of new religions that have successfully established branches outside Japan.

The vitality and dynamism of many of the larger new Japanese religions are linked to their close-knit organizational structure, within which members find camaraderie and counselling. In some new religions, such as Risshô Kôseikai, small cells of adherents serve as vehicles for the dissemination of teachings and are frequently the means of considerable growth within the religion. In such groups, senior members are often partly responsible for the spiritual development of junior members, and junior members are invited to emulate the examples set by the leaders of the religion.

The trend among many new religions that have arisen or gained prominence since the early 1980s, however, is towards a more individualized practice. Organizational structures are less fixed and are designed to appeal to those seeking a more personal spiritual experience. These more recent new religions spread through tape recordings of teachings, videos, and publications, rather than meetings, which allows the individual the freedom to select his or her own course of spiritual practice. Some groups, such as Kôfuku no Kagaku, have established their own publishing companies.

The new religions often deftly employ technology to help spread their message. In Shinnyoen, spiritual questions to mediums and their answers can be communicated through fax machines that link branch temples abroad with the headquarters in Japan, while the Golden Light Association and other groups have set up websites.

A sense of control over material and spiritual matters through the development and cultivation of spiritual faculties is one of the distinctive features among new Japanese religions and one of the main reasons they are attractive to a large number of people (approximately 10–25 per cent of the population). An emphasis on personal transformation, incorporating a wide range of individual and communal practices designed to refine the character, is common among the teachings of the new religions such as Ittôen and Ômoto. Practices may include meditation and other psychological techniques to reach higher levels of consciousness, and communal cleaning of parks and public toilets and other activities that involve voluntary work.

Experimentation with the spiritual dimension of life is also a hallmark of new Japanese religions. They offer followers the opportunity to develop their own spiritual faculties or supernatural powers that seem to enable them to perceive mysterious phenomena. The prominence of mystery and experimentation can also be viewed as an expression of the reaction against scientific materialism and increasing rationalism prevalent in modern society.

Many view the established religions of Japan as inadequate when facing the challenges of modern life and turn instead to the new religions in order to address problems of spiritual, social, and emotional malaise. In this regard, Japanese new religions are a product of and an impetus for religious change and dynamism in contemporary Japanese society.

Shintô priests at prayer in a sacred garden at Nara. Shintô is based on the worship of spirits of the natural world, and so rituals and ceremonies are usually held outside.

JUDAISM

JONATHAN MAGONET

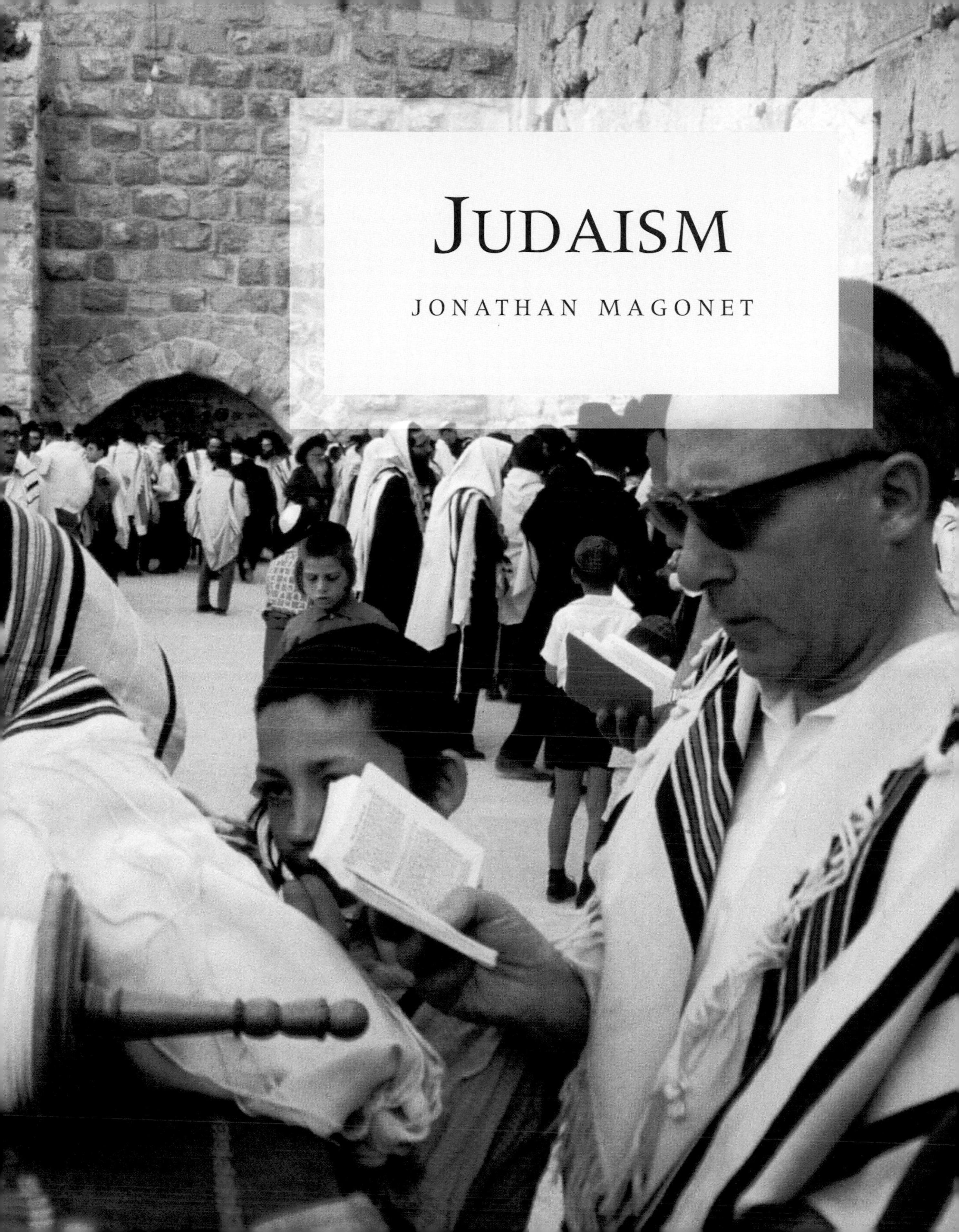

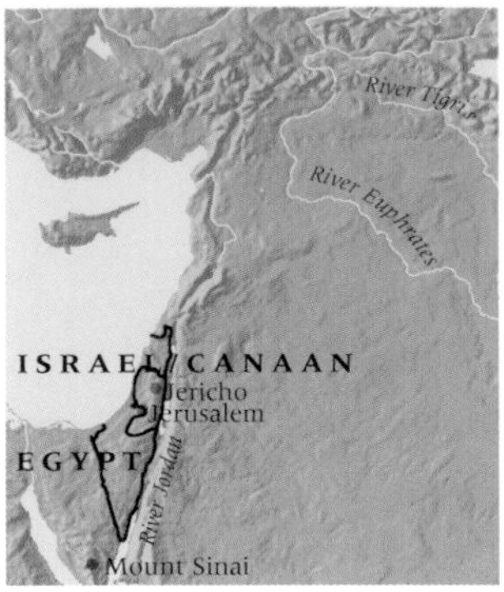

JUDAISM

JUDAISM IS ONE OF THE OLDEST RELIGIONS. The Jews believe that it was 4,000 years ago that God gave Moses the Ten Commandments and the Torah ('law') on Mount Sinai and so institutionalized the world's first monotheistic religion. Judaism places its emphasis on practice rather than belief: it is the way that one lives that defines one's religiosity. And it is these practices that have maintained a cultural identity through the 2,000 years of the dispersion of the Jewish people.

ORIGINS OF THE JEWISH PEOPLE, EXODUS, AND A NEW LAND

The only direct source for the origins of the Jewish people is the Hebrew Bible, compiled between the second century BCE and the second century CE, but this must be used with considerable care by the historian. Information about 'historical Israel' must be gleaned by reading between the lines of the biblical account, using a variety of critical tools introduced in the eighteenth century and refined thereafter.

Though the Hebrew Bible (the *Tenakh*) is presented as a historical record of Israel's origins, it includes some obviously mythological and legendary material. Moreover, the way in which the diverse material is composed and interwoven reflects the viewpoints of a succession of anonymous authors and editors. They interpreted Israel's past in terms of the nation's failure to live up to the covenant with God *(see page 187)* which they saw as leading to the punishment of exile in Babylon *(see pages 192–193)*. However, the material contains clues to alternative accounts and perceptions that have been edited out or suppressed in order to give a coherent point of view. To these the historian turns in attempting to achieve a more comprehensive picture, helped by the information supplied by archeological evidence.

However, here too caution is required. Much archeological research in the nineteenth century was aimed at proving the accuracy of the biblical record. Today, while there is a general acknowledgement that archeological evidence locates the Bible firmly within its Ancient Near Eastern context, in terms of the material culture of the different periods, very little relates directly to the named persons or events described within the Bible itself.

One key to understanding the history is the geographical location of Israel (both ancient and modern) along the Mediterranean coast: a land-bridge and meeting place between the great successive empires of Mesopotamia to the north and Egypt to the south *(see pages 226–229)*. In ancient times, the region was called Canaan, roughly corresponding to 'Palestine', a designation introduced by the Romans. Whoever controlled this territory controlled the great north–south trade and military route, as well as access to the sea and to the rich empires in the East, so it was subject to constant struggles between these major empires, as well as limited periods of independence and a degree of local autonomy when either was in a period of decline.

Early Stone Age settlements abound in the region. The neolithic period saw a shift from nomadic hunting and gathering to the establishment of settlements and the use of clay to produce vessels for storage and cooking. In the early Bronze Age, the first urban societies began to appear. Asiatic invaders, the Hyksos, established themselves in the territory and from about 1720 to 1580 BCE ruled over Egypt before being driven out, the Egyptians ruling Canaan throughout the late Bronze Age. The population of Canaan was largely Western Semitic and the inhabitants of the small city-states attempted to exert ever greater control over their local area. The Egyptians began to withdraw from the territory at the beginning of the twelfth century, their place being taken by the Philistines, 'Sea Peoples', who invaded the coastal region and maintained an enclave of city-states long after the Israelite conquest.

ABRAHAM AND HIS DESCENDANTS

The Bible traces the beginning of the Jewish people to Abraham who originated in 'Ur of the Chaldeans', a Sumerian city in Mesopotamia near the head of the Arabian Gulf, but who spent time in Haran, a major trading centre in Northern Aram (Syria). The biblical account has him reaching Canaan, only to be driven briefly down to Egypt by famine. The narrative explains that he marked out the territory that God had promised him by establishing altars, and that he was buried in Hebron. His son Isaac, associated with Beersheba in the south, continued his father's tradition, re-establishing the wells dug by Abraham. His grandson Jacob returned to Haran to find a wife before settling in Canaan, where he is linked to sanctuaries at Shechem and Bethel. Rivalries among Jacob's twelve sons led to the sale of one of them, Joseph, as a slave into Egypt, only to rise to a high position in the land. In a time of famine, Jacob and his remaining sons moved down to Egypt at Joseph's invitation.

These stories, with their highly-crafted details, create a seamless account, though historically they may reflect the amalgamation of legends associated with different tribal groupings and particular sanctuaries. In their present form they emphasize factors that became characteristic of the emerging Israelite religion. Abraham is to withdraw from his own family and cultural and religious surroundings and settle in a land that will one day be his, but in so doing he is to bring blessing to all the families of the earth. The basis of God's choice of Abraham is that he will promote 'righteousness and justice' and pass on these values to his descendants (Genesis 18:19). He epitomizes trust in God's promise of many descendants, even when challenged by God to sacrifice his son (thereby abolishing child sacrifice within the Israelite religion). Jacob, a more complex character, is also a religious visionary whose struggle with a mysterious figure (often identified as an angel) bequeaths to his descendants the name Israel, one who struggles with or on behalf of God.

A Jewish worshipper at the Tomb of Abraham on the West Bank at Hebron where, according to the biblical accounts, the father of Judaism is buried.

The Names of God

The Hebrew Bible utilizes several names and terms for God, most of which are derived from contemporary Mesopotamian religion although they became integrated into the biblical world view. The two most common terms are *Elohim* and the 'four-letter name', transliterated as YHWH, which is often translated as 'Lord' or written as 'Yahweh' in some modern non-Jewish Bible translations. The former term has a plural ending (*-im*) and is used as a plural noun to refer to gods in general – for example, the gods or idols of the surrounding nations – or to powerful people or semi-divine beings. However, it may also be used as a singular noun to refer to the One God of the universe, as worshipped by Israel.

This 'God' has a more intimate name, which is special to the Israelites. The *Tetragrammaton* (Greek for 'four-lettered') YHWH, made up of the four Hebrew letters *yod, hey, vav,* and *hey,* is derived, according to one biblical etymology, from the verb *hayah*, 'to be'. However, Jews were prohibited from pronouncing this name and substituted for it the word *Adonai*, 'Lord', a term which is also found in the Bible. (In texts of the Hebrew Bible, the vowels of the word *Adonai* were written under the letters YHWH as a reminder of this practice. This convention was misunderstood by European Christian scholars who misread the name as Jehovah.) Ha-Shem, 'the Name', can also stand in for the Tetragrammaton.

Jewish scholars seeking alternative ways of translating the name have focused on the idea of God's 'being'. In the eighteenth century, Moses Mendelssohn (1729–1786) gave it a philosophical emphasis, God's 'transcendence', translating it as *der Ewige* (the Eternal). However, in the twentieth century, Martin Buber (1878–1965) and Franz Rosenzweig (1886–1929) focused on God's 'immanence' or presence in the world, and used the personal German pronouns *Er* (He) or *Du* (You) in their influential German translation of the Hebrew Bible.

In modern biblical scholarship, beginning in the seventeenth century, the use of the two names for God was understood to reflect two different sources of the biblical text, 'Elohist' and 'Yahwist'. Rabbinic tradition and, in different ways, more recent literary biblical scholarship see the specific use of the divine names as reflecting different aspects of God, operating in particular passages. Thus, for the rabbis, Elohim expressed God's quality of justice and YHWH God's quality of mercy. Feminist studies have noted that 'Lord' is a masculine term which reinforces male authority and power, hence some recent Jewish liturgies have sought to translate the name by a particular divine quality, such as 'The Generous', 'The Compassionate', as appropriate to the particular context.

The Bible abounds with other names for God (El, El Elyon, El Shaddai, to name just three) derived from the Ancient Near East. It also contains images of God as, for example, 'father', 'shepherd', 'husband', 'nursing mother', and 'king'. However Judaism insists that behind this plurality of images and metaphors, God is 'One' (Deut. 6:5). A rabbinic homily asks, 'Why does the daily prayer say, "God of Abraham, God of Isaac, and God of Jacob", and not simply, "God of Abraham, Isaac, and Jacob"?' The answer: Each of the patriarchs had to discover God for himself and in his own terms. The same prayer begins, 'Our God and God of our fathers' – each generation too has to encounter the same God of Israel, but in ways that are appropriate to its own time and experience.

In synagogues the recital of the Torah is aided by using a pointer or 'yad' (hand). The scrolls are considered too sacred to be touched by the human hand, and a yad helps the reader to follow the text. The example shown here is made of gold, but they are more commonly made of silver or wood, and are often prized as intricate works of art.

EXODUS

In Egypt (page 183), the Israelites were enslaved. They were rescued in the Exodus. The biblical account tells of a new pharaoh ruling Egypt who 'knew not Joseph'. Worried by the increasing numbers of Israelites, he feared that they might ally themselves with an enemy, and he introduced a secret programme that at first enslaved them but which ultimately led to genocide among the Israelites, the murder of all male children. One child escaped this fate and was adopted by one of the Pharaoh's daughters who named him Moses. Moses grew up in the court of the Pharaoh but identified with an Israelite victim of brutality, killed the Egyptian taskmaster, and had to flee for his life. Forty years later, having settled in Midian, in south Transjordan, Moses returned at God's command to lead the Israelites out from Egypt back to the land promised to their ancestors, Abraham, Isaac, and Jacob. On Pharaoh's refusal to let the people go, God unleashed a series of ten plagues, culminating in the death of all the Egyptian firstborn, following which Pharaoh allowed the Israelites to leave. Changing his mind, Pharaoh pursued them to the 'Sea of Reeds' (possibly the Red Sea) which miraculously opened up to allow the Israelites to pass, closing behind them and drowning the Egyptian army.

Gilded silver Torah shield from the nineteenth century. The Torah scroll is rolled up on two staves called 'the trees of life'. The scroll is held shut with a binder, then covered in a decorated mantle and adorned with a crown or bells, and the shield.

The tradition of this miraculous rescue became so embedded in Israelite consciousness that the imagery was evoked to depict the hoped-for return from the exile in Babylon, as expressed in the latter part of the book of Isaiah (Chapters 40–55). In contrast with the Egyptian slave-state, the Hebrew people were to construct a new society in the promised land which valued the freedom of the individual. By the sixth century BCE at the earliest, the Passover festival (in Hebrew, *Pesach*; when God passed over the Israelites' houses) transformed a spring festival into a celebration of the journey 'from slavery to freedom', a central theme of Israel's self-understanding as a people.

Attempts to verify the historical reality behind this tradition encounter a number of problems. There is no record in Egyptian materials that speaks directly of the Israelites and such a massive escape of slaves. It is possible that someone like Joseph could have risen to power in the period when Egypt was ruled by the Hyksos; the restoration of an Egyptian regime would account for his descendants' fall from favour. More radical is the view that the Israelites were actually part of the local Canaanite population who rebelled and set up their own society. Only some among them might have spent time in Egypt but their legends became incorporated into a collective history. Nevertheless, it is unusual for a people to depict itself as having such a degrading origin as slavery, which would support elements of the biblical account, the Exodus having occurred between the thirteenth and twelfth centuries BCE.

COVENANT IN THE WILDERNESS

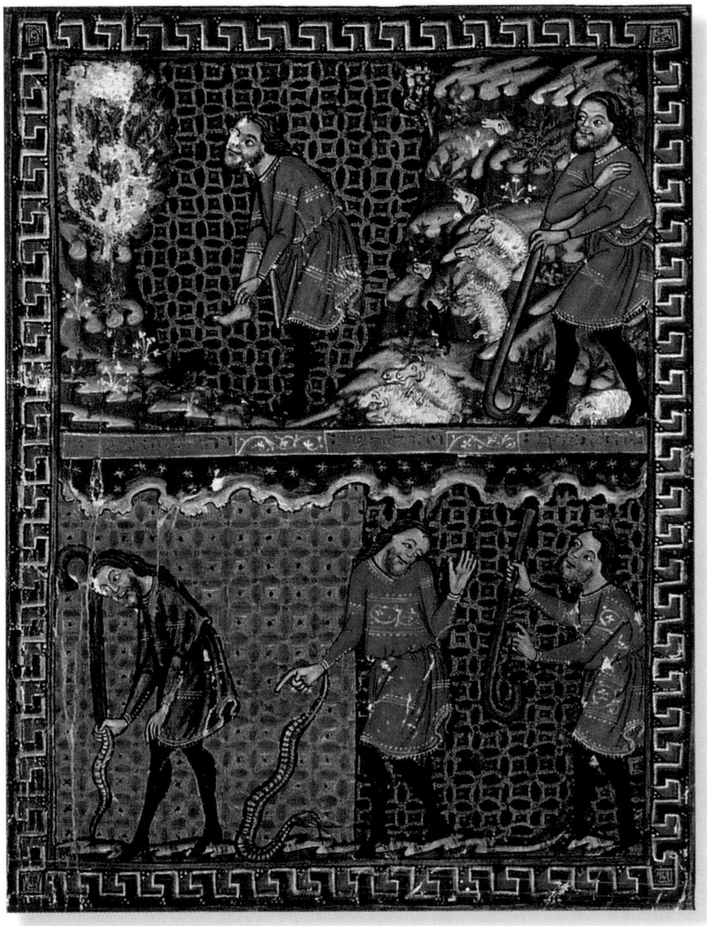

A page from a medieval illuminated *Haggadah*, the order of service used at the Passover meal. This page shows Moses and the burning bush from which God spoke to him, and Moses' staff turning into the snake at the court of Pharaoh, the first miracle God performed on behalf of the enslaved Israelites.

The Exodus is followed by an assembly of the people at Mount Sinai where Moses had received his call from God. Here the Israelites entered into a covenant, prefaced by the Ten Commandments, with the God of their ancestors who had redeemed them from slavery. Their task was to show exclusive loyalty to this God and build a model society based on justice and laws he gave them, in return for which God would establish them in their own land (identified as 'Canaan') and be their protector. Though the Sinai event may have had its origin in a separate strand of Israelite tradition, it became anchored in the Exodus story. In the rabbinic period (second century CE) it became associated with the harvest festival of Shavu'ot ('Weeks', or Pentecost) which occurs 50 days after Passover .

The rest of the Five Books of Moses (the Pentateuch: Genesis, Exodus, Leviticus, Numbers, Deuteronomy) are framed by the Israelites' 40 years of wandering in the wilderness between Egypt and Canaan. This followed a scouting expedition to Canaan that reported the land as too hard to conquer. The generation raised in Egypt, influenced in their worship by that culture and bearing the psychological scars of slavery, had to die out, for only the next generation, born in freedom, would be fit to enter the new land. The 40 years of wandering in the wilderness became associated with the major autumn harvest festival of Sukkot ('Booths', denoting the temporary structures the Israelites used during the harvest); this may have happened as late as the fifth century BCE. It completed the triad of 'pilgrim festivals' marked by a pilgrimage to Jerusalem, possibly initiated with the building of the first Temple there in the tenth century BCE.

The books of Leviticus and Numbers fill out the itinerary of that 40-year period, focusing on the beginning and the end. They describe through narratives and legal and cultic materials the establishment of institutions, in particular the priesthood, but also the legislature and prophetic vocation – for example, 'court prophets' – that would provide the basis for the governance of the new society. They recount the final stages and preparations before the entry into Canaan.

The book of Deuteronomy, introduced as a final speech by Moses, offers variations of earlier laws that reflect the practice of the time of the book's composition. The core of the book may have been the scroll discovered in the Temple during the reign of King Josiah of Judah (seventh century BCE) which sparked off his religious reforms, seeking to abolish all foreign cults and centralize worship in the Jerusalem Temple.

Canaan, or Palestine, the land to which God led the Hebrew people after their enslavement in Egypt. It was already occupied by the Canaanites, who had settled there c.3000 BCE, and it took almost 200 years of fighting before a united Kingdom of Israel was established.

SETTLEMENT OF THE ISRAELITES

The Bible contains two accounts of the settlement in the land of Canaan but they contradict one another. According to the book of Joshua, the twelve tribes of Israel under the leadership of Joshua, the man designated by Moses as his successor, made a triumphant entry into Canaan, conquering town after town in a well planned and well executed military campaign. They then divided the land between them. However, this account, which would suggest a date in the thirteenth century BCE, seems to be a later, probably post-exilic, composition, helping to create a cohesive history.

The book of Judges suggests a later period of settlement, between the twelfth to the eleventh centuries BCE, when the area was administered by local warrior-judges. It also points to a much slower infiltration, by nomadic families, initially in the sparsely populated hilly areas. As they consolidated their hold, they began to attack and conquer the Canaanite city-states, while avoiding confrontation with the Philistines who occupied the southern coastal region.

The first fifth of the book of Joshua is devoted to the crossing of the River Jordan and preparations for the first military engagement with Jericho. The parallels with the crossing of the Sea of Reeds affirms Joshua as the worthy successor of Moses. The act of circumcision, a sign of the covenant with God, not carried out during the wilderness period, and the celebration of the Passover, commemorating the exodus from Egypt, are undertaken, helping to establish divine support for and the religious significance of the conquest that is to follow.

The next section focuses on warfare in Canaan, introduced by the appearance of a heavenly messenger (5:13–15), again underscoring God's active support. The fall of Jericho is shown as successful precisely because of Israel's obedience to the word of God, and the ban on taking booty or any private gain reinforces this dependence on divine intervention. The violation of the ban leads to failure in the next battle against Ai, 'the ruin', until the guilty party is discovered. The Gibeonites, part of the local Canaanite population, enter into a covenant with Israel by means of a trick, pretending to have travelled from a distant land. This leads a coalition of neighbouring kings to attack them and Israel comes to their defence. With the defeat of the enemy, Israel consolidates its conquest of the south. Subsequent chapters describe further battles and conquests, in fulfilment of God's command to Moses that had been passed on to Joshua (11:15). There follows a brief summary of Joshua's triumphs, and the remainder of the book describes in detail the division of the land among the tribes, including setting aside cities for the Levites (cultic officials of the tribe of Levi who had had no land allocated to them) and asylum cities, where a manslaughterer could find refuge until tried, and would subsequently remain safe from revenge killing. The book closes with a solemn gathering at Shechem and the renewal of the covenant with God.

The book of Judges has three main parts: the first summarizes the conquest and final settlement (1–3:6); the second tells of the 'judges', local chieftains of the tribes who also functioned as judges (3:7–16:31), the main figures being Ehud (3:12–30), Deborah (4–5; the only female judge), Gideon (6–8), Abimelech (9), Jephthah (11), and Samson (13–16). The third part includes further stories emphasizing the internal conflicts between the tribes and a high degree of anarchy, thus setting the scene for the need to establish a monarchy, a theme already hinted at in the stories of Gideon and Abimelech, but shied away from because of its threat to theocracy.

The narratives about the judges are framed within a particular pattern. The Israelites sin by turning to and worshipping local Canaanite gods; God punishes them by sending an enemy; Israel repents and turns to God for help; God sends a judge who leads them to victory, establishing a period of peace during the judge's lifetime. However, following his or her death, the cycle begins again.

SAMUEL AND THE FIRST KINGS

The last of the judges is Samuel, who functioned also as a priest and 'seer', or prophet. He appears at a time of crisis. The Philistines inflicted a major defeat at a place later to be known as Eben Ezer, achieving not only the capture of the Ark of the Covenant (constructed to carry the tablets bearing the Ten Commandments in the wilderness) but the probable destruction of the sanctuary at Shiloh. Also mentioned in Egyptian documents, the Philistines invaded the coasts of Syria, Israel, and Egypt. When Egypt withdrew from Canaan the Philistines occupied five city-states along the southern coast. These were bound together in a strong military alliance, taking advantage of their monopoly on iron production in forging weapons. The dangerous military situation and the corrupt arrogance of Samuel's sons caused the people to demand the leadership of a king. Samuel was reluctant, seeing in their desire to have a king like the nations around them a rejection of God's rule. This ambivalence on his part led to tensions with the young man, Saul, of the tribe of Benjamin, whom he anointed as Israel's first king (1 Samuel 1–9), only to replace him later with David.

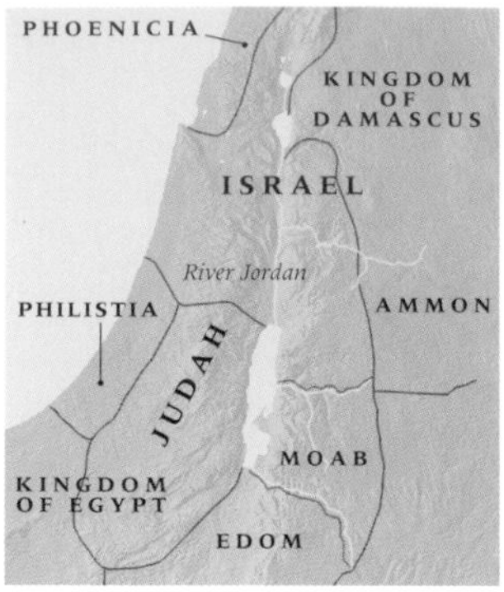

From a Kingdom to Exile and Subjugation

With the monarchy begins a period of written records and archival material, some of which was drawn on by the biblical narrators. Nevertheless, there is no extra-biblical evidence for the history of Saul or his successor David, who united all the tribal groupings under a single central government. The biblical story is contained in the book of Samuel.

DAVID AND SOLOMON

Early in the tenth century BCE, David established his capital in Jerusalem, which was located in a central position and not part of any tribal territory. It was also the site of an ancient sanctuary with traditions going back to Abraham's encounter with Melchizedek, 'King of Salem' (Genesis 14:18–20). The narratives about David paint a three-dimensional portrait of a complex figure, militarily successful, politically astute, artistic, the composer of many of the Psalms, yet humanly flawed with a tragic private life. His wish to build a magnificent temple for God was not granted. Instead he gathered the materials and purchased the site where his son Solomon built it.

The succession of Solomon after palace intrigues established the dynastic principle that was to give stability to the Southern kingdom of Judah for four centuries. Solomon, the exemplar of wisdom, built the bureaucratic infrastructure and the educational foundations needed to run the empire he inherited from David. To him are ascribed three books of the Bible – Proverbs, Song of Songs, and Ecclesiastes – although the last two are usually dated from centuries after his death. However, Proverbs contains material taken from Egyptian wisdom collections which could well be the result of Solomon's diplomatic and educational activities.

Chasidic Jew at the Western (Wailing) Wall in Jerusalem. It once formed the Western Wall of the courtyard of the Temple. In the eighth century CE, when Jerusalem was in Arab hands, Jews were permitted to gather at the wall on the evenings before the weekly Sabbath and feast days in order to hold services.

THE TWO KINGDOMS

The building of the Temple (circa 960 BCE) and the centralization of the religious cult in Jerusalem should have reinforced the unity of the kingdom, and for a while it did, but old tribal rivalries persisted and with Solomon's death the kingdom was again split by a revolt, this time over taxation. The Southern kingdom of Judah continued to be loyal to the Davidic line under King Rehoboam while the Northern kingdom of Israel, made up of ten of the tribes, was created under the leadership of King Jeroboam, its capital city Samaria being established later. The parallel history of the two kingdoms takes up the rest of the book of Kings and provides the full chronology for the prophetic books up to the Babylonian exile *(see below)*.

The biblical history of the period is recorded from the perspective of Judah, and its final editing followed the return from the Babylonian exile. It reads the history of the two kingdoms in the light of that experience, seeing the fall of the Northern kingdom *(see below)* and the exile as a punishment by God for the Israelites' failure to live up to the requirements of the covenant. Thus, when the Northern kingdom established new cultic centres at Dan and Bethel as pilgrimage centres in rivalry with Jerusalem, the account relates them to the 'golden calf' worshipped by the Israelites in the wilderness. Similarly, any acceptance of Canaanite or other gods by either kingdom is seen as a betrayal. The prophetic books (for example, Amos, Isaiah, Jeremiah) add to this accusation a powerful condemnation of social injustice whereby the exploitation of the poor is seen as a breach in the covenant requirement to create a just society.

The history of the two kingdoms is acted out against a backdrop of rivalries with local nations, in particular Aram (Syria), and the changing fortunes of the 'superpowers' of the region, Egypt to the south and the Assyrians, later the Babylonians, to the north. In contrast to the relative stability of the Davidic line in Judah, the Northern kingdom was subject to repeated coups, experiencing eight crises of succession during its 200-year history. The relationship between the two kingdoms varied from uneasy cooperation to outright hostility. Israel, astride the trade routes, was the more prosperous of the two nations. Although Israel was often at war with its neighbour, Syria, the two nevertheless collaborated in an attempt to throw off the yoke of the Assyrians. The result was disastrous; after a long siege, Samaria fell to the Assyrian army in 722 BCE and its population was deported, disappearing from history as the legendary 'ten lost tribes'.

Jerusalem nearly fell but an epidemic halted the Assyrians. Subsequently, King Josiah, seen in a positive light for the religious reforms he initiated following the discovery in the Temple of a scroll (which seems to have a strong relationship with the book of Deuteronomy), briefly regained some of the territory of the Northern kingdom, only to be killed fighting the Egyptians at Megiddo (609 BCE). The Babylonians succeeded the Assyrians, besieging Jerusalem and destroying the Temple in 586 BCE, taking the elite of the nation into exile. Others fled into Egypt, taking the prophet Jeremiah with them. New populations were brought into the conquered area by the Babylonians, the seeds of future conflict. The religious life of Judah had been centred on the Temple, with its daily sacrifices and special offerings of thanksgiving or atonement for sin. Now new forms of religious expression would be needed.

The menorah depicted on the Arch of Titus, built to celebrate the capture of Jerusalem in 70 CE, after a very long siege by the Roman Emperor Titus *(see page 196)*.

BABYLONIAN EXILE

The Babylonian exile marked a major transition for the Israelite nation in both political and religious terms. Nationalist elements, supported by prophets (Jeremiah 28) (later to be designated as 'false prophets'), could not accept that God would destroy Jerusalem and the Temple and assumed that the exile of the leadership of the people would be temporary. Though seen at the time as a traitor for predicting the Babylonian victory, the prophet Jeremiah composed a letter to the exiles telling them to put down roots in the new land as they would be there for a long time, a prophecy that proved correct. Moreover, they should pray for the welfare of the country to which God had exiled them, thus establishing a model of behaviour for all subsequent Diaspora communities and which continues in Jewish liturgy today.

From the gatherings of the exiles to discuss their situation eventually emerged the synagogue as the communal place of meeting, prayer, and study. From the prayers that sought to preserve the memory and timing of the daily sacrifices there developed the Jewish liturgy, which ultimately become a substitute for the Temple cult itself, a portable ritual that could be expressed wherever Jews settled. Here, too, began the gathering and editing of written stories and laws that would eventually coalesce into the collection of texts known as the Talmud *(see page 197)*.

Of importance were the development of theological speculations in response to the challenges posed by the influence of the Babylonian religion. Sections of the latter part of the book of Isaiah (40–55) address the vexed question: does military defeat also mean the defeat of Israel's God? No, comes the answer, Israel's God is simply using the Babylonians to punish Israel for breaking the covenant. When the time is right, God will bring them back to their land. The author grapples with the problem already debated by Jeremiah, about the apparent success of evil in the world. Rather than evoke separate divinities, good and bad, struggling with each other, the Isaiah of the exile asserts the 'Oneness' of God, 'who forms light and creates darkness, makes peace, and creates evil' (Isaiah 45:7).

Together with the hopes of return, here too was born the expectation of the restoration of the Kingdom under a descendant of David, remembered as the favoured one of God at a former time of national glory. The projection of this hope into the future developed into expectations of a 'Messiah', one anointed for the office of ruler, a descendant of David who would cast off the yoke of foreign rule, bring all exiles back to their land, and re-establish the nation. While this figure was to be a human political leader, some of the prophetic materials hinted at someone with divine gifts. His arrival would coincide with the establishment of universal peace and harmony between the nations and between humans and animals: a return to what once prevailed in the Garden of Eden.

RETURN AND TOLERANCE

In 539 BCE Babylon fell to King Cyrus of Persia (r. 559–530) who, in keeping with his usual policy of conquest, offered the Jews the opportunity to return to their land and rebuild their Temple. Not all chose to return, having been successfully established in Babylon for two generations. The books of Ezra and Nehemiah, which provide the historical background of the period, record that some 50,000 returned. They came back to conflicts with the mixed local population which delayed the rebuilding of the Temple. However, in 516 BCE, during the reign of Darius I, it was dedicated.

Nehemiah 8 records a gathering of the people 'on the first day of the seventh month' in which the entire Torah, the term that, by the first century BCE, came to be used for the Five Books of Moses, was read aloud by the Levites, 'clearly, translating and explaining the meaning so that the people understood'. Here was the beginning of the tradition of the weekly reading from the Torah with explanations that was to become a standard part of Jewish liturgy on Shabbat (the Sabbath, from Friday evening to Saturday sunset), Monday, and Thursday (market days).

Nehemiah, who had been cupbearer to the king of Persia, was appointed governor of Judah, with the task of rebuilding Jerusalem. The religious leadership was undertaken by Ezra, described as a priest and a scribe. Like Nehemiah, he was disturbed by the degree of intermarriage with local women and the intrusion of Canaanite and foreign rituals into Israelite worship. He decreed that these foreign wives and their children be expelled from the community, but it is not clear how much this actually occurred. It has been suggested that the book of Ruth, in which a foreign Moabite woman enters the community of Israel to become an ancestor of King David, was composed as a protest against Ezra's actions. The central role of the Temple gave a new significance to the priesthood, which would later come to replace kingship as the ruling power. Following the return and re-building of the society, little information is available about historical events until Alexander the Great.

With the conquests of Alexander the Great (ruled 336–323 BCE) and his successors, the Persian policy of giving religious autonomy to local peoples was maintained, allowing the Jewish communities in the Diaspora to follow their own religious tradition. Jewish settlements extended throughout the Greek world in Mediterranean, Mesopotamian, and the Egyptian territories. The Jews fell under the influence of Greek culture, Greek language became the vernacular, and knowledge of Hebrew diminished. One result of this was the translation of the Hebrew Bible into Greek, the Septuagint, during the third century BCE in Alexandria. Jews in Egypt adopted the Greek love of going to the gymnasium and the public baths. A major figure to emerge from this cultural mix was Philo of Alexandria (c.20 BCE–50 CE), whose numerous writings seek to reconcile Jewish religion with Greek philosophy through allegorical interpretations of the Torah.

Judea, which was frequently changing hands between the Ptolemaic and Seleucid kingdoms, depending on who currently controlled the area, was again governed by the hereditary high priests. Cultural assimilation led to the embracing of many Greek customs by the priestly and wealthier classes, whereas other parts of the population resisted these trends. (Since the Persian period, Israelites had been referred to as 'Judeans', a title that would later give rise to the English term 'Jew'.)

REPRESSION AND REBELLION

The situation changed dramatically with the reign of Antiochus IV Epiphanes (ruled 175–164 BCE) of Seleucia. His attempts to forcibly Hellenize Judea included a ban on religious worship, the rite of circumcision, and Sabbath observance. The book of Daniel speaks of the 'abomination of desolation', alluding to the placing of an altar to Zeus in the Jerusalem Temple. A revolution, led by the five sons of a priest called Mattathias, was finally sparked by the enforcement of the worship of idols throughout Judea. The sons fled to the hills where they slowly gathered around them other people loyal to God. The third son, Judas, called Maccabeus ('the hammer'), led a successful military campaign (recorded in the first and second books of Maccabees, and preserved in the Christian tradition in the Apocrypha). The Jews won and re-entered Jerusalem in 164 BCE. The devastated Temple was immediately cleared of foreign cultic objects and rededicated (hence the name *Chanukkah*, 'dedication', for the festival of lights that celebrates this event).

The last surviving brother, Simon, was sworn into office in 140 BCE as high priest, military commander, and ethnarch (national leader), the first of the Hasmonean dynasty. A formal alliance with Rome – the new rising force – ensured a degree of independence for the new Jewish state, which encompassed Syria and Palestine. The Hasmonaeans, however, were not content merely with the title ethnarch and were pleased to become known as kings. After Simon's murder, his son John Hyrkanos succeeded him (ruled 135–104), to be followed in turn by his sons Aristobulus (ruled 104–103) and Alexander Yannai (ruled 103–76). Alexander was succeeded by his widow, Salome Alexandra (ruled 76–67), but on her death, civil war broke out between her two sons, Hyrkanos and Aristobulus.

ROMAN RULE

With the siege and capture of Jerusalem by the Roman general Pompey in 63 BCE, Judean independence came to an end after less than 80 years. Reduced to a vassal state of Rome, the country lost the territories that had been gained under the Hasmoneans. Nevertheless, internal fighting continued until Herod, an Idumean (one of the people from the north of the Negev desert forcibly converted to Judaism by John Hyrkanos) and a son of Antipater, Hyrkanos's general, was proclaimed king of Judea by the Roman senate in 40 BCE. With Roman help he recaptured the land and ruled until his death in 4 BCE. Cruel and ruthless, Herod was also an effective ruler, his large building works including a magnificent restoration of the Temple in Greek style.

Two main religious parties emerged during this period, belonging to different social strata. The Sadducees (the name derives from Zadok, a priest in Jerusalem at the time of David and Solomon) were mainly upper-class, associated with the Hasmoneans and the Temple priesthood. Their ideology was based on the Written Torah, the Five Books of Moses, with its emphasis on the role of the priesthood. The Hakamim (Wise), also called by their opponents *perushim*, Pharisees ('separated ones' or perhaps 'interpreters') were politically opposed to the royal and priestly authority of the Hasmoneans. The two groups also disagreed fundamentally about the nature of religious authority and about such issues as the immortality of the soul, denied by the Sadducees because it is not mentioned in the Torah. The Pharisees based their authority on the Oral Torah, an oral explanation of the Written Torah which they believed had also been given to Moses on Mount Sinai and passed down to them through a chain of elders, prophets, and scribes.

Another group, the Essenes – the name is to be found in the writings of Flavius Josephus and possibly means 'the pious ones' – also objected to the authority of the Jerusalem priesthood and lived instead in rural communities devoted to ritual purity. The Dead Sea Scrolls, found at Qumran, reflect these values.

As well as sectarian disputes, this troubled time also saw the rise of a new kind of 'apocalyptic' religious literature, with its visions and speculations about the coming of the kingdom of God. An early example is to be found in the book of Daniel. Another powerful theme was an extension of the prophetic idea of the coming of a Messiah, one anointed with oil as a mark of royalty, to sit upon David's throne and throw off the yoke of foreign rule.

This period under Roman rule also saw the completion of the Hebrew Bible, the development of the synagogue as the communal meeting place for prayer and study, and the beginnings of liturgical prayer.

After Herod's death, Emperor Augustus divided the kingdom between Herod's three younger sons. However, a series of Roman governors (procurators), including Pontius Pilate (governed 26–36 CE), effectively administered the country. Roman rule was resented and anger was also directed against the aristocracy, associated with the Temple priesthood, for their loyalty to Rome and Hellenistic ways. Civil unrest and messianic hopes for the appearance of a political saviour were put down by the Romans. One such perceived troublemaker, who was executed by the Romans, was a Jew called Joshua (in Greek, Jesus) of Nazareth.

In 66 CE, riots occurred in Caesarea and Jerusalem, the high priest was assassinated, and fighting broke out between the Jewish and Greek populations. In the ensuing war, Emperor Nero appointed Vespasian to retake the territory. Vespasian besieged Jerusalem, but was then recalled to Rome on the death of Nero and proclaimed Emperor, leaving his son Titus to complete the task. In 70 CE, Jerusalem fell and the Temple was burned to the ground. Titus took the menorah, the seven-branched candlestick, from the Temple back to Rome for his triumphal procession; it is depicted on the Arch of Titus in Rome. Among the Jewish captives was a military leader who, taking the name Flavius Josephus, composed an important account of the events, *On the Jewish War*. Three years later, the last outpost of the rebels, Masada, was captured. The war cost in the region of 600,000 Jewish lives.

Yet another rebellion broke out in 132–135, this time fuelled by messianic fervour under the leadership of Simeon ben Koseba, renamed 'Bar Kochba' (son of the star) and acknowledged as the Messiah by the leading rabbinic authority of the time, Rabbi Akiba. This rebellion too ended in disaster. The Romans razed Jerusalem to the ground, rebuilding it as a Hellenized city, Aelia Capitolina. Surviving Jews were sold into slavery and forbidden to enter the city.

RABBINIC JUDAISM AND THE DIASPORA

With the loss of the Temple and the authority of the priesthood, the Sadducees disappeared as did the Essenes. Instead, the tradition of the Pharisees, now developed as 'Rabbinic Judaism' (*rabbi* meaning literally 'my master'), became the dominant form of Jewish religious thought and practice for most of the next 2,000 years. The synagogue became the centre of Jewish communal life; the home, with its domestic rituals, a focus of religious life. The synagogue liturgy included prayers for the restoration of the Temple and the return to Israel. Such hopes were to sustain the Jewish people throughout the succeeding centuries.

During the siege of Jerusalem, Yochanan ben Zakkai, a Pharisee leader, was smuggled out of the city and was then surrendered to the Romans. He was subsequently given permission to establish a small school in Yavneh, situated on the coast near Jaffa, which became a centre for studying the Torah and applying its teachings to the radically new circumstances of Jewish life.

Jewish communities spread throughout the Roman Empire, forming a sizeable minority, and were granted a degree of autonomy in regulating their affairs. The supreme authority in Jewish life, controlling political, religious, and judicial matters, was the Sanhedrin. After the destruction of the Temple, its functions were reconvened at Yavneh, moving to Galilee after the Bar Kochba revolt. The head of the Sanhedrin, the Nasi (Patriarch), held considerable power, representing the Jewish people to the Romans. He had the authority to ordain rabbis and pass laws, and maintained contact with Diaspora communities through his representatives. Under Judah ha-Nasi (c. 190 CE), the first codification of the Oral Torah, the Mishnah, was compiled and edited. The authority of the Sanhedrin was lost when the Romans abolished the patriarchate (c. 425 CE).

Outside the Roman Empire, the ancient Jewish communities in Babylon and Mesopotamia continued to flourish under Parthian and subsequently Sassanian Persian rule, and extended out along the main trading routes. A Resh Galutha, 'head of the exile', had similar powers to the Nasi. When the Roman Empire became Christian in the fourth century CE, many Jews moved to the established communities in the East. Religious freedom prevailed, although the final centuries of Sassanian rule before the onslaught of Arab conquerors in the mid-seventh century were a difficult period, when intolerance emerged. The quality of Jewish life in that early period is reflected in the editing of the Babylonian Talmud at the end of the fifth century, when centuries of rabbinic religious and legal debate within the academies of Babylon was incorporated. It is presented as a commentary on the Mishnah, each section elaborately constructed, and runs to almost 6,000 folio pages. In contrast, the Jerusalem Talmud, which was a smaller and less developed collection that was completed during the fourth century, points to the troubled history of the Palestine community. The wealth of religious creativity in all these different centres is further reflected in the many collections of Midrash, commentaries on the texts of the Bible, which developed legal and homiletic ideas.

The ruins of ancient Babylon, the place of exile and enslavement for the Jewish people after Nebuchadnezzar conquered Judah in 586 BCE and destroyed the Temple of Solomon.

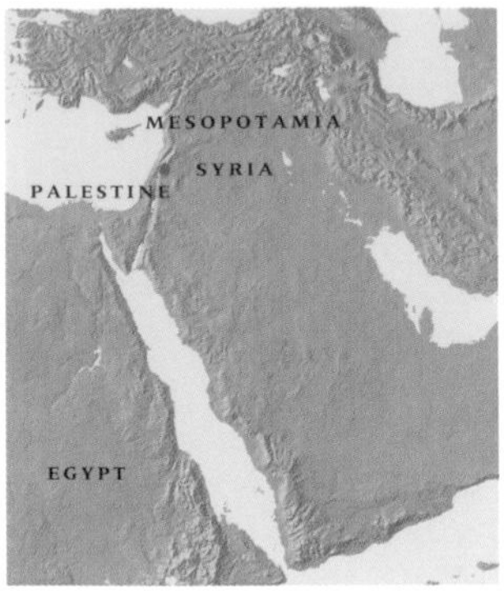

MEDIEVAL TO RENAISSANCE JUDAISM

IN THE SEVENTH CENTURY, Jewish communities in Palestine, Syria, Egypt, Mesopotamia, and Persia came under Muslim rule *(see page 290)*. Muhammad's early hopes that the Jewish tribes of Arabia would accept the new religion were not fulfilled, leading to early antagonisms, including massacres and expulsions. The Pact of Umar of the mid-seventh century formalized the status of Jews and Christians, the 'People of the Book', as *Dhimmīs*, 'protected' *(see page 278)*. They were exempt from military service and had restricted religious freedom. In return, they paid a poll tax and agreed not to insult Islam or convert Muslims. For the next 400 years, such regulations varied from place to place where Jews lived under Muslim rule.

An image of Jacob's Ladder, a significant metaphor in the mystical kabbalah. In Jacob's dream, he saw angels ascending and descending the ladder to heaven. In terms of the kabbalah, the Ladder represented the stages of spiritual ascent through worship.

During the early Middle Ages, many Jews moved into the major urban centres and became artisans, often with their own guilds. Baghdad, as the centre of the ʿAbbasid caliphate *(see pages 281–282)*, brought a large Jewish population into contact with the ruling powers. As merchants, Jews played a major role in trade, reaching India and China, creating new Jewish communities on the way. Those living in the Iberian peninsula (the name Sephardim applied to them derives from Obadiah 1:20) in the tenth to the twelfth centuries contributed to advances in the arts and sciences. As translators from Arabic into Hebrew, the Jews helped transmit Greek philosophic and other writings in their Islamic guise to the Christian world via other Jews who translated them into Latin.

Under the influence of Arabic poetry, Jews rediscovered the beauty of their own language. They uncovered the structures of Hebrew grammar, composed original poetry, both secular and religious, and wrote new commentaries on the Hebrew Bible, addressing philological, literary, and philosophical questions. The greatest Jewish philosopher of the period, Moses Maimonides (1135–1204), composed in Hebrew a major codification of the legal decisions of the Talmud using Islamic models, but also wrote in Arabic *The Guide to the Perplexed*, reconciling contemporary philosophical views with the Torah. Jewish mysticism, *kabbalah*, a term originally meaning 'tradition', also flourished during the Middle Ages. The most influential work, the *Zohar*, was published at the end of the thirteenth century.

The eighth to the twelfth century saw a major challenge to Rabbinic Judaism by a sect known from the ninth century as Karaites. They rejected the rabbinic concept of the Oral Torah and attempted to base themselves strictly on the Written Torah, drawing upon earlier schismatic movements and influenced by aspects of Islam. The intellectual struggle against Karaism was taken up successfully by Saadia Gaon (882–942) – the title 'Gaon' was given to heads of the rabbinic academies in Babylon. Though Karaite communities survived into the twentieth century, particularly in the Crimea and Egypt, they never attained more than a sectarian status.

THE RELATIONSHIP BETWEEN JUDAISM AND CHRISTIANITY

Compared with qualified Muslim tolerance, the situation for Jews under Christianity stands out in marked contrast. After Christianity gained political power in Rome, anti-Jewish polemic led to attacks on synagogues and later to laws that undermined the legal and economic basis of Jewish communities. The break-up of the Roman empire from the fifth century onwards brought some relief in certain areas, but Jews remained subject to hostile decrees and mob violence following anti-Jewish preaching. The economic usefulness of the Jews, particularly because of their international connections, gave them some measure of protection, but official edicts often led to local or even national expulsions (from England in 1290, France in 1394, Spain in 1492). The Crusades (1095–1270, *see page 248*) saw entire communities destroyed by would-be crusaders passing through the Rhineland, though both the Church and secular authorities ruled against such actions. The fourth Lateran Synod of 1215 decreed that Jews should wear special clothing to identify them; it also restricted them from high office, and imposed taxes on them. Jews could be found portrayed in medieval churches in the form of the the blindfolded figure of rejected Judaism and the 'Jewish swine'. Public 'disputations' (Paris, 1240; Barcelona, 1263; Tortosa, 1413–1414) were aimed at refuting Judaism; after the disputation in Paris, the Talmud was publicly burned. Jews migrated eastwards to Poland, Russia, and Ukraine (the term Ashkenazim applied to these communities derives from Genesis 10:3). In Spain, Jews who had converted to Christianity, often forcibly, became subject to the Inquisition and the auto-da-fé. In other places, the 'Jewish quarter' of the town became walled in as the ghetto. Superstitious accusations, that Jews had killed Christian children for ritual purposes, or that Jews had poisoned wells, were preached by Christian clergy, leading to attacks on Jewish communities. The Reformation *(see page 251)* offered some hope because Martin Luther initially expected Jews to convert, but when this did not happen he turned against them, leading to further expulsions and to the stricter implementation of earlier restrictions.

Nonetheless, the twelfth to fourteenth centuries saw important schools of Talmudic study in France and Germany associated with the descendants of the great Bible exegete (interpreter) Rashi (Rabbi Solomon ben Isaac, 1040–1105). His commentary on the Bible was to influence the authors of the English King James Bible (1611), while the commentary of Rabbi David Kimchi (Radak, c. 1160–c. 1235) in turn influenced Luther's German translation (1521–1534).

DEVELOPMENTS IN EUROPEAN JUDAISM

Many of the Jews who were expelled from Spain in 1492 subsequently found a new home in the Ottoman Empire, where they were welcomed for the skills that they brought with them, including commercial expertise. Many who had been forcibly converted to Christianity in Spain, called the Marranos, now resumed their Jewish faith. Within the Empire, which included Arabia, parts of North Africa, and the Mediterranean, new Jewish communities developed, particularly in the Balkans and Greece. Important communities also existed in Cairo, Damascus, Aleppo, and Izmir, and Jews returned to Jerusalem.

The impact of the Roman destruction of Jerusalem had found one response in the Mishnah, with the consolidation of legal traditions. A similar response to catastrophe can be found in the work of Joseph Caro (1488–1575). His code of Jewish law, *Shulchan Aruch*, 'The Prepared Table', reflected developments within the Sephardi tradition. To it were added glosses by a Polish talmudist, Moses Isserles (c. 1530–1572), noting differences within the Ashkenazi tradition, and the combined text became the authoritative expression of Jewish Law. Its impact was enhanced by the wide readership it gained from being one of the first Jewish books to be printed.

However, Caro's activities reflect another major trend within Jewish spirituality. He settled in northern Galilee in Safed, which had become a centre for a resurgent Jewish mysticism. Isaac Luria (1534–1572) was the foremost figure in this particular movement. In his system, Lurianic kabbalah, holy sparks from the divine were scattered through the world but could be restored, by means of human actions, to their divine source, the act of *tikkun*, 'putting right'.

The yearning for messianic redemption contained within these mystical notions of restoration found a more tangible expression in the appearance of claimants to be the longed-for Messiah. The most successful, and ultimately destructive, of these was Shabbetai Tzevi (1626–1676). A Turkish Jew from Izmir, his appearance coincided with hideous persecutions of Jews in Poland, so that he came to be seen as the promised saviour. Messianic fever gripped Jewish populations throughout Europe, many of whom sold their homes and businesses to follow Tzevi to the Holy Land. He threatened to march on Constantinople and depose the sultān, and was consequently arrested, converting to Islam to save his life. Even this did not prevent many believing in him, and in a later pretender, Jacob Frank (1726–1791), who converted to Catholicism.

When Christopher Columbus sailed to the New World in 1492, his crew included a number of Marranos, and in the following centuries, Jewish merchants and traders were to play a major part in the economy of the Americas. Yet others fleeing Spain made their way to Amsterdam where they flourished in the religious tolerance to be found there. The effect of the Reformation and Counter-Reformation had created a variety of religious movements, changing the previously unique status of the Jews.

Jews living in France and Germany in the thirteenth to the fifteenth centuries were subject to expulsions, Church decrees severely limiting their freedom, massacres, and accusations of ritual murder. Following the first outbreak of the Black Death (1346–1349), Jews were accused of poisoning the wells and mobs were incited to attack them and loot their property. This period saw the beginning of a new migration to Poland, encouraged by successive welcoming measures and favourable economic conditions, so that by the sixteenth century Polish and Lithuanian Jewry had become the largest Diaspora *(see page 20)* community. Their language, Yiddish, a mixture of Middle High German, Hebrew, and Polish, became the *lingua franca* of East European Jewry. Small towns, the *shtetls*, had mostly Jewish populations and community life was very well organized locally, as well as on a regional and national basis through the Council of the Four Lands (denoting provinces within Poland: Great Poland, Little Poland, Podolia, and Volhynia). Educational and welfare needs were supported and rabbinic scholarship flourished.

Touro Synagogue, Newport, Rhode Island. The oldest in the United States, this synagogue was built in the eighteenth century by Sephardic Jews from Portugal, the first Jewish settlers to come to America.

However, in 1648, the nationalist revolt of Ukrainian Cossacks, led by Bogdan Chmielnicki, led to the massacre of up to 100,000 Jews and the destruction of more than 300 communities. This disaster, as damaging in its way as the expulsion from Spain, was just the beginning of anti-Jewish activities in Poland over the following centuries. While many joined the movement back to Western Europe, a large Jewish population remained in Poland and continued to grow.

Against this background emerged a new movement within Judaism. The term *chasid*, perhaps best translated as 'pious', was applied to a movement in Germany in the twelfth century, the *chasidei ashkenaz*, who followed strict ascetic practices similar to those of their Christian neighbours. In contrast, the new popular Chasidic movement – followers of the Ba'al Shem Tov (Israel ben Eliezer, c. 1700–1760) and subsequent charismatic leaders, *zaddikim* (saints) – advocated spontaneity in prayer and joy in life. In part this was a reaction against the over-intellectualism of Rabbinic Judaism and it antagonized the traditional leadership, but it was also a response to poverty and ongoing assaults. Its emphasis on inner piety and avoidance of political messianic activity may have been a response to the disastrous effects of the false Messiahs.

INTO THE MODERN WORLD

The relationship of Jews to the wider society had been defined in the talmudic period under the rubric '*dina d'malchuta dina*', 'the law of the land is the law'. However, this apparent surrender to state authority did not include matters of religious law and, in its many different forms, effectively gave Jews a degree of autonomy in regulating the inner life of the community. The sixteenth and seventeenth centuries saw the consequences of fundamental changes in society and these affected Jewish life. The reduced power and authority of the Church was matched by the growth of tolerance to different kinds of religious expression, and Jewish communities flourished in the liberal atmosphere of Holland and England by the end of the seventeenth century.

For their part, Jews had become used to being closed off from the society around them by restrictive laws, ghettos, and persecution, reinforced by the thrust of their religious tradition that affirmed their special relationship with God. But increasing centralization within national administrations required consistent legal frameworks for the whole population, including the Jews. The new, more inclusive situation advanced the prospects of the Jewish individual as a citizen but threatened the power of the community. It opened doors to Jewish participation in the wider society but weakened the cohesion of the community and the dominance of the rabbis. An early example was the excommunication in 1656 of Baruch Spinoza (1632–1677) by the rabbinic authorities of Amsterdam for his unorthodox, free-thinking religious views.

During the Enlightenment, new thinking emerged about the status of Jews, ranging from the need to correct their inferior social status to hopes that such a process might lead to their conversion to Christianity. In Germany, of particular influence was Gotthold Ephraim Lessing's play *Nathan the Wise*, the character of 'Nathan' being modelled on his Jewish friend Moses Mendelssohn (1729–1786), an outstanding philosopher and thinker who was accepted into the intellectual circles of Berlin. Mendelssohn lived a traditional Jewish life but as a philosopher developed Enlightenment ideas, in particular believing in the supremacy of reason, a view which was to have a significant impact on Jewish religious thought.

The stages and degree of Jewish emancipation varied from place to place. In America, where many sectarian groups sought to create a new kind of society, it came with independence; the Bill of Rights of 1791 guaranteed freedom of religion, though social discrimination against Jews continued. Joseph II of Austria (ruled 1765–1790) was the first to grant equal rights for the Jews of Bohemia and Moravia, Hungary, and Galicia. In France, emancipation did not immediately follow the French Revolution of 1789 because of anti-Jewish sentiment. Napoleon brought equality to Jews in Holland, Italy, and certain German cities but was concerned about their cohesiveness as a people. He summoned an Assembly of Jewish Notables and later a Sanhedrin, in imitation of the Jewish court of the early rabbinic period, to exact a statement of patriotism to France. After Napoleon's downfall, the process of emancipation continued slowly in England, Holland, Belgium, and France. In Germany, the Romantic movement, allied to popular anti-Jewish sentiments, led to backward steps, including anti-Jewish riots in 1819. But the process was irreversible and by 1871 the German Imperial Constitution included the principle of religious freedom.

A young boy receives instruction in reading the Biblical text in preparation for his bar mitzvah.

With the door ajar, many Jews attempted swifter assimilation into the wider society by converting to Christianity, although this did not guarantee acceptance. On a more profound level, institutional changes had a major impact on Jewish self-understanding. Those who remained within the faith came to see Judaism as a purely religious identity, stripped of its national element, and saw themselves as citizens of their country, simply of the 'Mosaic persuasion' (i.e., following the religion of Moses).

Two opposing religious trends emerged. The diminution of rabbinic authority coincided with the need for Jews to adapt to life in this new open society so that observance of Jewish traditions, like the dietary laws and the Sabbath, began to break down. The emergence of the Reform movement, beginning in Germany in the nineteenth century and associated with Abraham Geiger (1810–1874), offered the possibility of retaining elements of Jewish religious practice, including a modified form of worship, while conforming to the conventions of the surrounding society. It was bolstered by the *Wissenschaft des Judentums* movement, which promoted the scholarly study of Jewish history and traditions. In contrast, the attempt to retain the primacy of traditional Jewish Law while finding a place in modern society was championed by Samson Raphael Hirsch (1808–1888) of Frankfurt. Both Reform and Orthodox seminaries were created at the end of the nineteenth century to train a new kind of rabbi – one with university qualifications as well as authority in Jewish traditional texts. In Eastern Europe, where the Enlightenment had arrived later than in the West, the Haskalah (a Hebrew term meaning 'enlightenment') movement cultivated the use of Hebrew while developing a secular Jewish literature.

The Jewish Calendar

The Jewish calendar is calculated from the creation of the world, a date based on the years recorded in the Hebrew Bible, and traditionally assumed to be 3761 BCE. The Jewish year is luni-solar, the months being calculated according to the phases of the moon but the years according to the sun. This produces an eleven-day discrepancy and so an extra month is added approximately every four years. This ensures that the three major 'pilgrim festivals' always coincide with the three harvests in Israel, thus maintaining a direct link with the land.

The Jewish festival calendar is built around a number of cycles of feasts, fasts, and solemn days. The three pilgrim festivals, Passover (*Pesach*), Pentecost (*Shavu'ot* – the Feast of Weeks), and Tabernacles (*Sukkot*), biblical harvest festivals, were given additional historical significance by representing three key events in Israel's history: the exodus from Egypt, the revelation at Mount Sinai, and the subsequent wandering in the wilderness.

Although the Bible speaks of two 'new years', in the spring at the beginning of the month of *Nisan* and the autumn at the start of the seventh month, *Tishri*, the latter has become dominant. A second cycle is built around the new year, the great penitential season. In the sixth month, *Elul*, a daily blast on the *shofar*, a ram's horn, calls people to repentance. On New Year's Day, *Rosh Hashanah*, the first day of Tishri, God judges the whole of creation. On the tenth day of the month, *Yom Kippur* or the Day of Atonement, when a solemn 25-hour fast is undertaken, the judgement on the year is sealed. The Ten Days of Penitence in between provide an opportunity to right wrongs and seek reconciliation for acts committed during the year.

The most powerful festival in the calendar is the *Shabbat*, the Sabbath, a day set aside each week for rest, prayer, and study. It begins at sunset on Friday and ends at sunset on Saturday. On this day a section is read from the Torah (the Pentateuch), the entire Five Books of Moses being completed and then begun again at a festival called *Simchat Torah* (Rejoicing in the Torah) that falls at the end of Sukkot.

Two minor festivals mark respectively the rescue of the Jews from possible genocide (recorded in the biblical book of Esther), *Purim*, and the rededication of the Temple by the Maccabees, *Chanukkah*. *Tu bi'Shvat* celebrates the 'new year' for trees. A series of minor fasts

commemorate the siege of Jerusalem during the biblical period, climaxing with *Tisha B'Av,* the ninth day of the month of Av, when both Solomon's and Herod's Temples were destroyed.

The twentieth century saw two significant innovations: *Yom Ha-Shoah,* commemorating the victims of the Holocaust, and *Yom Ha-Atzmaut,* a celebration of Israel Independence Day.

Children celebrate during the festival of Purim. The festival dates back to the fifth century BCE and commemorates the survival of Jews who were condemned to death by the Persians, as recorded in the biblical book of Esther. Today Purim is celebrated by exchanging gifts, making donations to the poor, and dressing up.

THE FURTHER DIASPORA

Biblical and Rabbinic Judaism share the notion that there are 70 nations in the world. The belief that God chose the Jewish people for a specific task only makes sense within the context of God's ownership of the entire world and all peoples. This universal concept, grounded in the biblical idea of the creation of a single human being at the beginning, helped Jews adapt and reconcile themselves to the experience of exile. The prophet Jeremiah advised those exiled in Babylon to pray for the peace of the city to which they had been taken. This provided the ideological backdrop that enabled Jews to make the most of their circumstances over the millennia while awaiting the promised return to their land. The empires and civilizations within which Jews have lived have provided opportunities for – or necessitated – the exploration of new regions and the creation of far-flung Jewish communities.

A family of Jewish immigrants newly arrived in the United States, seen at prayer on Brooklyn Bridge at the turn of the twentieth century. The bridge itself was an optimistic newcomer to the country; opened in 1883, it was known as the 'eighth wonder of the world'.

By the end of the nineteenth century, the world Jewish population was just under eight million, some 90 per cent of them living in Europe. A wave of pogroms in Russia beginning in 1881 triggered a massive migration of Jews to the West. Some found their way to South Africa, creating large communities in and around Johannesburg, to be extended by further immigration after the First World War. The United Kingdom received a large influx during the same period, the Jewish population growing from about 25,000 in the middle of the nineteenth century to nearly 350,000 by 1914.

However, the vast majority 'of migrants made the perilous sea voyage to the United States. Between 1881 and 1929, more than 2,300,000 Jews from Eastern Europe arrived in American ports. By the middle of the twentieth century, the Jewish population of the United States exceeded five million, two million Jews living in New York alone. Canada also benefited from this process of immigration, while Latin America attracted Sephardim from the Mediterranean region after the First World War and even larger numbers after the rise of Nazi persecution. The total figures for Latin America after the Second World War reached some three-quarters of a million.

North America saw the development of religious trends that had started in Western Europe, particularly Germany. In the second quarter of the nineteenth century, the main immigrants were German Jews, merchants who followed economic opportunities and helped to open up the Mid-West. During the Gold Rush they reached California and the Pacific. The freedom that they experienced there encouraged the expansion of Reform Judaism, with its emphasis on individual choice. Isaac Meyer Wise (1819–1900), a German-born rabbi, founded the Union of American Hebrew Congregations (Reform) in 1873 and two years later the Hebrew Union College (HUC) rabbinic seminary in Cincinnati. A series of 'platforms', beginning in Pittsburgh in 1885, sought to define the position of Reform Judaism. Liturgical changes, which were already under way in Germany, removed the traditional prayers for the restoration of the Jerusalem Temple and the sacrificial cult. Instead of feeling themselves to be in exile, the emphasis was on the Diaspora as part of a 'mission' to spread the knowledge of God to the wider world. Instead of the accent on the performance of the *mitzvot*, 'commandments', especially those concerning ritual, the movement looked back to the Bible and 'prophetic' Judaism with its engagement with social issues. The emphasis on Jewish 'peoplehood' was also reduced in line with the more universalistic mood of American society. Later platforms reversed some of these trends, particularly after the impact of the Second World War and the establishment of the state of Israel.

A reaction to the liberalism of the Reform movement, which had already been signalled in Germany, led to the creation of Conservative Judaism, with its own rabbinic training at the Jewish Theological Seminary (JTS) (1886). The movement saw itself as adhering to Jewish Law, Halakhah, and tradition, but developing and amending it. Within the movement, Mordechai Kaplan (1881–1983), who himself came from a traditional East-European Orthodox background, saw Judaism as an evolving religious civilization and emphasized the importance of its secular elements and humanist values. He established the Reconstructionist movement, which celebrated the rich diversity of Jewish cultural life but questioned some of its religious traditions, and founded the journal *The Reconstructionist* in 1935. The Orthodox community in the United States, although numerically the smallest, saw a resurgence during the closing decades of the twentieth century.

An example of the physical and religious journey that was undertaken by Jews during the twentieth century is shown by Abraham Joshua Heschel (1907–1972). Born in Eastern Europe, and descended from a leading Chasidic family, he obtained his doctorate at the Hochschule für die Wissenschaft des Judentums in Berlin. Deported by the Nazis in 1938, he then made his way to the United States, teaching first at HUC and from 1945 as Professor of Jewish Ethics and Mysticism at the JTS. He is celebrated for his writings on Jewish tradition, but also for the active role that he played during the early years of the Civil Rights movement.

SHOAH AND THE STATE OF ISRAEL

The emergence of Christianity brought with it the accusation of Jewish responsibility for the death of Jesus, despite the fact that he was executed by the Romans. This belief was to haunt Jewish communities whenever they lived within Christian societies, causing or fuelling anti-Jewish sentiment. The period of emancipation saw a new kind of anti-Jewish feeling as the times also saw emerging political nationalism which made the Jew yet again an anachronistic outsider. The term 'antisemitism', coined at the end of the nineteenth century, came to stand for economic, political, and ultimately racial theories that saw the Jew as a threat to the well-being of society.

Political antisemitism reached its peak in France at the end of the nineteenth century with the celebrated Dreyfus case. Captain Alfred Dreyfus (1859–1935), the only Jew on the French general staff, was accused of selling military secrets to Germany and was transported for life to Devil's Island. When it was discovered that the evidence against him had been forged, the ensuing struggle to free him divided the nation. A Hungarian-born Viennese Jewish journalist who covered the trial, Theodor Herzl (1860–1904), concluded that the only answer to antisemitism was for the Jews to be reconstituted as a nation in their own land. His political activity on behalf of this idea found an echo among groups in Eastern Europe that were promoting the colonization of Palestine. Political Zionism was established at the first Zionist Congress convened by Herzl in Basel on 29 August 1897, where he predicted that within 50 years the Jews would have a national homeland of their own. Herzl himself was ready to accept a British offer to establish it in Uganda in British East Africa, but the East Europeans were deeply imbued with the Jewish tradition of the land of Israel, and their view ultimately prevailed.

Small Jewish communities had existed in Palestine for centuries, but this new idea prompted waves of immigration, and East European socialist and Zionist ideas came together in the creation of agricultural settlements like the kibbutz and the moshav. The physical renewal was matched by a remarkable revival of Hebrew as a spoken language. The whole enterprise was not well received by the more assimilated Jews in Western countries, and both Orthodox and Progressive Jews rejected the idea. The former saw it as presumptuous to anticipate God's redemptive activity in restoring the land, while the latter viewed it as a backward step, given their universal values and new acceptance in society.

Stages in the evolution towards an independent Jewish state included the Balfour Declaration (1917), in which the British Foreign Secretary wrote a letter stating that 'His Majesty's Government views with favour the establishment in Palestine of a Jewish national home.' The same letter carried the caveat that this should not prejudice the religious and civil rights of the local Arab population. The ambiguities in this and subsequent British policy fuelled the conflict between Jew and Arab. After the First World War, the British had control over Transjordan by a League of Nations mandate. Arab hostility to Jewish immigration and unrest led to repeated restrictions imposed by Britain. The final restriction, in 1939, when Nazi oppression was at its prewar height, limited immigration to just 15,000, though the resultant illegal immigration doubled that number.

Undoubtedly, what gave the final impetus to the political establishment of the state of Israel was the latest and most destructive effect of European antisemitism, the attempt by the German Nazis to make Europe *Judenrein*, 'free of Jews'. The Shoah (calamity), the systematic segregation, transportation to concentration camps, and annihilation of six million Jews, one-third of the Jewish population of the world, in the period between 1933 and 1945, was a devastating blow, the effects of which still colour Jewish self-understanding, religious thought, and relationships with the rest of the world. However, it also gave the necessary political will to the international community to agree to establish the state of Israel in 1948.

Britain handed over responsibility to the United Nations and on 29 November 1947 the General Assembly, led by the United States and the Soviet Union, voted by 33 to 13 in favour of partitioning Palestine between the Jews and Arabs. On 14 May 1948 the British left and the state of Israel was declared by Prime Minister David Ben Gurion (1886–1973). Arab armies immediately invaded and in the subsequent war more than 650,000 Arabs fled. The following decades saw a massive immigration of Jews from all over the world and Israel emerged as a militarily powerful democratic state. As a result of the Six Day War in 1967, Israel took control of Jerusalem, some 2,000 years after the last Jewish dominion, but it also placed a large Palestinian population under Israeli occupation. Following the Yom Kippur War in 1973, a peace treaty was signed with Egypt, beginning a process of agreements with other states in the region. The unresolved problem of the Palestinian refugees from 1948 and the desire of Palestinians for their own state remain obstacles to creating a lasting peace.

Heaps of suitcases found at the concentration and extermination camp of Auschwitz-Birkenau in Poland bear silent witness to the millions who died.

The Jewish Family

The traditions and practices of the Jewish family have evolved across time, affected by Jewish law and also by the norms of the society in which Jews lived. The biblical patriarchs Abraham, Isaac, and Jacob were permitted to have several wives and concubines, building a large extended family. While the trend within the Bible was towards monogamy, bigamy and polygamy were allowed well into the talmudic era, although the sages advised that a man should have no more than four wives, otherwise he could not satisfy them equally. It was only in the twelfth century within Christian Europe that a ban on polygamy came into force, at least for the Ashkenazi if not the eastern Jewish communities.

The biblical world was patriarchal, with family authority vested in the 'father of the household'. This structure defined the relative roles of men and women, with men having major responsibilities as breadwinners but also in matters of religious study and public ritual practices, and women having major responsibilities within the domestic sphere, childrearing, and education, as well as in domestic religious rituals. This division of labour, both material and spiritual, provided a stable structure for family life throughout the centuries of exile, reinforced by the relative separation of Jews from outside society and the common need to survive as a small beleaguered community. Divorce rarely occurred and the extended family was an important unit.

This situation changed radically with the Jewish entry into modern, Western society. The changing status of women, who could enjoy greater independence, also had an impact on the internal dynamics of family life, highlighting the difficulties that were inherent in the traditional model. The classical example is in the matter of a religious divorce, which could only be granted by the husband. This had the effect of forcing women to stay within unsatisfactory marriages and could on occasion lead to blackmail, with the husband refusing to commence divorce proceedings without appropriate financial remuneration. Powers related to divorce exist within rabbinic courts, but Orthodox rabbis have often proved reluctant to use them. Increasingly, with the rise of the women's movement, this and other issues – such as the right of Jewish women to study traditional texts

and take a leading role in public ritual life (reading from the Torah in the synagogue service, functioning as rabbis) – have been challenged, with the Liberal, Reform, and Conservative religious movements taking a leading role in the debates. These changes, which parallel those in the wider society, have been accompanied by a greater rate of marital breakdown and divorce, putting the now standard nuclear Jewish family under considerable strain.

An Orthodox Jewish family in San Francisco, at the *Seder* table. Seder (order) governs the home ceremony used at the festival of Pesach (Passover). Non-Israeli Jews usually celebrate over two nights. The ritual includes prayers, recitations, readings, songs, special foods, and wine.

A traditional Jewish wedding in Paris, France. The bride and groom cover their heads with the *Tallit*, the prayer shawl, as the rabbi conducts the ceremony.

CONTEMPORARY JUDAISM IN CONTEXT

Judaism is the traditional faith of a particular people. In biblical times, the two components of peoplehood and religion came together through the concept of a covenant between the people and their God, and in the physical reality of a nation living on its own land. As a result of two exiles and the destruction of their religious centre, the Temple, their nation, and their land, the Jews managed to reconstitute themselves as a community of faith, existing for most of 2,000 years as a minority within many religious and political civilizations. In every new 'home' they had to adapt to the religious environment, preserving their core beliefs, rituals, and activities while selectively absorbing influences from around them, and reinterpreting their Judaism in response.

Post-Temple Judaism was rooted in the synagogue and the home, and Jews found their spiritual expression in the duties and celebrations of both domestic and communal life. A central religious value was the study of the Torah, the revealed word of God. Most significantly, Jews managed to preserve their trust in God despite the massacres, expulsions, humiliation, and degradation that they experienced on so many different occasions during their history.

With the emancipation of modern times, the cohesive quality that bound faith and peoplehood was weakened. The power of the community over its members was broken and with it the binding nature of Jewish Law. Religion became limited to the private sphere of life and with growing assimilation and intermarriage the Jewish world became increasingly divided. Questions of identity – 'Who is a Jew?' – came to replace those of the religious vocation of the Jewish people as a whole.

The nineteenth century saw the rise of new religious movements within Judaism along a spectrum from Orthodox to Liberal. But other Jews became ostensibly, and self-consciously, secular, acknowledging Judaism as their ethnicity alone. Thus, the messianic hope for the return of the exiles to the land of Israel became translated into political Zionism in its many forms. Prophetic traditions about the redemption of humanity found a secular expression in socialism and Communism. The quest for intellectual truth, the tradition of learning, found a voice through figures like Sigmund Freud, courageously exploring the new domain of the mind.

But are such examples to be understood simply as expressions of Jewish peoplehood and culture alone, or do they belong to a broader kind of religiosity in a secular age that is not determined only by statements of faith? Similarly, is the emergence of the state of Israel merely a late example of nineteenth-century political nationalism or itself of religious significance, a step in what was traditionally seen as the redemption of the Jewish people, as a stage towards the redemption of the world?

While the above remain important theoretical questions, at a deeper level, the Jewish people is still recovering from the impact of the Shoah. The Nazi assault destroyed the very fabric of the traditional Jewish society and culture of Eastern Europe, even though fragments of this have now reconstituted themselves. It also destroyed the experimentation with new expressions of Judaism in Western Europe, the world of thinkers like Martin Buber, Franz Rosenzweig, and Leo Baeck. Jews within that extraordinary culture made enormous contributions to the arts, sciences, and society. The first woman rabbi, Regina Jonas, was ordained in 1935, some 40 years before the first of the postwar wave of women rabbis appeared. A generation of leaders, teachers, and creators was destroyed, and with them their potential contribution to the advancement of Judaism. But as great as that loss has been, it is the religious questions, 'Where was God?' and 'What remains of the covenant with the Jewish people?', that have had, and continue to this day to have, the most profound impact on Jewish thinking.

The work of rebuilding communities, the struggle for the rights of Soviet Jews to emigrate, and the extraordinary adventure of creating the state of Israel, with all its internal and external problems, have absorbed Jewish energies since the war. The search for peace has proved easier with neighbouring countries like Egypt than with the indigenous Palestinians, and the status of Jerusalem remains a central issue. The need to respond to the gradual disappearance of Diaspora communities through assimilation and intermarriage; the bitter internal disputes between Orthodox and non-Orthodox movements, exacerbated by the political struggles within Israel; the changing nature of the relationship between the state of Israel and Diaspora communities; the opening up of the whole of Europe to Jewish life and interaction since the fall of the Soviet Union; and new spiritual movements ranging from fundamentalism to New Age to interfaith dialogue – all these raise questions about how Judaism is to respond and develop in the future. The unity of the Jewish people that could once be assured by Jewish Law is gone and it is too early to see what role Israel will play in the acceleration or reversal of the rifts. As so often in their past history, the Jewish people, bearing a rich tradition, are facing a radically new future.

ZARATHUSTRA AND THE PARSIS

JOHN BOWKER

ZARATHUSTRA AND THE PARSIS

The Zoroastrian Naujote 'new birth' ceremony. Children are initiated into the faith when they are old enough to choose for themselves, and receive the sacred white shirt *(sudre)* and lambswool cord (*kusti*), which is worn round the waist.

ZOROASTRIANS FOLLOW THE TEACHINGS of Zarathustra, whose name is often transliterated as Zoroaster. Little is known about him, not even his dates. His followers date him around 6000 BCE, and thus claim him to be the first of all the prophets in any religion. A more likely date is c.1200 BCE, though some have argued for the sixth century BCE. He lived, probably, in what is now northeastern Iran.

THE MESSAGE OF ZARATHUSTRA

Zarathustra's teaching related to the outlook of the Vedas, and especially *Ṛg Veda* in India (*see pages 29–31 and 34*). But Zarathustra's under-standing of God (unlike the Vedas and brahmanical religion) began with his conviction that he had seen God who had taught him personally. He called God the Wise Lord, Ahura Mazda.

His own teaching (of which little survives that has not been reworked) is contained in 17 hymns, or *Gathas*, found in a liturgical text known as *Yasna*. One of them asks: 'Who established the course of the sun and stars? Through whom does the moon wax and wane? Who has upheld the earth from below, and the heavens from falling?...Through whom exist dawn, noon, and eve?' (*Yasna* 44.3–6). Zarathustra answered that it is the Father of Order, Ahura Mazda. Who, then, created evil and disorder? Zarathustra lived at a time of great strife and he believed that war on earth reflects war in heaven: there co-exists with Ahura Mazda a creator of evil and destruction, whom he called Angra Mainyu, known as Ahriman in Pahlavi (Middle Persian, the language of the Sassanian Empire and thus of much Zoroastrian literature), the source of everything evil or destructive.

There is constant conflict between Ahura Mazda and Angra Mainyu, making Zoroastrianism an example of dualism. Human beings are a major battleground in this cosmic conflict, and they have the capacity (helped by Ahura Mazda) to defeat evil. Zoroastrianism is thus an optimistic religion, in the sense that it believes that people are capable of rescuing themselves and overcoming evil; and the final judgement is based on the issue of good works. The strong emphasis on personal responsibility has been an important characteristic in Zoroastrian history.

EARLY ADOPTION, SUPPRESSION, AND REINTERPRETATION

Zarathustra's teaching was initially opposed by the existing religious authorities, but when Cyrus the Great (died 529 BCE) established the Persian Empire in the sixth century BCE, Zoroastrianism became the official state religion and thus spread from northern India to Greece and Egypt. The Persian Empire, ruled over by the Achaemenid dynasty, created a stable society, with powers delegated to local rulers (*satraps*), a good network of communications and trade, and a strong legal system.

The Persians also tolerated the religions of the peoples over whom they ruled, and so the Jews were encouraged to return from exile in Babylon and rebuild their temple (*see page 193*). The contact of Jews with Zoroastrians may possibly have had an important influence on Jewish ideas (and thus subsequently on Christian beliefs) about angels, the devil, resurrection, and the end of the age.

Persian rule was well received by the Empire's citizens, but there was conflict with the Greeks, culminating in Alexander's conquest (334–330 BCE). He was 'the Great' to many but to Zoroastrians he was 'the accursed' because he destroyed the magnificent city of Persepolis and killed many of the Zoroastrian ritual experts, known as *magi*. The Greek influence (Hellenism) lasted for about 150 years, but in the second century BCE the old traditions recovered under a new ruling power, the Parthians. They restored much of the old Achaemenid empire and remained in power until the third century CE, during which time they resisted and frequently defeated raids and invasions from the Roman Empire. ('A Parthian shot' is a final and unexpected blow because the Parthians perfected the skill of seeming to retreat but then turning and firing over their shoulders a lethal volley of arrows.) Conversely, the Parthians raided the eastern territories of the Roman Empire, even on one occasion (40 BCE) capturing Jerusalem, until Herod the Great (*see page 195*) returned after two years with Roman help and forced them out.

The Parthians increased the number of temples in which the characteristic Zoroastrian rituals involving fire (one of the seven good creations of Ahura Mazda) were performed, and they began also the process of collecting the sacred oral traditions into a recognized canon of scripture, the *Avesta*.

In the third century, the Sassanians from the southwest managed to overthrow the Parthians of the north. The Sassanians gained support and sought to legitimize their rebellion by appealing to Zoroastrian sympathies and drawing upon the authority of the magi. State and religion were drawn so closely together that they became 'brothers, born of one womb, never to be divided'. Once the magi had been given official recognition and status in a governing role, opposing or disagreeing with them became not only heresy but treason. The Sassanian claim that their rule was based on Zoroastrianism has led many scholars to identify this 'reinvented' Zoroastrianism with the original teaching and religion. But in fact this official teaching varied greatly from that of earlier times, and is usually referred to as *Zurvan* (Time). Speculation on the nature of time began under Greek influence, leading to the belief that Time is the source of all appearance and being, including Ahura Mazda and Angra Mainyu – an unmoved Mover not unlike that of Aristotle. Because Time is itself unmoved and yet controls all things, it was believed that humans, far from having free will to fight against evil, are in fact predestined into their actions, a concept at variance with orthodox Zoroastrianism. The highly moral basis of Zoroastrianism was thus subverted, and the Sassanian period is the only one in Zoroastrian history where there is clear evidence of the oppression of other religions. Nevertheless, the Sassanian era was a time of splendour, with the building of great temples and palaces.

MUSLIM DOMINANCE

In the seventh century, the Muslims invaded Iran *(see page 278)* and the 1,200 years of Zoroastrian imperial history ended. The Iranians regarded the early battles as bedouin raids, but when the Muslims defeated the Sassanians at the battle of Nihavend in 642, the real threat was recognized. The last Zoroastrian king, Yazdegird III, fled and was killed (by one of his own people) in 652.

Muslim rule was imposed gradually, a process that was eased along by the fact that their taxes were lower than under the Sassanians. The teaching of Islam also seemed, on first hearing, simple and by no means hostile to the monotheism of the Zoroastrians. But as taxes increased and Arabic was imposed as the national language, and as Islam became more suspicious of Zoroastrian forms of worship (were they idolatrous?), so Zoroastrians came under increasing pressure. Theoretically, Muslims could regard Zoroastrians as *Ahl al-Kitāb*, a 'People of the Book' (as those who, like Christians and Jews, had received revelation from their prophet), and accordingly they could be regarded as 'protected people' (*dhimmīs, see page 278*). But their worship seemed like the worship of fire from which, according to the Qur'ān, Ibrahim/Abraham had fled long ago.

Muslim oppression increased, even though Iran itself suffered two major invasions, the first by the Seljuq Turks in the eleventh century *(see page 282)* and the second by the Mongols in the sixteenth. Both conquerors were eventually converted to Islam, but for Zoroastrians there was no alleviation of the great slaughter and persecution, and they retreated from the major cities near trade routes to the desert cities of Yazd and Kerman and their neighbouring villages.

Zoroastrian faith and endurance was tested to the limit under the Qajar dynasty, which prevailed from 1796 to 1925. Adherents were rarely protected by the law, the *jizya* (poll tax) was heavily increased, and travel was forbidden: they were humiliated, made to wear undyed cloth, forbidden to wear tight turbans or ride horses, and made to dismount in the presence of a Muslim. Many fled to India where they were known as Parsis (*see below*); some, offered inducements, converted to Islam; remarkably, many endured the tyranny and kept their faith.

ZOROASTRIANISM IN MODERN IRAN

In the twentieth century, the Zoroastrians in Iran were better treated. The *jizya* had been removed in 1882 and provision was made for their education and acesss to health services. In 1906, a parliament, the *Majles*, was established and a Zoroastrian was elected. In 1909, all minorities were given one representative in the government, and this included a Zoroastrian, Kay Khosrow Shahrokh. When the Majles deposed the last Qajar monarch and enthroned the prime minister as Reza Shāh Pahlavi (ruled 1925–1941), the status of Zoroastrians improved greatly. They were identified, with national pride, as being descendants of the original Iranians. The second Pahlavi Shāh, Muḥammad Reza (ruled 1941–79) gave further emphasis to this, and a Zoroastrian became a deputy prime minister; others achieved high positions in the armed forces and the professions.

When Ayatullāh Khumayni assumed power in 1979 and established the new Islamic Republic, the rights of Zoroastrians in law were restricted once more and many feared for their future. A new process of emigration began, especially to the United Kingdom, Australia, Canada, and the United States.

PARSIS

That process of emigration had begun long before, in the tenth century, when a number of Zoroastrians sought safety in India, where they became known as the Parsis, the people from Pars (Persia). The accepted date of their arrival on the west coast of India is 937 CE. The story of their migration is told in *The Tale [Qissa] of Sanjan*, but little is known of them through the next 700 years. They joined with Hindus in unsuccessfully resisting the Muslim invasions during the sixteenth century, but found that Muslim rule in India was not so brutal as the experience from which they had fled. They acted as middlemen when European traders arrived in the seventeenth century, and established in Bombay (now Mumbai) a network of influential and wealthy families. They remained detached from the British while prospering with them, and were active in the forming of the Indian National Congress from 1885 onward. Parsis remain prosperous and influential in India. Parsi religion in India developed in two main ways: in one, temples have been built to replace the home as the centre of worship, and reform has been sought to make the religion coherent with modern thought; in the other, an attempt has been made to create a kind of Theosophy, an esoteric wisdom called Ilm-i Kshnoom (Path of Knowledge), claiming to have guarded an ancient wisdom entrusted to a secret succession of Zoroastrian teachers. High levels of education have led to further emigration, especially to the United States, so that Parsi numbers continue to decline in India, with only about 60,000 still remaining there.

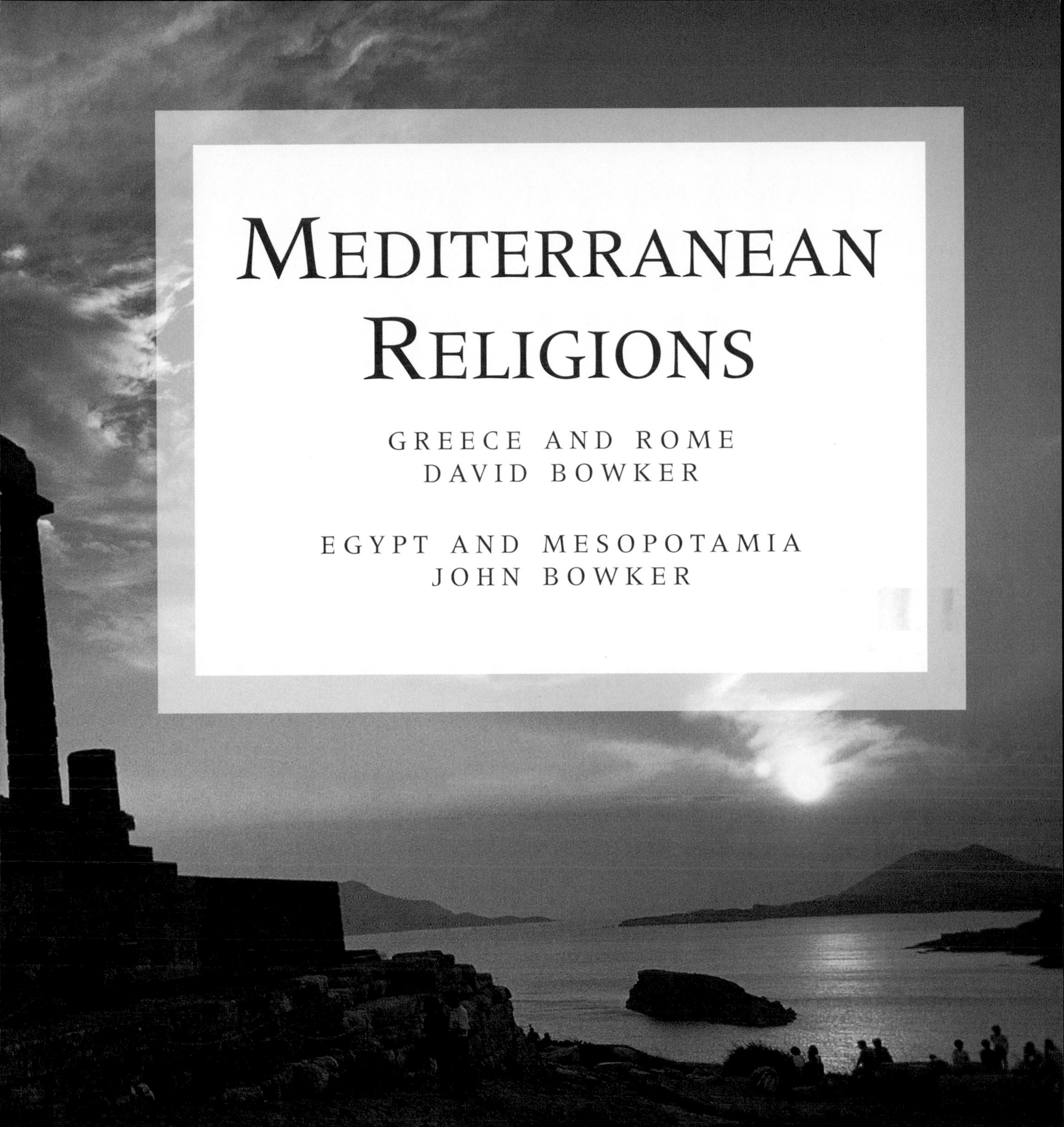

MEDITERRANEAN RELIGIONS

GREECE AND ROME
DAVID BOWKER

EGYPT AND MESOPOTAMIA
JOHN BOWKER

Classical Greek Religion

Classical Greek religion flourished during the heyday of the *polis* or Greek city state, which spanned a period approximately between 800 and 300 BCE. Its origins may lie earlier with the Minoan and Mycenaean civilizations which existed before 1200 BCE, but precise developments are unclear since there is little surviving literature or archeological evidence such as vase painting from before 700 BCE. Equally, the religion did not truly come to an end until the proscription of all pagan cults by the Roman Emperor Theodosius in 393 CE.

In its simplest form, Greek religion meant the worship of twelve deities whose home was Mount Olympus. Their leader was Zeus and each deity had different attributes. Thus, Athene was the goddess of wisdom, weaving, and war, yet also the patron of the city of Athens. The reality of the religion is more complicated because thousands of local gods also existed, many of whom became identified with these twelve Olympians. This was made possible by syncretism, or the fusion of cults. An individual could worship any number of deities provided the Olympians were acknowledged.

An essential feature of Classical Greek religion was its pervasiveness; although the Greeks had no word for 'religion', it underpinned almost every activity of the *polis*, the two becoming virtually inseparable, as shown by the many coins which represent a state through its leading deity or hero. There was no real distinction between the religious and the secular, and this can be seen in the festivals that dominated the Greek year. The most important were the four Panhellenic (national) festivals; these were dedicated to a variety of gods, but the central features were athletic and musical competitions. In Athens, almost half the year was taken up with festival celebrations, some of which lasted for several days. During the sixth and fifth centuries BCE, Athens experienced several building programmes and through the many fine temples constructed on the Acropolis ('high part of the city', the citadel containing the main temples and public buildings), the *polis* and the gods became indissolubly united.

The ceremonial aspect of religion can also be seen in the importance of sacrifice. Here, some gift such as the thigh of a selected animal was offered to a deity at an altar placed outside a temple. The purpose of the sacrifice might be to ask for a favour but more often it was to seek protection from harm through a display of dedication, since Greek gods by nature were jealous and unpredictable. The ritual had to be performed precisely if the sacrifice was to work. This involved careful selection of the victim and the method of sacrifice, as well as the correct use of all the cult names of the god. Such rites were also carried out at all the major oracles, sacred places where a deity could be consulted by worshippers on all manner of affairs, although the replies given were notoriously ambiguous.

The more private side of religion was also important. In the home, there were constant reminders of the gods. A cup of wine would not be drunk without some being poured out as a libation to a deity, while many houses had shrines to Hestia, goddess of the hearth. The gods were ever-present; if a coin was found in the garden, thanks would be offered to Hermes, god of treasure troves. There was a more secretive side to religion which can be seen in the various mystery cults which had initiation rites, such as those at Eleusis near Athens. Here Demeter, the Earth Mother who brought life to crops, and other divine beings were worshipped. The exact nature of these mysteries is unclear but it does seem that the devotees had an assurance of a good afterlife. This in itself is significant because such satisfaction was a remote prospect for most Greeks. Once their souls had been ferried across the River Styx by Charon, the boatman, they would enter a twilit world ruled over by Hades, the god of the dead (and by extension the name given to the Underworld itself), and simply exist as shadows. Another cult offering hope of an afterlife was that of Orpheus. Again, details are uncertain, but the participants or Orphics may have been inspired by Orpheus, the bard from Thrace. The cult had little impact on most Greeks but has historical importance since it and the philosophy of Plato (427–347) are held to have influenced the beliefs of some Christians that the body is a prison or tomb from which the soul has to escape. An Orphic had to lead a life of extreme asceticism to enjoy a reward thereafter.

Greek religion also had a darker side as evidenced in the worship of Dionysus, the vine god, who represented the wild, mercurial side of human nature. The Maenads, or female participants, would be uplifted by ecstatic moods and might even tear living animals to pieces. There was also a belief in curses, witchcraft, and ghosts. Many curse tablets, known as *katadesmoi,* have been discovered, each bearing a name and the hope that some disaster might befall the named person. Unburied souls were said to wander the earth in a kind of limbo and, according to Plato, those who were rich on earth might not die properly because of an over-attachment to riches.

Gates to the sanctuary of Dionysus at Delos. Dionysiac religion was passionate, fervent, excessive, and abandoned, embracing altered states and the creativity of chaos. It formed a complementary contrast to the Apollonian tradition of calm rationality and moderation.

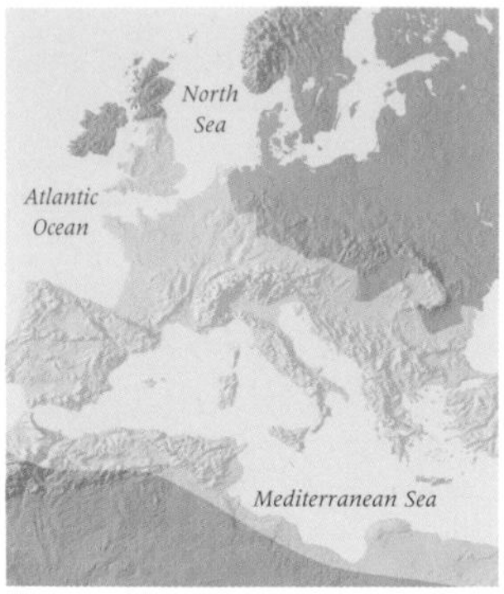

ROMAN RELIGION

ROMAN RELIGION IN THE PERIOD OF THE REPUBLIC (509–27 BCE) and early Empire (27 BCE–337 CE) was so diverse a phenomenon that it is impossible to say precisely when and where it began. It comprised many different strands, a reflection of the fact that, politically and socially, Rome was constantly changing during this period. Its development was aided by a process of adaptation of the Greek pantheon; and so the Roman Jupiter is the Indo-Aryan Dyaus-Pitr (the chief god in the pantheon of Vedism, *see pages 28 and 46–47*) and the Greek Zeus, while Venus, a horticultural deity, was identified with Aphrodite, the Greek goddess of beauty. This process of borrowing can be traced back to before the fifth century BCE, although native deities remained important. The woodland spirit Faunus became identified with Pan, Greek god of the countryside, but remained recognizably Italian. Indeed, flexibility was a characteristic of Roman religion.

As with Greek religion, the performance of cult acts was important. This was to preserve the *pax deorum* (the peace or favour of the gods) and while the Romans, like the Greeks, had no word for religion (the Latin word *religio* means 'scruple' or 'attention to detail', especially in ritual), the nearest equivalent, *cultus deorum,* means 'attendance on the gods'. Roman religion was closely associated with public life, to the extent that it overlapped with politics. Priests, who offered advice on religious matters and performed rituals and sacrifices, were a sub-group of the political elite; it was the Senate or Council that provided the link between the human and the divine, resolving religious problems and determining the significance of strange events such as androgynous births or showers of blood from the sky. Meetings of the assembly were always preceded by religious ritual in order to establish whether the gods approved of their being held, while augurs had the task of interpreting the omens. Roman gods, therefore, were not viewed as spectators but as deeply involved in Rome's changing fortunes. This can be seen in the Roman idea of a *bellum iustum* or 'just war', one fought with the support of the gods and under the protection of religious ritual.

This link between religion and public life is seen in the reign of the first Roman Emperor Augustus (ruled 27 BCE–14 CE) who assumed power after a turbulent period of political upheaval and civil war. He used religion effectively to strengthen his new regime, and his founding of a temple of Apollo on the Palatine Hill in Rome was appropriate because Apollo was the god of harmony and civilization, both apt for the new age. From the time of Augustus, much religious ritual became focused on the emperors themselves. This had a precedent since Romans traditionally believed that divine aid was crucial for success, and renowned figures such as Julius Caesar (c. 100–44 BCE) had claimed to be personally associated with the gods. In the time of the Empire, however, the emperor was even declared to *be* a god. All coins carried a

The Tiburtine Sibyl and the Emperor Augustus, painted in 1535 by the Venetian mannerist Paris Bordone (1500–1571). Julius Caesar and Augustus were the first to claim direct communication, and even kinship, with the gods for the rulers of Rome. Sibyls were female prophets who entered into trance-like states during which they transmitted the commands or wishes of the gods to mortals.

picture of the emperor's head and name while the reverse showed symbols illustrating his power and achievements. By the first and second centuries CE, the Empire covered a huge area, stretching from Britain to North Africa and Spain to Asia Minor, and worship of the emperor encouraged some degree of religious unity. A vast diversity of local practices remained, however, and there was frequently amalgamation of Roman and native deities.

The private side of religion was equally important, as seen in the worship of the Lares (ancestral spirits) and Penates (guardian spirits of the family larder). The latter were worshipped in conjunction with Vesta, goddess of the private and public hearth. There were also mystery cults with secret rites and initiations, such as that of Bacchus (equivalent to the Greek Dionysus) who attracted orgiastic worship. Others included those of Isis and Osiris from Egypt *(see page 227)*, and Mithras, a Persian deity of light and truth who became popular with soldiers and traders. These cults coexisted with the state religion, and yet when Christianity began to spread into the Empire at the beginning of the first century CE, early Christians suffered bouts of persecution. The answer to this may lie in their refusal to worship any god other than their own. Such refusal threatened the *pax deorum* and it was probably no accident that some persecutions coincided with disasters for which Christians could be blamed, such as the great fire of Rome in the reign of the emperor Nero in 64 CE. Despite this, Christianity gained ground and by the end of the fourth century had become the official religion of the Roman Empire. The influence of the Roman religions was still very apparent, however, especially in art where there was a conflation of Christian and pagan images, such as the Greek Orpheus being represented as the Good Shepherd.

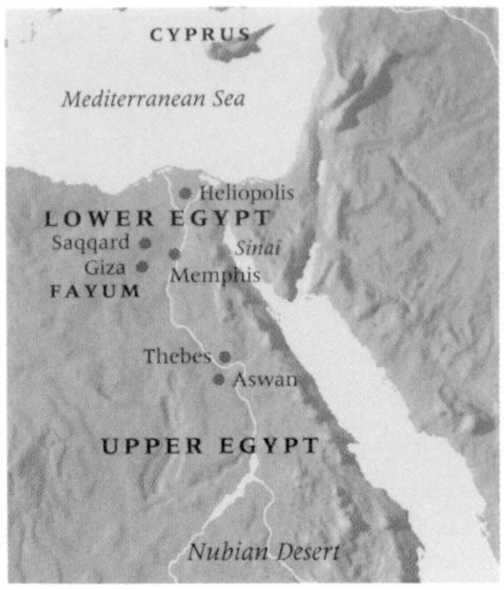

Manetho's Dynasties

The dynasties of Manetho do not always correspond with changes in the royal families. Dates are approximate.

Dynasties 1–2: 3100–2700 BCE (Archaic Period) Some signs of the cultic use of animals, later to become characteristic of religion in Egypt.

Dynasties 3–6: 2700–2200 (Old Kingdom) Major pyramid building at Saqqara and Gizeh/Giza; 'Pyramid Texts' (Fifth Dynasty).

Dynasties 7–10: 2200–2000 (First Intermediate Period) Conflict and division; rise of Thebes (Luxor).

Dynasties 11–12/13: 2000–1700 (Middle Kingdom) Control of Syro-Phoenician coast; execration texts curse Egypt's enemies; 'Coffin Texts'.

Dynasties 13/14–17: 1700–1540 (Second Intermediate Period) Conflict and division; infiltration of Lower Egypt by Asiatics under Manetho's 'Hyksos' *(see page 183)*.

Ancient Egyptian Religion

Egypt is a land strung like beads on the necklace of the Nile. An early Egyptian hymn says, 'Hail to you, O Nile, rushing from the earth and giving life to Egypt.' The 'beads' were held together by the Nile but originally by little else. Upper Egypt (the south, itself broken up by four major cataracts on the Nile) was surrounded by desert, while Lower Egypt (the Delta, to the north) was eventually opened to the Mediterranean world through trade and conquest. Upper Egyptian rulers conquered the Delta in about 3100 BCE and began to unify the country. The subsequent ruling houses were divided by the Greek historian Manetho into 30 dynasties, later increased to 31 *(see box)*.

To unify and hold the country together was the achievement of rulers known as *pharaohs* (meaning 'great house'); the first, according to Manetho, was Menes, the founder of the first dynasty *(see box, left)*. By the time of the Old Kingdom (2647–2124), the pharaohs were beginning to be regarded as divine – as God on earth and not simply, as in Mesopotamia *(see pages 228–229)*, the representatives of God on earth. They became, therefore, the focus of much Egyptian religion. Stone pyramids were built as the continuing and enduring (hence their massive size) home of the immortal god-kings after death.

A major unification strategy was to draw the gods of different regions together into a composite figure that would express the reality of the new alliance. This was effective because Egyptians were well known in the ancient world for being religious (the Greek historian Herodotus, writing in the fifth century BCE, observed, 'They are beyond measure religious, more than any other nation'). Thus, when Heliopolis ('city of the sun') became powerful during the Old Kingdom, its god Re rose to such prominence that by the fifth dynasty (2454–2311), the god-ruler was subservient to the priests of Re. The rulers subsequently moved their capital to Thebes under the god Amon but reconciled the priests of Heliopolis by creating the composite Amon-Re.

A more spectacular attempt to elevate a single god associated with the pharaoh was made by Amenhotep (Amenophis) IV (ruled 1353–1337) during the New Kingdom. His father Amenhotep III (ruled c. 1391–1353) built the great temple to Amon-Re at Luxor and also a shrine at Thebes to the new god Aten, the disc of the sun. Amenhotep IV decided to make Aten the one God from whom all other gods, including Amon-Re, derived their power; he changed his own name to Akhenaten, built a vast temple complex at Karnak devoted to Aten, and wrote the splendid hymn dedicated to Aten: 'You rise in perfection on the horizon of the sky, living Aten, who started life... You have made a far-off heaven in which to rise in order to observe everything you have made. Yet you are alone, rising in your manifestations as the Living Aten.'

The attempt failed. After Akhenaten's death the Karnak temples were destroyed, many of their huge stones being used to build temples to other gods. Many combined different manifestations of life: thus, Horus has a falcon's head, Hathor a cow's ears, Anubis an ibis's head, each with a human body. Aside from the centrali-zing cult focused on the pharaohs and the gods associated with them, popular religion sought the help of many other deities who would protect people in life – and in death.

Belief in immortality dominated, elaborated in the cult and myth of Isis and Osiris (Osiris was ruler of the underworld and judge of people after death; Isis was his sister-wife who sought him after his death and gave him new life); it was reinforced by the invention of mummi-fication during the third millennium BCE. Originally, reincarnation seems to have primarily involved the pharaohs (and their servants): the 'Pyramid Texts' *(see box, left)* contain rituals, hymns, prayers, and spells to secure the welfare of the pharaoh after death. But this belief extended to the wider population, based on the belief that pharaohs possessed *ka* (an indestructible principle of life contained in the body) which they dispensed to their subjects. Offerings made to the dead would mean they would not want to return to the body they had left, so to protect tombs and offerings, curses in 'Coffin Texts' were used to warn off robbers. One, from an Old Kingdom tomb, ends: 'I will seize his neck like a bird, and make all the living who are on earth fear the spirits who are in the far-off west.'

The consequences for morality and social order were great because the belief in immortality carried with it a belief in a final judgement based on *maat* (a just estimate of right or wrong living). As early as the sixth dynasty (2311–2140) this connection was clearly expressed, and it became even more apparent in the *Book of the Dead,* a New-Kingdom development of the Pyramid and Coffin Texts, preserved on papyrus. The 'negative confession' of Spell 125 gives a moving insight into the ideals of Egyptian life.

From the first millennium BCE, decline led to periods of foreign rule, initially by the Ethiopians, Persians, and Greeks, and then the Romans. Elements of ancient Egyptian religion persisted, as seen in the continued worship of Isis at Philae into the sixth century CE (thought by some to have influenced devotion to Christ's mother, Mary), and in the belief in many gods and a High God in pre-Islamic nomadic Arab communities *(see page 272)*.

Dynasties 18–20: 1550–1100 (New Kingdom) Ahmose expels Hyksos and begins an expansion that reaches the Euphrates; *The Book of the Dead*; Temple of Amon-Re at Luxor; Temple of Aten at Karnak (1350); major building by Rameses II (the Great); his defeat by the Hittites at Kadesh (c. 1299)

Dynasties 21–31: 1100–30 (Third Intermediate Period and Final Dynasties) Necho II is defeated by the Assyrians (606–605); Persian ruler Cambyses subjugates much of Egypt (525); Alexander the Great invades Egypt (332) and the Ptolemies are established as rulers; Egypt becomes a province of the Roman Empire (30), a situation that prevails until the accession of Constantine (324 CE).

The Great Pyramid at Gizeh (right), constructed c. 2500 BCE for the Old Kingdom pharaoh Khufu (Cheops) as a burial chamber. The pyramids next to it were built for Khufu's son Chafre (Chefren) and grandson Menkaure (Mycerinus). Old Kingdom pharaohs were considered gods.

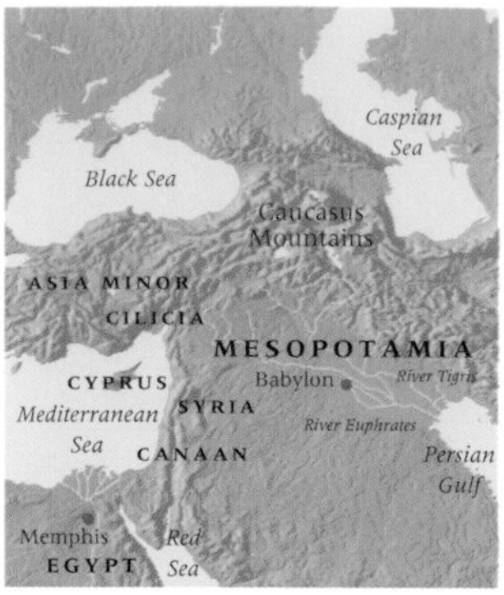

MESOPOTAMIA

MESOPOTAMIA (GREEK FOR 'BETWEEN RIVERS'), lying between the Tigris and the Euphrates, formed the western end of the 'Fertile Crescent', the inhabitable arc of land extending west through Syria and south into Palestine and Egypt. Home to many ancient civilizations, the most significant peoples of Mesopotamia were the Sumerians and the Babylonians from the south, the Assyrians from the north and later (in the sixth century BCE) by the Persians from the East (*see page 193*). However, there was much interaction between these people and numerous invasions from outside the territory, poorly served as it is by natural defences.

One of the 15,000 clay tablets, inscribed in cuneiform writing, found at Ebla, Syria. The tablets give a picture of Sumerian daily life and customs; some record the creation myths of the Sumerian religion.

The Sumerians formed the earliest influential civilization (third millennium BCE). Little was known about their culture until the 1970s when clay tablets, discovered at Ebla in present-day Syria, revealed a well organized city-state. The tablets recorded sections of several myths which showed that gods, such as Enki, were seen as the source of life and fertility. Enlil was the ruler of the gods but An (later Anu, 'sky') created human kings and delegated divine authority to them so that they played the part of gods in rituals of renewal and fertility. Even when the Babylonians under Hammarupi (1799–50 BCE) conquered most of Mesopotamia and the Sumerians lost their independence, their myths and rituals continued, especially the king's divine role. Such continuity was helped by the invention of cuneiform (Latin, 'wedge-shaped') writing, the characters being pressed into wet clay.

The name Babil first appeared during the Akkadian empire (2334–2193 BCE), becoming Bab-ilim ('Gate of God') then (plural) Bab-ilani, and was adapted into Greek as Babulon, hence Babylon. Hammarupi's empire was reduced after his death by Kassite invaders, then destroyed by the Hittites, a versatile people, under Mursili I (1620–1595). An extended period of conflict ensued, marked by the rise of the Assyrians in the north.

Assyrian independence and expansion began under Ashur-uballit (1363–28) and reached its height under Ashurbanipal II (883–859) and Shalmaneser III (858–824), when the empire reached the Mediterranean – receiving tribute from, among many, Jehu (c. 842–815), the king of Israel in 841, the subservience of Israel thenceforth being demanded. This could not always be enforced, but in 733/732 it was, and Galilee was made an Assyrian province (2 Kings 15:29). The last vestige of Israel's independence was ended by Shalmaneser V (726–722; 2 Kings 17:3–6). Judah survived, but only as a vassal of Assyria: attempts to break free against Sennacherib (704–681) led to a siege of Jerusalem (Sennacherib recorded that he caught the king Hezekiah 'like a bird in a cage') that ended with Judah paying an annual tribute.

The Assyrians were finally defeated and destroyed by the Babylonians. Babylonian revival had begun under Nebuchadnezzar I (1125–1104), although Assyria remained dominant in the north. In the ninth century BCE, a new coalition of tribes appeared in the south known as the Chaldeans. At first they paid tribute to the Assyrians but after the death of Adad-nirari III (783), Assyria became preoccupied with threats from the north. The Chaldeans took over Babylon which entered a long period of conflict with the Assyrians.

Assyria, threatened by the Medes from modern-day Iran and by the Chaldean Babylonians (the Assyrian capital, Nineveh, fell in 612) sought an alliance with Egypt. In 609, Josiah, King of Judah (647–609, *see page 191*), failed at Megiddo to stop the Egyptians who were on their way to reinforce the Assyrians, but his forces did weaken them. As a result, the Assyrians were defeated by Nebuchadnezzar II (604–562) at the decisive battle of Carchemish (605), the Babylonians gaining control of the whole region, besieging and capturing Jerusalem (588–586), and initiating the Jewish Exile *(see page 191)*. Nebuchadnezzar built spectacular palaces and temples in Babylon, including the Hanging Gardens, one of the Seven Wonders of the World, but thereafter Babylon declined and was overcome by the Persians under Cyrus II (559–530) who was welcomed as a liberator *(see page 193)*.

The religions of this long and turbulent period are impossible to summarize briefly. A consistent note was the belief that the gods of a conquered people had been defeated as well, a belief strongly denied by the prophets of the Exile (particularly in the book of Isaiah 40–55). Babylonia produced important texts, most notable being the Babylonian epics *(Enuma Elish* and *Atra-hasis,* which deal with creation, the latter following the sequence of human creation to the Flood, as in Genesis 1–9; and *Gilgamesh,* named after the legendary Sumerian king, which includes an account of the Flood), the Babylonian Wisdom literature *(Lulul Bel Nemeqi* and *The Babylonian Theodicy,* which deal with the undeserved suffering of the righteous), and the Law Code of Hammarupi. Babylonian ziggurats were stepped towers reaching to the gods in heaven, but there was little sense that they were steps leading to immortality. In strong contrast to the ancient Egyptian civilization, where belief in immortality led to the beginnings of enduring architecture in stone, they believed that nothing survived death except a vague shadow. As the historian Giedion put it, 'Architecturally, Mesopotamian tombs were without significance. Yet this was the period when the great pyramids of Cheops, Chephren, and Mycerinus were storming the heavens.'

CHRISTIANITY

DAVID L. EDWARDS

CHRISTIANITY

JESUS WAS A DEVOUT JEW born into a carpenter's family. The date of his birth is unknown, but it was probably a little before the beginning of the 'Christian' or 'common' era as calculated during the sixth century. His early years were spent in Nazareth, a village in Galilee in the north of modern Israel. When he was about 30 years old he was baptized in the River Jordan by John, an austere preacher, who demanded a cleansing of the heart in preparation for God's imminent judgement of the world.

In the midst of political and religious unrest *(see page 195)* Jesus began his own mission, but his emphasis was on the merciful love of God, who to him was *Abba* (Aramaic for 'Father'). Now a homeless wanderer, he gave joyful promises to the poor, treated women with a special sensitivity, and ate and associated with outcasts such as prostitutes and tax collectors. He assured listeners that their sins would be forgiven if they turned to God in repentance; there was no need for ritual purification followed by a sacrificial offering in the Temple.

Christ Addressing a Kneeling Woman, an early work (c. 1546) by the Venetian artist Paolo Veronese (c. 1528–1588). The woman may be Mary Magdalene or the woman suffering from 'an issue of blood' cured when she touched Christ's robe. Either way, it emphasizes the prominent role played by women in Christianity.

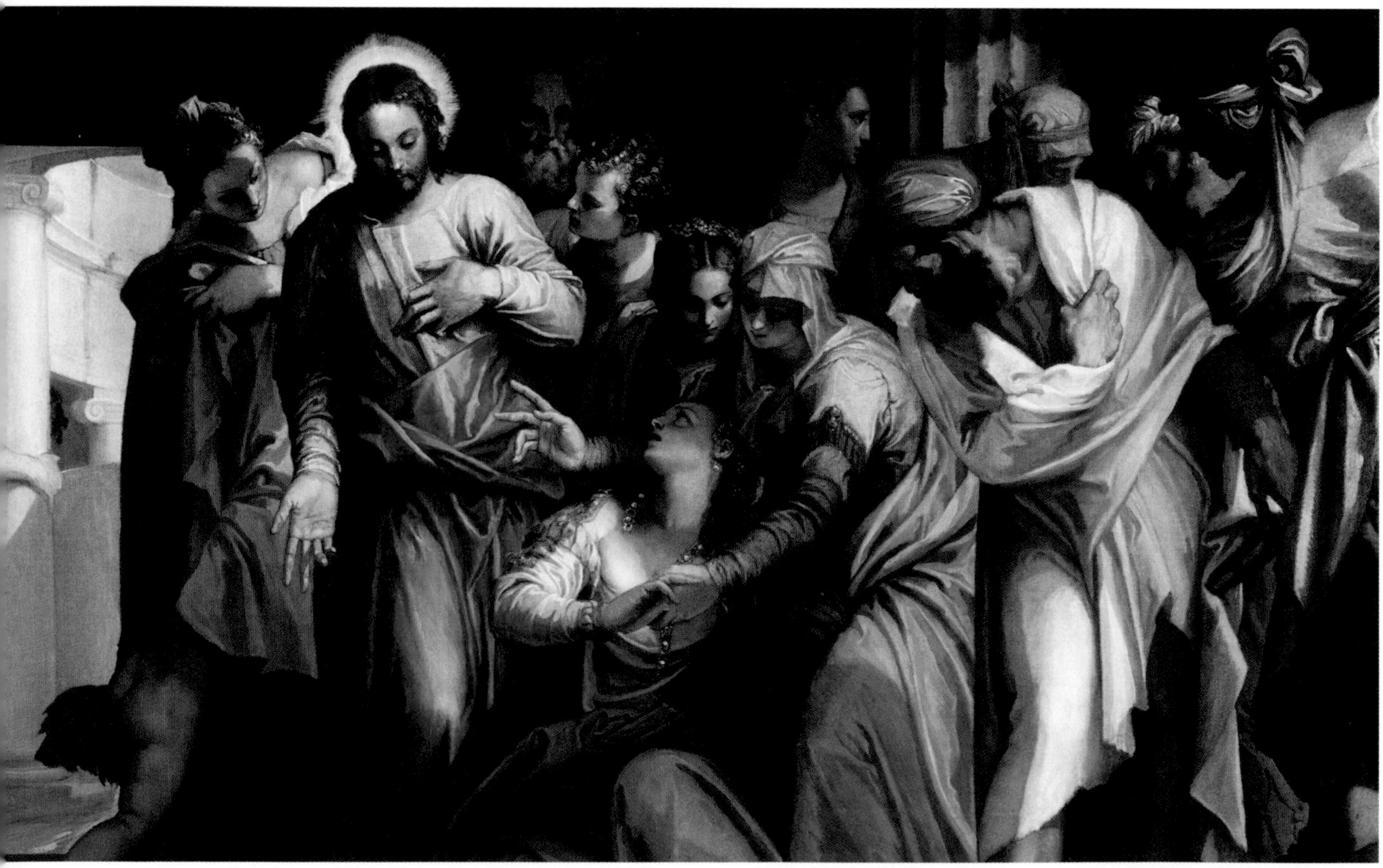

With his infectious faith in the power of their parent-like God, Jesus healed some of the mentally or physically sick – even on the Sabbath, which in the Jewish Law was to be kept as a day of rest apart from essential work. He told parables (very short stories, mostly based on rural life) and was equally remembered for succinct, sharp sayings, with the promise or warning that the 'kingdom of God' was beginning here and now. He claimed that these astonishing and controversial works and words came not from himself, but from God working through him.

He did not advocate rebellion against the Roman Empire but did demand a total revolution in daily life. The right response to the 'good news' he brought would be a life overflowing with love and generosity, in trusting dependence on God whose own generous love was breaking through all barriers. He did not issue detailed laws – he communicated a vision.

Jesus attracted followers, both men and women, and he picked twelve men to be his apostles (messengers); he looked forward to a new community, created by God as the twelve tribes of Israel had been, but not confined to Jews. He spoke of himself as 'the Son of Man' – in Jewish Scripture, one who must die (Psalms and the Book of Job), but who will be vindicated by God (Daniel, 7). He knew that he must suffer, like the 'Servant of the Lord' also found in the scriptures (Isaiah, 53).

Probably in the spring of 30 CE, Jesus came to Jerusalem during the festival of Passover (*see page 186*), which celebrated the past liberation of Israel from slavery in Egypt. When he entered the city, he claimed that his authority came from God, and some hailed him as Messiah, the hoped-for new liberator. In the Temple he challenged the authorities and disturbed the profitable trade that went on there during the pilgrimage. He warned his disciples that his own martyrdom was near, and at his last supper with them told them to repeat his actions in the future, washing each other's feet in humility, and consuming bread and wine in remembrance of his death and as a sign of the new covenant (i.e., a New Testament; *for covenants, see page 187*), gained by the sacrifice of himself.

One of his apostles, Judas Iscariot, revealed to the Temple authorities how they could quietly arrest him. When examined by the senior priests, Jesus did not accept their authority, and he was handed over to the Roman governor, Pontius Pilate, who also regarded him as a troublemaker. He was put to death by crucifixion, the agonizing and utterly degrading punishment which the Romans inflicted on rebels.

Despite this, some of Jesus' followers were sure that God had raised him from the dead and that he had appeared to them as the living 'Lord'. The exact nature of the resurrection cannot be recovered historically beyond the fact that those who had the experience certainly thought it real. It was this unique event, the beginning of the coming of the kingdom of God, that gave them new courage and spiritual power.

The Accounts and Impact of Jesus's Life

Jesus himself left nothing in writing, but countless books were to be written about him. The earliest surviving documents are letters, especially those of Paul. Accounts of Jesus's words and acts, and of how and why he was crucified, were made early, culminating in the Gospels (Good News): Mark was probably the earliest (c. 70 CE), used by Matthew and Luke for their narratives. John's gospel, while adding other traditions, followed the same pattern, and reflected the developing belief that Jesus could be called, in Greek, God's own *logos* (self-expression). The carpenter who had preached for a brief period – probably for not much more than one year – was tortured to death as a criminal, yet (as many non-Christians would agree) he became the most influential figure in the history of the world, certainly of the Western world. For Christians, to say that would be an understatement; to them, he is the one Saviour from sin and the one incarnation (embodiment) of God in a human life. The insistence of Judaism, and later of Islam, on One God is shared, but what lies within that 'Oneness' for Christians is a reality made known as Father, Son, and Holy Spirit – a belief expressed in the doctrine of the Trinity (*see page 240*). Christians believe that they enter eternal life through a relationship with Jesus, obeying his command, 'Follow me'.

St Paul by Etienne Parrocel (Il Romain) (1740s). Paul was the man who spread the Messianic message further than any other disciple. Born a Jew and a Roman citizen c. 10 CE, Paul (then known as Saul) became a zealous Jewish scholar, and his fanaticism so impressed the High Priest of Jerusalem that he appointed him to hunt out and arrest followers of Jesus. After his dramatic conversion, he suffered much persecution himself but poured his charismatic energy into formulating Christianity into a religion for all.

PAUL THE APOSTLE

Paul has been accused of making Christianity different from the faith Jesus had intended, but his own claim was that he was a servant and apostle of Jesus the *Christos* (the Greek term for 'Messiah', which became 'Christ' in English). Paul's life had been shattered and remade by an experience on the road to Damascus (c. 35 CE) when he had encountered Jesus after Jesus's resurrection. To his new Lord he dedicated all his talents and energies – but he did not merely repeat what Jesus had said. Jesus (his human name was still used) was known to have been crucified, yet he was seen immediately to be equal to God and worthy of worship.

A cultured man, brought up in Tarsus (in modern Turkey) as a Roman citizen, he was a Jewish scholar trained in Jerusalem as a strictly orthodox Pharisee. He now taught in circumstances very different from Jesus's villages in Galilee. In cities around the eastern Mediterranean, Paul developed a Jesus-centred interpretation of the Hebrew Bible and related it to problems of beliefs and behaviour, writing letters that came to be treated as holy scripture. His first base for this work was Antioch in northern Syria where the followers of Jesus were first called *Christianoi*. There Paul confronted Peter, the most prominent of the original apostles. At first, Peter had been willing to share meals with Christians who were Gentiles (non-Jews), but he withdrew after advice from James, the brother of Jesus, who now presided over the Christian community in Jerusalem. The warning came because some foods acceptable to Gentiles were unclean by Jewish religious ethics. Paul did not object to Christians who were Jews maintaining Jewish practices – as Peter did and as they did in Jerusalem – and he took a pride in his own Jewish heritage, hoping that one day 'all Israel' (the whole Jewish nation) would be saved. But he was convinced that Gentile Christians had no obligation to keep the Law of Moses, which would mean being circumcised if male and refusing to eat food deemed unclean in that Law. Peter, he insisted, ought to eat what was on the table in fellowship with Christians who remained Gentiles. By that stand, Paul, the 'apostle to the Gentiles', made Christianity a religion open to everyone – and, by expounding carefully what he believed, he made Christianity a religion full of profound arguments about the significance of Christ.

To him, faith was not essentially about accepting a community's traditions, nor was it about believing that a guess one had made was probably right. It was deciding to put one's trust in someone known: Jesus the Lord. Those brought into union with Christ by baptism were justified (treated as good) by God before being filled with the Holy Spirit (divine energy). This gift of God might induce 'speaking in tongues' (in a trance-like state) but, more importantly, it would inspire the calm virtues of love and joy, peacefulness and patience.

The new life 'in Christ', spiritually united with the Lord, would be lived in communion (partnership) with other Christians in a community that was the 'Body of Christ', carrying on Christ's work in the world. Christ did God's work with a unique power and was associated by Paul with God, although not in any sense which contradicted the Jewish belief in One God. His willingness to die because he loved sinners proclaimed God's own love and provided a means for humans to become God's friends. After Christ's self-sacrifice there was no need to sacrifice animals. That victory-through-death made the decisive change, like purchasing freedom for a slave (redemption). It was recalled whenever Christians shared bread and drank wine together with their faith fixed on their Lord, and whenever, at the beginning of his or her new life, a convert went down into the water during baptism. Baptism had its origins in the Jewish acceptance of a convert and in Christianity it came to represent rebirth, the washing away of sins, and the gift of the Holy Spirit.

To Paul, the small groups of Christians who met in houses were the Church in that place (he used the Greek work *ekklesia*, meaning a 'citizens' assembly', rather than *kuriakon*, the root of 'church', meaning 'belonging to the Lord'). They were nothing less than parts of God's 'new creation'. Jews and Gentiles, men and women, slaves and the free, educated or not, they were bound together by a faith stronger than any tensions between them. In spite of their human weaknesses, they were signs pointing to the future glory of God's kingdom; death should not dismay them. It seems that both Peter and Paul may have been executed in Rome in 64 CE.

The Words and Teachings of Jesus

In practice, have Christians largely ignored the teachings of Jesus, or have they applied them to living in different situations? Jesus's words reach us through the Christians of the first century. All four of the gospels that are regarded as authoritative (there are also several apocryphal gospels) give emphasis to Jesus's death and resurrection, but they also include his message, showing why he was crucified but in the end was victorious.

Scholars use the initial Q to refer to material collected before the gospels were written (abbreviated from *Quelle*, German for 'source'), which was used in common by *Matthew* and *Luke*. Here Jesus is a countryman who loves nature (including wild flowers) but teaches that what God is doing through him is greater than anything seen before. He is as homeless as foxes or birds but is also the 'Son of God' who reveals the character of God 'the Father'. The kingdom of God is beginning, with miraculous episodes of healing showing that a new start is offered to all. There must be complete trust in God; hesitation, anxiety, and hatred must be forgotten.

The gospel according to *Mark* (c. 65 CE?) is a stern challenge to follow Jesus as he goes in loneliness to suffering and death. The message echoes Q, with minor differences. The gospel ends with the words 'they were afraid'; this was a time when professing Christianity could bring hardship and death.

A quarter of the gospel according to *Matthew* (c. 75 CE?) is unique to this account and mostly concerns the relationship between Jesus and other Jews. The Hebrew Bible is quoted with reverence but some contemporary teachers are denounced as 'blind guides'. Jesus teaches a new morality and founds a new community. This is good news for the spiritually hungry, the pure in heart, the gentle, the merciful, and the peacemakers. The Sermon on the Mount teaches how to live in God's kingdom. The approach presents Jesus as the Messiah of the Jews, as the fulfilment of Hebrew prophecy, pointing the way to a new life in the early Christian Church.

A third of the gospel according to *Luke* (c. 80 CE?) is Luke's alone and concentrates on the good relationships Jesus developed with women and foreigners, his sympathy with outcasts and the poor, and the new power brought to the humble by the Holy Spirit. Here are the famous stories of the Prodigal Son and the Good Samaritan. A second volume written by Luke, the *Acts of the Apostles*, tells how this message began to spread throughout the Roman Empire. Both works point to the broad scope and potential of the religion.

The gospel according to *John* (c. 90 CE?) is unlike the other gospels. Jesus's speeches are long and much of what he says is about himself. Miracles are presented as signs of his glory, which is divine and therefore older than the world. Pharisees are denounced because they do not believe, but the Jews are shown making up their minds for or against. *John* stands further away from the historical Jesus, a Jew who said much more about God the Father than about himself and who was not eager to be called 'Messiah' because he knew that he must suffer before the victory of the kingdom of God. In *John*, it is significant that Thomas, who at first doubted the resurrection, called Jesus 'my Lord and my God', a title claimed by Roman emperors. Here are many expressions of a mature devotion to Jesus as the Word of God. He makes the eternal Father visible; he brings light to the blind, joy to the sad, and life to the dead. He makes the community of his followers clean and confident as they begin to share his glory. He brings them into a life which is already eternal because it will never end.

In different times and places, Christians have responded in diverse ways to Jesus, and the distinct pictures of him in the gospels have found favour accordingly. Those who feel his impact have found themselves attracted, fascinated, challenged, uplifted, and changed. To them, Jesus is human yet uniquely open to and inspired by God, so that in him the eternal God comes near. This faith has made some Christians outstanding saints while most have striven unsuccessfully in much of their lives but have been given a reason to hope.

St Matthew, apostle and evangelist, and author of the gospel that opens the New Testament. A collection of the sayings of Jesus is also traditionally ascribed to him.

THE EARLY CHRISTIANS

The triumph of the Christian Church in the Roman Empire was remarkable. In 303 CE, Christians probably represented less than a tenth of the Empire's population and, in his effort to restore unity under a strong government, the Emperor Diocletian (245–313) made them the target of systematic persecution. Yet in 313 the religion was declared lawful and by 325 the Emperor Constantine (c. 285–337) had announced that he owed his victory in the recent civil wars of his time to Christ's patronage, had strengthened his position by becoming the patron of the Catholic bishops, and was presiding over the first of the great Councils of the Church. Christianity was now given great privileges and was well on its way to becoming the Empire's only official religion, a step taken under Theodosius the Great, Emperor from 379 to 395.

Why did Constantine make this dramatic change? According to later reports, in a dream before the Battle of Milvian Bridge (312) that led to his becoming joint Emperor, he was told to fight under the cross (*'in hoc signo, vinces'* – 'in this sign, conquer'). Politically, part of the explanation is that Constantine, who was just as ambitious as Diocletian, saw that the Church's support could be almost as useful as the army's loyalty. But why did he choose Christianity, which in its earlier years had been regarded by government and public alike as a conspiracy against society? Why did he adopt the cross, the sign of a criminal's tortured execution? And why did this religion, which had been adopted by a minority with no hope of becoming anything else before the end of the world, prove capable of becoming the mother of Europe?

THE STRENGTH OF THE CHURCH In the 360s, the Emperor Julian (332–363), who was attempting to undo Constantine's work, urged that the traditional religion (called 'pagan' by Christians) must be revived by imitating the features which had brought the Church success. There must be leaders to match the bishops, who had emerged as the chief pastors and teachers of groups of local churches. Clearer authority must be given to the stories about the gods, so that they could rival the Christians' Bible. Worship in the temples must involve the people more, using sermons and hymns. Charitable work must be more extensive, for the Christians were active in caring for others as well as for their own sick. And educated non-Christians must work out a theology; it was not enough to accept conventions superficially while being deeply sceptical about the old gods.

Julian had been a Christian and knew that the Church's strengths had not been equalled. The teaching of Jesus was recorded or interpreted in the 27 documents which the Church had gradually added to the authoritative Jewish Bible as the New 'Testament' (the new agreement between God and humans). That still left room for some disagreements, but a firm interpretation came from the bishops. Their greatest struggle was with the Gnostics (Knowers), who linked Jesus with a series of emanations from God and with claims about the soul's origins and destiny, which could be understood only by a few. The bishops' teaching was about the one Creator of the real world and about the one Saviour who had been truly human. The all-involving worship which the bishops led was more than the sacrifice of an animal and was offered by more than an elite. The sharing of bread and wine in the Eucharist

Martyrs in the Catacombs, 1855, by Jules Eugene Lenepveu (1819–1898). During the early years of Christianity many believers were killed for their faith, or their refusal to renounce it. Some of them came to be regarded as saints; it came to be believed by many that saints were able to intercede with God on behalf of people on earth.

(Thanksgiving) was the whole Church's celebration of the triumph of the crucified and crowned Christ, and took place every Sunday. And from such worship flowed the new life of the 'new people', with some innovations in morality: baby girls must not be left to die; like women, men must not have sex outside marriage; divorce is wrong, so is luxury, so is violence, and so is hatred.

Also striking was the combination of this new life with intellectual work. The Church produced thinkers and writers (Origen of Alexandria, c. 185–c.254, was the greatest early Christian scholar and theologian) who developed Paul's restatement of what had originally been a Jewish faith. They entered into dialogue with other movements of thought in the Empire, particularly Greek philosophy with its emphasis on the eternal, and Roman law with its demand for precise language. Eloquent defences of Christianity were addressed to the ruling emperor.

Equally impressive was the bravery of the martyrs (meaning 'witnesses'). They refused to offer any token of worship to the Empire's many gods or to the images of the emperors. Men and women, young and old, slaves and their owners suffered cruel deaths in public and, as Tertullian (160–225) put it, 'we grow just as much as we are mown down by you, the seed is the blood of the Church', often cited as 'the blood of the martyrs is the seed of the Church'. But the bishops insisted that less courageous Christians who became traitors or were guilty of other serious sins must be allowed to repent and, after penitence, rejoin the faithful. Under its bishops, the Church was 'Catholic' (universal), with one hopeful message for all.

Thus even in its early years Christianity had developed clear leadership, sacred texts, uplifting worship, and an ability to appeal both to the educated and to the underprivileged. And, perhaps most decisively, death was not feared.

BYZANTINE ORTHODOXY

In 330 CE, seven years before his deathbed baptism, Constantine decreed that Byzantium, a town on the sea dividing Europe and Asia (now Istanbul in Turkey), was to be the new capital of the Roman Empire. Renamed Constantinople, it was unequivocally a Christian city. In the early fifth century, the western half of the Empire was invaded by various northern tribes; the city of Rome was sacked by Visigoths in 410. In little more than 50 years, the western empire was destroyed. But the eastern (Byzantine) empire survived into the fifteenth century. A society of great wealth, for centuries it was the scene of an elaborate attempt to make a single form of Christianity dominant over the whole of life. The idea was that the Emperor's chief duty was to support the Church and the Church's duty was to worship and lead a holy life according to orthodoxy (correct beliefs).

Orthodoxy was defined by councils of bishops (greatly influenced by the reigning emperor) who had developed the earlier links between Christian faith, Greek philosophy, and Roman law. Faith was now expressed in philosophical terms and the definitions were adopted by the imperial government and made compulsory for all. Large numbers of Christians rejected what Church and state tried to impose, but the creed (summary of belief) which emerged from these councils has been accepted very widely and is still used.

Constantinople, named for the Emperor Constantine, besieged by Turkish ships of the Ottoman Empire just before it fell in 1453. The city had been the eastern capital of the Roman Empire since the fourth century CE, becoming the sole seat of imperial power after the fall of Rome, its western twin, in 410.

A council in Nicaea near Constantinople (325) had decided that, in eternity, Christ is God the Son, 'of one substance' with God the Father and not merely a part of God's creation of the universe. This was rejected by a heretical group, the Arians, and when the 'barbarian' peoples conquered much of the old Roman Empire, for many years they accepted Christianity only in its Arian form. A council in Constantinople (381) defined the doctrine of the Holy Trinity: although one in substance, God is also three 'persons', Father, Son, and Holy Spirit. A council in Ephesus (431) decided that, since Christ is 'one person', his mother Mary should be venerated as the Mother of God, and a council in Chalcedon (449) agreed that after becoming human in his 'incarnation', Christ had two 'natures', still being divine but also perfectly human. These decisions were nevertheless rejected by many. After 431, Nestorians (who believed that the divine and human natures were separate within the incarnate Christ) fled to Persia and from there spread out to India and China. After 449, Monophysites (who believed that the incarnate Christ had only one nature, both divine and human) formed the main Churches in Egypt, Ethiopia, Syria, and Armenia. But the Orthodox Church was not shaken by these rejections, and in 681 a council decided that the incarnate Christ had two wills as well as two natures.

THREATS TO EMPIRE AND FAITH Such complications and controversies damaged Christian unity, with the result that soon after the death of the prophet Muḥammad in 632, Arab armies swiftly conquered Egypt and much of the rest of the old Roman Empire in the east of Africa *(see page 278)*, welcomed at first by Christians who thought that their domination would be preferable to rule by Constantinople. Some 400 years later the Turks began their advance, capturing Constantinople in 1453. Both Arabs and Turks owed much of their high morale to the relative clarity of their religion, Islam, with its practical teaching about obedience to One God.

Orthodoxy and the Byzantine Empire were threatened from another quarter. Its official version of Christianity was markedly different from the Catholicism that prevailed in Western Europe, centred on Rome. For a time, Byzantine emperors had been able to treat Roman bishops as their subjects, but in 1054 a new relationship was initiated when a representative of Rome visited and denounced Constantinople. In 1204 came a far more serious breach, when an army of so-called crusaders from the West occupied the city, looted it, and established a short-lived 'Latin' state. In 1274 and again in 1439 representatives of Orthodoxy accepted the authority of the pope (the bishop of Rome and head of the Roman Catholic Church), but it was only in the futile hope that the West would give military aid.

Orthodoxy was not doomed to total defeat, however. On the contrary, its survival after the end of the Empire showed that its spiritual strength had always come through its worship. The Liturgy (its form of the Eucharist) made the faithful feel close to the saints, represented in church and home by sacred paintings or icons. Indeed, people can feel close to heaven itself, for the emphasis in Orthodoxy has always been on the admission of the faithful to a share in the eternal glory of God. In monasteries, monks have been able to progress far in mental prayer and mystical contemplation, and by tradition only monks can become bishops. In theology, Athanasius (c. 296–373), bishop of Alexandria, stated what became the key doctrine: God the Son became human in order that humans might be immortal, even divine.

This spiritual strength kept the Orthodox Church alive during the long Turkish occupation of the Balkans and then again under communist rule. The Church of Greece has remained Orthodox and its customs lie at the heart of the traditional culture which has travelled with the many Greeks who have emigrated to North America and Australia. The suffering and victory of the Russian Church make an even more memorable story *(see page 242)*. Although Orthodoxy possesses elaborate doctrines, ceremonies, rituals, and buildings, its heartfelt prayers can be very simple, as in the Jesus Prayer which recites repeatedly: 'Lord Jesus Christ, Son of God, have mercy on me, a sinner'. Thus a tradition that is defiantly old-fashioned has survived into the modern world.

Russian Orthodoxy

In the 890s, a mission from Constantinople to central Europe led by the monks Cyril and Methodius was undertaken using the indigenous Slavonic language, in both spoken and written form. This innovation – Greek was the natural language of the Orthodox Church – helped the Slavs and Bulgars, who had settled in the Balkans, to accept Orthodoxy, and in the 980s it facilitated the conversion of some of the Rus people, led by the prince of Kiev, Vladimir.

Gradually, over many centuries, the whole of Russia – a vast area – was united politically and religiously with Moscow as its centre, and Russian Orthodoxy developed its own character. The tsar had even more power than the Byzantine emperor and the Church became even richer. Two reforming rulers, Peter the Great (1672–1725) and Catherine the Great (1729–1796), confiscated much of the Church's wealth and subjected it to strict control by the state, but right up to the triumph of Communism after the Russian revolution in 1917, it seemed that the alliance between Church and state would last forever, in control of a fervently devout people. But Russian Orthodoxy was not marked only by submission to power. There was also a tradition in the Church of closeness to the peasantry and the urban poor, such that humble monks and parish priests showed great sympathy for their hard lives. This was echoed in the nineteenth century when two great novelists, Dostoevsky and Tolstoy, wrote with force about the suffering of the people and advocated a religion in which the chief virtue would be compassion. And often the people worked out their own tough faith with love of the Church's traditions.

Orthodoxy survived when almost all of the 57,000 churches open in 1914 were closed by the communist government, tens of thousands of clergy were shot or imprisoned, the Church was forbidden to engage in any public activity except traditional worship, atheist propaganda was officially sponsored, and believers faced discrimination. Lenin, Stalin, and Khrushchev presided over persecution more severe than any other in the history of Christianity.

After this time of suffering in silence, 1,000 years of Russian Orthodoxy were celebrated in the 1990s with the knowledge that the Church had outlived Soviet communism. A regime that had seemed overwhelmingly strong, and which had been confident that Christianity could be replaced rapidly by a secular substitute for religion, had crumbled.

The tower and onion domes of St Basil's Cathedral, Moscow, the symbol of Russian Orthodoxy. Commissioned by Ivan the Terrible, it was completed in 1560.

CHRISTIANS IN INDIA

Did one of the apostles who had been commissioned by Jesus to carry his message become an evangelist and martyr in India? An old tradition says that this was the fate of St Thomas, and although proof is lacking, some 2,000 years later about a million Indians are called Malabar or Thomas Christians because they proudly trace their religious origins to that mission. However, many historians say that Christianity probably reached India through traders from Egypt and the Arabian Gulf *(see page 48)*.

For centuries Christianity was confined to communities near the coast in the south, but a wider impact was made in India by European traders and rulers from the sixteenth century onwards. Many Christian missionaries have been fascinated by India, the most religious country on earth. They have hoped that Christ would be universally accepted as the answer to India's prayers, but most of the conversions have come from groups with no great love for the social system associated with Hinduism: the badly underprivileged, such as tribal peoples, or low castes confined to menial jobs. And despite much good work done by Christian schools, colleges, and hospitals, there have been special factors hindering the growth of the religion in India. It took many years before the Portuguese colonialists based in Goa would let the papacy take charge of Indian Catholicism. Right up until Independence was achieved in 1947, there were losses as well as gains in the Protestants' links with British rule; and, above all, the arrogance of 'Christian' Europeans made a poor example to follow (Gandhi said that he objected not to Jesus but to Christians). However, the small group of more enlightened, receptive Europeans who had contact with India were impressed by the country's religious heritage, and Christianity's presence became more thoroughly Indian. When sensitive, Christianity has contributed to the nation in two vital ways: in the emphasis it lays on the unity and holiness of God, and in giving examples of practical concern for the welfare of the sick and the poor, women, and the young, as God's children.

The 1991 census suggested that Christians made up about 2.5 per cent of the population. About half of these were Roman Catholics, and the rest were made up of Syrian Orthodox Christians (originally from the Middle East) or, more numerously, Protestants belonging either to United Churches formed since Independence or to independent congregations. The future of Christianity in India seems to depend on its relationships with the majority Hindu traditions.

Indian Christians worship before the cross of St Thomas, the doubting apostle traditionally believed to have brought Christianity to the continent.

THE CONVERSION OF EUROPE

The western half of the Roman Empire collapsed largely because of invasions by peoples on the move, hungry for treasure and land. Then the Arabs swept through North Africa and Spain; they were halted in the middle of France but not before 732 (an account of that battle includes the first recorded use of the word 'Europeans'). And in the period 400–800, the weather was icy and devils seemed everywhere.

In response, much of the theology at this time was drawn from Augustine (354–430), bishop of Hippo in North Africa. He wrote *The City of God* when Rome had been occupied and looted by 'barbarians' in 410; he saw the Church rising from the ruins, human and therefore not perfect, but with a truth revealed by God in the Bible. To him, this was a truth about sinfulness from birth – indeed, from the parents' intercourse – and hopefulness through the undeserved gift of eternal life.

Also very influential was the Rule to guide monasteries drawn up in Italy by the monastic leader Benedict (c. 480–c.550). Benedictine monks became missionaries to non-Christian lands, they conserved non-Christian literature in their libraries, they taught Latin to the young, they improved agriculture – but all other work was subordinated to the Christian worship of God.

In 597, a mission from Rome landed in England, sent by one of the greatest of all the popes, Gregory I (c. 540–604). Slowly the Anglo-Saxons who had occupied England became Christians, and England sent its own missionaries to the Netherlands, Germany, and Scandinavia, always emphasizing the pope's authority. Ireland was converted by a succession of missionaries beginning with Patrick in the fifth century, and in turn sent missionaries to Scotland and other countries.

Christianity was legally recognized by Constantine I (c. 288–337 CE); the first ecumenical council was held at Nicea in 325, and what had been a persecuted, minority sect soon became the state religion of the Roman Empire. By the time the Empire had crumbled, Christianity was a significant unifying factor in a fragmented Europe.

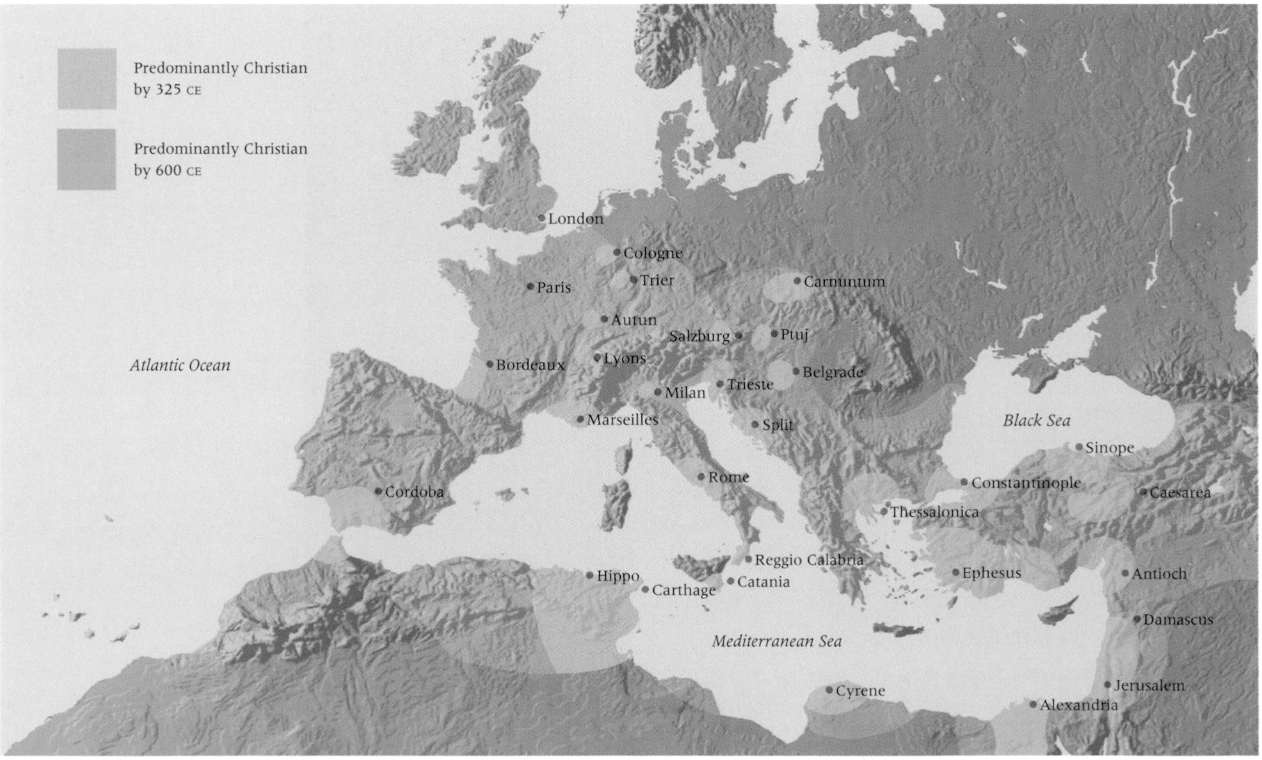

CHRISTIAN KINGS AND EMPERORS Other decisive moves were made when the most powerful rulers in France and Spain accepted the Catholic form of Christianity: Clovis (?466–511), the king of the Franks, was baptized during the 490s, and in Spain King Recared abandoned the Arian heresy in 587. The cooperation between the Church and the state came to a climax in the reign of Charlemagne (?742–814), who extended the power of the Franks over a wide area of Europe, with its centre in Germany. In 800 he was crowned by the pope as the first Holy Roman Emperor. He led a campaign to raise standards in Church life and in education – and, more brutally, a campaign to compel the Saxons to be baptized. In 962, a Saxon king, Otto I (912–973), was crowned Holy Roman Emperor. He and later emperors influenced the conversions of kings and peoples to the east, first the Poles and then the Magyars (in Hungary), and finally the Lithuanians when that kingdom was united with Poland in 1385.

The fact that this spread of Christianity in Europe needed such time before it was completed proves the strength of the local pagan religions. The expansion relied in part on the use of force; the Teutonic Knights, for example, used force without hesitation for their long 'crusade' against the Wends living along the Baltic Sea. But another part of the story is that Christians moved east as settlers, in a colonial expansion. A third factor was the prestige of *Romanitas*, the legacy of the Roman Empire in all the arts and crafts of civilization. 'Barbarian' rulers and peoples had to acknowledge *Romanitas* as a superior culture and richer way of life, and they entered into that heritage as they entered the Church. The Vikings, for example, had been ruthless pirates, but when they settled in new lands as farmers and traders they quietly accepted the Christianity of the Franks and the Anglo-Saxons; the conversion of their Scandinavian homelands included crusades as well as more peaceful means of conversion.

This reception of Christianity as the faith of Europe was made easier by the willingness of the Church to develop in a style not entirely different from the paganism that was slowly being replaced. Rulers were promised victory and wealth, and humbler folk were allowed to be religious in a manner that might be called superstitious. Pagan temples and festivals were adapted to Christian worship. The creation of saints – exemplary Christians who could be invoked in prayer – redoubled, and after their deaths their relics (bones) received much pious attention. Many stories of miracles were spread, and, after the recital of Latin words by the priest in the Eucharist (now called the Mass, after the concluding words of dismissal in Latin: *ite, missa est*), the bread was said to be changed physically into the body of God the Son.

Very gradually, the 'parish' churches, built for local use, enabled peasants to glimpse a mysterious glory amid their poverty. This adjustment to the habits of a society around the church also produced the so-called 'Celtic saints' of Ireland, Scotland, and Wales: humble people who were loved because they were rich in love, in cultures that valued heroic devotion, courage and simplicity. But the main emphasis was on power: the power of God, the power of Christian rulers, the power of bishops and priests, and the stirrings of power in a continent that had been poverty-stricken but was now gaining confidence as 'Christendom'.

St Patrick (c. 390–c. 460), now the patron saint of Ireland, was born in Britain but sent to Ireland as a missionary bishop. He is the subject of many myths and legends in which he is described as a miracle-worker.

Norse Religion

The origins of Norse religion are thought to lie in the Scandinavian Bronze Age (c. 1600–450 BCE) because the earliest figures of gods and goddesses date from this period. No written sources survive to tell us what language the worshippers spoke, and there is a gap in our knowledge after 450 BCE until the third to the sixth centuries CE (the Migration Period). At this time, there was a movement westwards and northwards of Celtic and Germanic peoples who brought new religious cults and symbols to Scandinavia. It was then that the cult of Wodan or Odin, the fierce god of death and battle, flourished. Paganism survived for several centuries in Scandinavia during the Viking Age. As the Scandinavians ventured further afield in the ninth and tenth centuries, they took the cults of their heathen gods with them. The evidence is fragmentary, but much can be learned from the *Poetic Edda*, a collection of Old Norse verse set down in the tenth and eleventh centuries, and the *Prose Edda* of Snorri Sturluson, a famous Icelandic poet and historian of the thirteenth century.

Viking religion was polytheistic and Odin was the chief of the pantheon, which was known as the *Aesir*. The religion is thought to have helped the Vikings understand a harsh and inhospitable world with long and cruel winters. Central to Viking mythology was the struggle against the forces of darkness and chaos that threatened *Midgard*, the realm of human beings. The *jotunn*, or frost giants, were intent on pelting the earth with snow and ice, and one of the Aesir, Thor the Thunderer and god of fertility, often ventured into their realm to destroy them with his hammer, Mjollnir. The religion is often characterized as warlike, but this is an over-simplification since it also gave a framework for conduct; Odin advised people to tread down the path to a friend's house so that it did not grow over with weeds, and to keep the door open for the tired traveller.

It was also a religion rich in symbolism. The universe was divided into nine worlds and stretching through these was a World Tree, *Yggdrasil*, commonly represented as a gigantic ash. *Asgard* at the top was the abode of the gods and goddesses, while around the trunk lay Midgard. Its roots stretched into spirit worlds which humans rarely penetrated. At the foot of the tree sat the three *Norns*, Fates who were arbiters of human destiny and spun the threads of life; they were very powerful, and even the Aesir had to bow to their will. The tree itself was linked with human fate as it was regarded as the source of unborn souls, and a Viking myth describes how its twigs dropped off to form shapes that became *runes*, ancient symbols used for magic and writing. Another important symbol was Thor's hammer,

Viking brooch featuring two goats and a thunderstone, symbols of Thor, son of Odin, god of thunder and fertility, one of the most important deities in the Norse pantheon.

which was often painted on barn doors to ward off evil spirits. As Vikings travelled and encountered new beliefs, they began wearing the hammer as Christians did the cross – as an emblem of their faith – thus learning practices from their Christian neighbours.

For most Vikings, the afterlife consisted of a sombre existence in the kingdom of Hel, a hag who was the offspring of Loki, the trickster god. Here the walls were a wickerwork of winding serpents; the plate in the banqueting hall was called Starvation and the knife Hunger. As with the Greeks, famous heroes gained immortality as they were remembered in the songs of bards for generations. Warriors who died in battle were rescued by Valkyries, the handmaidens of Odin, who took them to the hall of Valhalla.

A remarkable feature of Norse religion was its account of *Ragnarök*, the foretelling of a final, climactic battle in which the gods and forces of evil destroy each other. Out of this destruction a new earth arises, as well as two human beings called *Lif* (life) and *Lifthrasir* (the stubborn will to live). They worship not the old Aesir gods but God Almighty who dwells in *Gimlé*, the gleaming paradise. This tale probably represents the blending of Viking mythology with Christianity as the latter became firmly established in the countries of northern Europe during the ninth and tenth centuries CE. A similar fusion of the two can be traced in architecture; the tenth-century Viking-Christian cross at Gosforth, Cumbria, for example, shows both pagan and Christian influences.

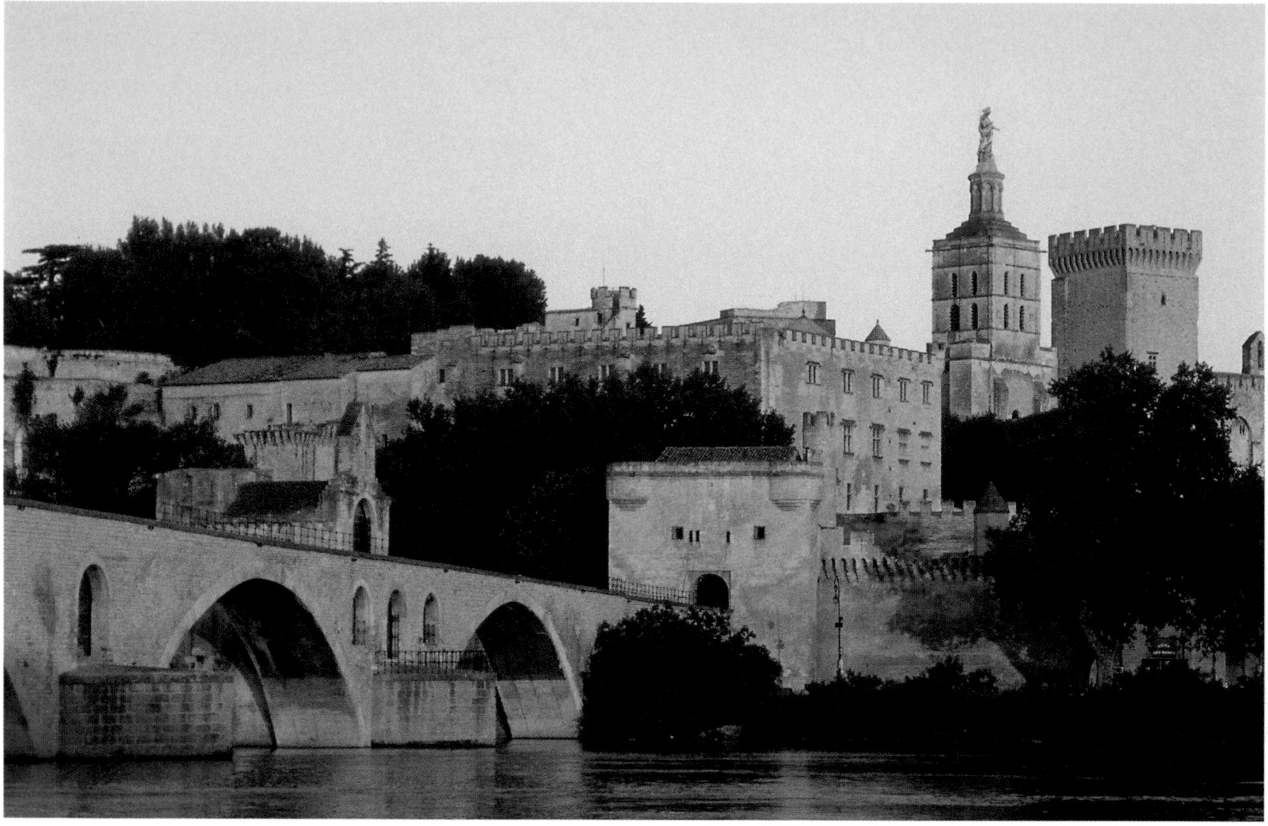

The papal palace at Avignon, France. The French-born pope Clement V (c. 1260–1314) set up his court here in 1309. His election to the papacy had been promoted by the French king Philip the Fair, who wanted a pliant ally to help him strip the Knights Templar of their wealth and land. The papacy remained at Avignon until 1377. Later two antipopes lived here, with French support, until 1408.

MEDIEVAL CHRISTIANITY

The Middle Ages (broadly taken as 500–1500, more narrowly 1000–1500) have been seen simply as the time between the civilization of the ancient world and the rebirth of the cultures of Greece and Rome in the Renaissance of the fifteenth century. Yet medieval Europe was, of course, itself a civilization, and one in which the whole of life was controlled or heavily influenced (in the west) by the Catholic Church.

In 1095, the pope summoned the knights of Christendom to launch the First Crusade against the Muslims who had for a long time been in control of the holy places known to Jesus in Palestine *(see page 282)*. Europe now had enough people, and enough prosperity and unity, for this adventure to be thinkable. It also had enough idealism, for its imagination had become Christian. But, in addition, its religion had become deeply involved in political and military struggles, so that the true history of the crusades was largely disgraceful and ended, in 1291, in complete failure.

Three of the popes were outstanding among the many who did their best to assert their authority over Europe's political rulers: Gregory VII, who became pope in 1073 and humiliated the Holy Roman Emperor at Canossa by forcing public penitence; Innocent III (1198); and Boniface VIII (1294). But popes also had troubles in Italy itself, because, like other rulers, they needed land to produce income and their land was usually the cause of conflict. For almost 70 years from 1309 they retreated from Rome to Avignon in France, and for almost 40 years from 1378 there were rival popes, supported by rival nations. The papacy's need for money was one of the reasons why popes claimed the right to appoint clergy to all bishoprics and parishes (their officials received fees), and why they developed a system of indulgences, involving payments in cash instead of due punishment for sin, even on the part of repentant sinners. But another and greater fact is that throughout the Middle Ages very few people in the west questioned the spiritual authority of the papacy. The Church was international and the pope was acknowledged as the successor of Peter, the 'rock' on whose faith Christ had built his Church.

Similarly, although many grumbles were heard about the clergy, only a few people refused to believe that priests had the power to forgive sins. In 1215 a council decreed that everyone should confess sins privately to a priest at least once a year. It was also accepted that the clergy had the power to decide legal cases connected with marriages and wills, with the laity's offences against morality, and with disputes about the clergy's own crimes or property. In England, the tomb of Thomas Becket, an archbishop murdered in Canterbury Cathedral in 1170 after a quarrel with King Henry II about the clergy's privileges, became the focus of pilgrimages.

INFLUENCE ON DAILY LIFE The number of churches built, rebuilt, and adorned with art was vast; each church was the centre of its community's life and festivities, and Church courts exercised wide control. The many 'holy days' celebrating saints were the only holidays that people had, apart from pilgrimages to saints' tombs and the weekly rest on Sundays, when almost all went to church to 'hear Mass' ('hear' because most people could not read, and so could not follow the service in a book). Some sermons were preached but not all priests were capable of preaching, and in any case the seven sacraments were more important: these were ceremonies consecrating a lifetime, from baptism soon after birth to unction (anointing) shortly before death. Christ was often feared as the stern Judge, or honoured as the victim whose self-sacrifice on behalf of all sinners had been needed to satisfy the Father as Judge; but his mother Mary was the most popular of all the saints, believed to be immaculate (sinless) and to have been assumed into heaven without dying.

Many resources were devoted to praying for the dead in many Masses, often understood as repeating the sacrifice of Christ. It might have been expected that people would doubt whether the Church on earth could influence the destiny of souls after death, but in fact many people paid priests to offer the 'sacrifice of the Mass' on behalf of the dead. The greatest poet of these centuries, Dante (1265–1321), who was highly critical of popes, expressed his passion for justice by an elaborate vision of the punishments of the dead in purgatory, a condition better than hell and a painful preparation for heaven. Encouragingly, the Church taught that time in purgatory could be shortened by prayers on Earth.

Tens of thousands of medieval churches are still used in Europe, and often the cathedrals (the bishops' own churches) are staggering examples of splendid architecture. Romanesque churches (ninth–twelfth century) are massive, as if they had been built by the Romans. Later Gothic churches (twelfth–sixteenth century) can be like forests of stone, rising into the sky with light pouring in through stained-glass pictures in the great windows.

REFORMING THE CHURCH

The vigour of the Church in the Middle Ages prompted many new movements. Often women became nuns, living in convent communities, or lay sisters (Beguines), living in small groups close to the people. The Cistercians were monks who protested against the wealth that had been given to Benedictine monasteries – and after an austere start became rich themselves, so efficient were their agricultural practices. Friars (holy beggars) belonging to the Franciscan and Dominican orders often tried to remain as poor as their founders, Francis of Assisi and Dominic (both living around 1215), had wished, but money was pressed into their hands because they were valued highly as preachers and spiritual guides.

The Franciscans and Dominicans provided able teachers in the universities, for medieval religion also had its intellectual side (which Francis, but not Dominic, scorned). Here the greatest names were those of Anselm (c. 1033–1109), who argued that the reality and justice of God were obvious to good reasoning and that Christ had been born and crucified in order to pay the penalty which sinners owed to God; Peter Abelard (1079–1142), who criticized crudities in traditional doctrines and argued that Christ had lived and died in order to attract sinners to God by love; and Thomas Aquinas (c. 1225–1274), who restated the whole of the Church's faith in dialogue with the philosophy of Aristotle. For example, Aquinas taught that the change in the Mass made the bread and wine into Christ's body and blood in their 'substance', not in an ordinary, physical sense. Later teachers were less confident, with more emphasis on the mystery of God's will.

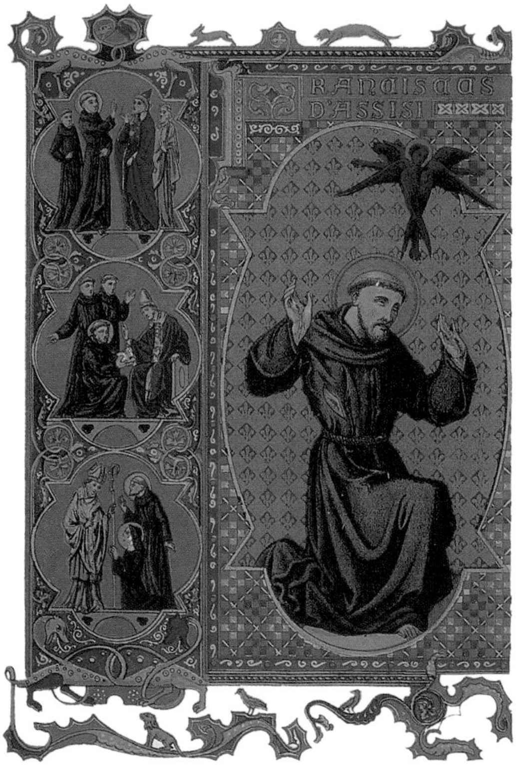

St Francis of Assisi (1181/2–1226), the spoiled son of a wealthy textile merchant, who in his early twenties publicly renounced his family and his wealth, and embraced poverty. He worked among lepers, started to repair ruined churches, and obtained food by begging. In 1208 he began to preach, basing his teachings on what Jesus said and did, and soon gathered followers. He established the order of Franciscans, a mendicant order that gave greater emphasis to radical action than to intellectual theorizing.

The brilliant revival of art and learning in Italy (c. 1350–1550) came to be known as the Renaissance because it seemed like a rebirth of the glories of ancient Greece and Rome, celebrating humanism (belief in human dignity and wisdom). It thrived within a society dominated by Catholic beliefs and images.

During the Middle Ages, achievements were both massive and enduring, but there were crises as well, and new thought which began to question what had been achieved in previous periods. During the 1330s, the Hundred Years' War broke out between England and France, a sign of the growing importance of nationalism. During the 1340s an epidemic that arrived from Asia (the Black Death) began to claim so many victims that the population of Europe did not return to the level it had achieved in 1300 much before 1600.

Bold criticism of medieval religion began to be heard from teachers such as John Wyclif in England in the 1370s and, in the early fifteenth century, from Jan Hus in Bohemia. But heresy was unpopular – and not only because people were terrified of being burned alive after an examination of their beliefs by the Church's judges of the Inquisition. Dangers could be seen by the far-sighted, and Church Councils debated proposals for reform, but little was changed. On the whole, the Church still seemed immensely successful and popular.

MARTIN LUTHER In 1517, a German monk and professor, Martin Luther (1483–1546), denounced the sale of indulgences promising forgiveness for the sins of the living and the dead. He gradually devised a campaign against almost the whole of the medieval system. The papacy was rejected together with everything which suggested that everyone apart from the clergy and nuns was a second-class Christian.

Luther went back to the theology of Paul and Augustine: humans are profoundly and helplessly sinful but can be saved if they put their trust in Christ, not in the saints, nor in any 'works' of their own, nor in any payments to the Church. The 'righteousness of God' is not the hostility of a judge; it is goodness that makes people good through faith in their Saviour. That gospel he preached to great effect, adding a German translation of the Bible, controversial pamphlets, and popular hymns to advance his challenge. He depended on the support of German princes (the original 'Protestants', from the Latin *protestari*, 'to protest' and also 'to avow'). He persuaded them to stand against the Pope and the Holy Roman Emperor, and allowed them great authority over everything except preaching. But he remained conservative in some matters, for example teaching that in the Mass the 'substance' of Christ's body and blood was added to the substance of the bread and wine.

From Germany, this Protestant Reformation spread to Scandinavia and elsewhere, but in England the rejection of the medieval system was influenced by politics rather than theology. Henry VIII (1491–1547) defied the pope in the 1530s because he was determined to rid himself of a wife who could not produce a son and heir, and he was supported by many of the landowners who wanted to seize the wealth of the monasteries. The first edition of *The Book of Common Prayer* was issued in 1549. Under Henry's daughter, Elizabeth I, the Church of England became Protestant, with Elizabeth as 'Supreme Governor', while retaining some Catholic practices.

Martin Luther rose from humble beginnings as the son of a copper miner to become the father of German Protestantism, a movement that effectively split Christian Europe into two.

Henry VIII, painted by Lambert Barnard in 1519, ten years after he became king of England. In 1534, Henry's desire for a male heir led him to confront and finally defy pope Clement VII over the annulment of his 20-year marriage to Catherine of Aragon. Once uncoupled from the power of Rome, Henry declared himself supreme head, under Christ, of the Church of England and dissolved England's monasteries.

RIVAL REFORMATIONS

Luther's influence was due partly to his rough, often crude eloquence, which could stir the emotions. But it was a Frenchman with a cool, logical mind, Jean Calvin (1509–1564), who replaced Catholicism with a theology that was systematically reformed – and the system he described in his great work *Institutes of the Christian Religion* (1536) he put into practice from 1541 as the chief pastor of Geneva.

CALVINISM Calvin based his reforms on the whole Bible; for example, he found in the New Testament clear instructions about how the leadership and discipline of the Church should be organized (this was to result in the Presbyterian system, without bishops). He had a strong sense of the majesty of the God revealed in the Bible and did not shrink from saying that God predestined the faithful to heaven and the sinners to hell. Paul and Augustine had sometimes said much the same but they had put more emphasis on God's love, and in the end most of Calvin's own followers decided that although God had a general policy of punishing sinners, and although all humans have been sinners since Adam and Eve, he did not settle the fate of individuals before their births.

Calvin's code was severe. Many people objected to the expulsion of all art from the churches (on the ground that it could lead to idolatry, the worship of statues, pictures, and saints, not God), and they also resisted the enforcement of the strict morality that he defined. They did so even in Geneva, and although Scotland accepted moral discipline more easily, in England the attempt to establish a Puritan (a biblically-based form of Protestantism) republic in 1649 under Oliver Cromwell did not last long. But the influence of Calvin was great on people who – often after a painful spiritual crisis – felt that they were the 'elect', chosen by God and promised blessings if they were pure in their lives and worked hard and honourably, with heaven to follow. To them life was a pilgrim's progress, resisting the temptations offered by an evil world.

Jean Calvin, theologian and reformer, was born in Noyon, Picardy, and studied in Paris, Orléans, and Bourges. His ideas and teachings led to exile from France. In 1536, while in Basel, he published the first edition of *Institutes of the Christian Religion.* He eventually settled in Geneva, Switzerland, where he produced successive editions of the *Institutes*, the final one appearing in 1559.

THE CATHOLIC RESPONSE Protestantism survived Catholic attempts to extinguish it but the conflicts brought great suffering. In France, the Huguenots who rejected Catholicism found that they were on the losing side in a long civil war. The Dutch Protestants won victory, but only after a bitter war against the Spanish army, which managed to keep the southern half of the Netherlands (modern Belgium) mainly Catholic. In central Europe, there were acute tensions even before the Thirty Years' War (1618–1648), which ended with the exhausted combatants agreeing to a settlement which decided that each region should accept its ruler's religion.

A more reflective response to the Protestant challenges has traditionally been called the 'Counter-Reformation' but is better called the 'Catholic Reformation', for it was not merely negative. It was expressed by the council of Catholic bishops which met in Trent at intervals between 1545 and 1563. It did not make any of the radical reforms that had been demanded, but it ordered the clergy to live and work in the places from which they drew their incomes, insisted that they should be trained, and asked for the preparation of revised editions of the Latin Bible and of the Church's doctrines and laws. Catholicism became more disciplined.

The St Bartholomew's Day Massacre by François Dubois. On 24 August 1572, Huguenot (French Calvinist) leader Henri de Navarre married Margaret de Valois, sister of the Catholic king of France Charles IX, an alliance that was intended to prevent further religious wars. However, the Huguenot wedding guests were massacred at the instigation of the king's mother, Catherine de Medici. Henri de Navarre was spared, but imprisoned and forced to renounce his faith. In 1576 he escaped and re-established himself as leader of French Protestantism. In 1594, he claimed the French throne as Henri IV, formally converting to Catholicism to do so, and four years later issued the Edict of Nantes, which guaranteed Huguenot rights and brought the religious wars in France to an end.

After this council, a number of famous bishops including Charles Borromeo (archbishop of Milan 1560–1584) breathed new life into the Church by injecting their tireless work with a new intensity of love for God and people. Architects and artists made grandeur and excitement visible, the Baroque style being a bold expression of confidence, and writers about the Christian life addressed the laity with a new realism and attractiveness.

The Society of Jesus was founded in 1534 by a Spanish former soldier, Ignatius of Loyola (1491–1556), who taught 'spiritual exercises' designed to bring people close to Christ in total devotion. These Jesuits created a network of schools and colleges that had a profound influence in Europe, and they threw themselves into the education of adults. They also grasped opportunities presented by the new European contacts with other continents. Francis Xavier (1506–1552) was a missionary in India, Sri Lanka, and Japan, and later Jesuits showed a similar courage; they accepted many of the customs of the elites in India and China, but after the 'rites controversy' they were stopped by Rome in 1704, 1717, and 1742 because they seemed too favourable to 'heathen' practices. Other Jesuits were pioneers in North and South America.

THE PAPACY IN CRISIS For a time, the papacy could inspire new and energetic work, but its authority was limited because national governments now held power in Europe. In Spain and its vast American colonies, popes had no administrative role. In France, kings persuaded popes to condemn various movements that encouraged the laity to develop their spiritual lives in personal ways. In 1733, a pope had to accept royal demands that the Society of Jesus should be disbanded; their success had made governments resent the Jesuits' influence. When, from 1789, the French Revolution destroyed the *ancien régime,* including the monarchy, there was talk that the pope who was then imprisoned would be the last.

NEW PROTESTANTS

There was another kind of Protestantism, often called a 'religion of the heart'. Luther could be interpreted as saying that nothing except faith in Christ mattered, and Calvin as saying that only God's predestination of the elect mattered (although Calvin did not emphasize this), so that what an individual could decide or do was of secondary importance. The teachings of these founders could be developed into intellectual systems almost as elaborate as those of Orthodoxy or Catholicism. But the new Protestants, while not denying the necessity of faith in response to God's mercy, emphasized that the individual must be converted in a deeply felt experience that resulted in a profoundly personal religion owing everything to the New Testament, nothing to any government, and very little to any organization larger than a congregation of believers. Pietists (led by Jacob Stener, 1635–1705, who sought a more godly life) and the Moravian Brethren (who sought to be an inspiration within existing Churches rather than a new Church) did much to deepen the spirituality of Protestants. The most sublime expression of Protestant piety (despite using Latin words from the Catholic tradition) may be found in the church music of Johann Sebastian Bach (1685–1750). Protestantism had become not a system, but a call to prayer and holiness.

Easter Morning at the Baptist Tabernacle Church in Beaufort, South Carolina, USA. Baptists first came to the United States in 1639, when the English Baptist Roger Williams began work in Rhode Island. Today there are about 27 million Baptists in the country. The majority of them belong to the Southern Baptist Convention; other groupings include the American Baptist Churches (mostly in the north), two National Conventions, and a number of smaller organizations.

ANABAPTISTS AND BAPTISTS From 1525 Luther and Calvin were given trouble by Anabaptists, who maintained that only believers who knew what they were doing – not children – should be baptized, and who usually added that true Christians should take no part in any war. Before the sixteenth century ended, many thousands had been put to death as heretics or traitors. Small congregations of Baptists formed in England and North America in the late sixteenth and early seventeenth centuries, also refusing to have their children baptized, but gradually winning the respect of other Christians and growing into a worldwide association of independent congregations of many millions, linked since 1905 through the Baptist World Alliance. From the 1580s, other congregations gathered, also rejecting supervision by bishops but not insisting on the strict Calvinism of most Baptists. In the twentieth century, most of these Congregationalists joined larger Churches.

METHODISTS The Methodist movement was founded in the late 1720s in England by John Wesley (1703–1791), a great preacher and organizer, and by his brother Charles (1707–1788). They were both priests of the Church of England but before their deaths it had become clear that their followers would leave the established Church. The Methodists resembled the Pietists; they were methodical in organizing small groups for mutual support and criticism, but they rejected the belief of strict Calvinists that Christ had died in order to save only the elect; Christ, they insisted, died in order to save all who would respond by repentance and faith (the Arminian position). In the United States, Methodism flourished in African-American and other communities, notably in the African Methodist Episcopal, United Methodist, and American Methodist Churches.

THE EVANGELICAL MOVEMENT The word *evangelical* is derived from the Greek for 'good news' (*euangelion*). In the English-speaking world, since the eighteenth century, it has generally been used to refer not to a Church but to a movement. Evangelicals stress the uniqueness of the atonement reconciling God and humanity achieved by Christ as Saviour. They rely on the Bible rather than any later teaching, often treating it as infallible in its message, although not necessarily in every detail. They also rely on sermons rather than sacraments. Their steady aim is to spread the gospel as they understand it, producing conversions such as those that resulted from the 'Great Awakenings' in North America and from many later campaigns for 'revival'.

PENTECOSTALISTS In the early years of the twentieth century, yet another new form of Protestantism exploded into activity, with the accent on the ecstatic 'speaking in tongues' which in the New Testament first occurs on the festival of Pentecost after the resurrection of Jesus. The Pentecostal movement began when this phenomenon was experienced by a congregation in Los Angeles, and from California it spread all over the world. The release of emotion is dramatic and it is especially attractive to people often frustrated in their daily lives, but there is more to Pentecostalism than excitement. The congregations formed by it are encouraged by their worship to live new lives as committed Christians.

The Society of Friends and the Salvation Army

In contrast with the Pentecostalists, the Society of Friends, often called Quakers, has preferred silence in its worship and has never drawn large numbers. The emphasis of its founder, the Englishman George Fox (1624–1691), was on the direct appeal of Christ to the 'inner light' or conscience in every individual, without any need for sacraments in churches or sermons by the clergy. It is a pacifist body. The Salvation Army, founded in 1865 by another Englishman, William Booth (1829–1912), is another movement that has become international and has won great respect for its charitable work. Its main difference from the Society of Friends is that it is strongly Evangelical, relying on brass bands and personal testimonies (statements in witness to Christ) to attract people from outside the Churches.

THE ENLIGHTENMENT

In many ways, the history of Christianity before the eighteenth century is similar to the history of other religions: the early years were comparatively humble and obscure, but the message aroused devotion and a change of life among the faithful, who celebrated the revelation of a reality supremely important and hopeful. A civilization grew around the religion and there were protests against its corruption, producing many attempts to return to early simplicity. But developments beginning around 1650 were unprecedented and seriously challenging. Christianity has had to state or drastically revise its claims in the context of the modern world of thought, where knowledge has been based on science and life on freedom. In this more secular atmosphere, religion has not disappeared but religious belief has become optional and often full of uncertainty, and in practice the Churches have become a minority.

In the seventeenth century, most scientists would have said that God was revealed both in nature and in the Bible, and that the Bible's teaching that the whole world was created by God made the whole world a suitable subject for truth-seeking study by Christians. This attitude encouraged modern science to develop in countries deeply influenced by Christianity. However, even in this period there were tensions. The Christian Bible includes the Jewish Bible (which Christians call the 'Old' Testament) containing the world-view of the early Hebrews, of a flat earth with the sun circling around it. And that was not what was being discovered as ships crossed the oceans and telescopes explored the sky.

The eighteenth-century German philosopher Immanuel Kant called what was beginning in his time the Enlightenment because the arrival of modern knowledge and freedom made the whole of the world's previous history look like darkness. The clergy were being deprived of power to control thought and behaviour, and basic questions about faith were raised in public as never before. What resulted was not, at first, widespread atheism, but there were denials that God had been revealed through any means other than human reasoning about nature and life; there could not be miracles. The teaching of Jesus could be admired – as vividly expressed common sense. The Church's doctrines about the supernatural were replaced by the individual's conscience, which condemned selfishness, for morality was what mattered. The clearest statement of this drastic reinterpretation of Christianity was provided by Kant's book on *Religion Within the Limits of Reason Alone* (1793).

THE CHALLENGES OF SCIENCE AND INDUSTRY In the nineteenth century, the attack on the Churches' traditional teaching grew stronger. Because this planet was very much older and the universe very much larger than the Bible said, and because humans had evolved (perhaps not very far) from other animals, it could seem that both the authority of the Bible and the dignity of Man, as they understood that word, had been destroyed. Was it now necessary for honest thinkers to conclude that only chance had produced human life and that only human decisions could give this life any meaning? Historical investigation could appear to discredit the old beliefs about Jesus. He was treated as a strange figure in ancient history. Some still praised him for being surprisingly modern in his teaching about ethics, but others were shocked to find that the gospels about him were not at all like modern biographies, and that he had shared the hope of his contemporaries that the kingdom of God would arrive in the near future, by a great miracle.

A challenge of a different kind came from the spread of modern industry. Because they no longer lived close to nature, depending for their existence on the weather and the soil or the sea, working people could well feel that customs and beliefs accepted in a village were out of place in the factory and the city; in Nietzsche's drastic phrase of 1887, 'God is dead'. And because most of the clergy seemed to be on the side of the employers who were exploiting them, people could feel that conventional religion was, in Karl Marx's word, opium – a drug to prevent the war between the classes and the revolution that Marxism predicted.

FAITH AND FELLOWSHIP OVERTURNED A still sharper challenge to the Churches came in the twentieth century when Europe was plunged into two great wars fought with modern technology and barbaric cruelty – and by nations with a long Christian history. The suffering included the deaths in concentration camps of six million Jews. Christianity was powerless to stop these horrors; indeed, nationalist and anti-Semitic teaching by the Churches had prepared for them. Was God also suffering, even powerless, if God existed?

In past centuries it had seemed that Europe was Christian and that Christianity was European. But in the modern age it was in Europe that Christianity faced its greatest challenge ever – the challenge of disbelief when there was any talk about God's being both powerful and good. The year 2000 marked the end of a century that had witnessed a huge drop in the number of regular churchgoers right across Europe.

A Dresden church lies in ruins after being bombed during the Second World War. After the war, especially in communist Eastern Europe, the Church did not recover its former status and importance in people's everyday lives.

THE AMERICAS

One of Christopher Columbus's motives for crossing the Atlantic in 1492 was to take Christianity over the ocean. The most obvious result was the deaths of many Native Americans (dubbed 'Indians' by explorers who were under the impression that they had landed in India) through violence, new diseases, and despair about the overthrow of their cultures. Millions died. But gradually new Christian civilizations were built – with very different histories in the two Americas, North and South.

NORTH AMERICA Most of the Europeans who migrated to North America before about 1860 were Protestants, although French Catholics settled in Quebec and Spanish Catholics in Mexico and California. The most famous were the Pilgrim Fathers who landed in Massachusetts in 1620 and 1630. These were Puritans *(see page 252)* who wanted religious freedom for themselves but not for others who did not share their Calvinism; however, over the next 150 years, 'freedom of conscience' for all became part of the American conception of democracy.

Many Americans were attracted by new movements which the historic Churches regarded as heretical: thus, in the nineteenth and early twentieth centuries, Adventists and Jehovah's Witnesses could claim that the end of the world was near (as the Early Christians had hoped), the Mormons could rely on a newly discovered holy book, and the Christian Scientists could draw inspiration from the teachings of Mary Baker Eddy (1821–1910). In due course, independent evangelists would reach huge audiences through television. But the Churches that originated in Europe were also given new life by American freedom: they became established not by the laws of the state but in the hearts of the people.

Preachers travelled with the people moving to and beyond the frontier in the West. Congregations in the industrial cities became spiritual homes for poverty-stricken immigrants. When the evil of slavery had been ended by civil war, preachers became the leaders of millions of Black people facing a long struggle for equality as citizens. And when, in the twentieth century, the United States had been dragged by events into great wars in Europe and the Pacific – and had then been confronted by another superpower, one with communist beliefs and its own nuclear weapons – the Churches were the institutions that did most to keep alive the 'American dream' of freedom and progress for all.

In the twentieth century, the Churches' role in the United States became more complicated. The Catholic Church was now the largest after a change in the pattern of immigration from Europe, but experienced tensions between its loyalty to Rome and its American instincts. The Protestant Churches were divided not only as separate denominations but also between conservatives, who retained a simple trust in the Bible, and liberals, who were more open to hearing the voice of God in the progressive movements that were transforming contemporary society (for example, the women's movement). And this society was more pluralistic, with many Americans preferring non-Christian forms of religion and spirituality, so that there were no more Christian prayers in the state schools. But the United States remained a churchgoing society in comparison with Europe, as did Canada.

A South American prays on the steps of a Mexico City church during the annual festival of Nuestra Señora de Guadelupe (The Virgin of Guadeloupe), when seven million pilgrims come to honour the vision first seen by Juan Diego in 1531.

SOUTH AMERICA In 2000 CE, South or Latin America also remained alive with traditional religion and wider spirituality than much of Europe, but regular attendance at a church was at the average European level, less than a quarter of the population.

The feeling that the Church does not really belong to the people goes back to Spanish or Portuguese colonial rule. The year 1492 saw the completion of the slow reconquest of Spain after Moorish occupation since the eighth century *(see page 280)*. Victory was achieved by force, but also through a militant Catholic faith, and that ideology inspired the colonization of South America from the sixteenth century to the early years of the nineteenth. Church life in the colonies was often marked by the energy of the Catholic Reformation, but close control was exercised by the governments of Europe through bishops who had been born and educated there. Most of the surviving indigenous 'Indians' became Christians who quietly retained many earlier beliefs and practices and who identified the official Church with the rich white men who oppressed them – and the whites who were not rich could also feel that Church and state were not their responsibility.

When colonial rule had collapsed, the new governments were for many years hostile to the bishops, and the revival of Catholic life between 1850 and 1950 could not completely change the people's old attitude towards the clergy; indeed, in the 1920s, a civil war in Mexico was the culmination of hostility between the elected government and the Church. Since 1950, however, great efforts have been made to renew Latin American Christianity as a religion of the poor, in both Catholic and Protestant (mainly Pentecostal) forms, and bishops have declared a 'preferential option for the poor' to be a Christian duty in a continent full of poverty.

American Christians

From the mid-seventeenth century in North America and since the mid-twentieth century in Latin America, it has been emphasized that the Church, whether Catholic or Protestant, must belong to the people. However, while it may seem undemocratic in this environment, strong leadership has been given by remarkable individuals, some of whom are discussed below.

Bartolome de la Casas (1474–1566) was the most prominent of the priests and bishops who became disgusted by the Spanish and Portuguese colonies in Latin America, and in particular by the cruel treatment of the 'Indians'. This, he said, made the Christians' God seem 'the most cruel, unjust, and pitiless god of all'. He proclaimed the fundamental equality of all humans and called for government with the consent of the governed, and 'respect for all who err in good faith'. His protests were prophetic but had little immediate effect.

John Winthrop (1588–1649) was the first governor of Massachusetts Bay Colony. During the voyage of the *Arabella* across the Atlantic to 'New England' in 1630, he preached to the other Puritans that their purpose must be 'to improve our lives to do more service to the Lord... We shall be as a city upon a hill, the eyes of the world are upon us'.

Abraham Lincoln (1809–1865) was the president who led the Northern states in the civil war (1861–1865) which was fought to secure the end of slavery in the United States. But with the Bible in his hand he thought deeply about the suffering on both sides. His speeches, which rose above the smoke of battle, did not make him popular and he was murdered on Good Friday, the anniversary of Christ's death.

Dorothy Day (1897–1980) included in her early years an abortion, a divorce, and an unmarried relationship. But gratitude for the birth of her daughter led her into a strong Catholic faith and 50 years of crusading on behalf of the poor and against the United States' involvement in wars.

Oscar Romero (1917–1980) spent most of his life living as a devout and conservative parish priest and bishop in various countries in Central America. He became the Archbishop of San Salvador at the age of 60, but the murder of one of his clergy opened his eyes to the brutality of the corrupt government's suppression of the protests that were being raised on behalf of the poor. He went on to join the protests, but was murdered as he began to celebrate Mass in the cancer hospital where he had been living.

Martin Luther King Jr (1929–1968) was the Baptist minister who led the civil rights movement demanding progress for the Black population (as African-Americans were then called) of the United States. Peaceful demonstrations gradually secured the end of segregation by race on public transport and in schools and restaurants, followed by the registration of African-Americans on the electoral roll. In 1963 King delivered his 'I have a dream' speech after a great march to the Lincoln Memorial in Washington, and the dream lived on when he was murdered.

Billy Graham (born 1918) is a Baptist minister, as was Martin Luther King. Graham began his career as a preacher of 'revival' in the 1940s, and his fame spread across the nation by means of 'crusades', radio and television appearances, and through the printed word; his voice and message were heard far beyond the United States. Graham's slogan remains 'the Bible says...', and his appeals for conversions to Christ are challenging. However, this evangelical leader also makes a point of cooperating with many Churches, pleads for justice in society, and – unlike some – is not hostile to modern knowledge.

Baptist minister and civil rights leader Martin Luther King Jr at a rally of 2,000 followers in Cleveland, Ohio, 1965. Two years after his famous speech at the Lincoln Memorial, King's famous 'dream' was no nearer realization; 98 per cent of African-Americans in Cleveland were still living in ghettos.

AFRICA

At the end of the twentieth century, the main success of Christianity outside the Americas was in Africa, south of the Sahara. For a long time such success seemed inconceivable. 'Negroes' were despised by Christian Europeans as being 'primitive' and, between the seventeenth and nineteenth centuries, about ten million of them were shipped across the Atlantic to work and die as slaves. By 1800, after the victories of Islam *(see pages 296–297)*, the only substantial Churches left in Africa were in isolated Ethiopia and (as a minority) in Egypt. The British slave trade ended in 1807, and when some former slaves who had become Christians in Britain or North America were brought back to their ancestral home in West Africa, they spread their faith there. Similarly, when Christian missionaries in the little English colony around Cape Town became interested in the exploration of the territory to the north, pioneers such as David Livingstone (1813–1873) opened the way for 'commerce and Christianity'. Both endeavours were preferable to the slave trade conducted by Arabs. In the 1860s, other European missionaries – most notably the White Fathers and Sisters from Catholic France – began to work extensively in the 'Dark Continent'.

These missionaries were valued chiefly because they introduced methods for improving agriculture and started schools and hospitals. But they also brought the Bible and with it Jesus as the best of chiefs. And in the Old Testament, Africans recognized a society not unlike their own, with a religion that was dramatic rather than intellectual, affirming life, health, and fertility, confirming that nature is full of the presence of the divine 'One', offering liberation from the fear of evil spirits, teaching harmony. From the 1890s, African Christians became effective apostles among their own peoples, always speaking in lives and words that could be understood, often starting their own denominations in what has been called the African Reformation. The best known were William Harris (c. 1860–1929) in West Africa, Simon Kimbangu (1889–1951) in the Congo, and the young Christians in Uganda who accepted martyrdom in 1885–1887.

Nelson Mandela (with Desmond Tutu, the Anglican Archbishop of Cape Town, on the left) shortly after his release from prison in February 1990. Both men have fought strenuously for the end of white supremacy in South Africa while advocating the non-violent principles of Christianity.

The growth of African Christianity began to be a significant phenomenon during the 1960s, when European colonialism was becoming only a memory. There was now less need for the Churches to provide modern education and medicine, but all the more need for what tribal traditions could not supply: a spirituality that could cope with a rapidly modernizing Africa. In South Africa, lay Christians such as the great President Nelson Mandela, and church leaders both black and white, were decisive in the replacement of white supremacy in the 1990s. In many new nations to the north, corrupt and ineffective governments disappointed the hopes that had been raised by independence, and problems of poverty and disease (including AIDS) increased along with the population, but African Christianity still aroused high expectations. Christ himself was its most attractive feature, but it also seemed to combine the best of being modern with the best of the continent before the arrival of missionaries. By the end of the twentieth century, African styles of worship, of theology, and of Christian behaviour were maturing, and Christians elsewhere were deeply impressed by the African combination of suffering and joy.

ASIA

In contrast with Africa, the traditional religions in Asia were highly developed, and when traders (associated with Christians) arrived from Europe in the sixteenth century, using violence to support their hunger for worldly goods, any mission to save Asians from hell seemed contemptible. In 1614 the ruler of Japan decreed the expulsion of the missionaries who had come with European traders, and Japanese Christians were persecuted *(see page 165)*. In 1721 the Emperor of China issued a similar decree *(see pages 130–131)*, which was enforced until, in the 1840s, Britain and France secured their readmission by defeating the Empire in war. It seemed very unlikely that Christianity would ever be viewed as a genuinely Chinese religion.

After the 1860s, missionaries had to be accepted as part of Japan's modernization programme *(see page 168)*, but the Churches have always formed small minorities and the impact of Christianity may be seen in less formal, more thoroughly Japanese movements which have often wanted discussion rather than baptism. More widely, Bibles have been read and customs such as Christmas have been enjoyed without membership of any specific Church.

In China, great efforts were made by European and American missionaries during the nineteenth century, with the Protestants founding schools and colleges and the Catholics starting Christian villages. But the Boxer Rising of 1898–1900 saw the massacre of many Christians, and when the communists triumphed in 1949, the expulsion of all foreign missionaries was popular. Significantly, however, Christians have grown in faith and numbers under communism, defying persecution but at the same time affirming patriotism. Eventually, from 1979, many Christian groups agreed to register with the government for permission to worship, although many did not: these were Catholics who refused to abandon the papacy's right to appoint all bishops, or Protestants who stoutly maintained that the Bible, not the Communist Party, deserved obedience in matters of religion.

The only large groups in Asia that have become predominantly Christian are to be found in the The Philippines. This Christian community dates from the 1560s when the Spanish colonialists introduced a more inclusive Church than their compatriots allowed in South America, and from 1909 to 1940 the country was, in practice, an American colony which encouraged religion to be popular rather than official. In South Korea Christians opposed the Japanese occupation (1910–1945) and then evangelized successfully during industrialization *(see pages 148–149)*.

THE CATHOLIC REVIVAL

The belief that the French Revolution had overthrown the Catholic Church, or at least the pope's control of it, proved wrong. In 1801 Napoleon ruled France, and he agreed a concordat with the papacy which lasted until 1905, followed by anti-clerical feeling that lasted less than a decade. However, the Industrial Revolution which transformed Europe and the United States in the nineteenth century presented a great challenge to a Church whose strength had been rooted in the countryside. So did the rise of democracy with its demands for religious freedom, including the freedom not to be religious. But many people disliked what they saw as an ugly new world, materialistic and without any sense of God, and they welcomed the Church's conservatism. Pius IX (pope 1846–1878) was the vigorous spokesman of this countermovement, and in 1869–1870 the bishops meeting in the First Vatican Council decreed that when teaching *ex cathedra* (with a special solemnity on matters of faith and morals), a pope was infallible and incapable of error. In the early twentieth century, Pius X (pope 1903–1914) led a crusade against Modernism, by which he meant the adjustment of traditional doctrine to modern thought.

This Catholic revival attracted converts. In Europe, the First and Second World Wars devastated the continent, but the prestige of the papacy grew because of its official neutrality. Postwar, a Catholicism with a firm creed seemed necessary as an alternative to communism. And in the global mission of Christianity, Catholics had many advantages, including colourful worship and the work of an army of unmarried priests and nuns. Some people loved the Church because it preserved their cultures: many of the Irish under British rule, and almost all the Poles under German or Russian occupation. Although popes no longer had their own kingdom (beyond the tiny Vatican state), religious loyalty to them was now a worldwide phenomenon.

Pope John Paul II uses his specially commissioned vehicle to mingle with the people in Vatican Square. The first Polish pope, John Paul has made it his mission to travel and meet people from as many different countries and backgrounds as possible, and has enjoyed a degree of success in raising the profile and boosting the popularity of Roman Catholicism.

THE NEED FOR FURTHER REFORM But, unexpectedly, the revival entered a second phase which in some ways contradicted the first. The 1960s was a time of ferment in many countries – and in the Church, where the Second Vatican Council (1962–1965) gave Catholicism a new face. Now the Bible was returned to the centre of the Church's life and the Church was called to take the side of the poor around the world, to welcome religious liberty and seek Christian unity, and to enter boldly into friendly dialogues with modern thought and with non-Christian religions. As part of the new emphasis on the laity, the Mass was no longer a mysterious drama with the central part in Latin; it was now in the language of the congregation, who ought to attend without compulsion and to be able to participate fully.

The years that followed showed that even after these radical changes many questions remained in the minds of the Catholic laity. Should married couples be allowed to use artificial contraception? Should priests be allowed to marry, and was it permissible for women to be priests? Should divorced people who made a second marriage be allowed to receive the sacred bread at Mass? Should the laity always be given the wine as well as the bread? Should the Mass be celebrated in a more local style in Latin America, Africa, and Asia? Should the pope always appoint and control the bishops – and the bishops the parish priests? And should some doctrines be restated, even revised? Two popes, Paul VI (pope 1963–1978) and John Paul II (pope from 1978), had the task of holding the Church together, but many would say that the twenty-first century came without a final answer.

LATIN AMERICA TAKES CENTRE STAGE The most promising development from the 1960s seemed to be in Latin America; more Catholics lived there than in any other region and the Church experienced renewal. But as the population grew, so did the poverty, and before wealth could begin to trickle down from the privileged to the poor, harsh rather than humanitarian solutions were sought. Repressive regimes of 'national security' were kept in power by the armies and the rich, and for the mass of the people it was a time of despair. Even in the continent's most prosperous country, Argentina, there was some admiration for the communist regime in Cuba. But around 1968, signs of hope for the future appeared – and they came more from the Church than from communism. Particularly in Brazil, groups of the Catholic laity called *communidades de base* (base communities) expressed their anger about poverty and found inspiration through direct reference to the Bible. They were supported by a 'liberation theology' that interpreted the Bible and the whole of history through the eyes of the poor. Many Catholic bishops became more proactive in working for the people. And the Protestants, previously few in number, began to grow rapidly through the popularity of Pentecostal worship – a hint to the Catholic Church about the need for further renewal. But the uncertainties had not been removed by the year 2000. Many millions are still very poor. Will they continue to turn to the churches for support? Will the bishops, priests, and Protestant pastors fully turn to them? And will the modern-minded middle classes find a religion that fulfills their spiritual or emotional needs? Latin America's future will be a vitally important part of Christianity's future, addressing both the very poor and the very modern.

MODERN CHRISTIANITY

In the modern age, there have been more practicing Christians than ever before – in the year 2000, almost two thousand million if we include people who try to pray (sometimes) and to live according to Christian moral standards even if they do not believe that all the traditional doctrines are true. For Protestants as well as Catholics the nineteenth century was a time of vigorous church life and of mission, and worldwide the numbers of Christians trebled during the twentieth century. But modernity has brought great challenges to the Churches, about which there has been much debate, itself a sign of the religion's continuing vibrancy.

Part of the debate has been about ending the divisions inherited from the past. In the Orthodox Churches, questions have been asked about whether all the traditions need to be preserved *ad infinitum*. In the past, persecution made the faithful defiantly conservative, but in a more tolerant atmosphere it can be argued that Orthodoxy should be more modern and, for example, more American in the United States. In the Protestant Churches there has been a greater willingness to be open to Catholicism, with more emphasis on the Eucharist (or Holy Communion) as the most important act of worship, and less determination to maintain the exact positions occupied by Luther, Calvin, or the Established Church when Protestantism was a new movement. Hopes of renewal, including reunion between Churches willing to overcome age-old divisions, have been encouraged by the World Council of Churches since 1948.

The twentieth century saw a growing desire for the expression of more enthusiasm of the Evangelical or Pentecostal type, with a simple message based on the Bible and informality in worship and preaching, using modern music and the modern media. These changes are even more dramatic when renewal within Roman Catholicism is added, and it has begun to seem possible that in the future there will only be two kinds of Church – one Catholic, with its centre in Rome but welcoming the insights of Orthodoxy and the Protestant Reformation, and the other still accepting the Bible's authority as the 'Word of God' but much less conservative in its atmosphere.

A MORE RADICAL VISION However, the debate within Christianity has also led some to conclude that many serious questions are not being addressed and that the changes in the Churches need to be far more radical. It can be argued that the challenges of modernity call for the development of styles of Christian faith and life very different from much found in the past. It can also be argued that these changes would be still in keeping with the essential message of Jesus.

When a society has been successfully modernized, should its Churches be changed? Long ago, Paul accepted the need to express the faith that 'Jesus is Lord' in a way that was Greek rather than thoroughly Jewish. Perhaps what is needed now is an expression of essentially the same faith, but in a modern way. There is a need to recognize that Christians are now most often in a minority, as the early Christians were, but it does not necessarily follow that it has become a mistake to obey Jesus, for a minority can be right. (Indeed, the acknowledged need to take minorities seriously forms part of postmodern thought.) In this new form of Christianity, spiritual development would be the main ambition and there would be less emphasis on the

Church as the institution that defines correct beliefs and behaviour; the solution of moral problems would be driven by the desire to undertake the most genuinely loving action, and belief would be driven by what is honestly thought to be true. There would be more reliance on the message of the Bible taken as a whole rather than insistence on the authority of a particular passage taken in isolation. There would be increased leadership from women and less dominance by the clergy. There would be more respect for scientific knowledge and a greater focus on the human rights of all; there would also be more of a welcome for the rich diversity of the world's cultures and a greater awareness that God has been at work everywhere, creating and inspiring; more joy in the widespread gifts of God, including responsible sexuality; and a redoubled commitment to fight alongside non-Christians in the battles against the well known evils of war, poverty, pollution, racism, addiction to drugs, and the breakdown of family life.

Those who advocate these changes in response to modernity see them as no mere surrender or comprise. While there would be less of a belief in the innate superiority of Christians, there would still be a profoundly decisive loyalty to Jesus. It would still be believed that he has never been equalled in his embodiment of God's love, in his spiritual power – which his death only increased – and in his vision of the Father's creation becoming the Father's kingdom.

St John's Evangelical Lutheran Church in Sam Houston Historical Park, Houston, Texas, nestling among the glass towers of a thoroughly modern city. Christianity in the twenty-first century is more likely to thrive if it can adapt to, accept, and address modern concerns and problems.

The Universality of Christianity and Jesus

Throughout history, encounters that have taken place between Christians and non-Christians have on many occasions been spoiled by a combination of arrogance, aggression, and exploitation, almost always on the part of the Christians. Even when human nature rather than the Christian faith itself is clearly to blame for such behaviour, non-Christians can still be troubled by the central tenets of the faith. How, they may ask, can a man, a human being, be called 'God' and 'the only Saviour'?

Christians believe that Jesus is unique because God acted through him, giving the world not just a holy book but also a whole life – a human life that included the experience of suffering in self-sacrifice, and which expressed the loving purpose that the one Creator has for every other human life. That purpose is creative rather than hostile; it brings a kind of joy and fulfilment that may be experienced without denying other kinds of goodness; it also saves humans from the power of evil and from despair. Christians who are witness to the action of God in Jesus Christ are like beggars who invite everyone to share food that has appeared miraculously: they want to share their good fortune with those around them. Anyone who wishes to can come to the feast, before or (as many Christians now believe) even after death. The traditional pictures of hell and heaven are not to be taken literally; 'hell' means the self-exclusion of the persistently wicked from eternity with God ('heaven'). Christians call Jesus 'Saviour' because they have known his power in their own lives, but God's purpose, as declared by Jesus, is to save everyone everywhere. Christians have a mission because they want to spread this good news.

Yet, in spite of the inherently inclusive nature of the religion and its message of salvation, Christianity has only just begun to defend the rights of the poor in Latin America, to express the spiritual life of Africa, and to be coloured in mind as well as skin by being Indian, Chinese, Japanese, or Korean. Only since relatively recently have more Christians actually lived in the southern hemisphere rather than in the northern, but

A Christian group in Peru, South America. Christianity was introduced to Peru by the Spanish conquistadors in the sixteenth century. Today Peru has a fast growing evangelical movement, which counts between 10 and 12 per cent of the population among its following, a figure that is predicted to rise to 16 per cent by 2005.

now the faith which began with Jesus, a Jew who lived in Asia, is no longer 'the white man's religion'. For example, in the small islands of the South Pacific, church life has become very strong; gratefully loving the Creator, rather than fearing the old gods, seems to fit the islands' beauty. In the future in this 'Two-thirds World', Christians will have much to learn from other traditions that thay encounter. They will also have much to say and contribute, as they make their way among the majority of the human race.

ISLAM

PENELOPE JOHNSTONE

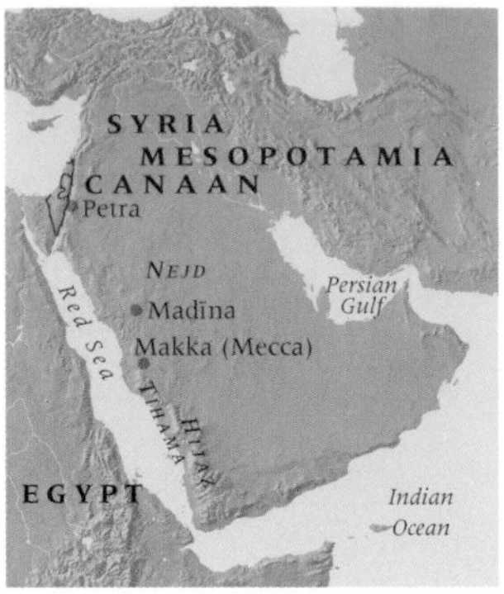

ISLAM

By the early years of the sixth century and into the seventh century, most of the then civilized world came under the sway of two great empires: the Greek Christian-Byzantine Empire situated in the West *(see pages 240–241)*, with its capital located at Constantinople; and the Persian Sassanian, mainly Zoroastrian, Empire situated in the East *(see pages 217–218)*. The intellectual, social, and economic influence of both these empires extended to the areas that lay between them, including the Arabian peninsula, which was the birthplace of Islam.

The Arabian peninsula is rectangular, covering around 3,250,000 square kilometres (1,250,000 square miles). It is bounded to the west by the Red Sea, the south by the Indian Ocean, and to the northeast by the Persian Gulf. The land mass to the north leads to the 'Fertile Crescent' of Egypt, Palestine, Syria, and Mesopotamia. The western coastal strip of the Tihāma gives way to the Ḥijāz (barrier) of mountainous uplands, and then inland to the plateau of the Nejd. The interior consists largely of sandy desert, with occasional oases. To the south and southwest, the rainfall permits agriculture and a settled population, and in ancient times there were kingdoms such as Saba and Ḥimyar. Further north, the kingdom of the Nabateans controlled a wide area from their capital Petra during the ancient Greek and Roman periods.

By the sixth century, most of the north was inhabited by nomadic tribes (*bedouin*), each led by an elected shaykh (sheikh) and a council of elders, who moved from one area to another with their camels and flocks in search of water and grazing. Two large tribes acted as 'buffer states' to the chief political and military powers: Ghassān on the west was a vassal of the Byzantines, and Ḥīra to the east a vassal of the Sassanians.

The decline in prosperity of the southern area around the fifth century is symbolized – or as the Arabs said, was caused – by the break-up of the huge Ma'rib dam which had made irrigation and agriculture possible. However, by the late sixth and seventh centuries, important trade routes existed, one of which led north from present-day Yemen along the Ḥijāz, passing through the city of Makka (Mecca).

Muslims traditionally speak of this period before Islam as the Jāhiliyya or 'time of ignorance' – not so much an absence of learning as a time of boorish behaviour and idolatry, of self-centred commercial greed among settled peoples with its attendant disregard for the underprivileged, and continual feuding, murder, and pillage among the nomads. At the same time, Muslims acknowledge the good qualities of the bedouin life: courage, generosity, hospitality sometimes taken to extremes, and intense clan and tribal loyalty. The Arab of the desert had a well developed perception of nature, not only for survival purposes but as an aesthetic appreciation, expressed in eloquent stylized poetry with precise rhyme and rhythm patterns and beautiful descriptions. For the bedouin, a kind of moral or religious feeling upholds honour and fidelity to one's word and recognizes the finality of *dahr* or 'fate'.

PRE-ISLAMIC BELIEFS

The nomadic Arabs believed in a multitude of deities and spirits, generally connected with rocks, stones, or springs, and each tribe had its own protecting deities. Above these were the goddesses Manāt, al-Lāt, and ʿUzza; there was also acknowledgement of the high god, called Allāh or sometimes al-Raḥmān.

Makka housed the most important monument in pre-Islamic religion (which helped to maintain a solidarity greater than that of a single tribe): a building called the the Kaʿba (cube). Islamic tradition holds that it was built by Abraham (Ibrāhīm) and his son Ishmael *(for Abraham, see page 183)*. In its side was the Black Stone, probably a meteorite. It brought wealth to the city, and the Kaʿba – said to have contained 360 idols – was a focus for local tribes, whose feuds were halted for three 'holy months' of truce during which pilgrimages and trade took place. Merchants, not shaykhs, had the most influence here, although the ruling party was of the tribe of Quraysh, into which Muḥammad was born.

Beside the pagan cults, Judaism and Christianity (both monotheistic) had settled in Arabia. Two Jewish tribes were based in and around Yathrib, while Jewish settlements were established elsewhere in the peninsula. The Christians had a bishopric at Najrān and so presumably quite a large community in the area. Although Christianity in Arabia would have largely followed the Eastern form, the controversies of the time did have an effect on the religion there. Some of the problems may have arisen from differences between Greek and the Semitic languages, but disagreements, particularly on the person of Christ, seem to have been widespread. The basic Christian message could be over-shadowed by sectarian disputes, for which the Qur'ān, here surely mirroring Muḥammad's own experiences, criticizes Christians. It also accuses them of worshipping Jesus rather than the One God, and of 'tampering with their scriptures'. Many Christians in the region may have felt alienated from their Byzantine religious leaders and ready to accept a simpler creed.

Worshippers at the Selimiye mosque in Cyprus. The mosque was created when the Ottoman Turks, who had conquered Cyprus in 1571, added two minarets to the Cathedral of St Sophia.

A camel caravan along the Nile. Before being called as a prophet by Allāh, Muḥammad may have worked as a trader and travelled with the caravans from Arabia to Syria.

MUḤAMMAD

In or around 570 CE, in Makka, Muḥammad was born into the Banū Hāshim, a branch of the tribe of Quraysh. Orphaned at an early age, he was brought up by a bedouin family in the healthier surroundings of the desert. As a young man, Muḥammad worked for his uncle Abū Ṭālib and is said to have accompanied trading caravans on their journeys into Syria. He became known as an exceptionally honest and upright man, and later was employed by a rich widow named Khadīja, who was so impressed by his character and personality that she married him, despite being some 15 years his senior. Until her death in 619, Muḥammad had no other wives.

Now leading a more settled life, Muḥammad took to spending long periods of time in reflection and meditation in a cave near Makka. Around the year 610, he received a startling visitation from a being who commanded him to 'Recite! in the name of thy Lord' (*iqra*ʾ meaning 'recite', the first recorded word in the Qurʾān, now forms the opening to sura 96). Although at first bewildered and reluctant, Muḥammad became certain that he was being sent to his own people of Makka to warn them of the Day of Judgement. The whole thrust of his early preaching in the streets and market-place of Makka was of the Oneness of God, against idolatry, and to encourage the duty of justice and care for the poor.

Not surprisingly, this message was not popular with the chief men of Makka, who saw Muḥammad as a threat to their wealth and status and tried ridicule, persuasion, and physical force to dissuade him from his mission. Apart from his wife Khadīja and his cousin ʿAlī ibn Abī Ṭālib, his first followers were mostly the less influential members of society. They gradually increased in number, people being won by the genuine quality and sincerity of his preaching. This developed in line with messages

Muḥammad received from the source which he now identified as the One God, through the intermediary of the angel Gabriel. These messages were carefully memorized and repeated, becoming the core of the Qur'ān and understood to be the Words of God.

A key element was 'submission' (Arabic root *s-l-m*) to the One God the Creator, Allāh, and from this root come both the name *islām* – not at first designating a separate religion – and *muslim*, one who has submitted. The content of Muḥammad's preaching expanded to include narratives of earlier 'prophets' – including Adam, Moses, and Noah – and references to former peoples and their punishment. A framework of theology was also revealed, as were some regulations for worship, fasting, almsgiving, and pilgrimage. These, together with the profession of faith (*shahāda*), form the 'pillars' of Islam.

Although Muḥammad saw himself as one of a line of prophets, in the Jewish and Christian tradition, he was unable to establish a rapport with the adherents of these two religions. His followers now included Abū Bakr, ʿUmar, and ʿUthmān, men of some standing, but increased opposition from the Quraysh led Muḥammad to negotiate with the people of Yathrib, who were looking for a reliable arbitrator for their own internal disputes. Finally in 622, Muḥammad and his followers travelled to Yathrib, in small groups to avoid suspicion. The *Hijra*, the 'emigration', is the first recorded date in the Islamic calendar, which begins from this year (thus the designation 'AH', 'Anno Hegirae' or 'After the Hijra', for dates in the Islamic calendar).

In Yathrib, later known as Madīna, 'The City' (of the Prophet), Muḥammad, as a respected arbitrator and leader, was supported by the majority of the Madīnans, his *Anṣār* (helpers). Those who accompanied him from Makka were known as *Muhājirūn* (emigrants). The Muhājirūn had no means of livelihood in Madīna, which was one motivation to launch raiding parties on the caravans of the Makkans, now their religious and political opponents. One raid, at Badr in AH 2 /624 CE, brought a great deal of plunder, and the Qur'ān sees this as a reflection of divine favour. An unsuccessful battle at Uḥud a year later was therefore a sign of the Muslims' lack of faith.

The community of the Muslims has always been both political and religious. The tone of the Qur'ānic utterances reflects the different circumstances of the last ten years of Muḥammad life. They contain legislation on inheritance, fasting, almsgiving and its distribution, marriage, the position of women, reflect religious disputes with Christians and Jews, and give guidance on military matters. In 8/630, the Muslims were strong enough to capture Makka, with very little bloodshed. The Kaʿba was cleansed of its idols, the pilgrimage rites were Islamized – in the form they still retain – and all the tribes of Arabia were united in oaths of allegiance to Muḥammad. It is a tribute to his character and political skill that Muḥammad was able to combine his role as prophet and founder of the new religion with that of tribal or super-tribal chief and leader of a whole new community.

However, Muḥammad's death in 10/632 prompted a crisis in the community. As a prophet, he was clearly irreplaceable. Yet the community needed a strong leader, and a consultative body of his close companions chose Abū Bakr, Muḥammad's father-in-law and one of his early supporters, as *khalīfa* (caliph, or deputy). He was the first of the four ar-Rāshidūn (The Rightly-Guided Caliphs) who ruled 11–40/632–661.

THE QUR'ĀN

The Qur'ān has been the single most important influence upon the development of the Islamic civilization and upon the life of the Muslim community and individual. Revered as divine speech, it became the measure and model of spoken and written Arabic. It is the source for theology, law, community affairs, commercial and personal conduct, and daily life. Its words have an incalculable effect upon hearers and readers alike. The Arabic has a rhythm and an eloquence giving it the status of 'inimitability', attested by the Qur'ān itself: unbelievers are challenged to 'bring one *sūra* like it' (10:38).

The Qur'ān emerged from Muḥammad's preaching, and the word itself means 'the recitation'. It is described as 'guidance', for humans need to follow the 'straight path'. The same themes recur repeatedly: the call to worship, the need for justice, the worthlessness of paganism, the inevitability of the Day of Judgement and the punishments awaiting the evildoer, and the reward of paradise for the just. Events such as the defeat at Uḥud, or issues of inheritance or divorce, called for reflection and renewed zeal, or gave guidance and detailed instructions.

The Qur'ān as we know it today is essentially the text brought together by 'Uthmān in the years around AH 30/650 CE *(see page 279)*. There are 114 *sūras* (chapters) made up of *āyāt* (verses) of varying lengths. *Sūras* are classified as Meccan or Medinan according to whether they were (at least mostly) revealed in Makka before, or in Madīna after, the Hijra. The *sūras* are roughly arranged by length, with the shorter, earlier ones towards the end of the book. The exception is the Fātiḥa, the 'opening' *sūra*, which is frequently recited as a prayer and is said to encapsulate the essence of the Qur'ān.

The Qur'ān was critical to the development of Arabic. When the text was first established, the outline script alone was written. Gradually a system of dots and marks was devised to distinguish individual letters and vowels,

while styles of calligraphy developed in different regions and successive periods. Important copies of the text were embellished with gold leaf and colour. In its written form the Qur'ān was now unchangeable, and came to be the arbiter of correct literary Arabic. Comment and exegesis in the early days concentrated upon grammatical form and precise meaning, since the Qur'ān's utterances form the main basis for law and theology, and 'obscure' verses needed clarification and interpretation.

The Qur'ān's status as eternal and uncreated means that its very words impart *baraka*, 'blessing'; to learn it by heart – to become a *ḥāfiẓ*, a 'preserver' of the Qur'ān – is a pious duty, bringing the respect of the community. Recitation of the Qur'ān is an art in itself, and specialist reciters may assist at times of mourning or celebration.

Although it is recognized that versions of the Qur'ān are needed in languages other than Arabic, Muslims consider such works as interpretations of the meanings of the holy book rather than as translations. The Qur'ān is the foundation of Muslim life, but its meaning is made clear in the acts, words, and silences of Muḥammad and his Companions, who become a kind of living commentary on the ways in which the Qur'ān should be understood and put into practice. Collections of Tradition (*ḥadīth*) concerning them were made, of which six have authority (the Sound, or Ṣaḥīḥ, Collections). Qur'ān and *ḥadīth* were gradually organized into codes of practice known as *sharīʿa* (the well-worn path: see Qur'ān 45.18). The Codes do not agree in all respects, so that Muslims live in slightly different styles according to which Code is being followed. The four Codes are: Mālikite (prevalent the Maghreb and West Africa); Ḥanafite (found throughout the Muslim world); Shāfiʿite (which is strong in Asia); and Ḥanbalite (which is strong in Saudi Arabia).

Young Nigerian Muslims read the Qur'ān. Its name means recitation; the Prophet Muḥammad could not write, and so he recited his visions and the words he had heard from Allāh for scribes to take down. In Islamic countries, the Qur'ān is the source of both religious practice and state law.

AR-RĀSHIDŪN, THE RIGHTLY-GUIDED CALIPHS

When Muḥammad died, many of the recently converted tribes considered their pact with Madīna was at an end. The Muslims, however, thought differently, and Abū Bakr was compelled to fight the wars of the *ridda* (apostasy) to restore the tribes' allegiance and to reunite Arabia. The next task was to spread the new religion, and the *Futūḥāt* (conquests) began, bringing in the whole of Arabia and reaching up to Damascus and Kufa, thus making inroads into both Byzantine and Persian territory.

On Abū Bakr's death in 12/634, the choice fell on ʿUmar ibn al-Khaṭṭāb, who continued the wars of conquest. Damascus was taken in 634–635 and Jerusalem in 638; across into North Africa, Fusṭāṭ (old Cairo) was conquered in 641 and Alexandria in 642. The Muslim armies spread along the North African coast and Berbers joined Islam and its fighting force. The campaign was equally successful against the Persians, and the Muslims captured their chief cities, including the capital Ctesiphon in 637; they founded their own military towns at Baṣra and Kūfa.

Islam as a religion, with its simple creed and precise duties of *ṣalāt* (prayer), *ṣaum* (fasting), *zakāt* (almsgiving), *ḥajj* (pilgrimage), and *jihād* (primarily striving in the way of God but also, where appropriate, against unbelievers), seems to have been easily absorbed by the conquered inhabitants of the region. *Ahl al-Kitāb*, 'People of the Book' – that is, those with a scripture: the Jews, Christians, and by extension Zoroastrians – were allowed to keep their religion and to have their own spiritual leaders, but they were grouped together as *dhimmīs* (protected persons) and were effectively second-class *(see page 198)*. They paid a *jizya* (poll tax), whereas Muslims paid *zakāt* (alms) and *kharāj* (land tax) where appropriate. Pagans had to convert to Islam.

'Umar's rule was severe but just; he followed strictly the directions of the Qur'ān and *ḥadīth* (accounts of the words and deeds of the Prophet and his Companions). The governors he appointed in outlying territories were directly answerable to him but were expected to use their initiative in following Islamic rulings.

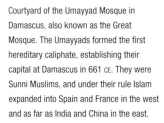

Courtyard of the Umayyad Mosque in Damascus, also known as the Great Mosque. The Umayyads formed the first hereditary caliphate, establishing their capital at Damascus in 661 CE. They were Sunni Muslims, and under their rule Islam expanded into Spain and France in the west and as far as India and China in the east.

POLITICAL INSTABILITY

On the death of ʿUmar in 23/644, a less than unbiased Shūra (group of advisers) chose ʿUthmān ibn ʿAffān, a pious but weak character who appointed relatives to key positions, including Muʿāwiya as governor of Syria. ʿUthmān's piety did not prevent sporadic revolts, culminating in 35/656 when a band of rebels attacked his home and murdered him – while he was reading the Qurʾān, according to tradition. Rumour suggested that ʿAlī ibn Abī Ṭālib, who was chosen as the next caliph, had been implicated in ʿUthmān's murder, and despite his denials he made no serious attempt to punish his predecessor's killers. It was ʿAlī, in the eyes of his companions and friends, who should have been chosen as the first caliph; he was Muḥammad's younger cousin and a very early convert, in addition to which he had married the Prophet's daughter Fāṭima. A brave fighter and a loyal follower, he may not, however, have been the ideal leader of a now very large community.

The political situation was becoming very unstable due to the rapid expansion of the Islamic empire, the influx of new Muslims and *dhimmīs*, and the increasing independence of provincial governors. Muʿāwiya managed to challenge ʿAlī to battle in 657, persuaded him to renounce his caliphate and submit to arbitration, then claimed the caliphate for himself. ʿAlī was accused of impiety by a group of his followers for having accepted arbitration, and these seceders (Khawārij, singular Khārijī) had to be defeated, distracting ʿAlī from the main threat, Muʿāwiya. The latter brought about the further weakening of ʿAlī's position in 659 at the arbitration proceedings. Already legally governor of Syria, Muʿāwiya next seized command in Egypt. In 40/661, ʿAlī was murdered and Muʿāwiya accepted as caliph, thus founding a century-long dynasty: the Umayyad caliphate.

Completion of the Qurʾān

ʿUthmān's greatest achievement was to have the Qurʾān recorded in its final form. Hitherto the revelations of the Prophet had been committed to memory and only partial *sūras* (chapters) were written down. As the early followers and 'keepers' of the memory died or were killed, it became vital to provide a more permanent record. ʿUthmān commissioned Zayd ibn Thābit, the secretary of the Prophet, and some others to carry out this task. Muḥammad himself had written nothing down and Islamic tradition describes him as 'illiterate', stressing that he had not received any book learning when the revelations came to him. Though shrewd and thoughtful, he was not a 'lettered' man, and like many of his contemporaries left writing to others. When the definitive text was completed, all the original copies and variant versions were destroyed, and seven copies of the 'standard' version of the Qurʾān were dispatched to the chief cities of Islam. These contained the same text that is used today.

THE UMAYYAD AND ʿABBASID DYNASTIES

The Umayyad dynasty, based in Damascus, ruled from 41/661 to 132/750. Later accounts speak of the Umayyads as being Arab 'kings' rather than true Islamic leaders, although this may be the result of propaganda by the ʿAbbasids (*see pages 281–282*). The Umayyads are known to have relied heavily on their Arab troops, and emphasized their Arab descent, expanding eastwards and westwards with further conquests. In public they upheld religious law, but as rulers they enjoyed a luxurious lifestyle, including hunting and drinking wine (forbidden under Muslim law). The Umayyad mosque in Damascus and the remains of their desert castles are witness to this contrast between official and private life, which was not exclusive to the Umayyads.

Muʿāwiya's son Yazīd became caliph in 59/680 on Muʿāwiya's death. In the same year, unrest in Iraq found a focus in ʿAlī's son Ḥusayn, but the revolt was a failure militarily. On another level, Ḥusayn's death at Karbalāʾ in Iraq marked the beginning of the Shīʿat ʿAlī ('party of ʿAlī', the Shīʿa), who saw the fallen warriors as martyrs and believed the true Islamic leadership was inherited by ʿAlī's family (*see pages 283–285*).

ADMINISTRATIVE REFORMS AND PRESSURES Family succession continued in this fashion, although Yazīd's two sons brought about a civil war that lasted from 683 to 684. In 65/685, ʿAbd al-Malik became caliph and began the real organization of government. The administrative systems inherited from the conquered Byzantines and Persians had been left in place, with Greek and Persian respectively as the official languages. Under ʿAbd al-Malik everything was centralized, Arabic was made the official language for correspondence and records, and an Arab coinage was established, with the gold dinar and silver dirham. As a sign of the caliph's piety, some of the treasury's wealth was devoted to erecting the original building of the Dome of the Rock in Jerusalem and, according to some accounts, an enclosure for the Kaʿba in Makka.

Under ʿAbd al-Malik's son Walīd (ruled 86–96/705–715), the conquests expanded even further, taking Islam eastwards to Bokhara and Samarkand and into India. To the west, a landing in southern Spain led to the occupation of much of the peninsula. In 114/732, the most northerly point of the Empire was reached when the Muslim forces were defeated by Charlemagne's grandfather, the Frankish ruler Charles Martel (ruled 715–741) near Poitiers. The Byzantine Empire was still powerful, and in Suleymān's reign (96–99/715–717) a naval expedition was sent against Constantinople, a Muslim failure that reflected badly on caliphal prestige.

Suleymān's successor, ʿUmar ibn ʿAbd al-ʿAbzīz (99–101/717–720), was claimed by some as the 'only true caliph' among the Umayyads, but his piety, combined with a bias towards the Arabs, led him to ban *dhimmīs* from administrative posts (although he admitted non-Arabs to the *amṣār* , garrison towns) and to increase the pay of Arab soldiers outside Syria. All these policies weakened the treasury. Besides the class of *dhimmīs*, there were the *mawālī* (singular *mawlā*), Muslims not descended from or affiliated with Arab tribes. At this time the *mawālī* suffered economic and social disadvantages, and as a disaffected group they were a potential threat to stability.

Around this time, too, the first Sufis are mentioned in historical sources (*see pages 285–287*). Asceticism was, at least in part, a continuation of an earlier tradition – such as the Christian Fathers of the Desert of the fourth century onwards – and partly a reaction of pious Muslims against the worldliness and wealth of many others who called themselves Muslims. *Ḥadīth* told of the prophet's poverty and simple lifestyle, while the Qur'ān's warnings were unequivocal.

The Empire was becoming too extensive and diverse for its administrative and political centre; successive caliphs were too weak to keep control of their governors; finances were shaky; the non-Arab *mawālī*, even more than the *dhimmīs*, became increasingly aggrieved at their second-class status; and followers of ʿAlī wished to install one of his family in the caliphate.

These last two factors came together in the revolt of Muḥammad ibn ʿAlī ibn al-ʿAbbās, a descendant of the Prophet's uncle, who banked on extremist Shīʿa support together with loyalty to the Prophet's line. On his death the organization of the revolt passed to his son Ibrāhīm, who sent an Iraqi, Abū Muslim, to Khorusan where the revolt began in earnest in 747. There was little effective opposition from government supporters and in the final great battle the Umayyads were decisively defeated.

Ibrāhīm's brother Abū al-ʿAbbās, known as as-Saffāḥ (the shedder of blood), was proclaimed caliph in 132/750. For the next five centuries the caliphate was to be based in Iraq and was no longer predominantly Arab.

Those Umayyads who escaped the battle were later murdered, with the exception of one, ʿAbd ar-Raḥmān, who made his way to Spain (al-Andalus) and there founded an Umayyad dynasty of *amirs* in Cordoba, which lasted until 422/1031. Their province was declared a caliphate by ʿAbd ar-Raḥmān III (300–350/912–961). The Great Mosque in Cordoba (dating from the late eighth century) remains a tribute to their power, culture, and influence.

THE ʿABBASIDS In 136/754, four years after as-Saffāḥ's victory, al-Manṣūr, his brother, founded Madīnat as-Salām (city of peace), Baghdad, between the Tigris and Euphrates rivers. The Empire was thus centred on a region of trade and agriculture inherited from the preceding settled civilizations of Babylonia and Assyria *(see page 198)*.

The administration became more Persian in character and Arabs ceased to be the mainstay of the army, which was now composed largely of paid troops rather than conscripts and at times became too powerful. A strong loyal army was vital to help crush the frequent rebellions, whether of pretenders to the caliphate or, more seriously, the uprisings of the Zanj (Black slaves) who, from 869 to 883, posed a severe threat and even captured Baṣra before being defeated.

Baghdad was the centre of a vast trading empire whose merchants travelled to the far north, even Scandinavia, and to India and China. Luxury goods brought wealth while staples and food were plentiful. As in the ancient civilizations, irrigation again allowed vast tracts of land to be cultivated; but, as so often, the peasant workers remained poor while employers and landowners flourished.

Of all the ʿAbbasid caliphs, perhaps the best known, through the stories of *The Thousand and One Nights*, was Hārūn ar-Rashīd, who ruled from 170 to 193 (786–809). On his death, civil war broke out between his sons; Maʾmūn was victorious, and during his reign (198–218/813–833) the prosperity of the Empire continued to grow. At the same time, however, internal and external tensions began to show; local governors claimed more power and some set up their own dynasties while paying only nominal allegiance to the caliph. The Umayyads in Spain were already independent *amirs*, and ʿAbd ar-Raḥmān III declared himself caliph in Cordoba in 315/928. In the third/ninth century, semi-independent rulers included Aḥmad ibn Ṭūlūn and his descendants in Egypt, and Ṭāhirids, Sāmānids, and Ṣaffārids in Persia. In the next century another Persian family, the Buwayhids (or Buyids), invaded Baghdad and took the real power from the caliph, to be replaced in the fifth/eleventh century by the Seljuq Turks.

Meanwhile, the Shīʿa began to assert their religious and political rights. The descendants of ʿAlī by his wife, Muḥammad's daughter, Fāṭima (hence the term Fāṭimids), and so doubly related to the Prophet, they considered themselves the true caliphs. In 148/765 a major split occurred within the Shīʿa between the relatively moderate 'Twelvers', who followed the *imami* line of Mūsā, and the 'Seveners' or Ismāʿīlīs, who were more extreme in their theological and political views *(see page 284)*.

The Ismāʿīlīs sent their representatives into many parts of the empire, most successfully to Tunisia, where in 296/908 the first Faṭimid caliph was proclaimed, and in 358/969 Muʿizz al-Dīn gained power in Egypt, from where further attacks were then made into Palestine, Syria, and Arabia. Muʿizz al-Dīn founded al-Qāhira (Cairo, 'the victorious city') beside the old capital Fusṭāṭ, and the mosque of al-Azhar was constructed as the religious and teaching centre of the Ismāʿīlī version of Islam. Fāṭimid power gradually declined, and ended in 567/1171 with the conquests of Ṣalāḥ al-Dīn (Saladin), a Sunni Muslim and Turkish commander of Kurdish origin, and a member of the Ayyubid clan, which took over Egypt and Syria from the Fāṭimid. Saladin himself fought the Franks (the Crusaders) and in 1187 he recovered Jerusalem for the Muslims.

ʿABBASID CULTURE AND CREED Under the ʿAbbasid caliphs, science, learning, poetry, and literature all flourished. Many of the most famous men of the time were not Arabs, and non-Muslims too could achieve fame and status, especially as physicians, although *dhimmīs* were still under legal disadvantages which were enforced from time to time.

The ʿAbbasids were careful to cultivate their image as pious rulers who were legitimized by their descent from the Prophet's family, and although life at court was clearly not a model of Muslim behaviour, individual caliphs took a close interest in religion and sometimes intervened in religious disputes. During the early ʿAbbasid years, the theology of Islam was codified and lively controversy sometimes degenerated into open conflict.

Philosopher-theologians known as the Muʿtazilites, attempting to reconcile the unity of God with his Word, declared that the Qurʾān was created, since otherwise it would be another divine being. The 'created Qurʾān' was the central point of their creed, and al-Maʿmūn subjected judges and theologians by decree to the *miḥna*, the 'test' of assent. A few outstanding men, notably Ibn Ḥanbal, refused to comply. Eventually there was great opposition to the reduced status of the Qurʾān, and a later caliph revoked the decree, allowing Muslims to believe again in the eternity and uncreatedness of the Qurʾān.

By the mid-eleventh century, the Europeans were beginning to regain land: in Spain the Reconquista was progressing, while Sicily (which had been conquered during the course of the late ninth century by the Tunisian dynasty of Aghlabids, and later came under the central ʿAbbasid government) fell to the Normans late in the eleventh century; and with the arrival of the Crusaders, the short-lived 'Latin Kingdoms' were established in Palestine and Syria. By Ṣalāḥ al-Dīn's death in 589/1193, however, most of the Crusader territory had been won back for Islam. Worse threats to the ʿAbbasid dynasty came from Central Asia, where the Turks were gaining strength; first from the Seljuqs, who in 447/1055 took Baghdad, then from the Mongols. Jenghiz (Genghis) Khan carried his campaigns westwards, and in 1221 entered Persia. On his death in 1227, Hulagu continued the conquest and captured Baghdad in 656/1258. The city was sacked and the caliph was killed, bringing to an end 500 years of the ʿAbbasid caliphate.

Shīʿa Muslims in Lebanon formed Hizballah (Hisbollah; the word means 'party of God') following the Lebanese civil war and the Israeli invasion of 1982. It takes seriously the demands of *jihad* (*see page 278*), claiming responsibility for the suicide bombings of French and US embassies in 1983.

THE SHIʿA

Today, the Shīʿa form a significant minority – perhaps 10 per cent – of world Islam. Their origins spring from the earliest days of the religion, their name indicating that they are *Shīʿat* ʿAlī, of the party of ʿAlī.

When Abū Bakr, ʿUmar, and then ʿUthmān were chosen to succeed Muḥammad, they set aside the man who, in his supporters' opinion, had the greatest right to be caliph – ʿAlī, Muḥammad's cousin and son-in-law, who, with his wife Fāṭima and his two sons Ḥasan and Ḥusayn, formed the *Ahl al-bayt*, the Family of the Prophet. ʿAlī did become caliph for a few years, but after his death power passed to the Umayyads.

In 680, Yazīd succeeded to the caliphate, but the Shīʿa supported Ḥusayn. On their way from Madīna to Kūfa, Ḥusayn and his small band, including close relatives, were defeated and slaughtered by the government forces at Karbalāʾ in Iraq. This 'martyrdom' was a foundation event of Shīʿa faith. The Shīʿa remained a small minority, subject to persecution on political grounds, and developed the principle of *taqīya*, 'pious concealment', allowing them to hide their true beliefs when it would be dangerous to declare them openly.

THE IMAMATE The term *imam* within Shīʿa Islam denotes the religious leader of the community, a position and title passed down through the generations. During the imamate of Jaʿfar al-Ṣādiq (733–765), the sixth in line, it was established doctrinally that the imam was divinely guided and as the leader of the community enjoyed infallibility and a state of *ʿiṣma*, sinlessness. He was able to give authoritative teaching and guidance and infallible interpretation of the Qurʾān on both the *ẓāhir* (outwardly apparent) and the *bāṭin* (inward, esoteric) meanings.

The status and hereditary principle of the imamate sometimes caused schisms, the most important divisions being the Imamiyya (*ithnā ʿashariyya*, or 'Twelvers', who followed the twelfth imam in line) and the Ismāʿīlīyya, (*sabʿiyya*, or 'Seveners'). When Jaʿfar died, his eldest surviving son, Mūsā, was accepted as imam by the majority of Shīʿa (the Twelvers), and the line passed through the family until the eleventh, al-Ḥasan al-ʿAskari (254–260/868–874), whose son Muḥammad al-Mahdī disappeared – or 'went into occultation' – in 329/940. The Twelver Shīʿa co-existed for the most part with the ʿAbbasid caliphs, while awaiting the messianic-style return of the Hidden Imam, their twelfth and last. The caliph al-Maʾmūn had appointed one imam, ʿAlī al-Riḍā, as his heir, but ʿAlī died a year later, and no Shīʿa thereafter came near to attaining the caliphate.

The other group of Shīʿa followed Ismāʿīl, Jaʿfar's eldest son who had died before his father, but who would have been the seventh imam in direct succession, and his son Muḥammad. Many subsects of Ismāʿīlīs arose, the main one today being the Nizaris, whose imam has been called Aga Khan since the late nineteenth century.

A branch of the Ismāʿīlīs developed into the line of the Fāṭimids, who claimed succession through their imams and who later became caliphs in Cairo. An extremist group of the Fāṭimids proclaimed the caliph al-Ḥākim (died 411/1021) to be divine. One of his supporters, Ḥamza ibn ʿAlī, developed the esoteric doctrines that formed the basis of the Druze religion. This took hold in the mountains of Syria and Lebanon, but the beliefs and practices of its initiates were so changed as to be no longer Ismāʿīlī. Another group of schismatics were the followers of Ḥasan-i Ṣabbāḥ, known as the 'Old Man of the Mountains', who, in the late eleventh century, seized the stronghold of Alamūt in the Daylam mountains of Persia from where assassins were sent out to kill political targets. Followers of Ḥasan were said to use *hashish*, the origin of the word *assassin*, by which name they came to be known. In the thirteenth century they were destroyed by the Mongols.

SHĪʿA BELIEFS AND THEIR DISTRIBUTION Shīʿa theology, like Sunni theology, is based on the Qurʾān and *ḥadīth* but incorporates additional *ḥadīth* and teachings of the imams. The most important written work is *Nahj al-Balāgha* (Path of Eloquence), a collection of teachings attributed to ʿAlī. Shīʿa devotions include pilgrimages to shrines of the imams, especially to Karbalāʾ and to Najaf. The *taʿziya* or mourning commemorating the death of al-Ḥusayn and his companions takes place annually around 10 Muḥarram, which is the first month of the Muslim calendar. Plays and processions to mark the event arouse intense emotion among participants and spectators.

Shīʿa have not always and everywhere been in a minority politically. The Ṣafavids began as a popular Sunni reform movement in the fourteenth century and by the fifteenth were a strong political organization in northwest Persia and eastern Anatolia. They adopted the Shīʿa cause and beliefs and the founder of the dynasty, Ismāʿīl (1487–1524), claimed to be the Hidden Imam. In 1501, Ismāʿīl was proclaimed Shāh (king) and Twelver Shīʿism became the official religion, accepted throughout Persia. The high point for the Ṣafavids occurred during the reign of Shāh ʿAbbas (1588–1629) whose capital was Isfahan. At this time, Persia enjoyed a thriving economy, and was widely famed for its high-quality carpets and crafts and beautiful architecture; many merchants from the English court came in search of trade. However, in 1736, the Afghans managed to defeat the last Ṣafavids. The Afghans themselves were, in turn, ousted in 1779 by the Qajar dynasty, which had originated in the Caspian Sea area and had first gained power in northern Persia, and they ruled until 1924. Iran today is strongly Twelver Shiʿī and there is a sizeable population in Iraq, with smaller groups elsewhere, including Syria and Lebanon.

Ismāʿīlīs, although forming a minority of Shīʿa, are more widespread, being found in Iran, Syria, Lebanon, East Africa, Pakistan, and particularly India, where the Bohra branch, which began in Yemen, migrated to Gujarat. Followers of the Aga Khan, who are mostly found in India, show none of the extremist tendencies of earlier Ismāʿīlīs, and are a highly organized, and quite wealthy, privileged group.

Shīʿite cemetery at Najaf, Iraq. As the burial place of ʿAlī ibn Abī Ṭālib, the founder of the Shīʿa sect, Najaf is a sacred place of pilgrimage. ʿAlī's actual tomb has never been found; he instructed his followers to put his corpse on a camel's back and to bury him wherever the camel first knelt to rest. A much rebuilt shrine, Mashad Gharwah was first established at Najaf in the ninth century by Hārūn ar-Rashīd.

SUFI ORDERS

The basic principles of *taṣawwuf* (Sufism) were first inspired by the Qurʾān itself and the Prophet's example; devotion to the One God and rejection of the world led to asceticism, at times extreme. There were outside influences, particularly from the ascetic tradition of the Christians and from the Gnostics, but Sufism is a specifically Islamic form of the mystic path. Initially, there was no organized system; individual holy men and women taught their pupils and devotees, and their sayings and actions were recorded and passed down. The name Sufi derives probably from *ṣūf*, wool, as they wore rough woollen robes.

Famous early ascetics included Ḥasan al-Baṣrī (died 110/728) in Iraq, Dhū al-Nūn al-Miṣrī, the Egyptian (died 247/861), and one of the best known women mystics, Rābiʿa al-ʿAdawiyya of Baghdad (died 185/801). Rābiʿa's life of poverty and devotion and her prayers expressing her complete abandonment to God and to worship for God's sake alone continue to inspire Muslims.

Asceticism was a preparation for the search for *maʿrifa* (wisdom or gnosis, rather than book learning), for a closeness to God, and for some it expressed a longing for union with God. Although most Sufis were quite pious and law-abiding, their experiences and their enthusiasm could lead some to ecstatic and unguarded utterances, as with Manṣūr al-Ḥallāj, whose words *anā al-ḥaqq* ('I am the Truth', that is, God) contributed to his condemnation and execution in 310/922. However, most Sufis held to a less extreme form of *fanāʾ* (interpreted as a 'passing away' in God).

Murīdūn (disciples) would gather around a shaykh or holy man in a *khānaqāh, zāwiya,* or *ribāṭ* (a house for a fraternity of Sufis, each word denoting a slightly different purpose). These disciples, known as the *sālikūn* (travellers), followed the *ṭarīqa* (path; plural *ṭuruq* or *ṭarīqāt*), a term that later came to denote the orders themselves.

Certain teachers from the tenth and later centuries were recognized as inspiring, although they were not founders of, a *silsila* ('chain' of affiliation) that would later become a *ṭarīqa*. Among the most famous were al-Junayd of Baghdad (died 298/910) and Yazīd al-Bistāmī (died 261/874) from Bistam in Khurasan. In the tenth century, al-Qushairī, Abū Naṣr al-Sarrāj, and Abū Ṭālib al-Makkī wrote about Sufism and its practitioners. A well-known writer who helped to make Sufism respectable was Abū Ḥāmid al-Ghazālī (died 505/1111), who abandoned theological teaching in the prestigious Niẓāmiyya college in Baghdad to seek 'certitude' of life and religion among the Sufis. His major work, *Iḥyāʾ ʿulūm al-dīn* (*Revival of the Religious Sciences*), composed over several years before 1105, gives his spiritual insight into Islam. Sufism could become a way of life, providing a more personal approach to the divine.

THE ṬURUQ In the twelfth and thirteenth centuries, the *ṭuruq* proper began, each named after a famous mystic or teacher. They had their own particular emphasis, prayers, and litanies, and, most importantly, their *dhikr*, literally 'remembrance' of God, generally expressed through communal recitation of the names of God or pious

Meditating sufi dervishes in Konya, Turkey. Sufis are those who seek direct experience of God. Sufis use many methods to reach a state close to God and free from external distractions, one of which is the whirling dance. 'Whirling dervishes' are called *Mevlevis*, or more accurately *Mawlawis*. The name comes from *mawlānā*, or 'master', a title given to Jalāl ad-Dīn Rūmī. Rūmī was one of the greatest poets and teachers of the Sufi way.

invocations. A new Sufi would receive the *khirqa*, robe, from his shaykh as a sign of membership. A less orthodox development was seen in excessive veneration of the Sufi shaykhs themselves, resulting in pilgrimages to shrines and tombs of holy men and belief in their intercession. Such practices brought the Sufis under suspicion.

The most famous orders include the Qādiriyya, named after ʿAbd al-Qādir al-Jīlānī (died 562/1166), and the Shādhiliyya, named after Abū al- Ḥasan ʿAlī al-Shādhilī (c.560–656/1196–1258), an inspiring and deeply spiritual teacher. The foundation of the Suhrawardiyya is attributed to Abū al-Najīb al-Suhrawardī (died 564/1168) but the *ṭarīqa* was developed by his nephew Shihāb al-Dīn al-Suhrawardī; this order spread into India. The Chishtiyya was founded in India by Muʿin al-Dīn Chishtī, who died in 634/1236 at Ajmer in Rajasthan. In Anatolia, the Mawlawiyya (or Mevleviyya in Turkish) *ṭarīqa* grew up around Jalāl ad-Dīn Rūmī (died 672/1273), known as Mawlānā (our master), whose Persian mystic poetry is much revered. It is these Anatolian Sufis, based in Konya, whose dance and music gave them the name of 'whirling dervishes'. The Naqshbandiyya is named after Bahāʾ al-Dīn Naqshband, who died in 792/1389 in Bukhara. Originating in Persia, this *ṭarīqa* became popular in Turkey and spread into India in the late sixteenth century. It is widespread today, has reached Europe, and often attracts Western converts to Islam. Although not founding an order, Muḥyī ad-Dīn Ibn al-ʿArabī (*ash-shaykh al-akbar*, 'the great shaykh', 560–638/1165–1240) from Spain, is probably one of the best-known names in the West, and his teachings had a great influence on later mystics. Any new Sufi fraternities since the Middle Ages have been mainly subdivisions or more localized groups.

In Egypt and elsewhere, the *ṭuruq* opened their doors to admit lay members (akin to tertiaries or oblates in Catholic Christianity) who followed the teachings and principles of the order and revered the shaykh, but continued their own secular occupations. This is still common practice today, and has the potential to inspire the everyday life of the Muslim with the high ideals of the Sufi brotherhood.

ISLAMIC SCIENCE AND LEARNING DURING THE MIDDLE AGES

'Thy Lord taught by the Pen', says the Qurʾān. Allāh is the fount of all knowledge, and the religious sciences take priority. However, the pen was not relevant at first. The Arabs possessed a long oral tradition, with tales of battles, feuds, and wars, and finely-tuned poetry celebrating the desert life. The Arabic language is their great pride, and the Qurʾān the greatest exemplar of that language, the model of rhetoric and clear speech, poetic though emphatically not 'poetry'. The Qurʾān, due to its status, was the first object of study for Muslims. Repeated and treasured orally, its content was soon collected and recorded, and the care needed to preserve precise grammar and pronunciation helped the development of the Arabic script and later the styles of calligraphy.

The science of *tafsīr* – Qurʾānic exegesis and commentary – demanded a high level of philological and grammatical expertise, and acquaintance with history and tradition. The best-known commentaries include those of the historian at-Ṭabarī (died 311/923), al-Zamakhsharī (died 538/1143), and al-Bayḍāwī (died 685/1286).

A girl student at school in the old Muslim Quarter of Jerusalem. Islamic tradition encourages female education in religious and academic subjects because it is believed that women should be able to read and understand the words of the Prophet for themselves. For Islamic women, marriage and motherhood are the ideal, and an educated woman is able to instruct her children correctly and help her husband to fulfil his religious duties.

The second source of theology and law was the *ḥadīth*, which conveyed the *sunna*, the custom or path of Muḥammad and his Companions. The *ḥadīth* was passed on orally at first. In theory at any rate, it reflects conditions at the time of the Prophet, giving his 'words, deeds, and silent approval'; it covers in quite minute detail many aspects of piety and of acceptable behaviour in public and private life, and sometimes also expands on certain Qur'ānic directives. In the third/ninth century, scholars compiled written collections of the sayings and narratives that they accepted as genuine: the two most respected are those of al-Bukhārī (died 257/870) and Muslim ibn al-Ḥajjāj (died 262/875), along with four other contemporaneous works, forming the 'six books' of reference.

The study of *ḥadīth* led to the development of biography; at first this was done in order to record the lives of *ḥadīth* transmitters, to verify their reliability, and then later *ṭabaqāt* (classes) were compiled of the lives of scholars, lawyers, scientists, and physicians, among others.

Territorial conquests led to the acquisition of older learning, both in Persian and especially in Greek. By the end of the first/seventh century, scholars were translating the corpus of Greek sciences, especially philosophy, medicine, astronomy, and mathematics, into Syriac, and translation soon took place into Arabic. This was encouraged in particular by the ʿAbbasid caliph al-Maʾmūn, who founded the Bayt al-Ḥikma (house of wisdom) in Baghdad for translation and study.

Some subjects were of obvious practical value: medicine was important, as were mathematics and astronomy, which were used for the purposes of navigation and exploration, and for the calculation of precise dates for religious purposes (as in Judaism, Islam follows a lunar calendar). The early centuries of Islam saw great scholarly 'all-rounders' such as al-Kindī during the third/ninth century (one of the few scientists of purely Arab origin), ar-Rāzī (Rhazes) in the ninth to the tenth centuries, Ibn Sīnā (Avicenna) in the eleventh century, and al-Bīrūnī in the tenth to the eleventh centuries.

Greek philosophy opened up new horizons for the theology of Islam and questioned the traditional self-sufficiency of the Qur'ān and *sunna*. The development of *kalām*, speculative or philosophical theology, extended the use of rational argument. Eventually, through the work of al-Ashʿarī (tenth century) and others, philosophy and reason were accepted as supporting revelation; the basics of Greek thought were retained but Islamic teachings were primary. Qur'ānic references to God's hands, eyes, throne, and the vision of God in Paradise were accepted literally but 'without asking how'.

Law is a characteristic science of Islam. The Qur'ān and *ḥadīth*, the two main sources, supported by *qiyās* (analogy), can dictate the most minute details of conduct. On major issues, four *madhāhib* (singular *madhhab*, generally translated as 'law schools') were developed by the second and third/eighth and ninth centuries. They are named after their founders, Abū Ḥanīfa, Ibn Ḥanbal, al-Shāfiʿī, and Mālik. The Ḥanbalī interpretation is usually the strictest; the Ḥanafī interpretation is the most comprehensive and widespread.

The Arabic medical texts and teachings of the medieval period were the most advanced of their time; a Muslim traveller during the Crusades wrote with horror of 'Frankish' medical practice. The Arabs used Greek works and developed their own expertise, and in pharmacy they added new *materia medica*. From the eleventh century on, Arabic medical works were translated into Latin, mostly in Spain and Italy, and continued to influence and instruct the West. Only with the work of such men as Vesalius and Harvey in the sixteenth and seventeenth centuries did they cede their position to Western medical science. In pharmacology, however, the Arabic tradition persisted until the nineteenth century; and today, in the Middle East, medical herbals and pharmacopeia are still published, as are editions of *Medicine of the Prophet*, combining folk lore, herbalism, and pious practice.

Western science in the modern world was accepted by Arab societies, especially with Napoleon's invasion of Egypt. His experts studied the ancient civilizations while Egypt acquired Western science, training, and expertise. More recently, in some Muslim countries there has been a reaction against the West, seen as the source of secularism, immorality, and irreligion. The more balanced view is to accept the discoveries and technology while attempting to avoid aspects of Western life that are seen as incompatible with Islam; mostly these would also be against Christian teachings, but there is a tendency to conflate 'Christian' with 'Western'. At the same time, Arabs and Muslims are recovering a proper pride in their scientific and cultural heritage and its place in the history of civilization.

THE SPREAD OF ISLAM

Islam describes itself as *dīn wa-dawla* (religion and state), indicating a reality that existed from the earliest days; unlike the Western tradition, there is virtually no separation between 'religion' and 'politics'. The drive to spread both religious and political control was evident in the zealous military expansion of the Empire during the religion's first century. From the mid-eighth century, much of Andalus, the Iberian peninsula, became a Muslim Umayyad power, which lasted until the early eleventh century. At the same time, Muslim armies were moving eastwards into Central Asia and to the borders of India. By 732, a century after Muḥammad's death, the Muslim empire had reached its furthest extent in terms of conquest and territory. The whole population did not become Muslim at once, but the culture, language, and legal structure formed the framework for an Islamic society.

However, in terms of Islam's goal to expand its sphere of influence, it is worth noting that, contrary to popular belief, Islam was not primarily 'spread by the sword'. A religion which started and was apparently rooted in the Middle East was able to spread not only along the lines of conquest and empire but in more peaceful ways. Despite the Arab nature of Islam, of its language and scholarship, the majority of Muslims today are not Arab: many millions are in Southeast Asia, Africa, China, and the former USSR. This did not come about by military means but through trade and travel, which are encouraged by Islam, and particularly through the example and influence of the Sufi orders. The annual *ḥajj* (pilgrimage) to Makka brings to the centre thousands of people from all parts of the world, Arabic supplying a shared language at least for religious observance.

AFRICA The initial spread of Islam was indeed a consequence of the conquests under the early caliphs. The Arab armies moved swiftly across the Fertile Crescent (Egypt, Palestine, Syria, Mesopotamia, *see page 198*) and along the North African coast. Where a Berber chief saw the advantage of becoming Muslim, the tribe would follow. North Africa – the home of St Augustine of Hippo and, in the fifth century CE, with a flourishing Church (*see page 244*) – soon became Islamized, and no indigenous Christians remain as they do in the Middle East (in spite of the Christian status of *dhimma*). Conversion to Islam was not encouraged at first as the religion was deemed to be Arab, but by the second/eighth century individuals and groups were attracted to the ruling religion, which brought distinct advantages, and a process of conversion began that lasted for several centuries.

Sub-Saharan Africa was accessible across the desert, or along the Nile into the Sudan, but Islam arrived mainly through maritime trade with the coastal cities. In East Africa, Arabic and Persian traders were frequent visitors from the seventh century onwards, and many settled along the coast. In both East and West Africa, trading contacts brought the ruling classes into Islam and the arrival of Sufis led to the conversion of local populations. In West Africa, some Islamic states were formed from the late tenth/eleventh century, although Islam remained largely the religion of the rulers and elite. In general, Islam was not exclusive, and to this day villages and even families may include both Muslim and non-Muslim members.

SOUTHEAST ASIA Southeast Asia as considered here comprises the Malay peninsula, Java and Sumatra (now Indonesia), Borneo, a number of smaller islands and island groups, and The Philippines. The area in all extends some 5,450 kilometres (3,400 miles) west to east and 2,000 kilometres (1,250 miles) north to south. Islam came to Southeast Asia more gradually than to the Arab world and it was absorbed over a longer period *(see page 22)*. The region had close trading contacts with Arabia and India, and Muslim merchants probably settled in trading ports, accompanied by missionary Sufis. They would thus establish an Islamic presence which, apart from its religious content, would appeal to the local rulers for its valuable commercial networks and to the local people for its unifying qualities. Indonesia began to become Muslim from the late seventh/thirteenth century through contacts between the coastal trading communities and Muslim merchants; conversion very gradually spread inland. There was travel not only for trade; students and scholars, Sufis, and holy men helped bring about the organization of Islamic society in a new environment. Local regimes were not replaced by Islamic rulers; rather, Islamic teachings were blended into the long-established and highly developed culture and society, and so the 'Arab' element was minimal. The religion in Southeast Asia acquired a distinctive local character, while remaining definitely Islamic.

Not much documentation exists for the earlier period, but a Muslim presence in Sumatra is recorded by Marco Polo in the late thirteenth century and in the mid-fourteenth by Ibn Baṭṭūṭa, the renowned Moroccan traveller. This region saw the first strong Muslim kingdom in Southeast Asia, Acheh (or Atjeh) in the northwestern tip of Sumatra, which was a powerful force by the end of the sixteenth century. By the early fifteenth century, Malacca on the Malay peninsula was a small independent kingdom with a Muslim ruler and extensive trading contacts; it was to become an

Muslims at prayer in the Isqal Mosque, Djakarta, Java. It is the largest mosque in Southeast Asia.

important centre for spreading Islam. Towards the end of the century, other rulers in the peninsula had become Muslim and Johore became a focus for the religion. On Java, the Muslim kingdom of Mataram was established and by 1625 had control of the whole island. Northeast from Java, Islam was accepted in the Molucca islands and part of Borneo at the end of the fifteenth century. During the century Islam reached The Philippines from Java and Sumatra, and a large population of Muslims remains today, although the majority religion is Christian. A Malay translation of the Qur'ān was made in the mid-seventeenth century by ʿAbd al-Ra'uf al-Sinkili. This translation perhaps highlights the way in which Islam was able to adapt to local situations, making the Qur'ān more accessible. Orthodox Islam in Malaysia and Indonesia has its individual character, with Sufism as a powerful influence.

In the sixteenth century, European traders entered Indonesia. Trade in spices and pepper prompted the need for ports and secure bases. The Portuguese were first, followed by the Dutch, and both acquired territory; between them they had control of the East Indies and Malaya until the nineteenth century. The European presence caused displacement of people, and the interchange of populations between the islands strengthened Islamic identity and cooperation. Dutch trading interests expanded and the Dutch East India Company established a firm foothold, with their new trading centre on the northwest coast of Java, named Batavia. In 1800, control passed to the Dutch government where it remained, other than for a brief period (1811–1816) when Java and its dependencies came under British control with Stamford Raffles as governor. In 1819, the British established a base at Singapore and held the Malacca Strait, between Sumatra and the Malay peninsula. By the mid-nineteenth century, the British and Dutch had possessions in Malaya and Indonesia respectively.

The early twentieth century saw the rise of indigenous movements that sought greater autonomy. Budi Utomo (Noble Endeavour), founded by a group of Dutch-educated Javanese, aimed to modernize the social system, which was based on traditional Muslim structures. Other movements followed, the most significant being Sarekat Islam (Islamic Union) in 1912. Within the Islamic movements, the Muhammadiyah (1912) was predominantly modernist and the Nahdatul Ulama (1926) was traditionalist. The Indonesian National Party (PNI) was founded in 1927 with Achmed Sukarno (1901–1970) at its head, aiming for a unified Indonesia that was independent of The Netherlands.

All such political activity was halted with the outbreak of the Second World War and the Japanese occupation from 1942 to 1945. After the war, Indonesia finally became an independent republic, with a coalition government made up of representatives of the Muslim and national parties and Communists, and with Sukarno as president (1945–1966). A national state was proclaimed based on the *Pancasila* (Five Principles), the ideals of belief in God, nationalism, humanitarianism, democracy, and social justice. In the 1960s, a civil war left the communists defeated, and General Suharto (born 1921) became President in 1966.

Although Indonesia is not officially Muslim, a Ministry of Religion safeguards the interests of Muslims and other believers; non-political Islam is encouraged and the Ministry of Education promotes Islamic education, with religious instruction in all schools. In 1951, the Islamic State University was founded, becoming in 1960 the State Institute of Islamic Religion. A similar process occurred on the Malay peninsula. In 1948, a Federation of Malaya was formed, then in 1957 an independent Malayan state established, with Islam as the official religion but with guaranteed freedom of worship. In 1963, the state was named Malaysia. The country is nominally Muslim, with a strong *dakwah* (*da`wa*) movement of missionary and educational endeavour.

The discovery and exploitation of oil have added greatly to the prosperity of the region; the Sulṭān of Brunei – a small Islamic state in northwest Borneo – is currently one of the richest men in the world. Mosques in the Indonesian-Malaysian region are large and beautiful, with a distinctive style of architecture that is more akin to the Indian tradition of temple-building than to the structure or geometrical ornamentation of Arab mosques.

ISLAM IN INDIA

At the time of the early Islamic conquests, the first inroads were made into India. An army dispatched by the governor of Iraq invaded and captured the Sind region in the lower Indus valley (93–94/711–712). Arabs established small independent dynasties in the new territory and some indigenous tribes became Muslim.

At the same time, in neighbouring Afghanistan, the Muslim Ghaznavids came to power, and the most capable of their kings, Maḥmūd (388–421/998–1030), made almost annual raids into India between 999 and 1027. Not merely a warrior, Maḥmūd brought back to his court Indian poets and artists as well as vast quantities of booty. The Ghaznavids were ousted by the Ghūrids who also raided northern India, as far down as the Ganges. In the late sixth/twelfth century, the local governor of north India became independent of the central authority, and the rulers of Delhi took the title of Sulṭān in the early thirteenth century, a sign of their power and autonomy *(see pages 40 and 42)*. In 639/1241, the Mongols overran the Punjab, but the sultanate recovered, repulsed the Mongols, and Muslim power moved southwards, through the Deccan. A number of sultanates co-existed, including those of Bengal, Kashmir, Gujarat, and Jawnpur. The year 720/1320 saw the rise of the Tughluqid dynasty in Delhi. Under Muḥammad ibn Tughluq (725–752/1325–1351), *ʿulamāʾ* (religious scholars) and holy men were sent to outlying areas to prepare the ground for Islam. Force was not used in the conversion; rather, the universality of Islam appealed to those disaffected with the caste system, while large numbers became Muslim through contact with the Chishtī Sufi order, founded in India during the late twelfth century and which valued learning, contemplation, and particularly music and songs of devotion as a way of approaching the Infinite. *Masjids* (mosques), *madrasas* (religious schools), and *khānaqāhs* (residences for Sufis) formed the basis of Muslim life and society in India. The Delhi sultanate itself was nominally Muslim, although the rulers varied from strict observance to open flouting of the law.

Muḥammad ibn Tughluq's son Fīrūz was a strong sultan and displayed tolerance towards Hindus. However, after Fīrūz's death in 790/1388, a succession of weak rulers led to the gradual disintegration of the sultanate, which was then attacked by

Tīmūr and his Mongol armies in 801/1397–1398. Delhi surrendered but Tīmūr then returned north. It was a descendant of Tīmūr, Bābur, who finally invaded and took over the sultanate in 932/1526, plundering, occupying Delhi and Agra, and moving on to become master of the whole of northern India. A man of letters as well as a soldier, he was succeeded in 937/1530 by his son Humāyūn and in 963/1556 by his grandson Akbar, the true founder of the Mughal dynasty. Akbar's reign is described as the 'golden age' of the Mughal empire; territory under Mughal control expanded, as Akbar's conquests took in Kashmir and Baluchistan to the north and the Deccan to the south. Although originally a devout Muslim, he was tolerant of the local religion and receptive to its tenets. He abolished the poll tax on Hindus and his chief financial adviser was a Hindu; the government accounts were kept in Persian, all of which reflected his openness and acceptance of non-Muslim influences. Debates on religious matters were held in his city of Fathepur-Sikri and he proclaimed a new style of monotheistic religion, Dīn-i Ilāhī, comprising elements from various religions (the faith died with Akbar).

At Akbar's death in 1014/1605, his son Jahāngīr *(see pages 66–67)* ruled until 1628 and was succeeded by Shāh Jahān (1037–68/1628–58), builder of the Tāj Maḥal in Agra. His son Aurangzeb came to the throne in 1658. A strict Muslim, he reintroduced the poll tax on Hindus and destroyed some Hindu temples. The reign saw continual unrest and fighting, the emperor leading his own campaigns. On his death in 1118/1707, his son Muʿazzam won power and reigned as Bahādur Shāh. The empire was weakening and in 1151/1738 suffered invasions by Nādir Shāh from Afghanistan. The Hindus gradually regained power and influence while the British and other Europeans became more powerful. In 1274/1858, the last Mughal was deposed on a charge of complicity in the Indian Mutiny/War of Independence, and India came under the British. Islam was no longer a dominant religion, and was frequently in conflict with Hinduism.

ISLAM IN PAKISTAN

In 1947, the Indian continent was partitioned. Pakistan (the land of the pure), under the leadership of Muḥammad Ali Jinnah (1876–1948), included the Muslim areas of West Punjab, the Northwest Frontier, Baluchistan, Sind, and – at first – East Bengal. The new country contained 80 million people, while some 50 million Muslims remained in India. In 1971, after a civil war, East Pakistan seceded and became Bangladesh. Islam has functioned in three different ways within Pakistan. Before the premiership of Zhulfiqar Ali Bhutto (1971–1977), it was a focus of national unity rather than a governmental programme. Under Bhutto, it was used to legitimize socialism. Under General Zia al-Haq's rule (1977–1988), the focus was on an Islamic system (*niẓām-i muṣṭafa*), lending legitimacy to his military regime. The Sufi element has a strong influence in modern Pakistan. Three orders are prominent: the Qadiriyya, the Suhrawardiyya, and the Indian order, the Chishtiyya. Shrines have grown up around the graves of *pīrs* (holy men and past sufis), and there is a belief in the inter-cession of saints, although orthodox Islam rejects this. The Barelwi (or Brelvi) tradition, founded at Bareilly in Uttar Pradesh by Ahmad Raza Khan (1856–1921), supports devotion to *pīrs* and their shrines. This is strongly opposed by the Deobandi, followers of a traditional *madrasa*, and hostility between the two groups can be extreme. The Tablighi Jama'at, founded by a former Deoband student, Māulānā Ilyās (1885–1944), concentrates on individual spiritual and moral renewal, also rejecting saint-worship. While townspeople and the more sophisticated may appear to be Muslim only in a cultural sense, in the countryside Islam regulates daily life, and for many Pakistani Muslims abroad, the link with the home country is represented and kept alive by their religion.

ISLAMIC OBSERVANCE IN INDIA AND PAKISTAN

Islam in India has been described as 'essentially a holy-man Islam'. As long as orthodox belief and practice held sway, the Sufi way of life fitted in with the tradition of Hindu holy men, while shrines and the veneration of tombs were accepted more readily than in the Islamic heartlands. Akbar's openness was criticized by some religious elders such as the traditionalist Naqshbandī shaykh, Aḥmad Sirhindī (971–1034/1564–1624). Later, another Naqshbandī shaykh, Shāh Walī Allāh (died 1763), sought a 'new spirit of *ijtihād*', the interpretation of Islam in the light of contemporary thought. In the nineteenth century, Muslim thinkers in India were aware of and wrestled with modern

Western ideas. Sayyid Ahmad Khan (1817–1898) saw the need for a modern version of *kalām*, religious dialectic. He founded the Aligarh college, rejected *taqlīd* (unquestioning following of tradition), called for a re-interpretation of the Qur'ān, and wrote a comparative study of Islam and Christianity. A little later, Muḥammad Iqbal (1876–1938), scholar and poet, wrote *The Reconstruction of Islamic Religious Thought* (1928). Like Muḥammad Ali Jinnah (1876–1948), the founder of Pakistan, he believed that Muslims needed their own nation. Finally, the tension between Muslims and Hindus erupted in the tragic slaughter and displacement of millions that accompanied Partition in 1947. Islam had its own nation, but at a terrible price.

In Asia, Africa, and the Indian subcontinent, European exploration, trade, and colonial expansion brought a new experience for Islam from the sixteenth to the nineteenth century: existence under non-Muslim rule. As seen in Southeast Asia, this led to mass migration, which in turn produced a new phenomenon: large numbers of Muslims living in the West and Europe (*see page 303*).

Muslims, some of them western converts, outside the mosque in Konya, Turkey. After World War One and the disintegration of the Ottoman empire, Islam experienced a period of repression in Turkey, but it began to regain status and adherents from the middle of the twentieth century.

THE OTTOMAN EMPIRE

The Ottomans were the last and by far the greatest and most long-lived of a series of Turkish dynasties that ruled over parts of the Islamic world from the fourth/tenth century onwards. Ultimately, they can be seen as the successors of the Seljuqs, who ruled the region now covered by Iran and Iraq in the fifth/eleventh century, establishing a subsidiary state in Anatolia following their victory over the Byzantines at Manzikert in 464/1071. This Seljuq Sultanate of Rūm was made possible by a large migration of Oghuz Turks from Iran.

The Ottoman (or Osmanli) dynasty is named after ʿUthmān (Osman, ruled 1281–1324), who, towards the end of the thirteenth century, established the nucleus of a state in northwest Anatolia. His son Orkhān (ruled 1324–60) consolidated and extended their possessions in Anatolia, captured Bursa and Iznik, and during the 1350s moved into Europe via Gallipoli and raided Thrace. The capital of the dynasty was moved in 767/1366 from Bursa to Edirne (Adrianople) on the European mainland, and the Ottoman armies gradually took control of the Balkans while simultaneously extending their hold in Anatolia. An invasion by the Mongol warrior Tīmūr (Tamerlane) in 804/1402 saw the defeat of the Ottomans and the capture of the sultan, Bāyezīd (ruled 1389–1402), but the Mongols did not occupy the region permanently. Ten years of civil war followed, but then the unity of the state was restored and Ottoman expansion continued once again. By degrees, the Christian population of Anatolia became largely Muslim, although Christians remained in the majority in the Balkans.

Ottoman fortress on Kekova Island off Turkey's Aegean coast. Under the Ottoman Turks, Islam spread further into the Balkans and eastern Europe.

THE EMPIRE'S HEYDAY Under Meḥmet Fātiḥ (the Conqueror, 855–886/1451–1481), the capture of Constantinople in 857/1453 was an event of enormous significance for the Ottomans; it united the two halves of their now substantial empire and symbolically gave the Ottoman sultan the status of successor to the Byzantine emperor. It was also a decisive blow to Byzantine and Christian power, pride, and confidence. The great church of Hagia Sofia was turned into a mosque and the nature of the city changed totally.

Under the Ottomans, who were Sunnī Muslims, *madrasas* (religious schools) and *waqfs* (pious endowments) performed the function of ensuring the perpetuation of learning and of charitable institutions, many of which were the inspiration for very beautiful and distinctive Ottoman architecture. The Islamic world achieved a unity that it had not known since the ʿAbbasids. In 924/1516 and 1517, the Ottoman conquests took in the Mamluk realms of Syria and Egypt, which remained in their control until the nineteenth century, and the Ottomans became responsible also for the maintenance and supervision of Makka and Madīna. Under Suleymān the Magnificent (ruled 926–974/1520–1566), the empire was at its peak in terms of both culture and power. Suleymān brought most of Hungary under his rule, and during this period the coastlands of Algeria and Tunisia also came under Ottoman suzerainty. Both Meḥmet and Suleymān introduced new administrative law codes which supplemented *sharīʿa* law.

One remarkable feature of the organization of the Ottoman state in its heyday was that a large proportion of the army and the senior state officials were recruited by compulsory levy from the non-Muslim population of the Balkans. Recruits were subjected to rigorous training which included conversion to Islam. The most famous force to be staffed by these former Christians was the infantry corps of Janissaries.

There was general tolerance towards *dhimmīs* (Armenians, Syrian and Greek Christians, and Jews), whose religious hierarchies were to some extent incorporated into the administrative system. The Ottomans encouraged the arts of Islam: architecture, distinctive styles of calligraphy, illuminated manuscripts, painting and craftwork. Literature, especially poetry, was of great importance to the educated elite, who drew their inspiration from Persia. Sufis and a number of *ṭuruq* *(see page 286)* played a central role in religious life and culture, the more orthodox in urban areas, the less orthodox in rural locations. In the sixteenth and seventeenth centuries, changing attitudes brought a more conservative form of Islam to the fore, and more extreme Sufi practices tended to be suppressed.

DECLINE OF THE OTTOMAN EMPIRE After Suleymān, it became difficult for the Ottomans to make further advances into Europe. Following a period of inconclusive warfare, a 1606 treaty recognized the Habsburg emperors as equals of the sultans; in 1683, the second Ottoman siege of Vienna was unsuccessful and led to their first substantial territorial losses in Europe, recognized by the 1699 Treaty of Karlowitz.

During the seventeenth and eighteenth centuries, the balance of power shifted further against the Ottomans and the empire proved too extensive for its central authority to control adequately. The Venetians, the Habsburgs, and the Russians gained former Ottoman lands. By the early eighteenth century, the sultans recognized the superior technologies of Europe and began to bring in foreign military advisers; even art and architecture showed a foreign influence. This foreshadowed a thoroughgoing programme of modernization in the nineteenth century, which failed to save the empire from final collapse during the First World War.

The nineteenth and early twentieth centuries saw the continuing decline and the eventual demise of the once powerful Ottoman empire. Napoleon's expedition to Egypt in 1798 – although his forces were expelled in 1801 with the help of the British – marked the beginning of wholesale European intervention. The appointment in 1805 of Muḥammad ʿAlī as governor made Egypt virtually independent of the Ottomans. Under him, Egypt gained control of western Arabia, including Makka and Madīna, extended its influence southwards into the Sudan, and in 1831 invaded Syria. In 1882, Egypt came under British occupation, which lasted until 1952.

From the mid-eighteenth century, nationalist movements in the Balkans became a serious threat to the empire; within a century, they had led to the disintegration of Ottoman power in the region and the birth of nation states. In 1830, the Greeks were the first to gain independence, after a bitter war involving European powers. After the Congress of Berlin in 1878, which saw the recognition of a number of these autonomous states, the process of disintegration accelerated and the major European powers appropriated various Ottoman territories.

Mosques

The word *masjid*, 'mosque', means any ritually clean place for prostration for the *ṣalāt* (worship). Traditionally, however, it is a place built for the purpose of communal prayer which may have a library or school attached.

Traditionally, mosques have a central entrance, often a *qubba* (dome), and a *manāra* (minaret) from which the *ādhān* (call to prayer) is given. The interior is almost empty, with carpets on the floor (shoes are left at the outer door), and at the far end is the *miḥrāb* (niche) marking the *qibla* (direction of Makka and of prayer). This is generally ornamented with calligraphic Qur'ānic verses and geometrical designs. There may also be Qurʾānic verses on the walls and around the dome, but no figurative art is allowed. Near the *qibla* is the *minbar* (pulpit) from where the Friday sermon is delivered by the imam, the prayer leader; Sunni imams are appointed by the community, sometimes acting as religious instructors, but with no charismatic or inherited role as in Shī ʿism. There is a separate area for *wuḍū*, ablutions, since ritual cleanliness is demanded. No Islamic ruling bars women from attending mosques although they will be separated from men, and in some places their presence is culturally opposed.

The *ṣalāt*, enjoined on all Muslims five times a day, is usually performed individually at home or at work. Assembly for the *jumʿa* (Friday) midday prayer is obligatory for free, adult males, as is gathering for major festivals such as ʿEid al-Fiṭr (breaking of the fast) at the end of Ramaḍān, and the ʿEid al-Kabīr (Great Feast of Sacrifice) during the *ḥajj* (pilgrimage) month.

The traditional method of teaching, where a learned shaykh sat by a pillar and his 'circle' of students gathered around him, can still be seen at al-Azhar in Cairo; however, earlier teaching by oral exposition and rote learning has evolved into a more structured curriculum, with modern methods and materials. Al-Azhar itself has long been one of the most influential centres of Islamic scholarship. Since the mid-twentieth century, the scope of its *jāmiʿa* (university) has extended to include medicine and various secular subjects.

Many mosques had – and in the Arab world still have – a *madrasa* attached. Originally, this was a religious school where young male Muslims learned to recite the Qurʾān by heart and to read and write Qurʾānic verses, and then to read Qurʾān commentaries by approved authors, *ḥadīth*, and biographies of *ḥadīth* scholars.

Worshippers at prayer in the al-Aqsa mosque in Old City Jerusalem, known as *al-Quds*, the Holy, to Muslims. Jerusalem is considered third in sacredness after Makka and Madīna.

Today, a *madrasa* indicates an ordinary primary or secondary school. The word can, however, still refer to traditional religious schools, some of which have been established beyond the Muslim world, such as those in northern England where there are large Muslim communities. The *madrasas* at Bury and Dewsbury are part of a network of some dozen Deobandi *madrasas*, where students follow a routine based on medieval instruction.

REFORMS AND INTERNAL CONFLICT In an attempt to stem the tide, Ottoman governments undertook several reform programmes, largely along European lines. Modernization began seriously during the reign of Maḥmūd II (1223–55/1807–1839), who abolished the Janissaries and succeeded in re-establishing central control over much of the empire. Reforms continued during the period of Tanzimat ('Reorganization', 1255–93/1839–1876), with the emphasis on government and law, and a system of secular education was instituted. Some law codes were based on European law, while the Mejelle (1870) was a codification of sections of *sharīʿa* law. During the 1850s and 1860s, non-Muslim Ottoman subjects were guaranteed rights under law, and in 1856 an imperial decree granted them equality with Muslims, a move which emphasized the concept of citizenship and could encourage Ottoman identity and loyalty.

The Tanzimat gave rise to a new administrative class, educated along modern lines. Within this class a group of intellectuals known as the Young Ottomans were resentful of what they saw as the leading statesmen's conciliatory attitude towards the European powers. They stirred up public opinion through the press and began openly to campaign for constitutional and representative government.

The reign of ʿAbd al-Ḥamīd II (1293–1327/1876–1908) began with his supporters forcing him to accept a constitution of a more democratic nature, but once in power he rejected it and initiated an autocratic and religiously conservative period of government. He emphasized the Islamic character of the state and even promoted himself as the natural leader of Muslims worldwide. The repressive conditions of his reign forced opposition elements to flee abroad, and in Paris in the 1890s the 'Young Turks' founded the Ottoman Society for Union and Progress, committed to overthrowing the regime. In 1907, army officers became involved in the opposition movement, leading to the 'revolution' of 1908 which forced ʿAbd al-Ḥamīd to restore the abortive constitution of 1876.

The last decade of Ottoman rule was a period of great turbulence and further territorial losses. It saw the centralizing and increasingly nationalistic policies of the 'unionist' Young Turks come up against more liberal, decentralizing tendencies. After the hiatus of the rule of ʿAbd al-Ḥamīd, further secularizing laws brought even religious schools and courts under the authority of the state. The sense of Ottoman identity was gradually moving towards one of Turkish ethnic identity: Anatolia as the home of the Turkish people, rooted in central Asia.

The First World War changed the map considerably. The Ottoman government, now under the control of the unionists (the Committee for Union and Progress), sided with Germany. Arabia under Ḥusayn, Sharīf (ruler) of Makka, pursued guerrilla warfare against the Turks, hoping for independence. Meanwhile, the British and French were dividing up the Middle East into 'spheres of influence'. When the Ottomans were defeated in 1918, the League of Nations granted Britain mandatory status over Palestine and Iraq and France similar powers over Lebanon and Syria.

Mustafa Kemal (later known as Ataturk), the Ottoman general who had repulsed the Allies at Gallipoli during the war, became the leader of the movement of national resistance against the powers occupying areas of the Turkish homeland. A three-year struggle, mainly against the invading Greeks, ended in 1923 with the Treaty of Lausanne which recognized Turkey as an independent state. The Ottoman Sultanate having been abolished already in 1922, the Republic of Turkey was proclaimed, with Mustafa Kemal as its first president (1923–1938). In 1924, the caliphate was formally abolished. Sufi orders were banned in 1925, and in 1928 the Ottoman Arabic script was compulsorily replaced by the Latin script. *Sharī ʿa* was replaced by law codes entirely of European origin, which radically altered the legal status of women in Turkey. Ataturk died in 1938, but the one-party regime which he had established continued until 1945. From the late 1940s, with the introduction of multi-party politics, Islamic religious expression was given much more freedom, and Islam was taught in schools. Since the 1970s, Islam has had a place in Turkish political life.

ISLAM IN THE MODERN WORLD

The twentieth century saw many changes in the Muslim world. World wars; the end of most colonial rule; the rise of nation-states in Asia, the Middle East, and Africa; the discovery of oil, the development of new industries, and their commercial exploitation by multinational companies; increasing ease and frequency of travel; communication by radio, television, and the internet; mass migration – all have brought Muslims into contact with foreign and non-Islamic communities and cultures. On an intellectual and religious level, Islam has had to acknowledge the rapid developments of modern times. The response to modernity varies widely within the Islamic world, according to geographical, historical, and economic circumstances. Grave doubts about the moral values of the West do not hinder Arab and Muslim countries from adopting whatever innovations and technologies they think beneficial.

The Emir of Kano and his entourage in Kano, Nigeria. Islam came to Western Africa via sea traders and was mostly confined to the elite.

Resistance to change has been called be outsiders 'Islamic fundamentalism', often with the term 'extremist', meaning 'using violent means to further political aims'. In fact, 'fundamentalism' is only appropriate if it implies 'a return to the foundations'. An early such reform movement, still operating today, was that of the Wahhābīs, founded in the eighteenth century by Muḥammad ʿAbd al-Wahhāb (1703–1787), a strict Ḥanbalī. He rejected Sufism and all kinds of *bidʿa* (innovation), and together with Ibn Saʿūd (1746–1765), an Arabian tribal chief, founded what became the Saʿūdī kingdom, which has continued to uphold orthodox Islam. The vast oil resources, first exploited in the 1930s, have kept Saudi Arabia and neighbouring states economically prosperous, while the annual *ḥajj* ensures the kingdom's Islamic prominence.

In Egypt, Muḥammad ʿAbduh (1849–1905), a leading judge and rector of al-Azhar, modernized the curriculum of this ancient, and by now Sunnī, influential seat of learning. In his view, religion, based on the Qur'ān, *ḥadīth*, and the example of *as-salaf as-ṣāliḥ* (the pious ancestors), was compatible with science and reason, and he expressed his wish for a reinterpretation of Islam in *The Theology of Unity* (1897). The so-called Salafiyya movement inspired by ʿAbduh was influential throughout the Middle East. At much the same time in the Indian subcontinent, another reformer, Sayyid Ahmad Khan (1817–1898), wrote an extensive commentary on the Qur'ān; later, Muḥammad Iqbal set himself the task of reviving Indian Islam and supported the idea of an Islamic state, which came about with the creation of Pakistan in 1947.

Rejection of the modern world is an element in the Ikhwān al-Muslimūn (Muslim Brothers), founded in 1928 by Ḥasan al-Bannā (1906–1949). He spoke out against the corruption in Egyptian politics, the growth of materialism, and (in his view) the failure of the scholars of al-Azhar to defend and represent Islam. The Ikhwān have been

Pilgrims complete their *ḥajj* at Makka, 1998. The *ḥajj*, the pilgrimage to the Kaʿba in Makka during Dhū'l-Ḥijja, the last month of the Muslim calendar, is a duty laid down in the Qur'ān that all adult Muslims must try to fulfil at least once in their lives. Rituals and celebrations last for almost two weeks.

officially banned several times in Egypt. Another reform movement, the Jamaat-i Islami, was founded in Lahore in 1941 by Abu al-ʿAlāʾ al-Mawdūdī (1903–1979). As with the Muslim Brothers, religious revival was combined with social action, and the movement is still important.

A truly Islamic state remains a distant goal. The overthrow of the Shāh of Iran in 1979 by a popular revolutionary movement headed by Ayatullāh Rūḥullah Khumayni (Khomeini)(1902–1989) introduced a strictly observant rule of law, under Shī ʿa principles, which restricted women's freedom and led to persecution of the Bahā ʾī community *(see page 307)*. The government had mellowed considerably by the end of the twentieth century, although a far more intolerant regime in neighbouring Afghanistan, the Ṭālibān, is Sunni and Wahhābī and not in sympathy with Iran.

MIGRATION TO THE NON-MUSLIM WORLD A new aspect of Islamic life seen in the twentieth century was the large-scale migration of individuals and groups, post-1945, to the non-Muslim West, especially to Europe, where the first wave was of migrant or 'guest' workers who intended to earn well and return home. From the 1960s, this changed, particularly in Britain, to the migration of whole families and communities, largely from Pakistan, India, and Bangladesh.

Migration tends to be related to colonial and trading links, so North African Muslims frequently migrate to France, Turkish Muslims to Germany, and East Indian Muslims to the Netherlands. Mosques and centres were built or adapted and governments had to provide special educational, welfare, and housing services. As the second and third generations have come through school and higher education and joined the workforce, there are inevitable tensions within the Muslim community: the generation gap is accentuated by the permissive wider environment, polarized attitudes towards the home country, and often the imam's lack of knowledge of the local language and social realities. This is changing for the better, with Islamic societies for students and professionals, training centres for imams, Islamic schools – which arouse mixed reactions – and the hard work and success of Muslims themselves. The Salman Rushdie affair, when Ayatullāh Khumayni issued a *fatwa* (legal opinion on Islamic law) ordering the death of the novelist for perceived blasphemy in *The Satanic Verses* (1988), highlighted a certain mutual incomprehension between the Muslim and non-Muslim worlds, but also brought about an awareness of the need for greater understanding and co-operation.

Associations representing various Muslim countries are found overseas, aimed at keeping the contacts alive between home and migrant communities and religious observances strong. The Muslim Brothers and particularly the Jamaat work in Britain. Muslims from the Indian subcontinent may belong to the Barelwi (or Brelvi) tradition, which particularly venerates the Prophet and holy men; there is also the strictly orthodox Deobandi tradition which rejects such devotions. Arising from the Deobandis is the Tablighi Jamaat, founded in 1927, which by preaching and example tries to bring Muslims back to a more fervent practice of their religion. With centres in Africa and Asia, the movement is also active in the United States, Britain, France, Germany and other European countries and has won over many converts.

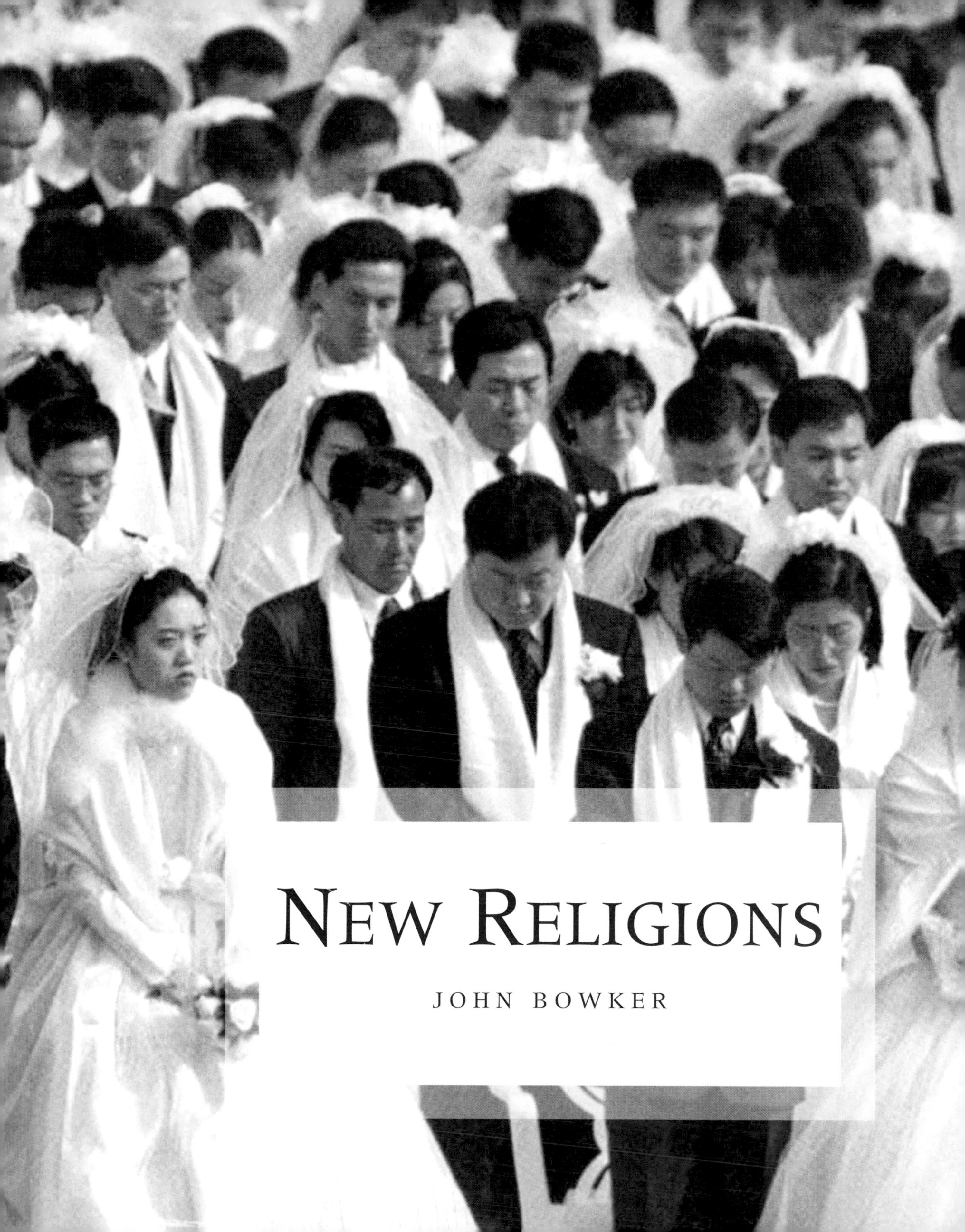

NEW RELIGIONS

JOHN BOWKER

New Religions

This book has been concerned principally with the major world religions. However, in every century there have been countless other religions which, when they first appeared, were called 'new'. New religions are in fact an old phenomenon, and while many have disappeared, others have endured and are no longer in any sense 'new'; furthermore, some recent religions, like Paganism and Wicca, claim to be restoring early beliefs and practices that have been underground for many centuries.

Paganism (the name neo-Paganism has been rejected by many Pagans, on the grounds that their beliefs are not new but represent instead the revival of an ancient religion) includes a large number of different movements and varied beliefs. The Pagan Federation was established in 1981 (on the basis of the earlier Pagan Front, which had been set up in 1970) in order to 'make Paganism accessible to people genuinely seeking a nature-based spiritual path'. In general, Paganism is a religious outlook that gives reverence to Nature and recognizes its animate or ensouled character. It emphasizes the spiritual resonance of particular places, as well as the spiritual significance of the earth.

Modern versions of traditional pagan artefacts on display at Laytonville, California, in the 1990s. The word 'pagan' comes from the Latin *pagus*, meaning 'village' – a country-place, as opposed to a town; hence the adjective *paganus*, 'belonging to the country' or 'country-dweller'. From that, it came to mean a civilian, as opposed to a soldier (*miles*). In Ephesians 6.11–17, Christians are instructed to equip themselves metaphorically as the soldiers of Christ, and in contrast referred to non-Christians as 'civilians', i.e., as pagans.

Wicca (Old English 'to bend' or 'to shape') underlies the word 'witch', but the movements gathered under that name dissociate themselves from what Starhawk (1979), a leader in the revival of Wicca, terms the caricature of witches as 'a kooky cult', and even more from horror-film associations with Satanism and evil. The twentieth-century revival of Wicca owes much to Margaret Murray (who did not use that word) and the claim of George Gardiner to have found people in England practicing witchcraft as an ancient religion that had been passed on secretly down many generations. The claims have been disputed, but Wicca regards itself as the recovery of an ancient European religion whose practitioners use rituals and techniques to recover power, especially within themselves, to change their lives for the better.

Paganism and Wicca are often associated with New Age beliefs and practices, although there are distinctions, especially in the case of Wicca. New Age is a label applied to many very different practices and movements of the late twentieth century. In 1996 the philosopher Paul Heelas identified four general characteristics in the midst of the enormous number and variety of New Age movements: 'you should exercise your own authority'; 'your lives are not working'; 'you are gods and goddesses in exile'; 'let go/drop it'.

The term 'new religions' first became familiar in the case of Japan, where such religions became known as *shinko shukyo* in relation to established religions (*kisei*). The upheavals of the nineteenth century led to the formation of many new religions *(see pages 178–179)*, so much so that in 1900 the Shrine Bureau (*jinja kyoku*) was established to supervise Shrine Shintô, with a separate Religions Bureau (*shukyo kyoku*) to supervise the many different religions and religious movements. Under the Meiji Constitution (1868–1912, but effective until 1945), new religions had to obtain official recognition in order to be legal and not to be called *ruji shukyo*, false religions. Notable new religions of the nineteenth century were Kurozumikyô, Konkôkyô, Omotôkyô, and Tenrikyô (which petitioned for recognition for 40 years). Important new religions of the twentieth century are Reiyukai, Soka Gakkai, and Seicho no Ie.

Outside Japan, new religions have been an equally widespread phenomenon, especially in Africa after the disruption of colonialism. Many – now known as African Instituted Churches – developed from the missionary Churches of Christianity, and include, among a very large number, Kimbangu, Lumpa Church, African Apostles, the Braid movements, the Harris movement, and Aladura churches.

Since 'new' religions are a constant and continuing phenomenon, R. Wallis, in 1984, tried to classify them into three groups according to their response to the world: world-affirming, world-denying, and world-accommodating. They can also be distinguished by their relationship to existing religions: extending, completing or fulfiling an existing religion *(see box, right)*; displacing existing religions; introducing an (or the true) alternative religion, often with a new revelation.

The Path to the Bahā'ī Religion

Of those new religions that complete or fulfil an existing religion, the sequence from Judaism to Christianity to Islam is an early example, with Islam claiming that Muhammad is the final prophet ('the seal of the prophets'). But in fact the sequence did not end there. Sayyid Ali Muhammad Shirazi (1819–50) claimed in 1844, after a series of revelatory visions, that he was the Bāb, or Gate, opening the way to the Imam of the Twelver Shī'ites *(see page 281)*; later he claimed to be the Imam himself. The Bābīs, as they were called, were persecuted by other Muslims, and the Bāb was executed in 1850. The majority of Bābīs gave their allegiance to Bāhā'u'llah, the religious title ('the Glory of God') adopted by Mirza Husayn Ali Nuri (1817–92), who became a Bābī in 1844, was imprisoned in the Black Pit of Teheran in 1852, and experienced his own revelatory visions. From him derives the Bahā'ī religion, with a worldwide membership of more than five million, affirming the oneness of God, religion, and humanity. It has continued to be persecuted by Muslims, who regard it as a contrdiction of the finality of Muhammad and the Qur'ān. It is an example of a world-affirming religion.

In India, religions exist in a coalition of possibilities, so that the completion or fulfilment of an existing religion is less common than the extension of existing religion into a new form in the present. An example is the International Society for Krishna Consciousness (ISKCON), which exists to develop consciousness of Krishna at all times, in work and in play. It was founded in 1966 by A.C. Bhaktivedanta Swami Prabhupada (born Abhay Charan De, 1896–1977), made familiar outside India by devotees chanting the *mantra* of Hari Krishna on the streets. Devotion to Krishna, focused on *Bhagavad Gītā* (see page 40), is deeply traditional, but it is extended by the many writings of Swami Prabhupada, including 30 volumes of *Srimad-Bhagavatam* on which he was still working when he died. In contrast, Transcendental Meditation (TM, founded by Maharishi Mahesh Yogi from 1961 onwards) draws far more eclectically on Indian traditions to bring into effect what are claimed to be neglected natural laws, and to create a science of creative intelligence, especially through its own version of *mantra* repetition. It is an example of a world-accommodating new religion.

Another example is the Church of Scientology, derived from the work of Lafayette Ron Hubbard (1911–86) who, in 1950, published *Dianetics: The Modern Science of Mental Health*, in order to promote the science and practice of Dianetics. Dianetics deals in the main with the 'reactive mind' (rooted in the subconscious), while the Church of Scientology is concerned mainly with the Thetan or everlasting spirit. The Church has been beset with controversy about its methods, especially of recruitment and of dealing with critics, but has vigorously defended itself.

Displacing an existing religion can be seen in the case of the Unification Church, founded by Sun Myung Moon (b. 1920). Born into a North Korean family that converted to Christianity, Moon experienced a vision of Jesus Christ on Easter Day, 1936. The revelations gathered in *The Divine Principle* and other works claim that the misunion of Eve with Lucifer before her union with Adam could not be put right by Jesus because he was killed before he could marry. A more complete redemption is effected through the mass marriages for which the Unification Church is well known. The movement seeks to unify the divided churches of Christianity, as the full title of the movement founded in 1954 indicates: The Holy Spirit Association for the Unification of World Christianity. It nevertheless represents a displacement or replacement of those churches.

Other new religions offer an alternative religion on the basis of a new (or newly discovered) revelation. An example is the Church of Jesus Christ of the Latter-Day Saints, better known as the Mormons. This derives from Joseph Smith (1805–44), who claimed that the angel Moroni had revealed to him where gold tablets were to be found, on which were written the words of God. The book, which Smith translated in 1830, tells of two migrations from the Middle East to America, of how Jesus made a post-resurrection appearance in America, and of how Mormon wrote the text on tablets which he then buried near Palmyra, New York, in 438 CE. Although Mormons insist that they are the restoration of the true Church that Jesus intended, and although many of their articles of faith are little different from those of Christians, at least two of them (that the Book of Mormon is the word of God, and that Zion will be built on the American continent) make it clear this is an alternative to other forms of Christianity.

World-denying new religions can be seen most dramatically in the case of those movements that lead their adherents into death – either their own or those of others. Of these, wide publicity attended the mass suicides that ended the People's Temple of Jim Jones in Guyana (1978), the FBI attack on the Branch Davidians under David Koresh at Waco (1993), the deaths of members of the Order of the Solar Temple (1994, 1995, and 1997), the sarin-gas attack on the Tokyo subway by members of Aum Shinrikyo (1995), and the decision by members of Heaven's Gate to leave their bodies on earth and go to find salvation in the spacecraft travelling in the wake of the Hale-Bopp comet (1997).

Controversy has surrounded many new religions, not just those that have led to a dramatic end. In particular, questions have been raised about the extent to which young people are manipulated or exploited – or, in more popular but inexact language, brainwashed. Groups have been set up to monitor cults and their methods, and even to rescue those who have become members. INFORM (Information Network Focus on Religious Movements) was set up by sociologist Eileen Barker in 1988 to make the results of academic research on new religions and cults available to enquirers. INFORM is neutral, but even so its pamphlet *Searching* warns of the risks to people at school or university: 'There are some new religious movements that promise solutions to life's difficulties but can land you with more problems than you started with! Some are dishonest or secretive about who they really are. Some demand much more of your time than you might have bargained for. Some could cost you a lot of money and get you into serious debt. Some might lead you into an emotional dependence, and you could find it harder to leave than to join.'

With so many risks, why do new religions continue to flourish, especially among the young? Many answers have been offered, but fundamental to them all is the fact that the capacity for religious belief and behaviour is deeply embedded in the human brain and body. It is inevitable, therefore, that people will be religious in some sense. It is this that makes religion so powerful and pervasive in human life and history. It does not follow, however, that people will necessarily take part in an existing religion (or indeed in any recognized religion at all). The human genius for religion leads to the constant development of new religions that seem to their adherents to meet their needs and fulfil their hopes. It leads also to a continuing history of existing religions for exactly the same reason.

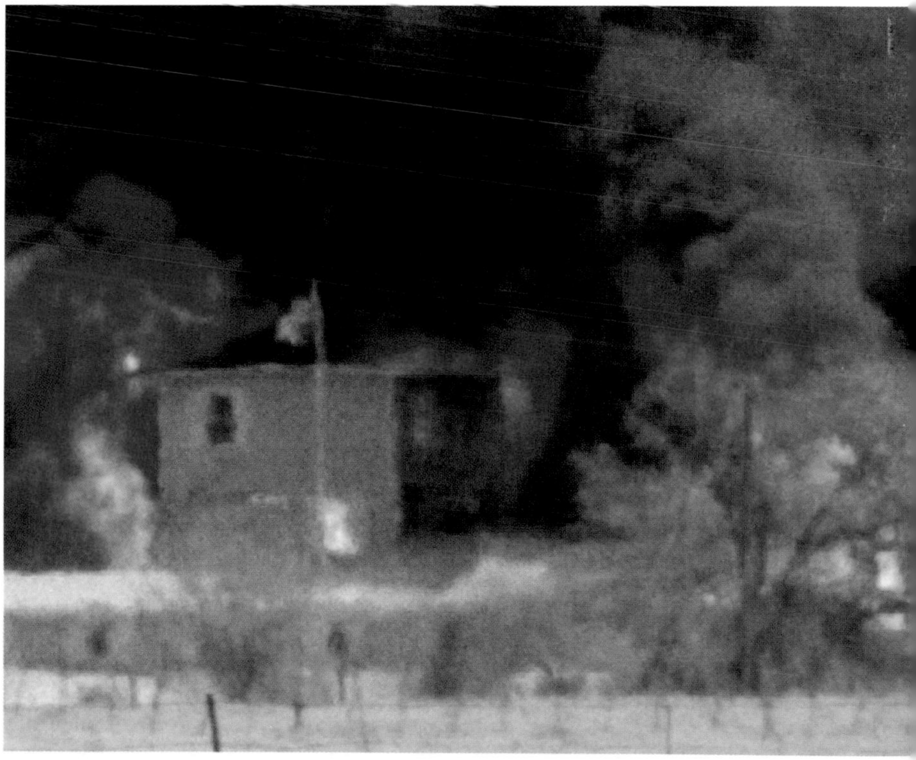

The disastrous aftermath of the 'Siege of Waco', which took place in April 1993. Government troops besieged the headquarters of a cult called the Branch Davidian sect: 80 members died, some by their own hand.

6000 5000 4000 3000 2000 1000 ◄BCE 0 CE► 100 200 300 400 500 600

Indian Religions and the Hindu Tradition

2800–2000 BCE • Indus Valley civilization

1200–600 BCE • *Vedas* composed
900–600 BCE • Brahmans are priests
800–300 BCE • *Upaniṣads* composed

c.320–500 • *Purāṇas* composed

Jainism

400s BCE • Mahāvīra founds Jainism

300–400 • *Tattvārtha Sūtra* compiled
400s • Jainism splits: Śvetāmbara and Digambara sects

Buddhism

480–c.370 BCE • Buddha
250 BCE • Buddhism splits: Theravāda and Mahāyāna
100–0 BCE • Theravāda *Tripiṭaka* compiled

200s • Buddhism in China
300s • Tantricism starts
372 • Buddhism arrives in Korea

500s • Buddhism in Thailand and Burma
550s • Buddhism enters Japa
600s • Buddhism in Tibet and Indonesia

Chinese and Korean Religions

500s BCE • Laozi writes *Daode Jing*
c.551–479 BCE • Confucius
200s BCE • Confucian *Analects* compiled
206 BCE–8 CE • Daoist *Taiping jing* written
145–86 BCE • Confucian *Records of the Historian* written

Pre-300s • Shamanism and ancestor worship in Korea
c.320 CE • Daoist *Baopuzi* written
372 • Buddhism arrives in Korea

631 • Christianity arrives in China
600s • Zoroastriani arrives in China

Japanese

500s • Confucianism and Daoism arrive
538 • Beliefs synchroni into Shintô

Judaism

c.2000 BCE • Biblical patriarchs
1200s BCE • Exodus from Egypt
1000 BCE • Jerusalem is the capital
c.960–586 BCE • First Temple
516 BCE • Second Temple built

0–100 CE • Tenakh is compiled
70 • Rome destroys the Temple
c.200 • Mishnah compiled

c.425 • Jerusalem Talmud compiled
500–600 • Babylonian Talmud compiled

Zarathustra and the Parsis

c.6000–1200 BCE • Zarathustra

500 BCE • Zoroastrianism is state religion of the Persian empire
100 BCE–200 CE • The *Avesta* is compiled

Mediterranean Religions

3000s BCE • Mummification and pyramids
1799–50 BCE • Epics written in Babylon
1540–1069 BCE • Egyptian *Book of the Dead* written

4th century BCE • Greek pantheon spreads in Near East
100s BCE • Rome adopts Greek gods
100 BCE–200 CE • Rome absorbs eastern cults

100–400 • Roman emperor cults dominate

Christianity

c.4 BCE–c.30 CE • Jesus
c.35 • Paul converted
c.70–90 • Gospel according to Mark, Matthew, Luke, and John written
100s • Christianity in India

325 • Christianity becomes the official religion of the Roman empire

Islam

c.570–632 • Muhamm
c.650 • Qur'an comp
680 • Islam splits: Sunni and Sh
Late 600s • Islam arrives in Africa, China, and Sp

0 800 900 1000 1100 1200 1300 1400 1500 1600 1700 1800 1900 2000

00–1000 • *Tantras* compiled
00–1600 • *Bhakti* movements founded
1540s • Christianity arrives
1895 • Vedānta Society formed
1915 • Gandhi works for independence using Hindi ideals
1947 • India partitioned

1600s • Sthānakvāsīs formed
1700s • Terāpanthīs formed

Sikhism

c.1499 • Gurū Nānak founds Sikhism
1552 • *Mohan Pothīs* compiled
1574 • *Harimandir Sāhib* built
1606 • *Akāl Takht* established
1675 • *Ādi Granth* compiled
1699 • *Khālsā* established
1799 • *Harimandir Sāhib* gilded
1950 • *Rahit Maryādā* issued
1984 • India storms Golden Temple

900–1300 • *Taejanggyong* compiled
1000s • Koryŏ *Tripiṭaka* and *Sokjanggyong* compiled
1251 • Second Koryo *Tripiṭaka* produced
1253 • Buddhism is Mongolian state religion
1300s • Buddhism in Laos
1578 • Sonam Gyatso made Dalai Lama
1959 • 14th Dalai Lama (Tenzin Gyatso) exiled

960–1279 • Neo-Confucianism develops in China
1500s • Three-in-One Religion founded in China
1795 • Christianity arrives in Korea
1945–54 • Unification Church in Korea
1949 • China bans all religions
Present day • Religions restricted in China

00s • Shintô *Kojiki* and *Nihongi* written
94–1185 • Shintô and Buddhism join: Shugendô
1549 • Christianity arrives
1925 • Reiyûkai founded
1941 • United Church of Christ in Japan founded
1946 • Hirohito renounces divinity
1970s • Islam arrives

00–1100 • Karaite sect flourishes
1040–1105 • Rashi
1100–1200 • *Chasidei ashkenaz* develops
1135–1204 • Maimonides
Late 1200s • *Zohar* compiled
1565 • *Shulchan Aruch* is written
1700s • Chasidism founded
1800s • 'Modern Orthodox', Reform Judaism, and Conservative Judaism founded
1926 • Progressive Judaism founded
1948 • State of Israel established

900 • Zoroastrians flee to India; known as Parsis
1800 • Parsi Zoroastrianism splits
1906–79 • Zoroastrians given a public voice in Iran
Present day • Parsis are influential in India

c.988 • Orthodox Christianity founded
1534 • Church of England founded
1549 • Christianity arrives in Japan. *Book of Common Prayer* compiled
1647 • Quakers founded
1740s • Methodists founded
1800s • Adventists, Jehovah's Witnesses, Mormons, Christian Scientists, Salvation Army founded
1869–70 • Pope declared infallible
Early 1900s • Pentecostalism founded

765 • Shi'ism splits: Twelvers and Seveners
800s • *ḥadīth* compiled
940 • Hidden Imam
996–1021 • Druze sect formed
1100s • Sufi orders established
1200s • Islam spreads in India
1400s • Islam reaches Asia
1700s • Wahhābīs founded
1800s • Salafiyya founded
1947 • Pakistan established
1979 • Shī'a Islamic Republic in Iran
1990s • Sunni Ṭālibān regime in Afghanistan

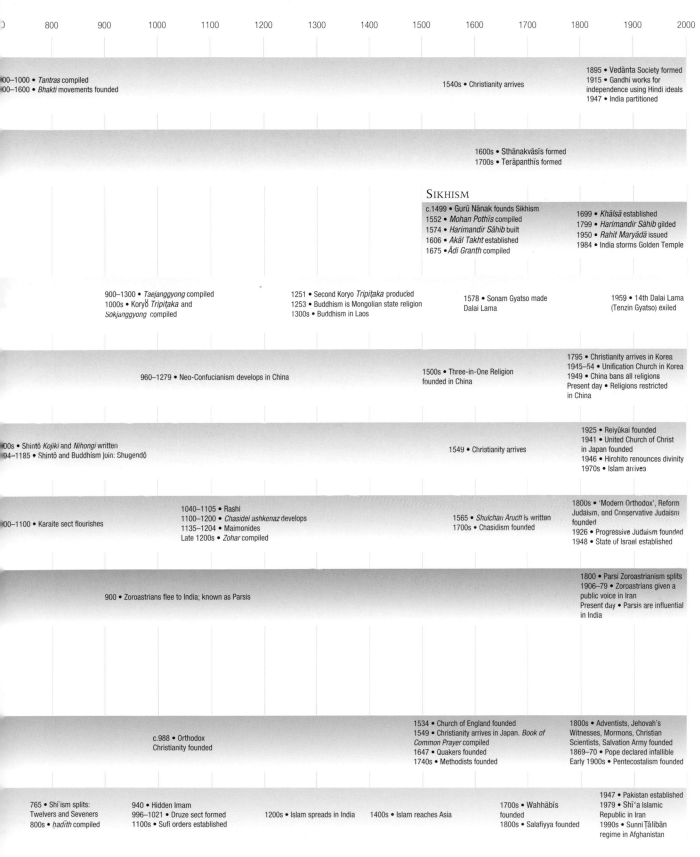

Chronology

Indian Religions

2800–2000 BCE • The Indus Valley civilization. Numerous figures and seals show similarities to Hindu traditions.
1200 BCE • Aryans migrate into southern Asia. They settle in the Punjab and western regions.
c.1200–900 BCE • Early Vedic period. The earliest *Vedas*, including the Hindu caste system, are compiled.
First millennium BCE • Brahmanical religion develops, emphasizing correct performance of ritual and adherence to social obligation or *dharma*.
c.900–600 BCE • Late Vedic period. Vedic culture continues. Brahmans perform rituals and govern religious ideology.
c.800–300 BCE • The 11 major *Upaniṣads* are composed. They express the idea of an unchanging self, passing from body to body depending on its actions.
500 BCE–1000 CE • The Epics and the Purāṇas documenting the rise of Viṣṇu, Śiva, and Devi develop.
c.320–185 BCE • Mauryan dynasty. Founded by Chandragupta (c.320–293 BCE). The idea of sacred kingship arises.
c.320–500 CE • The Gupta empire is the dominant power. The *Purāṇas* are composed.
c.500–650 CE • Fragmentation of the Gupta empire. Several southern kingdoms arise, including the Chalukya dynasty, the Pallavas, and the Pandeyas.
c.600–1600 • Rise of movements emphasizing devotion to Śiva and Viṣṇu, and equality of devotees. *Pūjā*, worship involving the offering of incense and food to a deity, becomes well established.
Seventh–eleventh centuries • Esoteric movements based on revelations found in texts known as *Tantras* develop.
c.870–1280 • Cholas dynasty. Hinduism arises in the south.
1498 • The arrival of Vasco da Gama, the start of European impact on southern Asia.
1540s • Portuguese missionaries arrive.
Seventeenth –nineteenth centuries • Hindu Renaissance. The Brahmo Samāj movement, f ounded by Ram Mohan Roy (1772–1833), seeks to restore Hinduism to pre-colonial greatness. The Ārya Samāj movement advocates a Vedic form of Hinduism rejecting image worship and later scriptures such as the *Epics* and *Purāṇas*.
c.1700 • The British East India Company is established.
1720 • The Mughal empire collapses. The British begin to take power.
1857 • The first National War of Independence (Sepoy) against the British occurs because of the use of pig or cow fat in guns, which goes against Hindu religion.
1876 • Queen Victoria becomes Empress of India.
1895 • The Vedānta Society by Vivekānanda (1863–1902) is formed. He promotes Hinduism as a world religion, the idea of India as a single nation, and influences the teachings of Mahatma Gandhi (1869–1948).
1915 • Gandhi joins the nationalist movement working for Indian independence using non-violence and passive resistance to the British.
1947 • India regains independence. It is partitioned, leading to conflicts between Hindus, Muslims, and Sikhs.
1948 • Gandhi is assassinated by a Hindu nationalist.
1950 • The Constitution of the Republic of India is inaugurated.
Present day • Hinduism brings many elements such as meditation, yoga, and gurūs to the Western world.

Jainism

Eighth–seventh centuries BCE • Jainism develops in east India. The *tīrthaṅkara* Parsva lives at this time.
Fifth century BCE • Traditional dates for Mahāvīra, the last *tīrthaṅkara* and the founder of Jainism.
c. third century BCE • A Jain community forms in the trading centre of Mathura.
c. fourth–fifth centuries CE • Umāsvāti codifies Jain texts in the *Tattvārtha Sūtra*.
c. fifth century CE • There is a schism culminating in the forming of the Śvetāmbara and Digambara sects.
Ninth–eleventh centuries • Digambara Jainism is frequently patronized by south Indian royalty.
Early–mid twelfth century • Caulukya dynasty of Gujarat. Hemacandra (1089–1172), a Śvetāmbara monk, is tutor to the two rulers Siddharāja and his nephew Kumārapāla.
Seventeenth century • The anti-iconic Sthānakvāsīs sect emerges.
Eighteenth century • The ascetic Terāpanthīs sect emerges.
Eighteenth–nineteenth centuries • Decline of the image-worshipping ascetic communities.
Present day • Revival of asceticism and development of mystical sects. Many emigrate to East Africa, the United Kingdom, and North America.

Sikhism

c.1499 CE • Gurū Nānak (1469–1539) founds Sikhism, becoming the first gurū.
1539 CE • Gurū Aṅgad (1504–52) becomes the second gurū.
1552 • Gurū Amar Dās (1479–1574) becomes the third gurū. He collects the gurūs' writings in the *Mohan Pothīs*.
1574 • Gurū Rām Dās (1534–81) becomes the fourth gurū. He founds Amritsar and begins construction of the *Harimandir Sāhib*, the Golden Temple.
1581 • Gurū Arjan Dev (1563–1606) becomes the fifth gurū. He installs the sacred text (later known as *Ādi Granth* and *Gurū Grānth Sāhib)* in the *Harimandir Sāhib*. His death by Muslim Mughals begins militaristic Sikhism.
1606 • Gurū Hargobind (1595–1644) becomes the sixth Sikh gurū. He assumes temporal and spiritual power over all Sikhs. He establishes the *Akāl Takht*, a platform facing the Golden Temple, from which edicts are issued.
1644 • Gurū Har Rāi (1630–61) becomes the seventh gurū.
1661 • Gurū Har Krishan (1656–64) becomes the eighth gurū.
1664 • Gurū Tegh Bahādur (1621–75) becomes the ninth gurū. He is executed by the Mughals.
1675 • Gurū Gobind Siṅgh (1666–1708, called Gobind Rāi until 1699) becomes the tenth gurū. He completes a compilation of the scriptures, *Ādi Granth*.
1699 • Gurū Gobind Siṅgh establishes the practices marking Sikh *Khālsā* commitment.
1708 • Gurū Gobind Siṅgh declares the *Ādi Granth* (*Gurū Grānth Sāhib*) as his successor, making him the last human gurū.
1799 • Maharaja Rañjīt Siṅgh (1780–1839) unifies the Sikhs and governs Punjab, 1799–1839. He gilds the *Harimandir Sāhib*, transforming it into the Golden Temple.
1873 • The first Siṅgh Sabhā is founded in Amritsar.
Late nineteenth–early twentieth centuries • Emigration to East Africa, the Far East, Canada, the United States, Europe, and Britain.
1909 • The Anand Marriage Act recognizes the Sikh rite.
1920 • The Akālī Party is established to free *gurdwārās* from corrupt management.
1925 • The Sikh Gurdwārās Act confers control of India's *gurdwārās* on the Shiromani Gurdwārā Parbandhak Committee (SGPC, founded 1920).
1947 • Indian partition. The Sikhs' homeland, Punjab, is divided between India and Pakistan. Sikhs flee to India.
1950 • A definitive code of *Khālsā* Sikh discipline, the *Rahit Maryādā*, is issued.
1966 • State boundaries are redrawn. Punjab becomes India's only majority Sikh state.
1973 • The Sikh Akālī Party issues religious and economic demands in the Anandpur Sāhib resolution. The Indian government does not concede.
1984 • Jarnail Siṅgh Bhindrānwāle (1947–84), a militant preacher, campaigns for autonomy. He is killed when the Indian army storms the Golden Temple.
Present day • Sikhism is a well-established world religion.

Buddhism

480 BCE • Buddha born in Kapilavastu, today Tilaurakot, Nepal.
c. mid-fifth century BCE • Buddha achieves enlightenment and delivers his first sermon to Hindu ascetics. Monastic communities develop in Nepal and India.
Fourth century BCE onwards • 'Lineage groups' develop because of disputes over the authenticity of teachers.
c. mid-fourth century BCE • The second Buddhist Council at Vaisali formulates monastic rules and practices.
c.370 BCE • Buddha entered *parinibbāna*, nirvāṇa-beyond-rebirth. The first Buddhist Council to systematize the Buddha's teaching is held at Rajagriha.
Early third century BCE • Buddhism arrives in South East Asia.
272 BCE • The Buddhist Mauryan emperor Aśoka (rules 272–232 BCE) ascends the Indian throne.
250 BCE • Aśoka presides over the third Buddhist Council at Pataliputra. It results in the Great Schism, which leads to the development of Theravāda and Mahāyāna Buddhism.
232 BCE • Aśoka dies. Buddhism declines in India.
Late first century BCE • Theravāda is influential in Sri Lanka.
End of first century BCE • The Theravāda Buddhist Canon (or *Tripiṭaka*) is completed in Sri Lanka.
Early first century CE • Indian Buddhists settle in South Asia. The Madhyamikas Buddhist school arrives in China.
c.220 CE • Chinese Buddhism develops into 'Buddho-Daoism'.
Fourth century • The Vijñānavādins (Yogācārins) start the Tantric synthesis of the Vajrayāna. They influence Tibetan and Far Eastern Buddhism. A relic, supposedly one of the Buddha's teeth, is brought to the Sri Lankan royal court.
372 • Chinese monks Sundao and Adao bring Buddhism to Korea.
384 • The Korean court receives an Indian monk, Marananta.
c.420 • Different schools appear in China. Tiantai and Huayan are scholarly, while Chan (Zen) and Jingtu (Pure Land Buddhism) are accessible to the people.
526 • Kyomik founds the Vinaya school in Korea, based on the Indian Vinaya (rules for monastic life).
527 • Silla (Korea) accepts Buddhism.
c.589 • Chinese Buddhism commentaries and lists of patriarchs are written.
Sixth century • Burma adopts Theravāda Buddhism. Nakhon Pathom in Thailand comes into use.
Mid-sixth century • Buddhism enters Japan from Korea. Prince Shôtoku (573–621) is revered as the 'founder'.

Early seventh century • Buddhism arrives in Tibet. King Songsten Gampo (c.609–650) makes it the state religion. Religious and political in-fighting with the original national religion, Bön, continues for centuries. In the Korean kingdom of Silla, the monk Won'gwang writes the *Five Commandments for Laymen*.

Seventh century • Mahāyāna Buddhism arrives in Indonesia patronized by the Srivijaya kings of Sumatra. In Korea the monks Uisang (625–702) and Wonhyo (617–686) found Haedong Hwaom, the Avatamsaka school.

Seventh and eighth centuries • Six Nara schools are established in Japan.

Seventh–fourteenth centuries • The Korean rulers use monks as state advisors. It also becomes customary for a member of the royal family to become a monk.

645 • The Vinaya Master Chajang builds the pagoda of Hwangnyong Monastery in the Silla capital, Kyongju.

668 • The role of Buddhism as state-protecting is established and the Korean peninsula is unified under Silla rule.

668–935 • Unified Silla period. Korean monks travel to China and India to bring back the latest Buddhist teachings.

Eighth century • Nara period (710–784) in Japan. Buddhism becomes the state religion.

Early eighth century • In Korea the Son Meditation school emerges from the Chogye Sect, becoming Nine Mountains of Son.

741 • In Japan Emperor Shômu orders temples to be built in every province.

Late eighth century • King Trisong Detsen (c.755–797) of Tibet establishes a monastic community at Samyé, based on Mahāyāna Buddhism. The Tibetan Nyingma school is also formed.

c.792–794 • The Great Samyé Debate decides that Indian Mahāyāna Buddhism is the preferred form for Tibet.

Ninth century • The Hindu Khmer assume control of Siam and Cambodia. They combine the worship of Mahāyāna bodhisattvas, indigenous spirits, and ancestors. In Japan the Tendai and Shingon schools are established.

836–842 • King Langdarma (c.803–842) of Tibet persecutes Buddhists. All monasteries are destroyed and thousands of monks and lay people murdered.

845 • The Chinese emperor Wuzong suppresses Buddhism.

Early tenth century • Koryŏ dynasty (918–1392) of Korea. T'aejo (rules 918–943) builds monasteries in Song'ak (present-day Kaesong) and institutes a Buddhist constitution.

Tenth–fourteenth centuries • Koryŏ dynasty in Korea. The Buddhist canon, *Taejanggyong*, is collected and printed.

Eleventh century • The king of Burma attempts to restore Buddhist monasticism to its original Theravādin form. Mahāyāna Buddhism declines.

Early eleventh century • In Korea the first Koryŏ edition of the *Tripiṭaka* is produced.

1042 • Atiśa (c.982–1054), Indian monk and teacher, arrives in Tibet. He inspires a renaissance of Buddhism.

1073 • The Tibetan Sakya school is established by Khon Konchog Gyalpo (dates unknown).

Late eleventh century • Taegak kuksa, National Preceptor of Great Awakening (1055–1101), founds the Korean Buddhist T'ien-t'ai school. In Korea Uich'on compiles the canonical scriptures, *Sokjanggyong* (the additional *Tripiṭaka*).

Twelfth century • The Kagyü school of Buddhism is established by Gampopa (1079–1153) in Tibet.

Early twelfth–late eighteenth centuries • Kings of Thailand act as protectors of Buddhist monastic communities, but rarely interfere in internal affairs.

Mid-twelfth century • Buddhism in India is virtually wiped out. Tibet is the centre for Indian Mahāyāna Buddhism.

Late twelfth century • The Korean National Preceptor of Broad Radiance (1158–1210), Pojo kuksa, combines the Kyo and Son schools. He founds the Suson Monastery in Chogye Mountain and the Chogye school.

1185–1333 • Kamakura period of Japan. Populist Buddhist schools evolve: Rinzai, Sôtô Zen, Jôdo Shu or Pure Land, Jôdo Shinshû or True Pure Land, and Nichiren Shu or the Nichiren school.

1231–59 • The Mongols invade Korea, destroying the *Tripiṭaka* and *Sokjanggyong*.

1251 • The second edition of the Korean Koryŏ *Tripiṭaka* is completed.

1253 • The Mongolian leader, Kublai Khan, accepts Tibetan Buddhism. It becomes the dominant religion of Mongolia.

Late thirteenth century • Tibetan Buddhism expands into eastern and central Asia.

Fourteenth century • Theravāda Buddhism is introduced into Laos. Laotian Buddhism retains popular elements.

Late fourteenth century • Accumulation of wealth and power lessens Korean Koryŏ Buddhist spirituality.

Fifteenth century • The Khmer kingdom is overthrown by the Thai. Theravāda Buddhism is dominant in Cambodia. Early Chosŏn period (1392–1910) of Korea. Neo-Confucian bureaucrats hold power. Buddhist privileges are reduced but it has the patronage of King Sejong (rules 1418–50). The Korean alphabet, *hangul*, is invented.

1409 • The Geluk school of Buddhism is founded by Tsong Kha pa (1357–1419) with the establishment of Riwo Ganden monastery in Tibet.

1461 • The Korean king, Sejo (rules 1455–68), establishes the Royal Superintendency for Sutra Publication to translate Chinese scriptures into *hangul*.

1578 • Sonam Gyatso (1543–88) is given the title of Dalai Lama by the Mongolian leader, Altan Khan. He applies the honour to his two previous incarnations, thus making Gendun Drub (1391–1475) the 'first' Dalai Lama.

1592–98 • The Japanese invade Korea and the Great Son Master, Sosan Hyujong (1520–1604), and his disciple Samyong Yujong (1544–1610) become national resistance heroes.

Seventeenth century • The Obaku school of Zen Buddhism arrives in Japan from China.

Seventeenth–eighteenth centuries • Buddhist rites and monasteries revive after Korea regains its independence.

Seventeenth–late nineteenth centuries • Tokugawa period (1603–1868) in Japan. Buddhism is the state religion.

Late eighteenth century–present day • Chakri dynasty in Thailand. Significant monastic reforms.

Mid-nineteenth century • Prince Mongkut (later Rama IV, rules 1851–68) makes changes to the monasteries in Thailand. He leads the *dhammayuttika* movement known as, meaning 'those adhering to the law'.

1868 • Shintô is reinstated as the state religion of Japan.

1898 • Buddhist monks are put in charge of a national programme of primary education in Thailand.

Early twentieth century • Taixu (1890–1947) leads a reformation movement of Chinese Buddhism.

1902 • The first Thai *saṅgha* act is passed. It sets out the duties and administration of monastic authorities.

1910–45 • Japanese colonial period in Korea. The monk-poet Han Yong-un (1879–1944) reforms Korean Buddhism.

1924 • In Korea Han Yong-un founds Chosŏn Pulgyo Ch'ŬngnyŬn-hoe and establishes a monthly magazine, *Pulgyo* (*Buddhism*).

1932 • Monarchy in Thailand takes on a constitutional form.

1941 • The second Thai *saṅgha* act introduces ecclesiastical democracy.

1945 • Religious freedom is introduced in Japan, with neither Buddhism nor Shintô being promoted by the government. A central office for Buddhism is established in Seoul, supported by provincial offices throughout Korea.

c.1949 • Buddhism is suppressed and controlled by the Chinese communist government.

1950 • Tenzin Gyatso (born 1935) becomes the fourteenth Dalai Lama. China invades Tibet. Buddhism is suppressed.

1959 • The Dalai Lama goes into exile.

1963 • The third Thai *saṅgha* act reflects the authoritarian policies of Sarit Thanarat (prime minister 1958–63). It concentrates power in the patriarch and replaces *saṅgha* committees with a council of elders.

1976 • The death of Mao. Buddhism begins to revive in China.

1995 • The Tibetan child Gedhun Choekyi Nyima is identified as the Panchen Lama. He is abducted by the Chinese authorities, who put another child on his monastic throne.

Late twentieth century • Buddhadāsa, *Putatāt* in Thai (1905–83), scholar and monk, reinterprets doctrines to give them a 'this-world' emphasis.

2000 • Urgyen Thinley (born 1984), the seventeenth Gyalwa Karmapa, the head of the Kagyü school, escapes from Tibet to India.

Present day • In Burma, Thailand, Cambodia, and Laos Theravāda Buddhism prevails. Mahāyāna Buddhism has diminished in these areas and Tantric elements have been suppressed. Theravāda monks have consolidated links with Sri Lanka and continue to study in India. Buddhism continues to flourish.

Chinese Religion

c.2070–c.1600 BCE • Xia dynasty. Religion is dominated by a belief in sacred kingship and mystical sovereigns.

c.1600–1046 BCE • Shang (or Yin) dynasty. Religious practices include oracles and divination, and ancestor worship. A pantheon of Di forms.

1046–256 BCE • Zhou dynasty. The worship of heaven, *Tian*, starts. Confucianism, Daoism, Moism, Yin-yang, and the Five Agents develop.

771–476 BCE • The Spring and Autumn period. Daoism is founded. It is codified by Laozi in his book, *Laozi* or *Daode Jing, The Book of the Way and its Power*.

551–479 BCE • Kong Fuzi (Confucius) founds Confucianism and compiles *The Book of History*, a religious history of early China, and *The Book of Poetry*, 305 poems of the Shang and Zhou dynasties.

479–438 BCE • Mozi (Modi) founds Moism, which dies out by the end of the third century BCE.

475–221 BCE • Warring States period. The *Lunyu* (*The Analects*) is compiled, collecting about 500 sayings and teachings of Confucius.

c.399–295 BCE • Zhuangzi develops Daoist philosophy.

c.372–289 BCE • Mengzi establishes a Confucian school claiming that humans are born good.

c.313–238 BCE • Xunzi founds a school of Confucianism claiming that humans are born evil.

c.305–204 BCE • Zou Yan combines the ideas of yin and yang with the Five Agents – water, fire, earth, wood, and metal – to form a systematic doctrine.

221 BCE • King Ying Zheng (259–210 BCE) becomes the first August Emperor of Qin, combining all the Chinese states.

221–206 BCE • Qin dynasty. New beliefs arise, including the worship of Heaven and Earth, and immortality.

221 BCE–220 CE • Qin and Han dynasties. The Xunzi form of Confucianism is popular.

220 BCE • Guan Yu dies. A famous general, he is worshipped as Guandi (Lord Guan), God of Wealth and Righteousness.

206 BCE–8 CE • Early Han Dynasty. Religious and political life is controlled by Huang-Lao and Legalism. Immortality Daosim is popular. Confucianism is the orthodox ideology. The Daoist text *Taiping jing* is compiled.

206 BCE–220 CE • Han dynasty. Syncretic State Religion is established, distinguishing between the religion of state and home. Buddhism is introduced.

202–195 BCE • Han Gaozu is emperor. He is the first to offer great sacrifices at the grave of Confucius.

179?–104 BCE • Dong Zhongshu, a Confucian scholar, is a councillor to Emperor Han Wudi (rules 141–187 BCE).

145?–86? BCE • Sima Qian writes the *Records of the Historian*, including a biography of Confucius.

141–87 BCE • Emperor Han Wudi makes Confucianism the state religion.

135 BCE • Grand Empress Dou dies. Confucianism gradually replaces Legalism and Huang-Lao.

113 BCE • Han Wudi is the first emperor to worship *Tai yi* (Grand Unity).

Early Common Era–1912 • The worship of Confucius is made compulsory in state schools and institutions. Offering sacrifices forms part of the duties of government officials.

25–220 CE • Late Han dynasty. Daoism evolves into Religious Daoism based on *Daode Jing* and other scriptures. A military movement based on Religious Daoism, called the Yellow Turbans, is formed by Zhang Jue.

142 • The Daoist Zhang Ling (Zhang Daoling) has a vision of Laozi. Zhang founds the sect of the Way of Five Bushels of Rice.

155–220 • Zhang Lu organises the Way of Five Bushels of Rice into religious communities, which become known as Daoism of Heavenly Masters.

226–249 • Wang Bi introduces Daoist concepts into Confucian learning.

251–334 • Wei Huacun is the first female 'patriarch' of the Daoist Shangqing sect.

c.320 • The Daoist Ge Hong (283–363 CE) writes *Baopuzi* (*The Master who has Embraced Simplicity*).

365–448 • Kou Qianzhi revives Daoism of Heavenly Masters.

406–477 • Lu Xiujing forms the Lingbao school.

456–536 • Tao Hongjing develops the Daoist Shangqing school.

589–906 • Sui and Tang dynasties. Buddhism and Daoism flourish. Religious pilgrimages become popular.

Seventh–eighth centuries • Islam is introduced.

618–626 • The emperor Gaozu builds a grand temple at the birthplace of Laozi.

618–906 • Tang dynasty. Many emperors take Daoism as their family religion. Trade introduces foreign religions.

631 • Nestorian Christianity arrives in China.

637 • The emperor Taizong (rules 626–649) issues an edict ensuring that Daoists take precedence over Buddhists.

691 • Empress Wu (rules 684–705), a Buddhist, reverses Taizong's policy. She builds Buddhist temples inside the imperial palaces at Luoyang and Chang'an.

694 • Manicheism is legalized. Its followers introduce the seven-day week.

Late seventh century • Zoroastrianism becomes established.

712–756 • The Daoist Xuanzong rules. He builds temples in Luoyang and Chang'an. Questions on the Daoist texts become a feature of civil-service examinations.

768–824 • Han Yu opposes Buddhism.

845 • Emperor Wu-zong (rules 840–846) persecutes Buddhists. All other non-Daoist religions also suffer.

960–1279 • Song dynasty. Neo-Confucianism arises, as do Perfect Truth Daoism and Orthodox One Daoism. The Confucian Mengzi school is popular. The Daoist canon is edited. Zhou Dunyi (1017–1073) and Cheng Yi (1033–1107) develop a rationalistic approach to Confucianism, while Lu Xiangshan (1139–1193) and Wang Yangming (1472–1529) are idealists.

1260–1368 • Yuan dynasty. The Mongols rule China. Nestorian and Catholic Christianity are present. The Christian Westerner Marco Polo holds a position at court.

1368–1661 • Ming dynasty. Confucianism becomes more idealistic. Catholic missionaries arrive. The state control of religion increases. The Temple of Heaven in Beijing is built. Manicheism is influential over religion and politics. Secret societies are banned but continue underground.

1420 • A revolution is started by Tang Saier (dates unknown), who claims to be *fo mu* (Mother of the Buddha).

Sixteenth century • *San yi jiao* (Three-in-One Religion) is started by Lin Zhaoen (1517–98) based on a synthesis of Confucianism, Buddhism, and Daoism.

1584 • A temple of the Three-in-One Religion is built for the worship of Confucius, Laozi, Buddha, and Lin Zhaoen.

Late sixteenth century • Jesuit missionaries arrive in China.

Late sixteenth–seventeenth centuries • The teachings of the Neo-Confucians Hayashi Razan (1583–1657) and Kaibara Ekken (1630–1714) help spread the doctrine in Japan.

1603 • The Jesuit missionary Matteo Ricci (1522–1610) writes *Tianzhu Shiyi* (*The True Meaning of the Lord of Heaven*), explaining Christianity to Confucians.

1644–1911 • Manchu Qing dynasty. New movements are founded within Daoism, Buddhism, and Christianity. The Pope condemns the proselytizing methods of Matteo Ricci. The Chinese court expels all Christians who do not follow Ricci. The Three-in-One Religion is persecuted. The emperors support Lama Buddhism from Tibet.

Early nineteenth century • Protestant missionaries arrive.

1851 • Hong Xiuquan (1813–64) founds the revolutionary movement, Heavenly Kingdom of Great Peace, based on Christian ideas.

1898–1900 • The *ye he tuan* (Righteous Harmonious Fists society) starts the Boxer Rebellion against missionaries.

Late nineteenth century • Violent clashes between Christian missionaries and the Chinese people occur.

1911 • Republican forces led by Sun Zhongshan (Sun Yat-sen, 1866–1925) bring down the Manchu Qing dynasty.

1912 • China becomes a republic. The government abolishes the teaching of Confucianism in schools.

1919 • The Fourth of May Movement is founded. It uses science to stamp out religions. Major intellectual leaders are Chen Duxiu (1879–1942), Hu Shi (1891–1962), and Lu Xun (1881–1936).

1920s–30s • New developments in Buddhism are made, and national Daoist organizations are founded.

1928 • Daoist and Buddhist temples are dismantled.

1930s • The New Life Movement is launched by the Nationalist Party of Jiang Jieshi (1887–1975), to revive traditional values.

1931 • Japan invades northeast China.

1934–35 • The Long March of the people's communist army takes place.

1937–45 • China is invaded and occupied by Japanese army.

1949 • The People's Republic of China is declared on 1 October. Mao Zedong (1893–1976) is chairman of the Chinese Communist Party and the first president of the People's Republic.

1950s • All societies connected to 'superstitions' or opposing political parties are banned. Religions that accept the communist government are permitted. They are observed and controlled by the government.

1958 • The Great Leap Forward is instigated by Mao.

1966–76 • The Cultural Revolution. The cult of Mao, which is started by Lin Biao (1907–1971), reaches its peak.

1976 • Mao dies, but his deification is discouraged.

1980s • Traditional religions flourish and the cult of Mao reappears. Temples to Mao are built.

1999 • Religions seen as superstitious, such as Falun Gong, the Practices of the Wheel of Dharma, are banned.

Present day • The government controls religious activities. Religious people are required by law to register their faith, but many do not. Prevailing practices include ancestor worship, Buddhism, Daoism, and Christianity.

Korean Religion

Pre-fourth century CE • Shamanism dominates. Agricultural spirits are worshipped along with ancestors.

Fourth century CE • Buddhism arrives and becomes widely accepted. (*See Korean Buddhism Chronology.*)

918–1392 • Koryŏ dynasty. Emergence of *Sŏn* (Zen) Buddhism. Folk religion and Buddhism mix.

1236–1251 • Creation of the *Tripiṭaka Koreanum*, an edition of the entire canon of Buddhist scripture.

1392–1910 • Chosŏn dynasty. The height of Confucianism. Attempy to create a model Confucian society. Buddhism and shamanism are suppressed.

1795 • The first Roman Catholic missionary, Father Chou Wên-mu (1752–1801), arrives. The Catholic Church forbids followers to take part in ancestral rites (*chesa*). This leads to the persecution of Catholics by the government for undermining social morality.

1801–71 • Thousands of Christians are martyred. This leads to the Catholic Church in Korea assuming a 'ghetto' mentality, which remains until the 1960s.

1882 • The Protestant John Ross translates the New Testament into Korean.

1884 • The first Protestant missionaries arrive in Korea.

1907 • Protestant revival movement starts in P'yŏngyang. Formation of self-governing Korean Presbytery.

1920s • Buddhist lay movements are initiated, leading to the revival of Buddhism.

1930 • An independent Methodist Church is created in Korea.

Late 1930s–early 1940s • Christians are tortured for refusing to participate in the Japanese colonial government's Shintô rites.

1960s • Rapid growth in membership of Christian churches.

1984 • Bicentennial of Roman Catholicism in Korea. Centennial of Korean Protestantism.

Present day • Christianity continues to grow.

Japanese Religions

6,000–300 BCE • Jômon period. Religious beliefs emphasize fertility, rebirth, and spirits.

300 BCE–300 CE • Yayoi period. Rituals linking rice growing to fertility arise. Burial objects suggest shamanism.

300–645 CE • Kofun period. A belief in the afterlife starts.

Sixth century • Confucianism and Daoism are influential.

538 • The native religion develops into Shintô as a response to the introduction of Buddhism.

538–552 • Buddhism is introduced from Korea.

574–622 • Buddhism becomes the state religion of Korea. Prince Shôtoku is a powerful sponsor.

Seventh century • En-no gyôja founds Shugendô.

604 • Nara period. The Seventeen-Article Constitution of Prince Shôtoku combines Confucian, Buddhist, and Shintô ideas.

607 • The Buddhist Prince Shôtoku proclaims the necessity of venerating the gods of Shintô.

Early eighth century • The Shintô texts *Kojiki* (712) and *Nihongi* (720) are written.

710–94 • Nara period. Buddhism receives government support and six schools are introduced to Japan from China: Jôjitsu, Kusha, Ritsu, Sanron, Hossô, and Kegon.

741 • Emperor Shômu (rules 724–749) institutes a network of Buddhist temples and nunneries.

745 • Emperor Shômu orders the building of a Buddhist temple in Tôdaiji, the religious focus of Japan.

788 • Saichô establishes Enryakuji, the Tendai temple on Mount Hiei.

794–1185 • Heian period. The assimilation of Shintô and Buddhism (*shinbutsu shûgô*) is formalized. Shugendô becomes more organized.

Ninth–tenth centuries • Cults of the dead (*goryô shinkô*) proliferate.

Early ninth century • The Shingon school of Buddhism emerges.

806 • Saichô returns from China and founds a Buddhist sect.

905–927 • Shintô prayers occur in the court records.

Twelfth century • Shugendô develops a hierarchy in centres of pilgrimage in mountain regions.

1185–1333 • Kamakura period. Natural disasters, civil wars, and the notion that *dharma* ('virtue') is in decline (*mappō*) colour Japanese religion. New Buddhist sects emerge, including the Pure Land and Zen. Anti-Buddhist movements emerge in Shintô.

1336–1573 • Ashikaga period. Chinese culture proliferates, facilitated by the Gozan temples, a system of Zen monasteries. Ryôan Keigo (1425–1514) introduces Wang Yang-ming Neo-Confucianism.

1484 • Yoshida Kanetomo (1435–1511) establishes Yoshida Shintô at Yamashiro, Kyoto.

1549 • Christianity is introduced with the arrival of the Jesuit missionary Francis Xavier. The Jesuits accommodate Christianity to Japanese traditions.

1571 • The Buddhist Enryakuji temple at Mount Hiei is destroyed. Christianity is encouraged to counteract Buddhist influence.

1593 • Franciscan missionaries arrive. They mission to the poor and are more confrontational than the Jesuits.

1597 • 26 Christians are crucified at Nagasaki.

1600–1867 • Tokugawa period. Japan is unified under the shôgunate. It closes its borders to the rest of the world. Buddhism is controlled by the government. Thousands of Buddhist temples are built. Shugendô is limited by restricting religious leaders to local villages. A form of Confucianism is made the official philosophy.

1612 • The Shimabara revolt. Foreigners are expelled and Christianity goes underground for 300 years.

1635 • The *danka* system is introduced. Families are required by law to register with Buddhist temples and state that they have no involvement with Christianity. All funerals and memorial services have to be performed at Buddhist temples.

1650 • The first mass pilgrimages to the Shintô Ise Shrine.

Mid-eighteenth century • A Shintô restoration movement begins to gain influence.

Early nineteenth century • A number of syncretistic religions – incorporating Buddhist, Christian, Shintô, and folk elements along with Western-inspired features such as spiritualism, the occult, and science fiction – emerge.

Late nineteenth century • The shôgunate crumbles. Western powers return to Japan. Significant Japanese emigration; religious customs are also transplanted.

1865 • 20,000 Kakure Kirishitan (hidden Christians) are discovered living in Nagasaki.

1868 • The *danka* system is abolished.

1868–1912 • Meiji period. Western ideas are adopted, but Shintô is the state religion, with Confucian ethical values.

1870s–80s • Buddhism is persecuted and temples are destroyed. It reforms to support the new government and accommodate the new technologies. Monks study at Western universities.

1871 • State Shintô is created and its priests become civil servants and its shrines instruments of the state.

1872 • Shugendô is abolished. Shugendô centres become either Shintô or Buddhist; *yamabushi* are imprisoned.

1873 • Early Meiji period (up to 1891). Persecution of Christianity stops. Buddhism takes on social welfare.

1876–1908 • *Kyôha* Shintô forms to recognize 13 schools.

1889 • The Meiji constitution is adopted on the date of the founding of the Japanese state in 660 BCE (11 February).

1890 • The Imperial Rescript on Education is written, combining Confucian and Shintô ideals and emphasizing social harmony and loyalty to the emperor.

1910s–20s • Christians help establish socialist and trade-union movements, but then lose influence.

1912–26 • Taishô period. Shintô is defined as a patriotic practice. There is a shift in emphasis to the worship of ancestors. Western influences grow, including seances, telekinesis, clairvoyance, and hypnosis.

1918 • The University Act (*Daigaku rei*) allows religious educational institutions to gain university status. Confucian movements are founded to combat Western materialism and the decline of public morals.

1920s onwards • New religions develop, including Seichô no Ie (1929), Sôka Gakkai (1930), and Shinnyoen (1936).

1925 • Reiyûkai is founded. It spawns a number of other new religions, including Risshô Kôseikai.

1926–89 • Shôwa period. Emperor Hirohito (1901–89) is enthroned.

1941 • The United Church of Christ in Japan is formed. It is the single largest Protestant body in the country.

1945 • Government restrictions on religion end. Shugendô is revived. Christian missionary activities resume. State sponsorship of Shintô ends.

Postwar years • New religions begin proselytizing campaigns.

1945–47 • Return of land previously owned by Buddhist temples is denied. Civil Code recognizes the nuclear family over the traditional system of households, thus eliminating sources of temple income. Buddhism diversifies into business and tourism.

1945–52 • Christianity makes significant inroads in Japan.

1946 • Emperor Hirohito renounces his divinity.

1964 • The religious organization Sôka Gakkai forms its own political party, the Kômeitô.

1970s • Islam becomes widely known.

Present day • Tensions between tradition, innovation, and international influence characterize religion. The Christian Church blends Confucian, Shintô, Buddhist, and folk elements. Shugendô continues to be practiced. New Age spiritual movements grow. Daoist and Confucian principles continue to colour Japanese life.

Judaism

c.2000 BCE • The period of the biblical patriarchs.

Thirteenth century BCE • The Exodus from Egypt.

Thirteenth–twelfth centuries BCE • The conquest of Canaan.

Twelfth–eleventh centuries BCE • The period of the Judges.

c.1000 BCE • King David unifies the tribes in Jerusalem.

c.960 BCE • Solomon succeeds and builds the First Temple.

c.920 BCE • Solomon dies. The kingdom divides into Israel in the north and Judah in the south.

Mid-eighth century BCE–Babylonian exile • The period of the pre-exilic biblical prophets, including Amos, Hosea, Isaiah, Micah, and Jeremiah.

722 BCE • Israel falls to the Assyrians. The people are deported.

609 BCE • King Josiah of Judah, who has inaugurated religious reforms, is killed fighting the Egyptians.

586 BCE • Judah is conquered by Babylon. The Temple is destroyed. The population is deported.

538 BCE • Babylon falls to King Cyrus of Persia. Judean exiles return to Israel.

516 BCE • The Second Temple is dedicated in Jerusalem.

Late sixth century BCE • The prophets of the exile and return include Ezekiel, 'Deutero', and 'Trito Isaiah', Haggai, Zachariah, Joel, and Malachi.

332 BCE • Alexander the Great (rules 336–323) conquers Palestine. Jewish communities develop throughout the Greek world.

175–164 BCE • Antiochus IV Epiphanes attempts to forcibly hellenize the Jews.

167 BCE • The Maccabean Revolt is successful.

164 BCE • Re-dedication of the Temple.

First century BCE • Two main religious parties emerge: the Sadducees and the Pharisees.

63 BCE • Pompey conquers Palestine. Jewish communities spread throughout the Roman empire.

40–4 BCE • Rome puts Herod on the throne of Judea.

First century CE • The compilation of the Hebrew Bible (*Tenakh*) is completed.

c.20–c.50 CE • Philo, a Jewish philosopher living in Alexandria, seeks to harmonize Greek philosophy with Judaism.

c.37–c.100 • Flavius Josephus, a soldier and historian, records Jewish history (*The Jewish War*, *The Antiquities of the Jews*).

50–135 • Rabbi Akiba ben Joseph dies as a martyr.

66–70 • The Jewish Revolt. Rome destroys the Temple.

c.70–85 • Yochanan ben Zakkai establishes an academy at Yavneh, the site of the Sanhedrin.

73 • Masada and the last of the rebels fall to the Romans.

132–135 • The Bar Kochba revolt. Jerusalem is razed and Jews are forbidden to live in the city.

c.200 • Completion of the Mishnah by Judah Ha-Nasi.

c.425 • The Romans abolish the patriarchate and Sanhedrin. Completion of the Jerusalem Talmud.

Sixth–seventh centuries • Completion of the Babylonian Talmud.

Seventh–tenth centuries • The Khazars, who rule a kingdom in the Volga-Caucasus region, adopt Judaism.

638 • The Muslim conquest of Jerusalem. The Pact of Umar makes Jews *dhimmis* ('protected persons').

Eighth–twelfth centuries • The Karaites, a Jewish sect based only on the written Torah, challenge Rabbinic Judaism.

Ninth–eleventh centuries • Jews flourish in the Rhineland.

Ninth–twelfth centuries • Jewish communities flourish in North Africa and Spain.

882–942 • Saadia Gaon translates the Bible into Arabic.

1040–1105 • Rabbi Solomon ben Isaac, 'Rashi', is the leading French commentator on the Bible and the Talmud.

1066 • The Norman Conquest. Jews settle in England.

c.1075–1141 • Judah Halevi writes the *Kuzari*, a debate between a Jew, a Christian, and a Muslim.

1089–1140 • Rabbi Abraham Ibn Ezra is the leading Spanish Bible commentator.

1096–99 • Jewish communities in the Rhineland are destroyed during the First Crusade.

Twelfth–thirteenth centuries • The pietistic movement *chasidei ashkenaz* develops among German Jewry.

1135–1204 • Moses ben Maimon, 'Maimonides' or 'Rambam', writes the *Mishneh Torah* (*Repetition of the Law*) and *The Guide to the Perplexed*.

1144 • First ritual murder libel at Norwich.

c.1159 • Benjamin of Tudela travels through Europe to Palestine, recording Jewish life in his *Book of Travels*.

1194 • The York Massacre. 150 Jews commit mass suicide rather than surrender to a mob.

1194–1270 • Moses ben Nahman, 'Nahmanides' or 'Ramban', debates in the Barcelona Disputation (1263).

1215 • The Fourth Lateran Council orders Jews to wear a special badge.

1240 • The Paris Disputation. The Talmud is burned in Paris.
1244 • Emperor Frederick II gives privileges to Austrian Jews.
1290 • The Jews are expelled from England.
End of thirteenth century • Publication of the *Zohar* (*Book of Splendour*). Compiled by Moses ben Shem Tov Leon, it is ascribed to the second-century Rabbi Shimon bar Yohai.
Fourteenth century • Jewish migration from western to eastern Europe begins.
1336–39 • The 'Judenschläger' massacres begin in Germany.
1348 • The Black Death. Jews are blamed and massacred throughout Europe.
1391 • Forced conversions to Christianity in Spain.
1394 • The Jews are expelled from France, but small communities remain under papal protection.
1437–1508 • Isaac ben Judah Abravanel is a leading Portuguese Bible commentator and statesman.
1438 • The first Jewish ghetto is established in Fez.
1475 • The first Hebrew book is printed, an edition of the commentary of Rashi.
1481 • The first auto-da-fé takes place in Seville.
1492 • The Jews are expelled from Spain; 160,000 depart.
1493 • The Jews are expelled from Sicily.
1497 • The Jews are expelled from Portugal and their children forcibly baptized.
Sixteenth century • Spanish Jews settle in the Ottoman empire and Holland.
1511–c.1578 • Azariah De Rossi, the greatest scholar of Hebrew during the Italian Renaissance, writes *Me'or Einayim* (*Enlightenment of the Eyes*).
1516 • The first ghetto is established in Venice.
c.1525–1609 • Rabbi Judah Löw ben Bezalel, the 'Maharal', is a Bohemian talmudist and moralist. He is the legendary creator of the Golem of Prague.
1527 • The Jews are expelled from Florence.
1534–72 • Isaac ben Solomon Luria, the 'Ari', is an influential Jewish mystic living in Safed in northern Galilee.
1542 • Martin Luther writes *Of the Jews and their Lies,* advocating destroying synagogues and forbidding rabbis to teach.
1553 • The Talmud is burned in Rome.
1555 • The Papal Bull *Cum nimis absurdum* renews all repressive, anti-Jewish laws.
1565 • The *Shulchan Aruch* (*The Prepared Table*), the most authoritative code of Jewish law, is written by Rabbi Joseph Caro (1488–1575), a Spanish talmudist.
1577–84 • Roman Jews are forced to attend conversion sermons in churches.
1580–1764 • The Council of the Four Lands ('provinces') is formed to provide leadership for the Jews of Poland.
1626–76 • Shabbetai Tzevi, the false Messiah, converts to Islam in 1666 in Constantinople.
1648–49 • The uprising led by Bogdan Chmielnicki in the Ukraine leads to the massacre of 100,000 Jews and the destruction of more than 300 Jewish communities.
1655 • Manasseh ben Israel (1604–57), a Dutch rabbi, unsuccessfully petitions Oliver Cromwell requesting the re-admission of Jews to England.
1656 • Benedict (Baruch) Spinoza (1632–77), the Dutch philosopher, is excommunicated.
1671 • The beginning of the Jewish community of Berlin.
1700–60 • Israel ben Eliezer, Ba'al Shem Tov (Good Master of the Name (of God) or 'Besht'), is a Polish pietist who founds the Chasidic movement.
1720–97 • Elijah ben Solomon Zalman (the Vilna Gaon), a Lithuanian talmudist, opposes Chasidim.
1729–86 • The German philosopher Moses Mendelssohn pioneers a new relationship between Jews and society.
1742 • The Jews are expelled from most of 'Little Russia' by Empress Elizabeth.
1757 • The Talmud is burned in towns in Poland and Russia.
1760 • The British Board of Deputies is founded to represent the Jewish community.
1782 • The 'Patent of Toleration' of Emperor Joseph II lifts restrictions against Jews in Bohemia and Moravia, Hungary, and Galicia.
1791 • In the United States, the Bill of Rights guarantees freedom of religion. The Pale of Settlement, where Jews may reside, is established in czarist Russia.
1794–1886 • The German Leopold Zunz is the first of the academics in the scientific study of Jewish history.
1801 • In Seesen, Germany, Israel Jacobson (1768–1828) introduces the first 'Reform' prayers in his school.
1802 • Solomon Hirschel (1762–1842) is appointed as the first British Chief Rabbi.
1807 • Napoleon convenes the 'Sanhedrin', made up of rabbis and lay leaders.
1808 • The Consistoire is founded by the French state to represent the Jewish community.
1808–88 • Samson Raphael Hirsch, a German rabbi, creates 'modern Orthodox' Judaism.
1810–74 • Abraham Geiger, German rabbi and scholar, leads Reform Judaism.
1819–1900 • Isaac Meyer Wise, a German-born rabbi, pioneers Reform Judaism in the United States.
1844–46 • Synods of Reform rabbis are held in Braunschweig, Frankfurt, and Breslau.
1847–1915 • Solomon Schechter becomes leader of Conservative Judaism in the United States.
1858–1922 • Eliezer Ben-Yehudah (Perelmann), a Lithuanian-born scholar, is the 'father' of Hebrew as a modern spoken language.
1860–1904 • The Austrian journalist and writer Theodor Herzl founds political Zionism.
1873–1956 • Leo Baeck, a German rabbi, is religious leader during the Nazi period.
1878 • The first agricultural settlement is established in Petach Tikvah, Palestine.
1878–1965 • Martin Buber, a Vienna-born philosopher, is a leading Zionist who acknowledges the rights of Arabs.
1881–1983 • Mordechai Kaplan, an American rabbi, founds the Reconstructionist movement, which in 1922 becomes the Society for the Advancement of Judaism.
1881–82 • Pogroms in Russia lead to massive emigration, particularly to the United States.
1894–1906 • The 'Dreyfus Affair'. A French Jewish army captain, Alfred Dreyfus, is falsely convicted of spying; he is eventually released.
1897 • The First Zionist Congress. Theodor Herzl predicts there will be a Jewish state within 50 years.
1917 • The Balfour Declaration. The British foreign secretary supports the idea of a Jewish homeland in Palestine.
1922 • The League of Nations places Palestine under the British Mandate; the British withdraw on 14 May 1948.
1926 • World Union for Progressive Judaism is founded.
1932 • Youth Aliyah, an organization for settling and educating Jewish children in Palestine, is created by Recha Freier in Berlin.
1933 • Hitler comes to power. He begins anti-Jewish actions.
1935 • Fräulein Rabbiner Regina Jonas (1902–44) becomes the first woman rabbi. She serves until she is deported by the Nazis and dies in Auschwitz Concentration Camp.
1938 • 10 November, 'Kristallnacht', the 'night of broken glass'. Jewish communities are attacked and synagogues burn throughout Germany.
1943 • 19 April, an uprising against the Nazis begins in the Warsaw Ghetto. Armed resistance continues until June, with some 50 ghetto fighters surviving.
1945 • By the end of the Second World War, six million Jews, one-third of the world Jewish population, have been killed by the Nazis in the Holocaust (*Shoah*).
1947 • 29 November, the United Nations votes for the division of Palestine between Jews and Arabs.
1948 • 14 May, David Ben Gurion (1886–1973) proclaims the creation of the State of Israel. Massive immigration of Jews begins.
1967 • June, the 'Six-Day War', against Egypt, Jordan, and Syria. Israel wins control of the Sinai peninsula: the Golan Heights, West Bank, East Jerusalem, and the Gaza Strip.
1979 • Peace Treaty between Israel and Egypt.
1987 • Controls over Jewish life in the Soviet Union are relaxed, leading to massive emigration to Israel.
1995 • Murder of the Israeli Prime Minister Yitzchak Rabin (1922–95) at a Peace demonstration in Tel Aviv.
Present day • Influx of Jews from the former Soviet Union into Germany rebuilds the community to about 100,000. Israel continues to accept Jews from all over the world.

Zarathrustra and the Parsis

c.6000 BCE • Traditional date for Zarathustra (Zoroaster).
c.1200 BCE • A more likely date for Zarathustra. His teaching is initially opposed by the existing religious authorities.
Sixth century BCE • Cyrus the Great (dies 529 BCE) establishes the Persian empire. Zoroastrianism is the state religion and spreads from northern India to Greece and Egypt. It is an important influence on Judaism (and Christian beliefs) concerning angels, the devil, resurrection, and the end of the age.
334–330 BCE • Alexander the Great conquers the Persian empire. He kills many Zoroastrian priests, the magi.
Second century BCE–third century CE • Zoroastrianism recovers under Parthian rule. The number of temples increases and the oral traditions are collected into a canon of scripture, the *Avesta*.
Third century CE • The Sassanians overthrow the Parthians, with the aid of the magi, who take on a governing role. Other religions are oppressed. Sassanian teaching is usually referred to as Zurvan (Time).
Seventh century • The Muslims conquer Iran, ending Zoroastrian imperial history. Seen as idolatrous worshippers of fire, Zoroastrians are persecuted.
642 • The Muslims defeat the Sassanians at Nihavend.
652 • The last Zoroastrian king, Yazdegird III, is killed.
Tenth century • Some Zoroastrians seek safety in India, where they become known as the Parsis.
Sixteenth century • Persecution forces Zoroastrians to the desert cities of Yazd and Kerman.
Seventeenth century • Parsis act as middlemen with European traders in India and establish an influential presence in Bombay (Mumbai).
1796–1925 • Qajar dynasty. Persecution, humiliation, and high taxes on Zoroastrians. Many flee to India, some convert to Islam, and others endure.
Nineteenth century • Parsi Zoroastrianism splits. One branch reforms to accommodate modern thought; the other, Ilmi Kshnoom (Path of Knowledge), becomes a form of esoteric wisdom.
1885 • Parsis are active in the formation of the Indian National Congress.
1906–79 • The Zoroastrians in Iran enjoy advancement.
1909 • A Zoroastrian, Kay Khosrow Shahrokh, is elected to the Iranian parliament, the Majles.
1925–41 • The Majles enthrones the prime minister as Reza Shāh Pahlavi. Zoroastrians are identified with national pride as descendants of the original Iranians.
1941–79 • Under the second Pahlavi Shāh, Muḥammad Reza, a Zoroastrian becomes a deputy prime minister.

1979 • Iran becomes an Islamic Republic. Zoroastrians are restricted once more and many fear for their future. A new process of emigration begins, especially to Britain, Australia, Canada, and the United States.
Present day • Parsis remain influential in India.

Classical Greek Religion

Pre-1200 BCE • Greek polytheistic religion starts during the Minoan and Mycenaean civilizations.
c.800–300 BCE • Period of the *poleis* or Greek city states. Greek politics and religion are inseparable.
Sixth and fifth centuries BCE • Temples are constructed on the Acropolis ('high part of the city') in Athens.
393 CE • Greek religion comes to an end with the proscription of all pagan cults by the Roman emperor Theodosius.

Roman Religion

Sixth century BCE–fourth century CE • Roman Republic (509–27 BCE) and early empire (27 BCE–337 CE). It is impossible to say precisely when and where Roman religion begins. Priests are a sub-group of the political élite and the Senate resolves religious dilemmas.
Pre-fifth century BCE • Roman religion incorporates the Greek pantheon – Jupiter is identified with the Greek Zeus, Aphrodite with Venus, and so on.
27 BCE–14 CE • The first Roman emperor, Augustus, uses religion to strengthen his regime.
27 BCE–476 CE • Much religious ritual now focuses on the emperors, who are regarded as gods.
Early first century CE • Christianity begins to spread into the empire. Early Christians suffer bouts of persecution
Late fourth century CE • Emperor Constantine I (c.288–337 CE) makes Christianity the Roman empire's state religion.

Ancient Egyptian Religion

5000–3000 BCE • Predynastic period. Egypt is split into two kingdoms, Upper Egypt and Lower Egypt. Hieroglyphic writing and monumental brick architecture are started.
c.3000 BCE • Upper Egypt conquers Lower. Subsequent rulers are divided into 31 dynasties of pharaonic periods *(for dynasties, see box, pages 226–227).*
Mid-third millennium BCE • Mummification is introduced.
2647–2124 BCE • The Old Kingdom. Pharaohs are regarded as divine beings. Stone pyramids are built to house the immortal god-kings after death.
2454–2311 BCE • Fifth dynasty. The sun god, Re, and his priests become more prominent than the pharaoh. The capital moves to Thebes and Re becomes the composite Amon-Re. The belief in reincarnation, and mummification, extends to the wider population.
2311–2140 BCE • Sixth dynasty. A belief in final judgement arises based on *maat* (a just estimate of right or wrong living), on which the fate of the dead rests.
1540–1069 BCE • The *Book of the Dead*, religious and magical papyrus texts from the New Kingdom, connects the final judgement and the fate of the dead.
1391–53 BCE • The New Kingdom. Amenhotep (Amenophis) III builds the great temple to Amon-Re at Luxor and a shrine to Aten, the disc of the sun, at Thebes.
1353–37 BCE • Amenophis IV introduces the monotheism of Aten. He changes his name to Akhenaten and builds a temple complex at Karnak. After his death, the Karnak temples are destroyed and orthodoxy re-established.
First millennium BCE • Late Dynastic period. Periods of foreign rule, by the Ethiopians, Persians, Greeks, and, by the beginning of the Common Era, the Romans.

Ancient Mesopotamian Religion

Third millennium BCE • The Sumerians inhabit Mesopotamia. Gods are seen as the source of life and fertility. Divine authority is exercised through human kings.
2334–2193 BCE • Akkadian empire. The name Babil first appears. It is adapted into Greek and becomes Babylon.
1799–50 BCE • The Babylonians under Hammarupi conquer Mesopotamia. The king's divine role continues. Babylonia produces important texts, including epics, wisdom literature, and the Law Code of Hammarupi.
1620–1595 BCE • The Hittites destroy Hammarupi's empire, adding their gods and myths to Mesopotamia.
1125–1104 BCE • Babylonian revival begins under Nebuchadnezzar I, allowing old cults to revive.
883–824 BCE • Assyrian power reaches the Mediterranean under Ashurbanipal II (883–859) and Shalmaneser III (858–824). The mingling of religious influences continues.
722 BCE • The Assyrians defeat and deport the Israelites, taking Jewish influences to the heart of the empire.
605 BCE • The Babylonians gain control of the whole region, capturing Jerusalem (588–586) and initiating the Jewish exile. The Jews maintain their religious identity.
Fourth century BCE • Alexander the Great conquers Mesopotamia, bringing Greek religion.

Christianity

c.4 BCE • Traditional date for the birth of Jesus. His early years are spent in Nazareth in northern Palestine.
c.29 CE • Jesus is baptized by John and begins preaching.
c.30 CE • Jesus arrives in Jerusalem for Passover. He is arrested by the Roman authorities and crucified.
c.35 • Paul becomes a Christian. He teaches a Jesus-centred interpretation of the Hebrew Bible in Asia Minor and Greece.
c.64 • Peter and Paul are executed in Rome.
c.70 • The Gospel according to Mark is written.
c.80 • The Gospel according to Matthew and the Gospel according to Luke are written.
c.90 • The Gospel according to John is written.
Late first century • Tradition has it that the apostle Thomas brings Christianity to India.
Early third century • Origen of Alexandria (c.185–c.254) starts the tradition of Christian theology.
245–316 • The reign of the emperor Diocletian. Christians are persecuted.
Early fourth century • Athanasius (c.296–373), Bishop of Alexandria, states the key doctrine of Christianity.
313 • Christianity is declared lawful by the emperor Constantine (c.285–337).
325 • The first Church Council is held at Nicaea.
330 • Constantinople becomes the capital of the Roman empire.
360s • The emperor Julian (332–363) revives traditional Roman religion. After his death the empire reverts to Christianity.
410 • Visigoths sack Rome. By the end of the century the western Roman empire is destroyed.
416–422 • Augustine (354–430), Bishop of Hippo in North Africa, writes *The City of God.*
c.432 • Patrick (c.390–c.460) begins the conversion of Ireland to Christianity.
Mid-fifth century • Rulings from Church Councils cause dissent. Nestorians flee to Persia and spread out to India and China; Monophysites form churches in Egypt, Ethiopia, Syria, and Armenia.
c.496 • Clovis (466–511), King of the Franks, is baptized.
Late fifth century • Irish missionaries begin the conversion of Scotland.
c.529 • Benedict (c.480–c.550) founds the Benedictine order.
c.540 • Benedict composes his Rule covering all aspects of Christian monastic life.
587 • King Recared abandons the Arian heresy.
597 • Pope Gregory I (c.540–604) sends a mission to England to convert the Anglo-Saxons.
690 • English missionaries begin their work in the Netherlands, Germany, and Scandinavia.
Eighth century • Muslims from North Africa conquer Spain.
800 • Charlemagne (?742–814) is crowned by the pope as the first Holy Roman Emperor.
890s • A mission from Constantinople takes Orthodox Christianity to central Europe.
962 • Otto I (912–973), a Saxon king, is crowned Holy Roman Emperor.
966 • Mieczyslaw, Prince of Poland, is baptized.
985 • Stephen, Prince of Hungary, is baptized.
c.988 • Vladimir, Prince of Kiev, is baptized. The conversion of Russia to Orthodox Christianity begins.
1054 • The Roman Catholic Church denounces the Orthodox Church.
1095–99 • The First Crusade takes place against the Muslims who control the Holy Land. Jerusalem is captured and the Latin Kingdom of Jerusalem proclaimed.
1097–98 • Anselm (c.1033–1109), Archbishop of Canterbury, writes, *Cur Deus Homo? (Why did God Become Man?).*
1098 • The first house of the austere Cistercian order of Roman Catholic monks is founded in Cîteaux, Burgundy.
Early twelfth century • Peter Abelard (1079–1142) is active as a philosopher, theologian, and teacher.
1147–49 • The unsuccessful Second Crusade takes place.
1187 • Jerusalem is conquered by the Muslim Saladin.
1189–92 • The Third Crusade is launched. The crusaders negotiate safe passage of pilgrims to the holy places, but Jerusalem is not retaken.
1202–04 • The Fourth Crusade is unsuccessful. The crusaders attack and occupy Constantinople, stronghold of the Orthodox Church, and establish a Latin empire (which lasts until 1261).
1209 • Francis of Assisi (1181/2–1226) founds the order of Franciscan friars.
1212 • The Second Order of St Francis, or the Poor Clares, is established for women.
1215 • Dominic (1170–1221) founds the Order of Friars Preachers, the Dominicans.
1215 • The Fourth Lateran Council decrees that all Catholics should confess their sins to a priest at least once a year.
1229–44 • Christian Crusaders rule in Jerusalem.
1265–73 • Thomas Aquinas (c.1225–74), a Dominican theologian, writes his *Summa Theologiae* as a dialogue between Catholic doctrine and Aristotelian philosophy.
1291 • The Latins are driven out of the Holy Land by Muslims.
c.1305 • Dante Alighieri (1265–1321) begins his *Divina Commedia* (*Divine Comedy*), a poetic vision of hell, purgatory, and divine justice.
1309–77 • Disturbances in Rome; the popes retreat to Avignon, France.
1370s • John Wyclif (c.1329–84), the English theologian, opposes the Catholic belief in transubstantiation and calls for the use of vernacular scriptures.
1378–1417 • The Great Schism. Rival popes strive to lead the Church, supported by rival nations.
1385 • The Lithuanians convert to Christianity.

Early fifteenth century • Jan Hus (1373–1415), a Bohemian priest, calls for Catholic reform. He is burned at the stake.

1492 • Spain is reconquered from the Moors.

Sixteenth century • European traders spread Christianity in India. South America is colonized by Spain and Portugal, introducing Catholicism. Exploitation of the indigenous peoples is denounced by Bartholomé de Las Casas.

Early sixteenth century • Desiderius Erasmus (c.1466–1536), a Catholic priest, criticizes ecclesiastical corruption.

1517 • A German scholar-monk, Martin Luther (1483–1546), writes the *Ninety-Five Theses*. marking the beginning of the Reformation.

1525 • Anabaptists decide to baptize only believers who know what they are doing, not children.

1534 • The Society of Jesus, known as the Jesuits, is founded by Ignatius of Loyola (1491–1556). Under King Henry VIII's instigation England breaks with the Roman Catholic Church. The king declares himself head of the newly formed Church of England.

1536 • Jean Calvin (1509–64) publishes *Institutes of the Christian Religion*, which replaces Catholicism with a systematically reformed Christian theology.

1545–63 • The Catholic Council of Trent inaugurates the Counter-Reformation, called the Catholic Reformation.

1549 • Francis Xavier takes Christianity to Japan. The Church of England's *Book of Common Prayer* is issued.

Late sixteenth and early seventeenth centuries • Baptist Congregations are formed in England and North America. French Catholics settle in Quebec and Spanish Catholics in Mexico and California.

1614 • Christians are persecuted in Japan.

1620 • The Pilgrim Fathers, Christian dissenters, set sail in the *Mayflower* and establish Plymouth Colony in America.

1647 • The Society of Friends, called the Quakers, is formed by George Fox (1624–91).

1675 • Pietism begins the spiritual renewal of Protestantism in Germany.

Eighteenth century • The Evangelical movement begins to be popular among English-speaking Christians.

1721 • The emperor of China bans Christianity.

1740s • The Methodist movement is founded by John Wesley (1703–91) and his brother Charles (1707–88).

1793 • Immanuel Kant (1724–1804) writes *Religion Within the Limits of Reason* against supernatural doctrines.

Nineteenth century • Dissenting Christian movements develop in the United States, including Adventists, Jehovah's Witnesses, Mormons, and Christian Scientists. European and American missionaries continue in their attempts to spread Christianity in the Far East, China, and the islands of the South Pacific.

1801 • Napoleon, as ruler of France, agrees a concordat with the pope.

Mid-nineteenth century • Start of the revival of Catholicism in South America. Christian missionary work begins to spread in Africa.

1858–1947 • British rule in India includes the promotion of Christianity.

1860s • Religious tolerance in Japan. Christian missionaries arrive.

1865 • The Salvation Army is founded by William Booth (1829–1912).

1869–70 • The First Vatican Council decrees that the pope is infallible.

1890s • The African Reformation begins. William Harris (c.1860–1929) in West Africa and Simon Kimbangu (1889–1951) in the Congo work as missionaries.

1898–1900 • The anti-foreigner Boxer Rising in China sees the massacre of many Christians.

Early twentieth century • Pope Pius X (pope 1903–14) works to stop the adjustment of traditional doctrine to modern thought. Pentecostalism is founded in the United States.

1920s • The communist government closes almost all the churches in Russia and tens of thousands of clergy are shot or imprisoned.

1934 • The Barmen Declaration protests against the replacement of Jesus Christ by Adolf Hitler in Germany.

1949 • Communism in China. Missionaries are expelled.

Mid-twentieth century • Catholicism resurges in South America. The Pentecostal congregations provide an alternative form of popular Christianity.

1950s • Christian evangelism in South Korea begins.

1960s • The growth of African Christianity begins to be a significant phenomenon.

1962–65 • The Second Vatican Council makes the Catholic Church and its observances more accessible to the laity through the use of the vernacular and the promotion of Christian unity and interfaith dialogue.

1980s • Christian groups register with the Chinese government for permission to worship.

1990s • In South Africa Christianity is decisive in the replacement of white supremacy. 1,000 years of Russian Orthodoxy are reached.

Present day • Christianity continues to flourish world-wide.

Norse Religion

c.1600–450 BCE • The origins of Norse religion are thought to lie in the Scandinavian Bronze Age.

Third–sixth centuries CE • Migration period. The movement west and northwards of Celtic and Germanic peoples brings new polytheistic cults to Scandinavia. The cult of Wodan or Odin, the god of death and battle, flourishes.

Sixth–eleventh centuries • Viking age. Paganism continues to survive in Scandinavia.

Ninth and tenth centuries CE • Scandinavians venture further afield, taking the cults of their pantheon of heathen gods with them.

Islam

SIGNIFICANT AH DATES ARE GIVEN IN THE MAIN TEXT

Sixth and seventh centuries CE • The Jāhiliyya or 'time of ignorance'. Allāh or al-Raḥmān is the high god in a pantheon of deities, and Makka houses the most important monument, the Kaʿba (cube).

c.570 CE • Muḥammad is born in Makka into a branch of the tribe of Quraysh. He marries Khadīja, a rich widow.

c.610 • In a cave near Makka, Muḥammad receives a vision of a being who commands him to warn his people of the Day of Judgement.

c.610–622 • Muḥammad preaches on the Oneness of God. The rulers of Makka see him as a threat. A key message is 'submission' (Arabic root *s-l-m*) to Allāh, from which root the words Islam and Muslim derive. Muḥammad's preachings include narratives of earlier 'prophets', Jewish and Christian figures; a framework of theology is revealed and rules of conduct, worship, fasting, almsgiving, and pilgrimage.

622 • Growing opposition in Makka causes Muḥammad and his followers to move to Yathrib (later Madīna). This emigration, *Hijra*, begins the Islamic calendar, year AH 1 (Anno Hegirae).

624 • The Muslims make a successful raid on Makkan caravans at Badr.

625 • The Muslims are defeated by the Makkans at Uḥud.

630 • The Muslims capture Makka. The Kaʿba is cleansed of idols, the pilgrimage rites are Islamized, and all the tribes of Arabia take oaths of allegiance to Muḥammad.

632 • The death of Muḥammad brings about a crisis. Abū Bakr, Muḥammad's father-in-law, is chosen as *khalīfa* (caliph or deputy). He is the first of the four ar-Rāshidūn (The Rightly-Guided Caliphs) who rule 632–661.

c.632–633 • The wars of the *ridda* (apostasy) are fought to restore allegiance to the capital of Madīna and Islam and to reunite Arabia.

633 • The *Fūtuḥāt* (conquests) begin, to spread the new religion, bringing in the whole of Arabia and making inroads into Byzantine and Persian territory.

c.633–642 • Muslim Arab armies move across the Fertile Crescent (Egypt, Syria, Palestine, Mesopotamia), along the North African coast, and further into Persian and Byzantine territories.

c.650 • ʿUthmān ibn ʿAffān has the Qurʾān recorded. This becomes the accepted authorized version.

656 • ʿUthmān is murdered. ʿAlī ibn Abī Ṭālib, Muḥammad's cousin and son-in-law, is chosen as the next caliph.

657 • Battle of Ṣiffīn. Muʿāwiya, governor of Syria, challenges ʿAlī and claims the caliphate.

659 • Arbitration at Adruh is opposed by a group of ʿAlī's supporters. The political situation becomes increasingly unstable.

661 • ʿAlī is murdered and Muʿāwiya is accepted as caliph, founding the Umayyad caliphate (661–750).

680 • Unrest in Iraq finds a focus in ʿAlī's son Ḥusayn. The death of Ḥusayn marks the beginning of the Shīʿat ʿAlī ('party of ʿAlī'), the Shīʿa.

685–705 • The reign of ʿAbd al-Malik. The administrative system is centralized, Arabic becomes the official written language throughout the Muslim territories (replacing Greek and Persian), and an Arab coinage is established.

Late seventh century • The ruling classes in East and West Africa convert to Islam, and the arrival of Sufis leads to the conversion of local populations.

Eighth and ninth centuries • Groups of Muslim ascetics and mystics begin to form.

710 • Arab armies enter al-Andalus (southern Spain) from North Africa.

732 • A century after Muḥammad's death, the Muslim empire has reached its furthest extent in terms of conquest and territory. At the Battle of Poitiers (Tours), the Franks check any further advance northwards.

747 • A revolt inspired by descendants of the Prophet's uncle, supported by the Shīʿa, sees the Umayyads decisively defeated.

750 • Abū l-ʿAbbās is proclaimed caliph in Iraq.

754 • Madīnat al-Salām ('city of peace'), Baghdad, is founded as the new capital of the ʿAbbasid empire.

755 • ʿAbd ar-Raḥmān, the sole surviving Umayyad, reaches Spain (al-Andalus) and founds an Umayyad dynasty of amirs in Cordoba.

765 • Shīʿism splits. The majority become the moderate Imamiyya (*ithnāʿashariyya*, or 'Twelvers'), who co-exist with the ʿAbbasid caliphs, and a minority breaks away to become the more religiously extreme Ismāʿīlīyya (*sabʿiyya*, or 'Seveners').

786–809 • Reign of Hārūn ar-Rashīd, best known through the stories of *The Thousand and One Nights*.

Ninth century • Written collections of the *hadīth*, sayings associated with Muḥammad, are compiled. The most important are those of al-Bukhārī (dies 870) and Muslim Ibn Ḥajjāj (dies 875). Local governors set up their own dynasties. Sicily comes under Muslim rule.

813–833 • Reign of Maʾmūn. Theological controversy

centres around the 'created' or 'uncreated' status of the Qur'ān. A centre for the translation of texts from Greek to Arabic is founded in Baghdad, the Bayt al-Hikma.

869–883 • Uprisings of the Zanj (black slaves) pose a severe threat, but are eventually defeated.

908 • The first Fāṭimid (Ismāʿīlī) caliph in Tunisia.

928 • The Umayyad amir ʿAbd ar-Raḥmān III declares himself caliph in Cordoba.

940 • The twelfth imam of Twelver Shīʿite Islam, Muḥammad al-Mahdī, disappears, or 'goes into occultation'. The messianic-style return of the Hidden Imam is still awaited by Twelvers.

945 • The Buwayhids (or Buyids), a Persian family, invade Baghdad and take power from the caliph.

969 • The Fāṭimids gain power in Egypt, from where they attack Palestine, Syria, and Arabia. Al-Qāhira ('the victorious city'), Cairo, is founded and the mosque of al-Azhar is built as the religious centre of the Ismāʿīlīs.

996–1021 • The reign of the Fāṭimid al-Ḥākim. Hamza ibn ʿAlī develops the esoteric doctrines that form the basis of the Druze religion, which takes hold in the mountains between Syria and Lebanon.

Late tenth–early eleventh centuries • West Africa, reached via the Sahara, begins to accept Islam.

1030 • The Umayyad caliphate in Cordoba is defeated by the Christian Reconquista.

1055 • The Muslim Seljuq Turks take Baghdad, leaving the ʿAbbasids as nominal rulers.

Mid-eleventh century • The Christians begin to regain land: in Spain, the Reconquista is progressing; Sicily falls to the Normans; and short-lived Crusader 'Latin Kingdoms' are established in Palestine and Syria.

1071 • The Seljuq Turks defeat the Byzantines at Manzikert and establish a subsidiary state in Anatolia.

1099 • The Crusaders take Jerusalem.

Late eleventh century • The 'Assassins' form around Hasan-i Sabbāh, the 'Old Man of the Mountains', who in 1090 seizes Alamūt in the Daylam mountains of Persia.

Twelfth and thirteenth centuries • The Sufi *ṭuruq* (orders) are established; the most famous include the Qādiriyya, the Shādhiliyya, and the Suhrawardiyya. Other *ṭuruq* include Chishtiyya, which is founded in India, and the Mawlawiyya in Anatolia.

1171 • After a gradual decline, Fāṭimid power ends in Egypt with the conquests of Ṣalāḥ al-Dīn (Saladin), a Kurdish soldier.

1174 • Saladin declares himself Sultan of Egypt and Syria.

1193 • By the time of Saladin's death, most of the Crusader territory has been won back for Islam.

Thirteenth century • The Assassins are wiped out by the Mongols.

Thirteenth–sixteenth centuries • In India, Muslim power moves southwards through the Deccan. A number of sultanates exist, including Bengal, Kashmir, Gujarat, and Jawnpur.

Early thirteenth century • In India, the Delhi rulers take the title of Sulṭān. The Spanish Muḥyī al-Din ibn al-ʿArabī (*al-shaykh al-akbar*, the great shaykh, 1165–1240) has a great influence on later mystics.

1221 • The Mongols, under Jenghiz Khan, enter Persia.

1241 • The Mongols overrun the Punjab but are repulsed by the sultanate.

1258 • The Mongols under Hulagu capture Baghdad. The city is sacked and the caliph killed, bringing to an end 500 years of the ʿAbbasid caliphate.

Late thirteenth century • ʿUthmān (Osman, rules 1281–1324) establishes a state in northwestern Anatolia and founds the Ottomans (or Osmanli), the greatest Turkish dynasty to rule the Islamic world. Muslim merchants and missionary Sufis begin to settle in South East Asian trading ports.

Mid-fourteenth century • The Ottomans capture Bursa and Iznik and move into Europe via Gallipoli. The Naqshbandiyya Sufi *ṭarīqa* is founded in Persia and becomes popular in Turkey.

1366 • The capital of the Ottoman dynasty is moved from Bursa to Edirne (Adrianople) on the European mainland.

Late fourteenth century • The Ottoman armies gradually take control of the Balkans while simultaneously extending their hold in Anatolia.

Fifteenth century • Islam reaches the Philippines.

Early fifteenth century • Malacca on the Malay peninsula becomes an independent Muslim kingdom. It is an important centre for spreading Islam in South East Asia.

1453 • Constantinople is captured from the Christians by Mehmet Fāṭih (the Conqueror, rules 1451–81), thus uniting the two halves of the Ottoman empire and making the sultan the Byzantine emperor.

1492 • The armies of Castile and Aragon capture Granada. All Muslims are expelled from the peninsula.

1501 • Ismāʿīl (1487–1524), founder of the Shīʿa Ṣafavid dynasty, claiming to be the Hidden Imam, is proclaimed Shāh (king) of Persia, where Twelver Shīʿism becomes the official religion.

1516 • The Ottomans conquer Syria and Egypt, which remain in their control until the nineteenth century.

1517 • The Ottomans become responsible for the maintenance and supervision of Makka and Madīna.

1520–66 • The reign of Suleymān the Magnificent. The Ottoman empire reaches its zenith, achieving a unity it has not known since the ʿAbbasids. Most of Hungary and the coastlands of Algeria and Tunisia come under Ottoman rule.

1526 • The Mongol Bābur (rules 1526–30) invades and takes over the Delhi sultanate, becoming master of the whole of northern India.

1556 • Akbar (dies 1605) founds the Mughal dynasty in northern India.

1580–1629 • The high point for the Safavid dynasty in Persia. The reign of Shāh ʿAbbas.

Late sixteenth century • Acheh (or Atjeh), in the northwestern tip of Sumatra, becomes the first powerful Muslim kingdom in South East Asia.

Seventeenth and eighteenth centuries • The Venetians, the Habsburgs, and the Russians divide European Ottoman lands between them.

1625 • The Muslim kingdom of Mataram takes control of Java.

1699 • The Treaty of Karlowitz confirms the first substantial territorial losses for the Ottoman empire in Europe.

Eighteenth century • Muḥammad ʿAbd al-Wahhāb (1703–87), founder of the Wahhābīs, rejects Sufism and all kinds of *bidʿa* (innovation). With Ibn Saʿūd (1746–65), he founds what becomes the Saudi Arabian kingdom, containing Makka and Madīna. The Hindus regain power in northern India from the Mughals. Europeans also become a significant presence.

Early eighteenth century • The Ottoman sultans begin to bring in foreign military advisors in their wars in Europe.

1736 • The Afghans defeat the last Ṣafavids in Persia.

1738 • The Mughal empire is invaded by the Afghans.

1779 • The Afghans are ousted by the Qajar dynasty, originating from the Caspian area, which rules Persia until 1925.

1798 • Napoleon's expedition to Egypt marks the beginning of wholesale European intervention in the Ottoman empire.

1805 • Muḥammad ʿAlī is appointed governor of Egypt, which becomes independent of the Ottomans. Under him, Egypt gains control of western Arabia, including Makka and Madīna, and extends its influence into the Sudan.

1807–76 • The Tanzimat period. The Ottoman empire undergoes an extensive programme of modernization in government, law, and education.

1830 • Greece is the first Balkan territory to gain independence from the Ottomans.

1850s • Non-Muslim Ottoman citizens are granted equality with Muslims.

1858 • The last Mughal is deposed in India and the country comes under British rule.

1876–1908 • The reign of ʿAbd al-Ḥamīd II. An autocratic and religiously conservative period for the Ottomans.

1878 • The Congress of Berlin recognizes a number of autonomous Balkan states that were previously ruled by the Ottomans. Major European powers appropriate various Ottoman territories.

1882–1952 • Egypt is occupied by the British.

Late nineteenth century • Muḥammad ʿAbduh (1849–1905), the rector of al-Azhar university in Egypt, modernizes the curriculum. He inspires the Salafiyya movement.

Early twentieth century • Muḥammad Iqbal (1876–1938) seeks to revive Indian Islam and supports the idea of an Islamic state.

1908–18 • The last decade of Ottoman rule. The nationalistic 'Young Turks' arise. More liberal policies develop, with a sense of Turkish ethnic identity emerging.

1912 • Sarekat Islam (Islamic Union), the most significant modernizing Muslim movement in South East Asia, is founded.

1918 • The Ottoman empire falls. The League of Nations grants Britain mandatory status over Palestine and Iraq, and France similar powers over Lebanon and Syria.

1923 • The Republic of Turkey is proclaimed, with Mustafa Kemal (later known as Ataturk) as its first president (1923–38).

1927 • The Tablighi Jamaat movement is founded in India to encourage Muslims back to a more fervent practice of their religion without undue devotion to the Prophet and holy men.

1928 • The Ikhwān al-Muslimūn (Muslim Brothers) is founded in Egypt by Ḥasan al-Bannā (1906–49).

1941 • The Jamaat-i Islami reform movement is founded in Lahore in India by Abu al-ʿAlā ʾal-Mawdūdī (1903–79).

1945 • Indonesia becomes an independent republic, with a coalition government of Muslims, national parties, and communists.

1945–60s • Mass migration from Asia, Africa, and India sees Islam spread to the West. Most migrants intend to earn money and return home.

1947 • Partition occurs in India. Islam has its own nation in Pakistan, founded by Muḥammad Alī Jinnah (1876–1948), and becomes a minority religion in India.

Late 1940s • The introduction of multi-party politics in Turkey. Islam is given more freedom and is taught in schools.

1957 • An independent Malayan state is established, with Islam as the official religion but with guaranteed freedom of worship.

1960s onwards • Whole families and communities begin to emigrate to the West, notably from South East Asia and North Africa to Europe and North and South America.

1979 • The Shāh of Iran, Muḥammad Reza Pahlavi (1919–80), is overthrown by a popular movement headed by Ayatullāh Rūḥullah Khumayni (1902–89). A strict fundamentalist rule of Shīʿa principles is introduced.

Late 1990s • The Ṭālibān come to power in Afghanistan, establishing an intolerant and extreme regime.

Present day • Sunnis form the majority of Muslims. Iran is strongly Twelver Shīʿī, and there is a large population in Iraq. Ismāʿīlīs are found in the Middle East and India.

BIBLIOGRAPHY

INTRODUCTION

A. F. Aveni, *Nasca*, London: British Museum Press, 2000.

W. Bosman, *A New and Accurate Description of the Coast of New Guinea*, London: J. Knapton; D. Midwinter, 1705.

J. Bowker, (ed.) *Oxford Dictionary of World Religions*, Oxford: Oxford University Press, 1997.

J. Bowker, World Religions: *The Great Faiths Explored and Explained*, London: Dorling Kindersley, 1997.

P. Carr-Gomm, *The Druid Renaissance*, London: Thorsons, 1996.

J. Clottes, D. Lewis-Williams, *The Shamans of Prehistory: Trance and Magic in the Painted Caves*, New York: Harry N. Adams, 1998.

D. Drew, *The Lost Chronicles of the Maya Kings*, London: Weidenfeld & Nicolson, 1995.

E. Durkheim, *The Elementary Forms of Religious Life*, London: Allen & Unwin, 1915.

M. Eliade, *Shamanism: Archaic Techniques of Ecstasy*, London: Routledge, 1964.

The Encyclopedia of Asian History, New York: Scribners, 1988.

M. J. Harner, *Hallucinogens and Shamanism*, Oxford: Oxford University Press, 1973.

J. Hawes, 'God in the Machine', *Antiquity* XLI, pages 174–80, 1967.

A. B. Kehoe, *The Ghost Dance*, New York: Holt, Rivehart and Winston, 1989.

J. Lubbock, *Prehistoric Times*, London: Williams & Norgate, 1913.

J. Lubbock, *The Origin of Civilization*, Chicago and London: Chicago University Press, 1978.

A. Marshall, 'The Old Generation of Economics and the New', *Quarterly Journal of Economics* XI, page 121, 1897.

M. Müller, *Natural Religion* in *Collected Works*, vol. I, London: Longmans, Green and Co., 1907.

A. J. Raboteau, *Slave Religion*, Oxford: Oxford University Press, 1980.

S. M. Shirokogoroff, *The Psychomental Complex of the Tungus*, Rhode Island: AMS Books, 1982.

N. Smart, *The World's Religions*, Cambridge: Cambridge University Press, 1989.

J. Smith, *Tapu Removal in Maori Religion*, Wellington: The Polynesian Society, 1974.

T. Swain, *A Place for Strangers: Towards a History of Australian Aboriginal Being*, Cambridge: Cambridge University Press, 1993.

D. Tedlock, *Popol Vuh*, New York: Simon and Suster, 1996.

G. W. Trompf, *Melanesian Religion*, Cambridge: Cambridge University Press, 1991.

C. Waldman, *Encyclopedia of Native American Tribes*, New York: Checkmark, 1998.

INDIAN RELIGIONS AND THE HINDU TRADITION

J. Brockington, *The Sacred Thread*, Edinburgh: Edinburgh University Press, 1981.

F. Clooney, *Hindu Wisdom for All God's Children*, Maryknoll: Orbis Books, 1998.

M. Eliade, *Yoga: Immortality and Freedom*, Princeton: Princeton University Press, 1970.

G. Flood, *An Introduction to Hinduism*, Cambridge: Cambridge University Press, 1996.

C. Fuller, *The Camphor Flame*, Princeton: Princeton University Press, 1992.

W. Halbfass, *Tradition and Reflection: Explorations in Indian Thought*, Albany: State University of New York Press, 1991.

J. Heesterman, *The Inner Conflict of Tradition,* Chicago: University of Chicago Press, 1985.

T. Hopkins, *The Hindu Religious Tradition*, Belmont: Wadsworth, 1971.

W. Johnson (trans.), *The Bhagavad Gita*, Oxford: Oxford University Press, 1994.

R. King, *Indian Philosophy: An Introduction*, Edinburgh: Edinburgh University Press, 1999.

K. Klostermaier, *A Survey of Hinduism*, Albany: State University of New York Press, 1994.

K. Knott, *Hinduism: A Very Short Introduction*, Oxford: Oxford University Press, 1998.

J. Lipner, *Hindus*, London and New York: Routledge, 1994.

D. W. Lopez (ed.), *Religions of India in Practice*, Princeton: Princeton University Press, 1995.

W. D. O'Flaherty (ed.), *Textual Sources for the Study of Hinduism*, Manchester: Manchester University Press, 1988.

P. Olivelle, *Upanisads*, Oxford: Oxford University Press, 1996.

J. Parry, *Death in Benares,* Cambridge: Cambridge University Press, 1994.

I. Peterson, *Poems to Siva: The Hymns of the Tamil Saints*, Princeton: Princeton University Press, 1989.

A. K. Ramanujan, *Speaking of Siva*, Harmondsworth: Penguin, 1973.

D. White (ed.), *Tantra in Practice*, Princeton: Princeton University Press, 2000.

JAINISM

M. Banks, *Organizing Jainism in India and England*, Oxford: Oxford University Press, 1882.

P. Dundas, *The Jains*, London and New York: Routledge, 1992.

P. S. Jaini, *The Jaina Path of Purification*, Delhi: Motilal Banarsidass, 1979.

SIKHISM

W. O. Cole and P. S. Sambhi, *The Sikhs: Their Religions, Beliefs and Practices*, Brighton: Sussex Academic Press, 1995.

J. S. Grewal, *The New Cambridge History of India II.3: The Sikhs of the Punjab*, Cambridge: Cambridge University Press, 1990.

W. H. McLeod, *Historical Dictionary of Sikhism: Religions, Philosophies and Movements no. 5*, Lanham: Scarecrow Press, 1995.

W. H. McLeod, *Sikhism*, London: Penguin, 1997.

H. Oberoi, *The Construction of Religious Boundaries*, Delhi and Oxford: Oxford University Press, 1994

K. Singh, *A History of the Sikhs*, Delhi and Oxford: Oxford University Press, 1977, 2 vols.

N.-G. K. Singh, *The Name of My Beloved: Verses of the Sikh Gurus*, San Francisco: Harper SanFrancisco, 1996.

P. Singh and N. G. Barrier (eds), *Sikh Identity: Continuity and Change*, Delhi: Manohar, 1999.

D. S. Tatla, *The Sikh Diaspora*, London: University College Press, 1999

BUDDHISM

E. Conze (ed.), *Buddhist Texts Through the Ages*, Boston: Shambhala Publications, 1990.

D. L. Gosling, *Religion and Ecology in India and Southeast Asia*, London and New York: Routledge, 2001.

P. Harvey, *Introduction to Buddhism*, Cambridge: Cambridge University Press, 1990.

K. N. Jayatilleke, *The Message of the Buddha*, London: Allen & Unwin, 1975.

C. Kabilsingh, *Thai Women in Buddhism*, Berkeley: Parallax Press, 1991.

W. J. Klausner, *Thai Culture in Transition*, Bangkok: Siam Society, 1997.

S. Murcott, *The First Buddhist Women*, Berkeley: Parallax Press, 1991.

M. Pye, *The Buddha*, London: Duckworth, 1979.

C. S. Queen and S. B. King (eds), *Engaged Buddhism*, Albany: State University of New York Press, 1996.

N. Thera, *The Patimokkha*, Bangkok: Mahamakut Academy, Social Science Association of Ireland, 1966.

P. Williams, *Mahayana Buddhism: The Doctrinal Foundations*, London and New York: Routledge, 1996.

TIBETAN BUDDHISM

A. Abbotts, *Naked Spirits: A Journey into Occupied Tibet*, Edinburgh: Canongate, 1997.

H. H. The Dalai Lama, *The Heart of the Buddha's Path*, London: Thorsons, 1999.

D. Norbu, *Tibet: The Road Ahead,* London: Rider, 1998.

Patrul Rinpoche, *The Words of My Perfect Teacher*, London: HarperCollins, 1994.

J. Powers, *Introduction to Tibetan Buddhism*, New York: Snow Lion, 1995.

W. D. Shakabpa, *Tibet, A Political History*, New York: Potala Publications, 1984.

T. Shakya, *The Dragon in the Land of Snows*, London: Pimlico, 1999.

Sogyal Rinpoche, *The Tibetan Book of Living and Dying*, London: Rider, 1992.

R. A. F. Thurman, *The Tibetan Book of the Dead*, London: Aquarian Press, 1994.

R. A. F. Thurman, *Essential Tibetan Buddhism*, San Francisco: HarperCollins, 1996.

CHINESE BUDDHISM

K. Ch'en, *Buddhism in China: A Historical Survey*, New Jersey: Princeton University Press, 1964.

Francis H. Cook, *Hua-yen Buddhism: The Jewel Net of Indra*, Pennsylvania and London: Pennsylvania State University Press, 1970.

H. Dumoulin, *Zen Buddhism: A History* (trans. J. W. Heisig & P. Knitter), New York: Macmillan, 1988; London: Collier Macmillan, 1990.

J. Foard, M. Solomon, R. K. Payne (eds), *The Pure Land Tradition: History and Development*, Berkeley: University of California Press, 1996.

C. B. Jones, *Buddhism in Taiwan: Religion and the State 1660–1990*, Honolulu: University of Hawaii Press, 1999.

P. L. Swanson, *Foundations of T'ien-t'ai Philosophy: The Flowering of the Two Truths Theory in Chinese Buddhism*, Berkeley: Asian Humanities Press, 1989.

PERFECTION OF WISDOM

E. Conze (trans.), *Buddhist Wisdom Books: The Diamond Sutra; The Heart Sutra*, London: Allen & Unwin, 1958.

E. Conze (trans.), *The Large Sutra on Perfect Wisdom with the Divisions of the Abhisamayalankara*, Berkeley and London: University of California Press, 1975.

D. S. Lopez, Jr, *The Heart Sutra Explained: Indian and Tibetan Commentaries*, Albany: State University of New York Press, 1988.

HUAYAN

G. C. C. Chang (trans.), 'On the Golden Lion' in *The Buddhist Teaching of Totality*, University Park/London: Pennsylvania State Press, 1971.

T. Cleary (trans.), *Entry into the Inconceivable: An Introduction to Hua-yen Buddhism*, Honolulu: University of Hawaii Press, 1983.

T. Cleary (trans.), *The Flower Ornament Scripture*: Boulder and London: Shambhala, 3 vols: vol. 1, 1984; vol. 2, 1986; vol. 3, 1987.

W. T. de Bary et al., 'Fa-Tsang: A Chapter on the Golden Lion' in *Sources of Chinese Tradition*, New York and London: Columbia University Press, 1960.

TIANTAI

N. Donner and D. B. Steenson, *The Great Calming and Contemplation: Study of an Annotated Translation of the First Chapter of Chih-i's Mo-ho chih-kaun*, Honolulu, University of Hawaii Press, 1993.

B. Kato et al. (trans.), *The Threefold Lotus Sutra,* Tokyo: Kosei Publishing Company; New York and Tokyo: John Weatherhill, 1975.

Sangharakshita, *The Eternal Legacy: An Introduction to the Canonical Literature of Buddhism*, London: Tharpa Publications, 1985.

K. Yamamoto (trans.), *The Mahayana Mahaparinirvana-sutra*, New Delhi: International Academy of Indian Culture, 1990.

CHAN (ZEN)

N. W. Ross *The World of Zen*, London: Collins, 1962.

D. T. Suzuki, *Manual of Zen Buddhism*, London: Rider, 1983.

T. Hoover, *Zen Culture*, New York: Random House, 1977.

JINGTU

L. O. Gómez (trans.), *The Land of Bliss: The Paradise of the Buddha of Measureless Light*, Honolulu: University of Hawaii Press, 1996.

H. Inagaki with H. Stewart, *The Three Pure Land Sutras: A Study and Translation from the Chinese*, Kyoto: Nagata Bunshodo, 1994.

F. M. Müller (ed.), *The Sacred Books of the East*, vol. XLIX, Oxford: Clarendon Press, 1894.

JAPANESE BUDDHISM

W. La Flure, *The Karma of Words: Buddhism and the Literary Arts in Japan*, Berkeley: University of California Press, 1983.

A. Matsunaga, *The Buddhist Philosophy of Assimilation*, Rutland, Vermont: Charles E. Tuttle, 1969.

A. and D. Matsunaga, *Foundations of Japanese Buddhism*, Los Angeles: Buddhist Books International, 1972, 2 vols.

R. E. Morrell, *Early Kamakura Buddhism: A Minority Report*, Berkeley: Asian Humanities Press, 1983.

P. K. Robinson Ariai, *Women Living Zen*, Oxford: Oxford University Press, 1999.

E. D. Saunders, *Buddhism in Japan*, Philadelphia: University of Pennsylvania Press, 1964.

KOREAN BUDDHISM

R. E. Buswell, Jr, *Tracing Back the Radiance: Chicul's Korean Way of Zen*, Honolulu: University of Hawaii Press, 1991.

R. E. Buswell, Jr, 'Buddhism under Confucian Domination: The Synthetic Vision of Sosan Hyujong' in *Culture and the State in Late Choson Korea* (ed. J. Kim-Haboush and M. Deuchler), Cambridge, Massachusetts, and London: Harvard University Press, 1999.

S. Y. Iryon, *Legend and History of the Three Kingdoms of Ancient Korea* (trans. Tae-hung Ha and G. K. Mintz), Seoul: Yonsei University Press, 1972.

Korean Buddhist Research Institute (eds), *The History and Culture of Buddhism in Korea*, Seoul: Dongguk University Press, 1993.

L. R. Lancaster, K. Suh, C. S. Yu (eds), *Buddhism in Koryo: A Royal Religion* (Korea Research Monograph 22), Berkeley: Institute of East Asian Studies, University of California, 1996.

L. R. Lancaster and C. S. Yu (eds), *Introduction of Buddhism to Korea: New Cultural Patterns*, Berkeley: Asian Humanities Press, 1989.

L. R. Lancaster and C. S. Yu (eds), *Buddhism in the Early Choson: Suppression and Transformation* (Korea Research Monograph 23), Berkeley: Institute of East Asian Studies, University of California, 1996.

P. H. Lee (trans.), *Lives of Eminent Korean Monks: The Haedong Kosung Chon*, Cambridge, Massachusetts: Harvard University Press, 1969.

Y. Pak, 'Illuminated Buddhist Manuscripts in Korea' in *Oriental Art*, vol. 33, no. 4 (winter 1987–8), pages 357–74.

CHINESE RELIGION

S. Allan, *The Shape of the Turtle: Myth, Art, and Cosmos in Early China*: Albany: State University of New York Press, 1991.

D. Bodde, *Festivals in Classical China: New Year and Other Annual Observations during the Han Dynasty 20 BC–AD 220*, Princeton: Princeton University Press, 1975.

S. Breslin, *Mao*, London and New York: Longmans, 1998.

R. Bush, *Religion in China*, Niles: Argus Communications, 1977.

W. Chan (ed.), *A Source Book in Chinese Philosophy*, Princeton: Princeton University Press, 1963.

J. Ching, *Mysticism and Kingship in China: The Heart of Chinese Wisdom*, Cambridge: Cambridge University Press, 1997.

W. T. de Bary and I. Bloom (eds), *Sources of Chinese Tradition*, vol. 1, New York: Columbia University Press, 1999, second edition.

R. Eno, *The Confucian Creation of Heaven: Philosophy and the Defense of Ritual Mastery*, Albany: State University of New York Press, 1990.

J. Gernet, *China and the Christian Impact: A Conflict of Cultures* (trans. Janet Lloyd), Cambridge: Cambridge University Press, 1985.

A. C. Graham, *Disputers of the Tao: Philosophical Argument in Ancient China*, La Salle: Open Court, 1991.

L. Kohn, *Taoist Mystical Philosophy – The Scripture of Western Ascension*, Albany: State University of New York Press, 1991.

D. C. Lau (ed.), *A Source Book in Chinese Philosophy*, Princeton: Princeton University Press, 1963.

M. Loewe and E. L. Shaughnessy (eds), *The Cambridge History of Ancient China*, Cambridge: Cambridge University Press, 1999.

D. Lopez, Jr (ed.), *Religions of China in Practice*, Princeton: Princeton University Press, 1996.

D. McMullen, *State and Scholars in Tang China*, Cambridge: Cambridge University Press, 1988.

H. Maspero, *Taoism and Chinese Religion*, Amherst: University of Massachusetts Press, 1981.

D. J. Munro, *The Concept of Man in Early China*, Stanford: Stanford University Press, 1969.

D. S. Nivison, *The Ways of Confucianism: Investigations in Chinese Philosophy*, Chicago: Open Court, 1996.

J. Rawson (ed.), *Mysteries of Ancient China: New Discoveries from the Early Dynasties*, London: British Museum Press, 1996.

I. Robinet, *Taoism: Growth of a Religion* (trans. Phyllis Brooks), Stanford: Stanford University Press, 1997.

G. Rozman (ed.), *The East Asian Region: Confucian Heritage and Its Modern Adaptation*, Princeton and Oxford: Princeton University Press, 1991.

J. K. Shryock, *The Origin and Development of the State Cult of Confucius: An Introductory Study*, New York: Paragon Book Reprint Corp., 1966.

D. Sommer (ed.), *Chinese Religion: An Anthology of Sources*, Oxford: Oxford University Press, 1995.

M. Spiegel, *China: State Control of Religion*, New York: Human Rights Watch/Asia, 1997.

R. L. Taylor, *The Way of Heaven: An Introduction to the Confucian Religious Life*, Leiden: E. J. Brill, 1986.

L. Thompson, *Chinese Religion: An Introduction*, Belmont and London: Wadsworth, 1996.

D. Twitchett and M. Loewe, *The Cambridge History of China: Volume I*, Cambridge: Cambridge University Press, 1986.

E. Wong, *The Shambhala Guide to Taoism*, Boston and London: Shambhala, 1997.

C. K. Yang, *Religion in Chinese Society*, Berkeley: University of California Press, 1961.

X. Yao, *Confucianism and Christianity: A Comparative Study of Jen and Agape*, Brighton: Sussex Academic Press, 1996.

X. Yao, *An Introduction to Confucianism*, Cambridge: Cambridge University Press, 2000.

KOREAN RELIGION

R. E. Buswell, Jr, *The Korean Approach to Zen: The Collected Works of Chinul*, Honolulu: University of Hawaii Press, 1983.

R. E. Buswell, Jr, *The Zen Monastic Experience: Buddhist Practice in Contemporary Korea*, Princeton: Princeton University Press, 1992.

D. N. Clark, *Christianity in Modern Korea*, Lanham and London: University Press of America, 1986.

W. Theodore de Bary, J.-K. Kim Harboush (eds), *The Rise of Neo-Confucianism in Korea*, New York: Columbia University Press, 1985.

J. H. Grayson, *Korea: A Religious History*, Oxford: Oxford University Press, 1989.

L. Kendall, *Shamans, Housewives, and other Restless Spirits: Women in Korean Ritual Life*, Honolulu: University of Hawaii Press, 1985.

D.-H. Kim, *A History of Religions in Korea*, Seoul: Daeji Moonhwa-sa, 1988.

J. Kim, *Korean Cultural Heritage: Thought and Religion*, Seoul: Korean Foundation, 1996.

JAPANESE RELIGIONS

H. B. Earhart, *Japanese Religion*, Belmont: Wadsworth, 1982.

H. Hardacre, *Kurozumikyo and the New Religions of Japan*, Princeton: Princeton University Press, 1986.

H. Hardacre, *Shinto and the State*, Princeton: Princeton University Press, 1989.

J. M. Kitagawa, *On Understanding Japanese Religion*, Princeton: Princeton University Press, 1987.

M. Mullins, *Christianity Made in Japan*, Honolulu: University of Hawaii Press, 1998.

M. Mullins, S. Shimazono and P. L. Swanson, *Religion and Society in Modern Japan*, Berkeley: Asian Humanities Press, 1993.

I. Nobutaka (ed.), *New Religions: Contemporary Papers in Classics*, Tokyo: Kokugakuin University, 1991.

I. Reader, *Religion in Contemporary Japan*, Honolulu: University of Hawaii Press, 1991.

I. Reader and G. J. Tanabe, Jr, *Practically Religious*, Honolulu: University of Hawaii Press, 1998.

N. Tamaru and D. Reid, *Religion in Japanese Culture*, Tokyo: Kodansha, 1996.

JUDAISM

BIBLE & COMMENTARY

A. Cohen (ed.), *The Soncino Books of the Bible*, New York: Soncino Press, 1945–61, 14 vols.

J. M. Hertz, *The Pentateuch and Haftorahs*, London: Soncino Press, 1969.

JPS Hebrew–English Tanakh, Philadelphia: Jewish Publication Society, 1999.

W. G. Plaut and B. J. Bamberger, *The Torah: A Modern Commentary*, New York: Union of American Hebrew Congregations, 1981.

N. M. Sarna (ed.), *The JPS Torah Commentary*, Philadelphia: Jewish Publication Society, 1989–96, 5 vols.

Tanakh, The Holy Scriptures, Philadelphia: Jewish Publication Society, 1988.

Torah: Five Books of Moses, Philadelphia: Jewish Publication Society, 1985.

OTHER BOOKS

The Authorized Daily Prayerbook of the United Hebrew Congregation of the Commonwealth ('Singer's'), London: Eyre and Spottiswoode, 1962.

H. Beinart, *Atlas of Medieval Jewish History*, New York and London: Simon & Schuster, 1992.

W. G. Braude, *The Midrash on Psalms*, New Haven: Yale University Press, 1959, third edition 1976, 2 vols.

A. A. Cohen and P. Mendes-Flohr, *Contemporary Jewish Religious Thought: Original Essays on Critical Concepts, Movements and Beliefs*, New York and London: Free Press, 1972.

H. Danby (trans.), *The Mishnah*, Oxford: Oxford University Press, 1933.

I. Elbogen, *Jewish Liturgy: A Comprehensive History,* Philadelphia and Jerusalem: Jewish Publication Society of America; New York: Jewish Theological Seminary of America, 1993.

I. Epstein (ed.), *The Babylonian Talmud: Translated into English with Notes, Glossary and Indices*, London: Soncino, 1935–52, 35 vols.

Forms of Prayer for Jewish Worship, London: Reform Synagogues of Great Britain, 1977, 1985, 1995, 3 vols.

D. H. Frank and O. Leaman (eds), *History of Jewish Philosophy*, London and New York: Routledge, 1997.

H. Freedman and M. Simon (trans and eds), *Midrash Rabbah*, London: Soncino Press, 1939, reprinted 1961, 10 vols.

D. J. Goldberg and J. D. Rayner, *The Jewish People: Their History and Their Religion*, London: Penguin, 1989.

I. Greenberg, *The Jewish Way: Living the Holydays*, New York: Summit Books, 1988.

J. Harlow (ed.), *Siddur Sim Shalom: A Prayerbook for Shabbat, Festivals and Weekdays*, New York: Rabbinical Assembly/United Synagogue of America (Conservative), 1985.

D. Hartman, *A Living Covenant: The Innovative Spirit in Traditional Judaism*, New York: Free Press, 1985; Woodstock: Jewish Lights, 1998.

B. W. Holtz (ed.), *Back to the Sources: Reading Classic Jewish Texts*, New York: Summit Books, 1984.

L. Jacobs, *A Jewish Theology,* New York: Behrman House, 1973.

L. Jacobs (ed.), *Jewish Law,* New York: Behrman House, 1968.

L. Jacobs (ed.), *Jewish Biblical Exegesis*, New York: Behrman House, 1972.

Kol Haneshamah, Elkins Park: Reconstructionist Press, 1999.

F. Lachover and I. Tishby, *The Wisdom of the Zohar: An Anthology of Texts* (trans. David Goldstein), Oxford: Oxford University Press, 1989.

N. de Lange, *Atlas of the Jewish World*, Oxford: Phaidon Press, 1984.

J. Magonet, *The Explorer's Guide to Judaism*, London: Hodder & Stoughton, 1998.

C. G. Montefiore and H. Loewe (eds), *A Rabbinic Anthology*, Philadelphia: Jewish Publication Society of America, 1963.

J. Neusner, *The Misnah, A New Translation*, New Haven: Yale University Press, 1988.

L. I. Newman, *The Hasidic Anthology*, New York: Bloch, 1944.

J. Plaskow, *Standing Again as Sinai,* San Francisco: Harper and Row, 1990.

H. M. Sacher, *The Course of Modern Jewish History*, London: Weidenfeld & Nicolson, 1958; New York: Vintage Books, revised edition 1990.

G. Scholem, *Major Trends in Jewish Mysticism*, London: Thames and Hudson, 1955.

Siddur Lev Chadash, London: Union of Liberal and Progressive Synagogues, 1995.

A. Steinsaltz (ed.), *The Talmud (The Steinsaltz Edition)*, New York: Random House, 1990–, several vols).

Y. H. Yerushalmi, *Zakhor: Jewish History and Jewish Memory*, Philadelphia: Jewish Publication Society of America, 1982.

ZARATHUSTRA AND THE PARSIS

M. Boyce, *Zoroastrians: Their Religious Beliefs and Practices,* London: Routledge, 1979.

M. Boyce, *A History of Zoroastrianism*, Leiden: Brill, 1975, 1982.

J. R. Hinnells, *Persian Mythology*, New York: P. Bedrick Books, 1985.

P. Nanavutty, *Gathas of Zarathustra: Hymns in Praise of Wisdom*, Ahmedabad: Mapin, 1999.

P. Nanavutty, *The Parsis*, Delhi: Delhi Parsi Anjuman, 1992.

MEDITERRANEAN RELIGIONS

GREECE AND ROME

M. Beard and M. Crawford, *Rome in the Late Republic*, London: Duckworth, 1985.

J. Boardman, J. Griffin, O. Murray, *The Oxford History of the Roman World*, Oxford: Oxford University Press, 2001.

W. Burkert, *Greek Religion*, Oxford: Blackwell, 1985.

P. Cartledge, *The Cambridge Illustrated History of Ancient Greece*, Cambridge: Cambridge University Press, 1998.

P. E. Easterling and J. V. Muir (ed.), *Greek Religion and Society*, Cambridge: Cambridge University Press, 1985.

J. H. W. G. Liebeschuetz, *Continuity and Change in Roman Religion*, Oxford: Oxford University Press, 1979.

R. Parker, *Athenian Religion: A History*, Oxford: Oxford University Press, 1997.

A. Wardman, *Religion and Statecraft at Rome*, London: Granada, 1982.

EGYPT AND MESOPOTAMIA

J. Baines, *Religion in Ancient Egypt: Gods, Myths, and Personal Practice*, Ithaca: Cornell University Press, 1991.

J. Baines, J. Malek, *Atlas of Ancient Egypt*, London: Thames and Hudson, 1984.

J. Bottero, *Religion in Ancient Mesopotamia*, Chicago: University of Chicago Press, 2001.

I. Gershevitch, *The Cambridge History of Iran*, Cambridge: Cambridge University Press, 1985.

A. J. Hoerth, *Peoples of the Old Testament World*, Cambridge: Lutterworth Press, 1996.

J. G. Macqueen, *The Hittites and their Contemporaries in Asia Minor*, London: Thames and Hudson, 1986.

J. N. Postgate, *Early Mesopotamia*, London: Routledge, 1992.

M. Roaf, *Cultural Atlas of Mesopotamia and the Ancient Near East*, New York: Facts on File, 1990.

G. Roux, *Ancient Iraq*, Baltimore: Penguin, 1992.

B. Shafer, *Religion in Ancient Egypt*, Ithaca: Cornell University Press, 1991.

CHRISTIANITY

The Bible, New Revised Standard Version, London and New York: Thomas Nelson, 1989.

E. Cameron, *The European Reformation*, Oxford and New York: Oxford University Press, 1991.

D. Chichester, *Christianity: A Global History*, London and New York, Penguin, 2000.

G. Davie, *Religion in Modern Europe*, Oxford and New York: Oxford University Press, 2000.

E. Dussel, *The Church in Latin America*, Tunbridge Wells: Oates; Maryknoll: Orbis Books, 1992.

D. L. Edwards, *Christianity: The First Two Thousand Years*, London: Cassell; Maryknoll: Orbis, 1997.

R. Fletcher, *The Conversion of Europe: From Paganism to Christianity 371–1386*, London: HarperCollins, 1998.

W. H. C. Freud, *The Rise of Christianity*, London: Darton, Longman & Todd, 1985.

S. Gilley and W. J. Sheils (eds), *A History of Religion in Britain*, Oxford and Cambridge, Massachusetts: Basil Blackwell, 1994.

V. Green, *A New History of Christianity*, Stroud: Sutton Publishing; New York: Continuum, 1996.

A. Hastings (ed.), *A World History of Christianity*, London: Cassell; Grand Rapids: Eerdmans, 1999.

E. R. Hambye, *A HIstory of Christianity in India*, Bangalore: Church History Association of India, 1982–, 6 vols.

E. Isichei, *A History of Christianity in Africa*, London: SPCK, 1995.

H. Küng, *Christianity: Its Essence and History*, London: SCM Press, 1995.

J. Le Goff, *Medieval Civilization*, Oxford and Cambridge, Massachusetts: Basil Blackwell, 1988.

J. McManners (ed.), *The Oxford History of Christianity*, Oxford and New York: Oxford University Press, 1990.

S. Moffat, *A History of Christianity in Asia,* London and New York: HarperCollins, 1994–, 2 vols.

M. A. Noll, *A History of Christianity in the United States and Canada*, London: SPCK; Grand Rapids: Eerdmans, 1992.

R. E. Olson, *The Story of Christian Theology*, Leicester and Downers Grove: Inter-Varsity Press, 1999.

D. Pospielovsky, *The Orthodox Church in the History of Russia*, Crestwood: St Vladimir's Seminary Press, 1998.

E. P. Sanders, *The Historical Figure of Jesus,* London and New York: Penguin, 1993.

T. Ware, *The Orthodox Church*, London and New York: Penguin, 1993.

NORSE RELIGION

H. E. Davidson, *Gods and Myths of Northern Europe*, Harmondsworth: Penguin, 1964.

J. A. MacCulloch, *Celtic and Scandinavian Religions*, Chicago: Academy Chicago, 1998.

ISLAM

QUR'ĀN & VERSIONS

A. Y. Ali, *An Interpretation of the Holy Qur'ān, with full Arabic text*, Lahore: Shaikh Muhammed Ashraf, 1975.

A. J. Arberry, *The Koran Interpreted*, Oxford: Oxford University Press, 1998.

R. Bell (revised W. M. Watt), *Introduction to the Qur'ān*, Edinburgh: Edinburgh University Press, 1970.

A. K. Cragg, *The Event of the Qur'ān*, London: Allen & Unwin, 1971.

N. J. Dawood, *The Koran*, London: Penguin, 1999.

H. Gatje, *The Qur'ān and its Exegesis*, Oxford: One World, 1998.

M. Pickthall, *The Meaning of the Glorious Koran*, London: Allen & Unwin, 1957.

N. Robinson, *Discovering the Qur'ān*, London: SCM Press, 1996.

OTHER BOOKS

A. Ahmed, *Postmodernism and Islam*, London: Routledge, 1992.

R. Ahmad, *Islamic Modernism in India and Pakistan, 1857–1964,* Oxford: Oxford University Press, 1967.

C. E. Bosworth, *The Islamic Dynasties*, Edinburgh: Edinburgh Surveys, Edinburgh University Press, 1967.

W. C. Chittick, *A Shi'ite Anthology*, London: Muhammadi Trust, 1980.

W. C. Chittick, *Sufism: A Short Introduction*, Oxford: One World, 2000.

J. Esposito, *Islam: The Straight Path*, London: Routledge, 1992, third edition.

M. Fakhry, *A history of Islamic philosophy*, London: Longman, New York: Columbia Press, 1983.

G. S. P. Freeman-Grenville, *The Muslim and Christian Calendars*, London: Oxford University Press, 1962.

B. Gascoigne, *The Great Moghuls*, London: Jonathan Cape, 1987.

M. Gilsenan, *Recognizing Islam: Religion and Society in the Modern Middle East*, London: Croom Helm, 1982.

P. Hardy, *The Muslims of British India*, Cambridge: Cambridge University Press, 1972.

M. Hodgson, *The Venture of Islam*, Chicago: University of Chicago Press, 1974.

S. H. M. Jafri, *Origins and early development of Shi'a Islam*, London: Longmans, 1979.

G. H. A. Juynboll, *Muslim Tradition: studies in chronology, provenance and authorship of the early hadith*, Cambridge: Cambridge University Press, 1983.

I. M. L. Lapidus, *A History of Islamic Societies*, Cambridge: Cambridge University Press, 1988.

B. Lewis, *The Arabs in History*, London: Hutchinson, 1966.

B. Lewis, *The Assassins: A Radical Sect in Islam*, New York: Octagon Books, 1967.

I. M. Lewis (ed.), *Islam in Tropical Africa*, London: Hutchinson [for the] International African Institute, 1980, second edition.

P. Lewis, *Islamic Britain: Religion, Politics and Identity among British Muslims, Bradford in the 1990s*, London: I. B. Tauris, 1994.

M. Lings, *What is Sufism?*, London: Allen & Unwin, 1975.

M. E. Marty and R. S. Appleby (eds.) *Fundamentalists Observed*, Chicago: Unmiversity of Chicago Press, 1991.

S. H. Nasr, *Introduction to Islamic Cosmological Doctrines*, Albany: State University of New York Press, 1993.

I. R. Netton, *A Popular Dictionary of Islam*, London: Curzon Press, 1997.

J. Nielsen, *Muslims in Western Europe*, Edinburgh: Edinburgh Surveys 20, Edinburgh University Press, 1992.

F. Rahman, *Islam*, Chicago: Chicago University Press, 1979.

F. Rahman, *Major Themes of the Qu'ran*, Minneapolis: Bibliotheca Islamica, 1980.

J. F. Richards, *New Cambridge History of India vol I: 5: The Mughal Empire*, Cambridge: Cambridge University Press, 1993.

R. Roolvink, *Historical Atlas of the Muslim Peoples*, Amsterdam: Djambatan, 1957.

M. Smith, *The Way of the Mystics*, London: Sheldon, 1976, revised edition.

J. S. Trimmingham, *The Influence of Islam upon Africa*, London and New York: Longman and Librairie du Liban, 1980, second edition.

C. W. Troll, *Sayyid Ahmad Khan: A Reinterpretation of Muslim Theology*, New Delhi: Vikas Publishing House, 1978.

M. Ullman, *Islamic Medicine*, Edinburgh: Edinburgh University Press, 1978.

D. Waines, *An Introduction to Islam*, Cambridge: Cambridge University Press, 1995.

W. M. Watt, *The Formative Period of Islamic Thought*, Edinburgh: Edinburgh University Press, 1973.

W. M. Watt, *Islamic Philosophy and Theology*, Edinburgh: Edinburgh University Press, 1962.

W. M. Watt, *Muhammad Prophet and Statesman*, Oxford: Oxford University Press, 1961.

NEW RELIGIONS

E. Barker, *New Religious Movements*, London: HMSO, 1992.

D. V. Barrett, *The New Believers*, London: Cassell, 2001.

J. Bowker, *God: The Human Search*, New York: Dorling Kindersley, 2002.

P. Heelas, *The New Age Movement*, Oxford: Blackwell, 1996.

R. Wallis, *Elementary Forms of the New Religious Life*, London: Routledge, 1984.

INDEX

Contributors

Professor John Bowker
John Bowker is renowned for his religious writings, and has written or edited more than a dozen books in this area. Formerly Professor of Religious Studies at Lancaster University, he is a Fellow of Gresham College, London, Adjunct Professor at the University of Pennsylvania and North Carolina State University, and a Fellow of Trinity College, Cambridge. His books include *What Muslims Believe* (1995), *The Oxford Dictionary of World Religions* (1997), *World Religions* (1997) and *The Complete Bible Handbook* (1998).

Professor Gavin Flood
Gavin Flood teaches in the Religious Studies Department at the University of Stirling. His research interests include Hindu Tantra, asceticism, and theory and method in the study of religion. He has published a number of articles and books including *An Introduction to Hinduism* (1996) and *Beyond Phenomenology: Rethinking the Study of Religion* (1999).

Dr Paul Dundas
Paul Dundas has spent most of his academic career at the University of Edinburgh, and has written widely on Jainism, including *The Jains* (1992).

Dr Eleanor Nesbitt
Eleanor Nesbitt is a lecturer in Religions and Education at the University of Warwick. Her publications include *The Religious Lives of Sikh Children: A Coventry-Based Study* (2000), *Guru Nanak* (with Gopinder Kaur, 1999), and *Hindu Children in Britain* (1993).

Dr David L. Gosling
David L. Gosling has taught both physics and religious studies at university level, specializing in Southeast Asian Buddhism at the University of Hull, and the Hindu and Buddhist traditions at the University of Cambridge, where he was the first Spalding Fellow in Religions at Clare Hall. He has published extensively in the area of south Asian religions and ecology, his most recent book being *Religion and Ecology in India and Southeast Asia* (2001).

Adrian Abbotts
Adrian Abbotts is Head of Religious Studies at Coombe Dean School, Portsmouth. His account of his recent journeys in Tibet was published in 1997 under the title *Naked Spirits: A Journey Into Occupied Tibet.*

Emeritus Professor Roger Corless
Roger Corless is Professor of Religion, Emeritus, at Duke University. He studied at King's College, University of London and the University of Wisconsin at Madison. He is a co-founder of the Society for Buddhist–Christian Studies and its journal *Buddhist–Christian Studies* (University of Hawaii Press).

Professor Paul Ingram
Paul Ingram is Professor of Religion at Pacific Lutheran University, Tacoma, Washington. His two most recent books are *Wrestling With the Ox: A Theology of Religious Experience* (1997) and *The Sound of Liberating Truth: Buddhist–Christian Dialogues in Honor of Frederick J. Streng* (1999), edited with Sallie B. King. From 1997–1999, he served as President of the Society for Buddhist–Christian Studies.

Dr Youngsook Pak
Youngsook Pak is a Lecturer in Korean Buddhism at the School of Oriental and African Studies, University of London.

Dr Xinzhong Yao
Dr Xinzhong Yao is Reader in Religion and Ethics and the Chair of the Department of Theology and Religious Studies at the University of Wales, Lampeter; he is also the Adjunct Professor of Religious Ethics at Renmin University in Beijing, China. He has been teaching courses on Chinese religions and philosophy in Wales since 1991. Dr Yao has published widely in the area of religion and ethics, both in English and in Chinese. His most recent English publications include *An Introduction to Confucianism* (2000) and *Confucianism and Christianity* (1996), and the Chinese translation of the latter is being published by China Social Science Publishing House, Beijing (2001).

Dr James Huntley Grayson
James Huntley Grayson is Reader in Modern Korean Studies, Director of the Centre for Korean Studies in the School of East Asian Studies of the University of Sheffield, and Dean of the Faculty of Social Sciences. Dr Grayson lived in Korea for 16 years where he taught anthropology and the history of world religions at Kyongbuk National University in Taegu, then at Kyemyong University in Taegu, and finally in the Methodist Theological College in Seoul. He was decorated by the Korean Government with the medal of the Order of Cultural Merit in 1995. Among his writings are *Early Buddhism and Christianity in Korea: A Study in the Emplantation of Religion* (1985), *Korea: A Religious History* (1989), and *Myths and Legends from Korea: An Annotated Compendium of Ancient and Modern Materials* (2001).

Professor Jay Sakashita
Jay Sakashita teaches religions at the University of Hawaii. His publications include entries on 'New Religions', 'Christianity in Japan', 'Sôka Gakkai', 'State Shintô', and 'Religion and the State' in *Encyclopedia of Japan* (2002).

Rabbi Professor Jonathan Magonet
Jonathan Magonet studied at the Middlesex Hospital, Leo Baeck College, and the University of Heidelberg. He is the principal of Leo Baeck College and its professor of Hebrew and Biblical Studies; he is vice-president of the World Union for Progressive Judaism; he is the co-editor of *European Judaism*; and his many publications include *A Rabbi's Bible* (1991), *Bible Lives* (1992), *Jewish Explorations of Sexuality* (editor, 1995), *The Subversive Bible* (1997), and *The Explorer's Guide to Judaism* (1998).

David Bowker
David Bowker studied Classics at Cambridge University, and is now a teacher of Classics at the Haberdashers' Aske's School for Girls in Elstree, Hertfordshire. His previous publications include contributions to the *Oxford Dictionary of World Religions* (1997) and *World Religions* (1997), and he has also presented programmes for the BBC World Service.

continued

Contributors continued

Dr David L. Edwards

David L. Edwards was a Fellow of All Souls College, Oxford, from 1952–1959, the Dean of King's College, Cambridge, from 1966–1970, a Canon at Westminster from 1970–1978, and Dean of Norwich and then Southwark until 1994. He has written many books, including *Christian England* (three volumes, 1981–1984), *The Future of Christianity* (1987), and *Christianity: The First Two Thousand Years* (1997).

Dr Penelope Johnstone

Penelope Johnstone has lived, worked, and travelled in the Middle East, and teaches Arabic at the Oriental Institute of Oxford University. Her previous career included posts at the universities of Manchester and Birmingham, and her publications include *The Medicine of the Prophet* (translator, 1998).

Acknowledgments

AKG, LONDON: pps. 51,186, 223 Erich Lessing, 228, 239, 240, 251, 253.

THE ART ARCHIVE: pps. 74, 95, 96.

PAUL BAHN: p. 11.

CORBIS: pps. 2 Annie Griffiths Belt, 5 Danny Lehman, 6 Roger Wood, 12 Earl & Nazima Kowall, 14 Gunter Marx Photography, 17 Enzo & Paolo Ragazzini, 18 Charles & Josette Lenars, 21 Swift/Venuga Images, 24/5 Chris Lisle, 27 Diego Lezama, 29 Ric Ergenbright, 30/1 Sheldan Collins, 33 David H.Wells, 37 David Samuel Robbins, 41 Lindsay Hebberd, 42 Brian Vikander, 44/5 Bob Krist, 46/7 Eye Ubiquitous, 48 Lindsay Hebberd, 53 Zen Icknow, 54/5 Chris Lisle, 56 Sheldan Collins, 58/9 Hans Georg Roth, 61 Robert Holmes, 71 Earl & Nazima Kowall, 72/3 Nevada Wier, 75 Chris Lisle, 76 Eye Ubiquitous, 77 Luca I.Teltoni, 78 Jeremy Horner, 78/9 + 81 Brian Vikander, 84 Tim Page, 87 Chris Lisle, 89 Christine Osborne, 97 Pierre Colombel, 99 Bettmann Archive, 101 Dave Bartruff, 102 Michael Freeman, 104/5 Ric Ergenbright,110/1 Kevin Fleming, 113 Macduff Everton, 114 Archivo Iconographico, 116 Kevin K Morris, 118/9 + 121 Lowell Georgia, 125 Nevada Wier, 126/7 Royal Ontario Museum, 134 Todd Gipstein, 137 Hulton-Deutsch, 138 + 140 Bettmann Archive, 143 Dave G.Houser, 144/5 Nathan Benn, 146 Earl & Nazima Kowall, 147 Catherine Karnow, 148 + 150/1 Chris Lisle, 153 Michael Freeman, 154 Chris Rainer, 156 Michael S.Yamashita, 159 Pierre Columbel, 162/13 Chris Rainer, 164 + 168 +172 Michael S.Yamashita, 166 Ric Ergenbright, 174 Michael Freeman, 176 Chris Lisle, 179 C & J Lenars, 180/1 Ted Speigel, 183 David H Wells, 185 Richard T. Norwitz, 188 David Lees ,190 + 192 Richard T. Nowitz, 197 Nik Wheeler, 201 Nathan Benn, 203 + 204/5 Hanan Isachar, 206, 209 Michael St. Maur Shiel, 210 Roger Ressmeyer, 212 Owen Franken, 214/5 Lindsay Hebberd, 216 Tim Page, 220/1 Richard T.Nowitz, 225 Alexander Burkatowski, 227 Richard T Nowitz, 230 Nathan Benn, 232 The National Gallery – by kind permission of the Trustees of the National Gallery, London, 234 Christies, 242 Farrell Grehan, 248 Gail Mooney, 254 Jules T Allen, 257 Owen Franken, 259 Stephanie Maze, 260 Bettmann Archive, 262 David & Peter Turnley, 264 Vittoriano Rastelli, 267 Lowell Georgia, 268/9 Daniel Laine, 270/1 Owen Franken, 274 Jonathen Blair, 276/7 Paul Almasy, 278 Carmen Redondo, 283 Francoise de Mulder, 285 Kurt Michael Westermann, 286 Dave Bartruff, 288 Annie Griffith Belt, 291 C & J Lenars, 295 Chris Hellier, 296 R T Nowitz, 298/9 Ted Spiegel, 301 Paul Almasy, 304 + 309 Reuters New Media inc, 306 Phil Schermeister.

DR JOHN REYNOLDS: pps. 90, 92.

PROFESSOR JAY SAKASHITA: pps. 160, 171.

TRIP/ART DIRECTORS: pps. 1, 62/63 F. Good, 66 + 69 Helene Rogers.

WERNER FORMAN ARCHIVE p. 246/7.

DR XINZHONG YAO p. 128.

PROFESSOR JOHN BOWKER would like to express his thanks to all the contributors, and to all those at the Ivy Press, particularly Rowan Davies, Sarah Polden, Tony Seddon, and Vanessa Fletcher.

THE IVY PRESS would like to thank Professor Bowker for his patience and expertise, and Kevin Taylor at Cambridge University Press. Thanks also to Oxford University Press for permission to reprint two passages from the *Oxford Dictionary of World Religion.*